Mirror
of
Intimacy

Daily Reflections

on Emotional

and Erotic Intelligence

ALEXANDRA KATEHAKIS

—

TOM BLISS

"The daily meditations speak to me. The words that are chosen seem to hit a target spot—sometimes a bruised and sore spot—deep within me. By identifying and giving context to what I'm feeling, the reflections help me become a more whole person, connected to my inner consciousness, which then radiates into my environment and those around me."

— Kristin Rose
Detroit, Michigan

"Going through the daily reflections of *Mirror of Intimacy* is a fascinating experience. This is a book to experience and savor one day at a time. I see *Mirror of Intimacy* as a 'vade mecum,' **one of those books which you don't let out of your sight** and use for daily reflection because, centered on sexuality, it touches every aspect of being human. I also see it as breaking through the area of sexual mindfulness, a new positive focus on our complex humanity through our sexuality.

As a psychologist, I am happy to have this magnificent creation to use with clients and patients in need of healthy sexual 'recovering' leading to their enrichment, joy and celebration of life. The many people who are sexually unhappy will find in *Mirror of Intimacy* a real help to discover the beauty of healthy sexuality. **The book will soon be one of the important therapeutic tools in our field.**"

— Dr. Daniel L. Araoz, Ed.D
Author of *Integrating Hypnosis with Psychotherapy: The Legacy of Buddhism and Neuroscience*

"I enjoy and look forward to reading your Daily Reflection. My wife of 19 years and I are going through a very rough patch in our marriage and it's uncertain what the outcome will be. **Your comments have hit the core of our marital issues;** mostly related to our respective sexual identities, desires and the need to communicate, understand and accept each other for our differences. She reads and looks forward to your writings as well. It definitely has made a positive difference at home while we struggle to decide which outcome is best for us and our children."

— D.J.L.

"Having worked in counseling for the past 10 years, **I've yet to encounter any material as powerful, concise and direct as your meditations. I use them in couples therapy** in lieu of assigning long articles or books. My couples enjoy the 'straight talk' of the meditations, backed up with personal 'homework' at the end of each meditation."

— Dr. Carmelia Lowman, LPC
Savannah, Georgia

"*Mirror of Intimacy* **stands out from the clutter of meditation books.** The writing of Alexandra Katehakis & Tom Bliss is deep and thoughtful, shedding a warm light on healthy relationships. Highly recommended."

— Jeff Jay
Co-Author of *Love First: A Family's Guide to Intervention*

"As a gay man, my sexually sober life has been rebuilt a day at a time with prayer and meditation as an essential element. These daily meditations enable me to interact with my emotional, spiritual and sexual life on a new level. Which has helped me discover the true purpose of my sexuality. Recovery is a WE process, and **my husband and I are very grateful to have Alexandra and Tom as a part of our team.**"

— Paul M.

"The meditations I received on a daily basis were like a balm to my soul. Each meditation gave me something to reflect upon, especially in light of the fact that I experienced living with one who was sexually addicted. I was able to look beyond the situation to really ask myself how the daily meditations applied to me. **They gave me insight which helped me look beyond the addict to see the person.** Although we are divorcing, these meditations continue to give me food for thought as I move into a future intimate relationship."

— Alice
Scottsdale, Arizona

"This book of daily reflections is a comforting gift. **Thoughtful, spiritual, caring, renewing.**"

— Chaplain Trey Littlejohns, M.Div

"For myself and for my husband of 57 years, as well as for my patients, your daily reflections are a splendid reminder of what's important as we go through our busy days. They provide wonderful conversation starters as well as bonding opportunities and perhaps most importantly, they serve to motivate us to focus on our intimate relationships. Thank you for a brilliant job, well done."

— Marilyn Loevy Spiro, PhD
Richmond, Virginia

"I use these wonderful meditations as a practitioner's resource to help my sex and love addicted clients practice daily mindfulness. This homework intervention has proven to be extraordinarily empowering to them and to me as a practicing counselor. I highly recommend these meaningful meditations as a resource for therapists to share with their clients."

— Howard Baumgarten, LPC
Denver, Colorado

"These reflections are an integral part of both my professional and personal life. I often refer to them when particular issues arise. They are thought-provoking, interesting and healing. Well Done!"

— Kris Herron, M.Ed
Digby, Nova Scotia, Canada

"These meditations, written with the wisdom of a sage, have been the perfect daily dose for healing on my spiritual path to recovery from love addiction. The words are wise, profound and modern. I hope to continue strengthening my character with this thoughtful advice as I begin anew with a healthy love relationship."

— Sandra

"I can't say enough about how your meditations have helped me in my recovery from sex addiction and in my relationship with my wife. Nowhere on the planet are these issues being discussed or taught; yet I find your comments essential to building a true connection with my partner and lover. Your work is therapy and nourishment for my soul and for my relationships with the rest of the world."

— Peter S.

"Each morning I rush to open my meditation for the day. They have inspired my partner in life and me to grow closer emotionally, intimately and spiritually. Some have described our love relationship without a blemish and others, used as a tool and guide, better our personal growth to bond tighter as a loving couple. Thank you for the writers for their efforts and amazing talent. I cannot go through my day without reading my meditation. Truly a gift for me."

— Joanie, RN
Clinical / Surgical Director
New York, New York

"I have read every daily reflection, and they all have provoked insight and meaning. More than stirring emotional awareness, your meditations relate heartfelt clarity and also thoughtful reactions, digestible even in the midst of catastrophic trauma or in the peace of happy contentment. Great work!"

— J.Y.

"I have found the daily topics often mirror issues that I am struggling with at that moment. This enables me to see a different and healthier perspective than my own which leads to emotionally healing benefits. I have shared this resource with all of my friends."

— Jon A.

"In a world that is often all too quick and content to shame individuals who want to explore and understand their sexuality and sex, these meditations provide healthy, beautiful and accessible approaches to a healthy, beautiful and crucial part of the human experience."

— Noah Michelson
Gay Voices Editor, Huffington Post

"Your sensibilities are heart and truth made manifest. Each day's writing pushes my bounds of being human, adding breadth to my breath, and affirmation to my healing, tripping and endless flight."

— Faye Y.

ACKNOWLEDGMENTS

Before publication, books exist in the experiences and minds of the people who gather together to create them. In the case of this book, the seed was planted by Douglas Evans, nurtured by Alex Katehakis, and cultivated by Tom Bliss, and our complementary talents ushered in what sits before you as a published work. But we're thankful for the many persons, famous or obscure, whose emotional and erotic intelligence informed our own and who supported this project in thought and in actuality. We are grateful to our online subscribers who, one by one, circulated our messages so we could reach an erotic army of daily readers. Special recognition goes to our readers, whose collaboration titled the work, *Mirror of Intimacy.* We owe a debt of gratitude to Alisa Reich for her masterful editing and to Mike Ellison and X-tine Goodreau for their inspired cover and layout designs. Finally, we deeply appreciate the endless enthusiasm, camaraderie, and love from our Center for Healthy Sex staff.

I, Alex, especially want to thank my steadfast husband, lover, and business partner, Douglas Evans, who courageously embarked on a journey of marriage with me fourteen years ago and who always challenges the best in me to show up. I also thank my dear nephew, Eddie, for making me laugh and for being patient with the writing process that stole much of my time from the pleasures of raising him.

And I, Tom, would like to thank my support group friends and mentors, and my kind family—with a special nod to my sister Mara Levarre for her inspiring chats exploring loving relationships and to my Grandma Merna Levinthal for her unwavering encouragement and wisdom. I'm beyond grateful to Douglas and Alex for giving me the opportunity, in such a nurturing environment, to embark on the great work of understanding the complexity and poetry of our universal, and individual, eros.

Mirror of Intimacy: Daily Reflections on Emotional and Erotic Intelligence
© 2014 Alexandra Katehakis, Inc.

Edited by: Alisa Reich
Book design by: Ellison / Goodreau
Published by: Center for Healthy Sex
10700 Santa Monica Boulevard
Suite 311
Los Angeles, CA 90025
(310) 843-9902
www.CenterforHealthySex.com

Printed in the USA
First Printing, 2014

CONTENTS

FOREWORD

Dear Seeker,

We don't know you, but we're willing to make a significant wager the book in your hands will enrich your life. And we're not gambling. Our wager is based on one crucial clue: You are reading or at least checking out this book.

We also know the expertise, sensitivity, and compassion that led the authors to offer these life-changing nuggets of inspiration, information, and practice. We first heard Alex lecture at a professional conference on Sexual Addiction, a controversial topic with complex treatment issues. We were astounded at how her hands-on, *heart-on* experience working with this painful problem let her cut through myths and misperceptions to integrate their emotional, psychological, and biological aspects.

But if you're like most people, you don't have a sexual, or any, addiction. So why would this book interest you? We think it's because you want to learn about your own soul, mind, body and sexuality. And in the same way that you'd rather be on board ship with a captain who's weathered the worst storms instead of one who's sailed only on the calmest days, you'll appreciate having the most expert of guides to help you navigate your quest for self-understanding. In Alex's presentation we saw just such an

experienced, wise captain we wanted to learn from. She and her extraordinary co-captain, Tom Bliss, create one heck of a teaching team. They're the trustworthy pilots anyone would want on the passage to emotional and erotic intelligence.

Wonderful insights await you. Even better, those insights mesh with practical exercises—reflective practices that can free you from shame, ignorance, self-obsession or dependence to attain genuine, generous human connection. Alex and Tom appreciate the tough inner wrestling needed for such personal growth. So each of the book's thought-provoking daily meditations opens with a gem of age-old wisdom and closes with doable activities to stretch your reflection and enrich your erotic and emotional life.

Read, ponder, apply. You have in your hands a treasure map. But you yourself must cross the landscape full of emotional risk and demanding sustained effort—like every other significant endeavor you've done. Yet you no longer struggle alone to know your mind and heart. This marvelous book is a reassuring and wise companion on your journey of erotic and emotional discovery. Free of judgmentalism or sugarcoating, it's won our highest endorsement as we eagerly tell you, our clients, and thousands of therapists we train around the world, "You gotta read this book."

Ellyn Bader, PhD and Peter Pearson, PhD
Co-founders The Couples Institute
Menlo Park, California

INTRODUCTION

by Alexandra Katehakis and Tom Bliss

Sex. No matter our upbringing or culture or education, no matter whether we're relatively free of hang-ups or riddled by shame, none of us ever quite shakes doubts about our sexual normalcy or knowledge. Worse, we torture ourselves by believing that other people have it "right." And it's no wonder, given the barrage of (mis) information and images being blasted at us from movies, Internet pornography, and best-sellers on the subject. The Sexual Revolution of the 1960s freed us to express ourselves sexually, but left a loaded legacy: the conviction that we should all be sexual masters knowing exactly what to do, when to do it, what we like, what we don't like, and how to communicate it perfectly to a partner.

Indeed, the current expectation of sexual expertise has become a new oppression, because sex is never simple and unencumbered. Teenagers agonize over who "likes" them and when and how to "do it." Singles party until dawn, driven by the promise of sensual paradise or finding "the one." Couples with young children scramble to fit sex into their demanding family life; elders struggle to redefine their sexuality, or grieve their loss of ability or interest in it. Even in the prime of life sex confuses us by bringing us to heights of ecstasy, then leaving us

thirsty for more or giving up altogether. Yes, sex is troublesome *and* beautiful. And only when we drop our expectations, and know that we'll have moments of great sex and moments when our sexuality confounds, pains, or infuriates us, will we be liberated to enjoy it in a way that's true to ourselves.

The basic question, "What comprises hot, healthy sex?" set us on a quest. We knew no single answer to this highly individual query could, or should, apply to everyone. So we chose a medium that we hope will speak to almost every one of us, one by one. Unfettered by cultural, social, or religious norms, we set our intention to examine 366 topics related to sex and sexuality that, together, might point us in the direction of what comprises healthy, great sex. Tom matched eloquent quotations (famous or obscure) to each subject; we divvied them up according to personal resonance, and occasionally wrote together. Thus we composed a (leap) year's worth of daily reflections that explore and support the range of human sexualities as a divine gift and a human right.

When I, Alex, first began to write I was surprised by the words' easy flow and was excited to see what came from my experience and beliefs. In time, though, my thinking grew more critical and I began to question my own statements. With each passing month, my increasing vigilance made writing more complicated and demanding. Ironically, as our readers generously sent messages about how deeply our meditations were touching their love lives and sexual recovery, I became even more cautious about how I was creating meaning. Just as with sex itself, I felt that I knew very little and had to be even more scrupulously honest in the sacred task at hand. But every day, Tom's uniquely intricate, philosophical, philological, context-sensitive and soulful style inspired my own. Many times I was astonished at how aligned our ideas and feelings were; although we wrote alone I began to feel an energetic interconnection as if we were writing with one voice.

And I, Tom, also had to confront long-held beliefs, as well as recurring emotional blocks, while writing this book. Our shared vision for *Mirror of Intimacy* required deep introspection to discern the sacred and sublime usually overlooked in these familiar themes. The reflections also reference a rich array of approaches: attachment theory, mind/body nexus, neurobiology, 12-step principles, meditation techniques, Eastern and Western philosophy, and ancient world myths. At first, I found it intimidating—as I did my successful collaborator! Alex possesses such extraordinary perception,

intelligence, and knowledge—all wrapped up in personal and scientific modesty—that a unique grace infuses her every effort. Finally, when I started work at Center for Healthy Sex, I was in recovery for various sex and love issues. Many of Alex's meditations challenged me to the core. Now that the book is finished, I'm a paradigm of healthy sexuality! Just kidding, but certainly my sexual identity and relationships have been transformed for the better, and I believe these pages will erotically enlighten you and your world.

It occurred to us and many readers that these reflections apply to matters well outside the sexual. But we've learned that in order to have great sex, we must first aim to be good human beings. Eventually, we realized that these meditations provide not directions, but aspirations, for our readers and ourselves. To reach off the page and into the heart of our common issues, we followed the therapeutic practice of *empathic attunement:* the rigorous training in self-awareness which guides the therapist to heed his or her own somatic responses in order to attune to the inner state of the client. We've tried to embrace this practice in these daily reflections, to touch each and every one of you with healing kinship, and so to grant you the autonomy and adoration you deserve by virtue of your heroic quest for hot, healthy sex.

"*Words saturated with sincerity, conviction, faith, and intuition are like highly explosive vibration bombs, which, when set off, shatter the rocks of difficulties and create the change desired.*"

— Paramahansa Yogananda

January

"As far as inner transformation is concerned, there is nothing you can do about it. You cannot transform yourself, and you certainly cannot transform your partner or anybody else. All you can do is create a space for transformation to happen, for grace and love to enter."

— Eckhart Tolle

1 JANUARY

INVITATION

The prospect of an intimate relationship and healthy sex life inspires us to reflect profoundly on ourselves, our experiences, and our purpose. Like an enchanted mirror, what we send out is what we receive. So to seek sexual and relational intimacy through neediness, coercion or manipulation will unconsciously invite those qualities into any relationship. We can invite the potent force of eroticism only if we stop grasping or trying to control. With open hands and hearts, the energy of the passionate depths we all share can flow through us, igniting our love with lasting vitality and mutual affinity.

What values do we cherish in a loving sexual connection? Attraction. Passion. Respect. Autonomy. Expression. These gifts and others exist as potentialities within us all. But we are powerless to receive them unless we first abundantly nourish them within ourselves. Just as a professional party planner expertly sets the stage for a celebration, we draw intimacy and eroticism into our lives by creating a sacred space for them. Every invitation we extend—holiday feast, public performance, romantic date—materializes only as the result of our intention to sustain our guests' well-being, whether through delicious repast, delightful experience, or treasured closeness. Similarly, eroticism arrives as a result of the intentions we've set, our willingness to be open to new experience, and our true desire to connect more deeply with ourselves, with others, and with life.

DAILY HEALTHY SEX ACTS

- Are you inviting others into your inner world? Within you is a buried treasure. Your every interaction is the map that shows the way. Invite the special people you trust to share in the adventure of your unknown depths today by revealing your most sacred thoughts and feelings.

- Without knowing it, we can invite shame, conflict, chaos, and misfortune through unhealthy habitual behaviors. Shine the light on your every intention. Let go of resentment and fear, live in your loving integrity, and with time your conscious acts will invite encouraging reciprocity.

- Start inviting eroticism with an open-minded, open-hearted intention, ritual, or meditation right this moment.

> *"They enveloped each other within the folds of their thoughts, holding each other with an intimacy no physical embrace could replicate."*
>
> — Christopher Paolini

EMOTIONAL INTIMACY

The word *intimacy* is often described as "into me see" to make the direct point that intimacy begins with knowing the intricate nooks and crannies of oneself. Only by knowing yourself well can you then really "see" or know another. So emotional intimacy demands a big risk: a willingness to traverse the corners of one's own personal reality, which means an earnest commitment to recognize and track bodily-based feelings.

Repeatedly feeling unsafe in a family teaches a child to "leave" his or her body—to dissociate—as a way to survive. The process of dissociation is an elegant mechanism built into the human psychological system as a form of escape from (sometimes literally) going crazy. The problem with checking out so thoroughly is that it can leave us feeling dead inside, with little or no ability to feel our feelings in our bodies. The process of repair demands a re-association with the body, a commitment to dive into the body and feel today what we couldn't feel yesterday because it was too dangerous.

Connecting to your bodily-based feelings really allows you to "see" inside yourself. How often have you had a "gut" feeling, felt tight in your chest, or had "butterflies" in your stomach when you knew something bad was happening or going to happen? All of these are your reality, which is different than what you *think* is going on. Connecting with another from this deep place inside you, where your truth and reality reside, is the beginning of emotional intimacy. Communicating your deepest feelings and risking being known—fears and all—will have you feeling closer and more in love with your partner than you can imagine. When the body speaks the truth, you're in your center. And it's from that center that you can love and be loved.

DAILY HEALTHY SEX ACTS

- Take a moment to check in with your body. Notice what you're feeling even if you feel "nothing": Where is the numb or empty feeling? Is it in the center of your being? If so, does it have a size, shape, temperature? See if you can dive into it and become it. How does that affect you? Pay attention to any images or other bodily-based feelings that come up.

- Give a voice to the feelings in your body. If your gut could speak, what would *it* say?

- Get a sheet of paper and draw whatever feelings or non-feelings you encounter and don't worry about what your drawing means. Share it safely with another.

> *"We tend to think of the erotic as an easy, tantalizing sexual arousal. I speak of the erotic as the deepest life force, a force which moves us toward living in a fundamental way."*
>
> — Audre Lorde

3 JANUARY

EROTICISM

Eroticism points to the deliberate seeking of pleasure in an exotic land that emerges through the synergy between you and your partner during love-making. Begin your journey into this territory with a conscious commitment to venture into the unknown with your loved one, trusting your heart and soul to be your guide. When trust is the foundation of sex, you and your partner will resonate as one, creating a mystical third. Stay open and fluid. Watch your erotic connection deepen and take different forms as you develop and grow your sexuality both individually and together.

Trusting yourself is key to the expression of your eroticism and will be made evident when you challenge yourself to be honest about your sexual arousal. This includes times when you pleasure yourself without a partner present. Until you can release the shackles of self-judgment about what brings you to sexual heights, you won't be able to reveal your erotic desires to a partner.

A big part of aspiring to erotic sex means challenging your limiting beliefs and fears about certain sexual acts. Addressing your own inadequacies and the parts of your partner that turn you off requires a certain kind of mettle. Forge forward, warrior-like, as you take a trip to the erotic landscape of your lover's body to discover yourselves and your erogenous zones together. Your intent is to give up control and be in service of the other so as to make contact with the depth of your life force.

DAILY HEALTHY SEX ACTS

- Familiarize yourself and your partner with your erogenous zones.

- Ignite your carnal desires during sex by using all five senses.

- Pick one of the senses to focus on next time you have sex, such as smell, then investigate your lover's smell or introduce a new scent into your sensual practices.

"No act loses us; no violence we're subjected to destroys us; no debasement chases out the divine, and no one can take the divine from us."

— Daniel Odier

When you replay your darkest moments, experiencing the hurt and injustice of your worst pain, there's one aspect of every tragic memory that's easy to overlook. This particular aspect survives all your worst times, and will attend any possible suffering to come. What could possibly be present for all your trauma, you ask? *You.* Your consciousness is the integrating factor in every second of your life—the *you* who is reading these words right now. *(Hello!)* You are here. This self-awareness of yours today was surely with you in every twinkling of your history, and is made possible by your personal integrity.

The word *integrity* comes from the Latin *integritas*, meaning whole or complete. In mathematics, *integers* are whole numbers, either positive or negative (or zero, the very real quality of no-thing.) To integrate is to unite separate parts into a whole. Life, the ultimate unity, accordingly expresses integrity, and we are part of that whole. And that greater integrating force propels us onward through all our experience. Psychologically we're driven toward *individuation*—the emergence of a fully differentiated, integrated, central Self. In such a master scheme, every step you take leads to this goal either through validation or correction.

To operate outside one's integrity really means to be ruled by dualistic extremes—to lose track of one's personal through-line. Without the transparency of intimacy, our desires and motives stay irreconcilably partitioned, separate and secret, until we can't tell our selves from our shadows. Just as the integrity of an object signifies its soundness, the same may be said for persons. What we truly know in life, whether positive, negative, or naught, becomes reflected via the integrity of our consciousness and the conscious acts it creates.

DAILY HEALTHY SEX ACTS

- Do you follow through on your intentions? Today, for the sake of integrity, stick to the plan. If you say you're going to do something at a certain time, do it. Notice how often throughout the day you casually undermine *your own* plans.

- On each corner of a piece of paper, write one *complete* sentence retelling: your earliest memory; your worst memory; your best memory; and your most recent memory. Circle all the times you wrote "I," "me," "mine," or "my" and draw a line from each circle to the center of the paper. Cultivate a sense that you are not your experiences. You're the all-embracing human being centering and integrating all you experience.

> *"A person's approach to sexuality is a sign of his level of evolution. Un-evolved persons practice ordinary sexual intercourse. Placing emphasis upon the sexual organs, they neglect the body's other organs and systems. Whatever physical energy is accumulated is summarily discharged, and the subtle energies are similarly dissipated and disordered. It is a great backward leap."*
>
> — Lao-Tzu

5 JANUARY

SEXUALITY

Sexuality is a core component of personal identity as well as a determining factor in sexual behavior. But *sexual behavior* is often mistaken for *sexuality*, just as the external actions of our lives—career, relationships, social activities—are mistaken for the inward experiences of our lives. Both mistakes confuse *what we do* with *how we feel*. Sexuality includes much more than actions: our sexual orientation, gender identity, arousal template, and beliefs.

Our culture does not provide a process to develop conscious sexuality. Sexual education is usually limited to a hasty discussion of biological development, with no mention of its varied expression or of ways to measure functionality and fulfill sexual potential. In fact, three out of every four teenagers in a nationwide survey cited friends and television as their main sources of sexual education! If we're getting our cues about sexuality from popular media and the locker room, we don't have a very conscious way of imbibing knowledge about sexuality.

Many of us learned about our sexuality in casual or frantic states. And this mode of learning creates an attitude in which, even if we collect the basic info regarding what goes where and why, we might still experience the same underlying panicked or repressive response. People can, and often do, engage in copious sexual activity while utterly repressing their core sexuality. That's why sexuality (our true sexual nature) and sexual behavior (what we do sexually) can sometimes be at odds. Especially when one's sexuality has been wounded, one grasps for help anywhere, often through partners that are struggling with the same wound. But sexuality is a sacred aspect of our being that deserves at least the same level of care and commitment as our primary relationship.

DAILY HEALTHY SEX ACTS

- If your sexuality were a country, would it be a developed nation or a desert island? Write some descriptive words you associate with your sexuality.

- What do you know about your sexual self, and how did you gain this awareness? As you consider this, note signs of discomfort, confusion, or blankness. Write a list of affirmative words you'd like to associate with your sexuality.

- Partners are the obvious helpers in exploring sexuality and healing sexual wounds. A qualified sex therapist can also help by providing safe, educated discussion. Whom can you trust to explore as-yet unknown aspects of your sexuality? Conceive a plan for how you might fulfill your sexual potential.

> *"Your task is not to seek for love, but merely to seek and find all the barriers within yourself that you have built against it."*
>
> — Rumi

Poets and scholars have pondered the meaning of love from the beginning of time. The Greeks delineated three types of love: Agape, Philia, and Eros. Agape is a love that is so deep and profound it includes the universe; it is a feeling that emerges from inside our being and encompasses the depths of our soul. Philia is the love we feel for our friends—the warm, familial gentleness that brings security, laughter and kindness to our lives. Eros, or romantic love shot from Cupid's arrow, is the love that starts wars, moves mountains, and makes star-crossed lovers like Romeo and Juliet die for one another. Eros is passionate and sexual and, like a powerful drug, sends us into a swoon (and sometimes out of our right minds). It inoculates us to our lover's imperfections so that we enter the commitments of everlasting love which are necessary for building a family.

In the game of tennis "love" is a score of zero, suggesting that when we're in love the score is even and all is well. But how often do we keep a competitive score in love relationships? This "tit-for-tat" score-keeping holds the ball in play so that we don't have to look at ourselves. Research shows that when contempt, defensiveness, blame and shame are in the forefront of a couple's style of relating, divorce is surely on the horizon. Conversely, utterances of love and appreciation are antidotes to nasty, "I won, you lose!" words that eat at the foundation of love. Keep the score zero in your love relationship: Give generous doses of gratitude, make caring gestures to your partner daily, and watch the passion and abundance grow.

DAILY HEALTHY SEX ACTS

- Keep a healthy score by counting how many times you utter something loving and positive to your partner in a day.

- Tell your friends and family members that you love them, and follow that by a loving action.

- Give thanks to your Higher Power (whether spiritual or philosophical) by making a gesture that has meaning to mankind, such as holding a door open for someone, offering a smile, or making a donation to a charity or person in need.

> *"I long, as does every human being, to be at home wherever I find myself."*
>
> — Maya Angelou

7 JANUARY

SECURITY

Relational security cannot be pointed to as a *thing* we possess. We're not sexually or romantically secure because we've built the perfect bodies, homes, or lives. And even material success is relative at best. Of course, the relative security of fit bodies, safe homes, and fulfilling lives are often the result of hard-won inner work. But history (and gossip) presents an endless parade of people who "had it all" and either threw it away or lost everything. Any security deriving from outside of us cannot be expected to be permanent. The only lasting security results from self-trust, self-care, and choosing the people and actions that fit our values. Security is a spiritual quality we can share with others only after we've achieved it for ourselves. Likewise, we may share love, honesty, integrity and all our ideals only if we've secured them first within.

The survival instinct is one of our strongest drives and the single greatest reason children can withstand terrible circumstances rather than risk abandonment. From youth to adulthood, we instinctively spend incredible time and effort plotting our security in every situation. Especially if we've ever felt genuinely unsafe, we will feel an urge to grab at any straw: People who have endured trauma often create a whirlpool of chaos as they flail about for a foothold, like persons who feel they are drowning. If we don't heal our wounds from within, the survival instinct will goad us to seek external forms of security, however undependable these may be. Casting another in the role of rescuer devalues the authentic self of both parties and impedes intimacy. The trade-off often requires turning a blind eye to character defects, which creates simmering internal conflict. Ask yourself just how secure it feels to relinquish personal power, and at what price?

DAILY HEALTHY SEX ACTS

- Watch yourself for signs of wanting to be rescued in your relationships. Do others give you security? In what form? Does this devalue either of you?

- Release yourself from the bondage of using others to feel safe. Write an inventory of all the ways you seek out security, and how each has worked out for you.

- What gifts or superpowers have you uncovered in yourself? True inner security will see you through any storm. Today, face your fears and lovingly confront any relational conflict that blocks your light in order to increase your spiritual security in this world.

> *"How difficult, how tragic even, must often be the fate of those whose deepest feelings are destined from the earliest days to be a riddle and a stumbling-block, unexplained to themselves, passed over in silence by others."*
>
> — Edward Carpenter

AWKWARDNESS

Not having grace or sexual skill is often a result of a childhood marked by emotional invisibility. People who feel awkward in life, and especially in sex, were typically not seen, heard, understood, or cherished as children. Moreover, many others were sexually shamed or, worse yet, sexually abused. Shame creates sexual awkwardness, so overcoming sexual trauma is the first step on the road to recapturing our natural grace and ease.

Once you've done the major work of reclaiming your sexuality and pulled it out of the grip of shame, feeling awkward in sex can be overcome. Like a beginning dancer or musician with no technique, you may feel that any attempt to make a sexual move is impossible for you. Yet with practice and with patience—from both yourself and your lover—the "impossible" will become merely "difficult" as your nervous system recalibrates to read sexual contact as something good rather than a set-up for danger or rejection. Eventually the "difficult" becomes "easy" and, with time, you will experience your sexual ease as a thing of beauty.

DAILY HEALTHY SEX ACTS

- Set sail on a course of sexual healing by committing to address just one issue that will help you move out of awkwardness. Does this mean going to therapy for the first time to address sexual abuse you experienced as a child? Or does it mean you feel awkward around a certain sexual act you need to talk to your partner about? Today's the day to take action.

- Make a list of activities that make you feel awkward. What about them most creates anxiety in you? Is there a theme that emerges from your list?

- Try one activity on your list and pay attention to your self-consciousness. Surrender your critical voice and turn toward a natural play state. See what happens.

"Sex lies at the root of life, and we can never learn to reverence life until we know how to understand sex."

— Havelock Ellis

9 JANUARY

DEPTH

We think of depth as a descent to the ocean floor or soaring into limitless space. And while liberating ourselves from emotional blocks certainly empowers healthy expression in the human world *out there*, it also allows us to plumb the internal depths of our reality *in here*. Sadly, many cannot identify even with their *capacity* for attaining such depth. Wounding messages that one is superficial and lacks depth, or distorted associations of spiritual depth with moroseness and depression, can create an unwillingness to go deeper. We may fear that trauma lurks in the depths or entertain the false idea that going deep requires uncovering and solving every mysterious secret.

But at its heart, depth of experience or knowledge simply requires the expenditure of patient, quality time. Just being present in this moment, connecting these very words in this sentence to grasp their meaning, signifies an incredible depth of comprehension using the reading skills that were once impenetrable to you. Likewise, with loving attention you will learn to read your own and your lover's body and soul in bed.

Depth is your due, the thread that binds life together, your through-line, the all-inclusive perspective of your life. Sexuality is not separate from this, your exceptionally profound vantage point. Your past sexual feelings and experiences bestow sexual maturity in the present, and they're all part of who you are. Realize when you meet another in sex, you're giving a singular gift that no one else can give—and avoid the flipside where you see yourself as God's gift! Let your depths reveal your sexual potential, like the maps of ancient travelers gradually discovering the corners of the world, like a puzzle disclosing its own image.

DAILY HEALTHY SEX ACTS

- Do you affirm your depth? What messages prevent you from doing so? Depth is one area where voiced affirmations can have incredible power. Tell yourself: "I affirm my depth." Let your partner know: "I want us to experience deeper fulfillment."

- Take a risk, and share your feelings—not with sentences but with direct sharing. You probably know how to silently express your anger, nervousness, or frustration. Today, show the depth of your love with unrepressed feeling.

- Involve your whole body in every action. Rather than isolating body parts, make love with your entire being.

"When I have sex with someone I forget who I am. For a minute I even forget I'm human. It's the same thing when I'm behind a camera. I forget I exist."

— Robert Mapplethorpe

SEXUAL ABANDON

Sexual abandon—the idea of surrendering to carnal desire popularized by movies, books, music videos, and myth—is a romantic notion. When people feel sterile and aimless in their lives, sexual abandon seems to promise entry into a divine state. In Greek mythology, Dionysus rules irrational, chaotic passion while rational, orderly reason is ruled by Apollo. All civilizations have their Dionysian side, many of which openly celebrate it with orgiastic rites and festivals. We each experience some chaotic passion—orgasm is a moment of sexual abandon. But our culture's current thirst for sexual abandon usually means anonymous promiscuity, risk-taking, or going past one's own limits. That sort of sexual abandon does not result from a sober decision reached by consulting with experts and ironing out details: "planned sexual abandon" is a contradiction in terms! Pursuing sexual abandon as an ultimate goal requires relinquishing mental control over our lives while rushing headfirst into sensual gratification.

Any cautious contemplation of sexual abandon in our culture might be dismissed as sex-negative and puritanical. Certainly, past generations would have interpreted much of what we take for granted today—sleeveless shirts, group dancing, explicit sex talk—as shameless abandon. So we can't ignore the repressive threat of sex-negativity. Still, it's valuable to look at exactly *what's being abandoned* during a sexual binge. If it's a committed relationship, or protecting our sexual health, or responsibilities like work and family, then the flipside of sexual abandon may be that it's really a form of avoidance or self-abandonment. Understood that way, sexual abandon, ironically, perpetuates the greatest of inhibitions because it's being used to block real experience and to numb our highest functions. So sexual abandon, while touted as the very symbol of emotional and sensual growth, can in fact paralyze our spiritual being and our sexual potential.

DAILY HEALTHY SEX ACTS

- What allure do you find in the romantic notion of sexual abandon? Think of clear examples of sexual abandon in your life, in the lives of others, or in movies and books. Then consider the surrounding circumstances. What underlying issues were being abandoned?

- There are structured ways to invite abandon—certainly, artists and performers can experience creative abandon without destroying themselves or their productions. How can we invite divine sexual ecstatic experiences into our lives without completely disrupting our living?

"Come, woo me, woo me; for now I am in a holiday humor, and like enough to consent."

— William Shakespeare

CONSENT

Healthy sex requires consent, *without exception*. In new relationships, partners usually seek out each others' full and free participation. But as time progresses, explicit statements of consent get reduced to shorthand signals, and it's all too easy to ignore a partner's true wishes or even to override them through coercion. True relationship, of course, requires continuing attentiveness to a partner's concerns, including unspoken ones. But asking consent, as well as giving it, assumes the person's autonomy. And those who grew up in controlling environments where their autonomy wasn't respected might have difficulty both seeking consent and bestowing it. Intimacy, of course, is impossible without the consent of both parties. Forced emotional intimacy—a contradiction in terms—is found whenever one party claims to nurture an emotionally honest relationship while actually disrespecting the other's boundaries. It is nothing less than psychological hostage-taking.

Sadly, during much of history consensual sex was the exception rather than the rule, and the horrors of human trafficking and child brides remain in too many parts of the world. But in our society, having a legal age of consent asserts that no sexual activity involving a minor is ever consensual, regardless of the circumstances. A child does not have the capacity to make mature, informed decisions nor to understand the social stigma and long-term psychological consequences of sexual acts. But even in our culture, definitions of consent can vary. In a 2005 sexual assault research survey, over 25% of respondents blamed a woman for being raped if she was drunk, wore revealing clothing, or acted flirtatious beforehand. These appalling statistics reveal a society-wide deficit of autonomy, because public attitudes reflect personal struggles. And until we can be sympathetic to our own right and need for wholehearted and unforced assent, we cannot show more than token concern for another's consent.

DAILY HEALTHY SEX ACTS

- How do you confirm a partner's consent? Have you ever felt that someone owed you sexual favors?

- If you've ever committed any kind of sexual assault, seek help through a therapist, 12-step program, or spiritual practice. Your inner world will become a safer place *for you* once you do. Make amends for misdeeds, and volunteer your time or money to a women's shelter or charity fighting domestic violence.

- Today, seek others' consent in all your interactions. Avoid unilateral decisions, ask for input, and listen with respect and care.

"The fear of appearances is the first symptom of impotence."

— Fyodor Dostoyevsky

IMPOTENCE

Anxiety about how we look to others is the enemy of psychic freedom. In fact, the moment we step outside our selves into self-consciousness, we become impotent. Whether we're talking about sexual performance or public speaking, impotence ensues when we lose our center—our solid sense of self. How much time do you spend agonizing about how you come across to your lover or other people? Some Shamanic cultures believe that when we compare ourselves to others we steal a piece of their soul and abandon our own. Like a thief who can't see he already has what he needs, comparison makes you ignore your own self and steal another's.

It works the same in sex. We're conditioned to think we're responsible for our partner's orgasm, and ignore ourselves while becoming anxious about performing for our partner. But our pleasure, our orgasm, and our sexual experiences are ultimately our responsibility. When we think of impotence, we usually think of men losing their erections during a sexual experience. Has that ever happened to you? If so, were you willing to stop and take care of what you needed? Did you notice what was happening in your body, where your attention was, and whether or not you were anxious? Did you talk to your partner about it or did you shrink into shame, hoping that s/he didn't notice?

If you live in fear that you'll be impotent, you'll create a vicious cycle. Stop. Notice what you're feeling and talk about what you need. The act of calming yourself down and connecting with your partner will help restore your personal potency. Bodily-based pleasure is one of the most luscious experiences we can have. Don't ruin your physical pleasure by putting pressure on yourself to perform.

DAILY HEALTHY SEX ACTS

- Spend one day noticing how you compare yourself to others or how you worry about what others think of you. How much energy are you wasting and how much of your life is passing you by? Minutes, hours, days...

- Next time you have sex, surrender to receiving pleasure. Notice any preoccupation you have or self-judgments you make about being "selfish" or about "getting it right."

- Pay attention to performance anxiety and how that impacts your capacity for potency.

"We are meant to learn this great truth, that giving fulfills us, while withholding and trying to get causes us to feel empty and even more needy."

— Gina Lake

13 JANUARY

WITHHOLDING

Withholding love or sex is psychological abuse and results from early trauma. Withholding is altogether different from *not having* sex or *not reciprocating* love. People *don't have* sex for many reasons. They might be traumatized. They might suffer from sexual dysfunction. They might be practicing self-care and setting appropriate boundaries *for them*. They might even be engaging in the political act of a sex strike in an effort to enact social change. There are equally many reasons why people might *not reciprocate* love. But to *withhold sex or love as a punishment* is a different matter altogether, and is always the result of learned emotional or mental abuse. Manipulating loved ones might appear to be a thought-out strategy, but it's always compulsive.

Withholding exemplifies how deeply we hurt ourselves when we try to hurt others, and how deeply hurt so many of us have been. The phrase, "This hurts me more than it hurts you" (commonly uttered before corporeal punishment), is actually true. A caregiver doling out physical pain literally experiences the punishment along with the person they are hurting. Unfortunately s/he is also reinforcing a psychological pattern that brings psychic agony and isolation. Likewise, those who purposefully withhold love or sex certainly feel the pain and isolation of their actions.

Like any addiction or compulsion, such habitual behavior doesn't just disappear. Because withholding is often masked by denial, it can be difficult to confront. Withholding is a very human quality; most of us at one time have given and received "the silent treatment." Since most solutions to human troubles involve caring, attention, and love, to withhold means to deny solutions. Such withholding is probably a leading factor in many personal, social, and global conflicts.

 DAILY HEALTHY SEX ACTS

- Think of times you withheld love or sex. Know that we all have the capacity to do this. Where will you find help breaking your own pattern of withholding?

- Contemplate examples of others' withholding sex or love from you. What was your response? Know that what others say and do is about *them*. Let yourself feel compassion for whoever wronged you this way, wholly acknowledging right now the pain they must have been repeating.

- Let cold hearts thaw. Breathe into all impossible pain, and be free of repeating old stories. Today, choose love and acceptance. Resolve to embody your vitality and your desire to connect.

"We must embrace difficulty and change if we are to create a fulfilling life for ourselves. If a boat is not rocking, it's not going anywhere."

— Yehuda Berg

DIFFICULTY

It can be difficult dealing with the world, which stymies us with constant, unpredictable obstacles. It can be difficult dealing with inner worlds, too. Our brains, bodies, thoughts, and feelings swirl in a constant flux of neurophysiological and psychological reaction and regulation. Of course, we've outgrown many challenges. If we went back in time with our current abilities intact, how simple it would be to ride that bike, bake that cake, or hit that home run! Yet these and similar activities weren't always easy.

Other difficulties remain challenging forever, such as battling an illness or balancing inner truth with outer circumstance. We must learn the crucial difference between facing difficulties in order to resolve them, and fomenting difficulties out of compulsion, such as seeking conflict in a relationship. Sex and love addicts seek out complications for a thrill. They know that life's normal satisfactions never last long enough, but the rush of unnecessary friction? There's nothing more effective to resurrect the ego and distract from reality.

So how do we face difficulty with grace? It helps with a trusted other. Knowing we share problems may not make them any easier, but it makes them bearable. Through sharing our difficulty, we learn to listen and receive—which is what life and love is all about. Through the delicate act of intimacy, we can bear our most indelicate burdens. To heal yourself from perpetual feelings of hopelessness and persecution, let your difficulties be the guiding light to the inner growth you seek. They bring the opportunity to practice acceptance and loving-kindness, to affirm connection and courage, to summon endurance and true purpose. These precious virtues manifest only through effort. All that we know, express, and become springs from great difficulty. Through difficulty, we never stop evolving to greater levels of being.

DAILY HEALTHY SEX ACTS

- Recall having to do difficult homework as a child. How did you get through it? We can call on the healthy coping skills we learned growing up. Now remember a personal triumph when you worked your way through a tough task. How can you apply this proven problem-solving process to your daily life?

- Recognize the growth made possible in you through difficulty. How have your hardest, most challenging times changed you for the better?

- Get out of self-pity, blame and resentment. Embrace any difficulties today with positive certainty that they deliver the spiritual transformation you're seeking.

"Here in this body are the sacred rivers: here are the sun and moon, as well as the pilgrimage places. I have not encountered another temple as blissful as my own body."

— Sarahapāda

15 JANUARY

BODILY PLEASURE

How blissful do you feel in your own body? Slow down and be aware of the pleasures and sensations you experience in your body while being touched or massaged, when feeling the wind in your hair or the sun on your back, or during sex. Be aware of how much you feel your own bodily pleasure during sex versus how much you're preoccupied with your partner's pleasure. See if you can abandon control while receiving touch from your partner and relax into the sensations of your body. What happens to you when you do this? Do you feel entitled to receive bodily pleasure or do you feel ashamed?

Many have experienced repeated squelching of bodily enjoyment in childhood by critical messages instilling shame and guilt about corporeal pleasure. Don't believe those messages! It's time to take back your sexuality from the shaming communications you may have received, and to remind yourself that those are not your thoughts, but the thoughts of misinformed others. Your pleasure belongs to you and is a celebration of the unique temple known as your body. Celebrate and rejoice in your bodily pleasure, and share your revelry with your beloved.

DAILY HEALTHY SEX ACTS

- Today, notice all the sensations in your body and note which areas respond most pleasurably to touch.

- Make yourself familiar with your erogenous zones so you can communicate that knowledge to your partner. Massage, tickling, gentle touch, and whispering softly into a listening ear all create pleasurable sensations in the body.

- Take a chance and discover a new pleasure zone today, then share it with the one you love.

"Anything that's human is mentionable, and anything that is mentionable can be more manageable. When we can talk about our feelings, they become less overwhelming, less upsetting, and less scary. The people we trust with that important talk can help us know that we are not alone."

— Fred Rogers

TRAUMA

"The beginning of love is to let those we love be perfectly themselves, and not to twist them to fit our own image. Otherwise we love only the reflection of ourselves we find in them."

— Thomas Merton

17 JANUARY

AUTONOMY

One of the greatest gifts people can give their partners, and themselves, is to love them and, at the same time, to let them go. Autonomy is not the opposite of attachment, but its teammate. Without one, we can't have the other and we need both for us and our partners to flourish. The task of love is to continue to accept those we love for who they are, even as they evolve and change independently. On the other hand, demanding that someone change his or her basic nature to conform to our ideas is an act of emotional terrorism. Such ultimatums and other manipulations don't support autonomy in our partners or in ourselves.

Everyone has the right to explore who s/he is, to search for truths about the meaning of life, and to shift and change along the way. Do you have the strength and courage to risk living an autonomous life while staying attached to the ones you love? Do you have the patience and character to support your partner's search for autonomy?

Sexual growth and development demands the willingness to explore and define who we are and what we do and don't like throughout our life span. Stand on your own two feet and tell your partner what you do and don't like sexually. Then, listen without judgment as your lover shares the same with you. Be bold and stay curious.

DAILY HEALTHY SEX ACTS

- Risk being boldly autonomous today and talk to your partner about your sexual desires, fears, preferences, and fantasies.

- Invite your partner to do the same, and listen and ask questions with an open and curious mind.

- What are the autonomous activities you engage in that you cherish? How do you distinguish healthy autonomy from those activities that isolate you from people you care about?

"I admit, I have a tremendous sex drive.
My boyfriend lives forty miles away."

— Phyllis Diller

It's said that "distance makes the heart grow fonder." Distance measures how far apart objects are in time and space, like lovers who separate occasionally. The further away from each other you and your lover are, the more you may actually miss one another, stoking fantasies of reunion. Missing your lover can add a level of excitement to your eventual meeting because the absence of the other's body, soul, essence, and personality has stirred a deeper yearning. This intermission can offer perspective on the relationship so you can ponder what you want, who you've become in the partnership, and who you are when you're alone.

But distance can conveniently create aloofness—an emotional space for disconnection. Often, people with intimacy issues can tolerate only either long-term distance or short-term proximity in relationship. That is, they can maintain long-distance relationships for a great length of time, but can maintain relationships in proximity to one another only briefly. Intimacy demands tolerating geographical closeness *and* time as both are necessary components of a long-term relationship.

Using distancing strategies to heat up a relationship or to leverage power just creates drama—a form of relational game-playing. The idea that distance is necessary to spice up a romance can seem to validate both partners' repeated leaving as a way to create novelty. But when two people invite their mutual sexual attraction in order to reveal themselves more deeply, heat and passion are kindled from a different source. The key to maintaining healthy distance is for both partners to maintain their individuality while under the same roof. Commit to developing yourself, and risk sharing who you are with your partner, even when it threatens the illusion of security in your relationship. Dare to be yourself in proximity to your lover. Don't run away; instead, stand still.

DAILY HEALTHY SEX ACTS

- Make a list of the distancing strategies you use to create separation from others. Do you distance within your current relationship? If so, how do you do this?

- Do you distance yourself from certain types of people, such as from anyone to whom you feel attraction? If so, why? If not, what's the difference between the people you distance from and those you don't?

- Take a good look at the number of friends you have and the length of your longest friendships. Do you need to examine your capacity for intimacy?

"Happiness is a sunbeam which may pass through a thousand bosoms without losing a particle of its original ray; nay, when it strikes on a kindred heart, like the converged light on a mirror, it reflects itself with redoubled brightness. It is not perfected till it is shared."

— Jane Porter

19 JANUARY

HAPPINESS

Happiness is a peculiar feeling. Most of us long for happiness when it's gone. Yet when life pleases, some of us anxiously treasure and fanatically document our joy. There's even a word for the irrational fear of excessive happiness—*cherophobia*—recognizing that such an exalted state carries the potential for disappointment or consequent tragedy. Material happiness refers to a temporary state depending on outside factors, and being based in externals results in a dual experience. In the physics of the material world, what goes up must come down. Similarly, material pleasures have a beginning and end, a rise and decline. That's why we can chase after every desire and peak experience and it doesn't necessarily create long-term happiness. The core belief that happiness will inevitably trigger displeasure may strike us as familiar, because we all know fluctuating cycles and the pain of polarity. But this is clearly a falsity, a mental distortion to ever think that happiness and pain must be received in equal measure.

Is there a possibility for everlasting happiness, perpetual grace? We certainly do seem to seek the happy ending as a species, and the right to the pursuit of happiness is even indoctrinated in the U. S. Declaration of Independence, although the right to the fulfillment of said happiness is noticeably absent except in assorted religious promises of the afterlife. We do know that true inner happiness is an act of communion because it results in identification and connection to the flow of life. This happiness must involve intimacy, the ability to make oneself known. Receptivity to the experience of personal happiness is a form of self-knowledge. To be capable of self-knowledge, intimacy and communion manifests fulfillment, a deeply enduring happiness.

DAILY HEALTHY SEX ACTS

- When you seek happiness from something outside of yourself, first seek the inner values promised by your object of desire: A vacation promises freedom and novelty; a new lover might promise eroticism or esteem. Cultivate lasting happiness by focusing on these inner values, which you can work toward any and every day, with or without that object of desire.

- Today, practice smiling for two minutes nonstop. How long can you last? If your habitual mental loop spasms to negativity (anxiety, fear, or sadness) you'll feel your facial muscles twitch. Even if you don't feel happy, the physical act of smiling can trigger neurotransmitters to induce a healthy surge of happiness.

"Love is an irresistible desire to be irresistibly desired."

— Robert Frost

VALIDATION

The self-centered need for validation may be the single greatest motive for sexual and romantic hook-ups. Having narcissistic caregivers leaves an individual endlessly seeking validation to fill the hole of invisibility, the lack of recognition and empathy. Similarly, when people feel inadequate in areas such as beauty, potency, or worthiness, sex can become a playing field to disprove—or prove—these negative core beliefs. For while many seek validation through others' praise or worship, even more unknowingly seek to confirm *negative* internal messages.

Expecting others to compensate for your perceived inadequacies prevents true relational sex. It's akin to a conversation where you're just waiting for someone to finish talking so it's your turn. These interactions lack adult intimacy, and any validation they convey is never enough. Then there are people who seek validation in theory: "Would you still love me if...?" By pushing the envelope, they hope to gauge another's feelings. At its worst, this is the partner on the receiving end of relational injury who concludes irrationally that abuse equals caring. Typically s/he can't receive genuine validation, since her or his thought process defensively blocks healthy support with a plethora of reasons for its inauthenticity. So any supposed validation gets ferreted out circuitously: "He/she didn't reject me, ergo I have worth."

Honest—not compulsive—validation is a healthy human need. One method to counter our compulsion for validation is to ask safely for honest appraisals, and prepare actually to receive new information about ourselves. Others can validate our perspectives and experience without necessarily agreeing with them. True reflection presents things as they are, and if our loved ones share truths about us, we can welcome them as letting us know we are not invisible—they really *do* see us.

DAILY HEALTHY SEX ACTS

- What do you need validated in your life that perhaps was not validated in the past—beauty, likeability, intelligence, choices, beliefs? List them, underline them, know them. Get them down on paper to lessen your need for compulsive validation.

- Set an intention to receive validation where you need it. Start with personal affirmations, and when you can accept these, ask others for validation. A loving sentiment fully received can be restorative.

- Validate others, even if you disagree with them—especially if you disagree with them. This can be as simple as repeating their statements to let them know you hear them.

"We need not become fixated upon our own suffering, whatever its origin. We offer it up, thus participating in the well-being of the universe. When we experience an illness or depression not as our own but as the universe's, we are one with all beings who experience this kind of suffering."

— Jean-Yves Leloup

21 JANUARY

COMMUNION

By offering up our pain to the world—marking it as holy because it is communal—we touch everyone who has similar pain, and thus become human. Our heartbreak is the world's heartbreak; our inadequacy, the world's inadequacy. We never suffer in our own private hell if our pain brings us into greater relation with humanity. Likewise, how we treat others' pain affects us as well. Dismissing others' poverty points to our denial of our own areas of impoverishment. Symbolically, we are truly one world. Communion reveals our greater nature, for to lift up others is to be lifted up.

We are unconsciously driven into the circumstances of our lives. So we may even subconsciously seek out pain to become closer to people. How many times in relationships do we provoke negative actions in hopes of an open airing and greater honesty and closeness? Only through conscious communion can we break through that round-about program and enter deeper oneness with the living world we inhabit. By knowingly pursuing this connection, we attain the communion we long for without self-destructive struggles.

Life affords all of us momentary glimpses of a vision of the greater good that's produced by considering everyone's existence. However, we rarely wholly cross the threshold into other people's lives, or let their stories deeply affect ours. Communing with human nature lets us embrace the vital spirit of all who enter our lives, allows the breadth and depth of all experiences to touch us. As we endeavor to heal ourselves, our endurance through dark days becomes a beacon of hope to others. We are none of us here by our own hand. Interconnectivity builds the body of our being and supports us; communion transforms and roots us.

DAILY HEALTHY SEX ACTS

- Recognize world sorrow. Until you realize how disconnected from and defended against other people's suffering you are, you will not realize how much you are suffering. For we bear, and even know, our pain together. Today, let every fleeting moment of negativity bring you into greater communion with others in distress.

- We commune with others through love and light as much as through darkness and shadow. Receive others' feelings as aspects of your own. Their joy is your joy. Their laughter lightens your way. Give freely of your spirit and let yourself be part of life's circle, a person among people.

*"True love is a discipline in which each divines the secret self
of the other and refuses to believe in the mere daily self."*

— William Butler Yeats

EXALTATION

Exaltation signifies a peak experience—functioning at full capacity in an elevated state. In astrology, a planet is *exalted* when it's in the sign allowing its greatest expression (so, only 1/12 of the time). We, too, long for exaltation, but like the planets, our lives achieve it only rarely. In love and sex, exalted feelings can easily overpower other emotions and experiences—and thank the stars for that, since initial infatuation helps us overlook personal differences long enough for a loving bond to take root. We all have euphoric recall for our exaltations: when we hit the ball out of the park, when our words had meaning and were felt and understood, when our jokes made people laugh, when we thrived in joy.

Conversely, recalling peak experiences can dishearten us, convincing us that normal life is colorless or has passed us by. The vitality we feel one day to fulfill our potential can easily dissipate into doubt and despair. But the simple practice of acceptance is a great antidote for these fluctuations. True transpersonal exaltation is by definition bigger than any of us; it's not a state we can will or manipulate into being. Still, while much of the work we do to grow our hearts is an inside job, and while the experience of exaltation cannot be commanded, it can be encouraged through a benevolent focus on others. Through affirming others' potential with gentle, persistent knowing and support, we exalt the qualities we hold dear. And in time we will realize that we love in others exactly what we value in ourselves. Judgment or separation cannot coexist in true exaltation, which is the very best of us. And what's the best of us? It's all of us. Altruism is a distinct aspect of exaltation that we can all nourish and invite.

DAILY HEALTHY SEX ACTS

- Recall the exalted states and peak experiences of your life so far. Does the euphoric recall of your past inspire or inhibit your present?

- If you were to invite exaltation, what part of your life would you most like to thrive right now? Exalt in others that which you most desire in yourself. Make room to receive from life by freely giving your time, your truth and your love.

- Today, see the best in others. Imagine a warm, golden glow around everyone you meet. See beyond personalities to share in their spirit.

"Each has his past shut in him like the leaves of a book known to him by heart and his friends can only read the title."

— Virginia Woolf

23 JANUARY

NARRATIVE

Studies have shown that those who learn to express a "coherent affective narrative"—a clear story of their emotional life—can earn a secure attachment, psychological health, and happiness. This relational skill is the ability to communicate your personal life story accurately and with appropriate feeling and thinking. People with this skill can correctly assess the adversity they've faced, and have learned a reliable process for repairing past relational challenges. Conversely, a person lacking narrative coherence is instinctively driven to repeat key mistakes. This is so because destructive tendencies are propelled by destructive self-perceptions, which can't be examined and disproved consciously without the ability to understand and talk about your life journey.

How have the running narratives imparted to us by primary caregivers impacted our own narrative? Most of us receive second-hand information throughout our lives and get into the habit of taking it as the gospel truth. If the life narratives of our primary caregivers were inaccurate or inarticulate—totally self-centered or simply missing—they didn't help us learn a working process for correctly interpreting and integrating new experiences using honest interactions and observation.

Think of your caregivers' previously expressed views of themselves. How did they see themselves and describe themselves to you? What are your current perceptions of those narratives? Can you assess whether they reflect the truth of the actual circumstances, or are you repeating someone else's narrative, taking it for granted? Talk therapy sessions and 12-step recovery shares help develop the ability to present a coherent life narrative through the safe structure of clear rules of communication that support healthy self-expression and self-awareness.

DAILY HEALTHY SEX ACTS

- Take a blank piece of paper and set a timer for five minutes to write your entire life story, filling the page any way you want.

- Try this exercise on a daily or weekly basis for a month. At the end of the month, consider what you learned about yourself from this exercise. How does the act of writing out your story within a limited space and time impact the way you share yourself with others?

"The worst loneliness is to not be comfortable with yourself."

— Mark Twain

LONELINESS

We always hear that getting love begins with loving our self. Depending on others to ease our pain or erase our loneliness eventually weakens us and, therefore, proves dangerous. If our self is weak and needs other people to prop it up, it can become unable to function and can keep us from attaining emotional self-reliance. This form of weakness keeps us in toxic relationships where mutual using marks the drumbeats of the codependent dance. On the other hand, the absence of family, community and friendship can lead to isolation and depression. Lack of companionship, while seemingly the opposite of emotional dependency, withers our soul equally.

When loneliness is a constant state of being, it harkens back to a childhood wherein neglect and abandonment were the landscape of life. Without consistent, caring contact with adults, a young person will be left with emptiness, uncertainty about personal identity, and a fear of being alone. As is natural for such a child, either using other people to feel better or isolating into an inner world will be the "go to" survival options. But both these choices fail to allow them, as adults, to reach out to others for love, comfort, and companionship as a healthy way of validating and meeting their needs.

Both using people and isolating from them pale in effectiveness compared to seeking genuine human relatedness. If you had to use either of these maladaptive options and now live with loneliness, choosing to fill that void is a herculean feat requiring courage and diligence. Start now. Set the intention to change your pattern, then take one small step to connect sincerely with one other person or with a community. That's all it takes to begin your ascent out of loneliness. When two people gather with honesty, magic can happen.

DAILY HEALTHY SEX ACTS

- Take a moment to think about your closest relationships. Are they a two-way street? Do they strengthen and nurture both of you, or are you taking advantage?

- Do you know the difference between loneliness and being alone? Being alone and enjoying your own company is a sign of mental health. When you are alone, do you always have the TV or music on for distraction? Can you tolerate silence or does it raise your anxiety? Challenge yourself to a silent experiment this week and turn off all distractions. Are you alone or lonely?

"For attractive lips, speak words of kindness. For lovely eyes, seek out the good in people. For a slim figure, share your food with the hungry. For beautiful hair, let a child run his fingers through it once a day. For poise, walk with the knowledge you'll never walk alone."

— Audrey Hepburn

25 JANUARY

GROOMING

Looks alone do not necessarily constitute beauty, for beauty emanates from within, but perceivable attractiveness is what moves us toward one another sexually. Grooming, the act of caring for oneself through cleanliness, dental hygiene, and tending to health concerns are habits learned in childhood. A neglected child will have difficulty as an adult with grooming habits such as flossing his teeth or tending to her hair and appearance—difficulties which can leave them feeling shameful and can thereby keep others away. Ironically, over-grooming (wearing make-up to bed or too much cologne) can be another way of avoiding being seen and creating intimacy.

Your standard of grooming is part of defining yourself as a functional adult. As a child, being forced to brush your teeth may have felt like an assault on your autonomy, but as an adult you have to make choices about your self-care and what you want to attract in your life. Once you've set your standard for self-care, then it's okay (and even a good idea) to adorn yourself for your lover. Find out what your partner likes, and see if that fits your self-perception. Maybe your partner tells you that s/he likes the color red on you. Challenge yourself to wear red one day, notice any discomfort you may experience and whether you can adjust, and remember that we sometimes unconsciously bring people into our lives that activate certain issues we secretly need to deal with. If, however, wearing red goes against your value system or taste, don't compromise yourself but do talk about it with your partner. It's good to have a healthy discussion about grooming rather than let any concern build up and become a turn-off or a resentment.

DAILY HEALTHY SEX ACTS

- What areas of bodily self-care do you need to tend to? What do you know about why you let your general hygiene or medical care take a back seat to other activities in your life?

- Plan a discussion with your partner about what turns each of you on and what turns each of you off about grooming and appearance. Be truthful about your preferences without being judgmental, mean, or hurtful. Listen to your partner's responses without reacting out of hurt or shame.

> *"Boys and girls in America have such a sad time together; sophistication demands that they submit to sex immediately without proper preliminary talk. Not courting talk—real straight talk about souls, for life is holy and every moment is precious."*
>
> — Jack Kerouac

COURTSHIP

Whether we're ready or not, nature brings adolescence—prime time for learning love's "rules of engagement." Sadly, many of us weren't taught how to win a person's favor appropriately through flirting or how to read sexual cues about when it's time to hold hands, touch, or kiss. Our culture offers no courses teaching young people how to send interest signals to a crush or what to do afterwards. Courtship know-how is stunted for many, leaving them frozen in time and repeating the same dead-end patterns, unable to become truly intimate or connected. They're stuck in immature patterns and clueless about which traits and personalities in others complement their own. Being attracted isn't enough, especially if you have a faulty, shame-based love map that distorts your natural attraction to someone who's right for you, causing you to make poor love choices. But healthy attraction is essential to the success of a long-term relationship, so healing the past is necessary in order to choose wisely.

Blossoming romance sets up the possibility of sexual contact. Risks are taken through deeper conversations and sharing vulnerabilities, and you start to get a sense of whether the other person is a good match for you or not. Making a good choice may mean saying, "Good-bye." But if your courtship progresses, you'll find yourself moving towards non-genital touch, and will likely start feeling more connected or attached. To create real relational intimacy, you need to pay attention, at every stage of the courtship, to the question of whether the person you're courting, and who's courting you, is really right for you. Finally, movement towards foreplay and intercourse suggests you've moved the relationship into deeper commitment. Choosing well comes from taking each stage of the courtship slowly and deliberately and heeding the cues along the way.

DAILY HEALTHY SEX ACTS

- What stages of courtship did you experience during adolescence? Did you skip a stage? If you feel stunted, briefly write about what steps you need to take to be more vulnerable with your partner or date.

- Have you repeated patterns, such as being stuck in the flirting stage? Were you always the "best friend?" If so, what did you do differently to become a girlfriend or boyfriend?

- Do you need to put effort into courting your current partner? Take time to flirt with your partner; become curious about who they are today. Plan a special evening or romantic dinner.

> *"I have found the paradox, that if you love until it hurts, there can be no more hurt, only more love."*
>
> — Daphne Rae

27 JANUARY

TOLERANCE

Tolerance commonly means accepting differences. It can also signal our ability to accept intimacy, which means we have learned to tolerate discomfort, stress, anger, and grief as well as positive feelings. Those of us who grew up in dysfunctional households learned to tolerate dysfunctionality and never learned to tolerate emotional honesty, security or well-being. But all of us resemble Semele, the mortal lover of Zeus, who was tricked into asking the god into revealing his true nature in all its glory—his godhood—and was burned to a crisp. We must all learn, gradually and in *tolerable* doses, to tolerate the potent forces of spirituality and sexuality.

There are some experiences for which we don't want to build a tolerance. We can easily become desensitized to violence, including not just physical abuse but also emotional, intellectual, psychological and spiritual abuse. Like alcoholics and junkies, sex and love addicts build up a tolerance for their behavior so that they need greater hits and increasing novelty to feel any arousal. We often hear of people who can't stop viewing pornography or performing sex acts they previously considered unappealing. Similarly, love addicts will no longer be satisfied with compulsive texting or cyber-stalking and will take ever greater risks that they themselves consider irrational. Ironically, while addicts build up a tolerance for unhealthy behavior, they remain unable to tolerate the stress underlying their behavior—the stress of loneliness, disappointment, or rejection.

How do we tolerate that which is intolerable, and perhaps should be? In any situation, we can at least learn to tolerate our own process, and the fact that sometimes we find ourselves in very difficult circumstances. We may thus tolerate any situation without *submitting to* it. It might be counter-intuitive, but the only way to create healthy tolerance in the world... is to have healthy tolerance for the world.

DAILY HEALTHY SEX ACTS

- We can learn to tolerate love, to tolerate peace. How long can you tolerate sitting in a peaceful moment? How about in traffic? How often can you get to a peaceful place today?

- For some people it can be difficult to tolerate another person's touch or eye contact. Can you tolerate a good rhythm or mood during sex without wanting to make it better (and sometimes ruining it!)?

- Expand your ability to tolerate intimacy through a physical act with your beloved today, whether holding hands or avowing your love.

"There is no easy way out of our circumstances. Sometimes you stick it out even when you want to give up because you know that on the other side is either a better situation or a better you."

— Krissi Dallas

CIRCUMSTANCE

The conditions we're living in at any given moment color our perceptions of our own and others' lives. We're all born into unique circumstances, and cannot ever completely understand another's situation, no matter the depth of love and intimacy shared. This includes our life partners and even our own children because every individual's circumstance combines so many levels of life: material, emotional, mental, and spiritual. It always sounds a bit funny to hear people gossip about the personal lives of celebrities, as we seldom know the real-life situations of our own friends and family, much less of people we've never met. In fact, we rarely know our *own* lives half the time. We're continually faced with confounding circumstances that try our patience, perhaps giving us unending opportunities for spiritual refinement.

When it comes to the circumstances that set the stage for our lives at birth, we may wonder whether caregivers create, or react to, a child's personality. The dispute between nature versus nurture is longstanding but in recent years we've come to believe that a child is shaped by both. Perhaps all potential influences on us co-exist in a symbiotic state—a house of mirrors from personal to interpersonal to planetary. Ultimately one of the only knowable truths is your own circumstance, which includes your actions as well as your perceptions. Perceiving that others suffer more or less than we suffer can be as much a part of our circumstance as the home we live in, the work we do, or the relationships we've built. May we hold a place of compassion for the circumstances of others, as we know from experience the overriding importance of our own.

DAILY HEALTHY SEX ACTS

- What are your current circumstances? List the first five that come to mind on a blank piece of paper. Now draw a circle, and create a pie chart to show the amount of "pie" each circumstance eats up in your life.

- Did you list only material circumstances or did you include emotional or mental circumstances, too? How much do love, anger, grief, and other feelings emerge on any given day?

- Do you have dominant thoughts? How does your mindset inform your circumstance?

- Reflect on the outer circumstances that indirectly affect your life—the perceivable circumstances of your lover, family, friends, community, and world. Do you recognize their circumstances as yours by association?

"Dreaming or awake, we perceive only events that have meaning to us."

— Jane Roberts

29 JANUARY

MEANING

The search for the meaning of life isn't the realm of poets and philosophers alone. We all seek our true purpose, and if we fail to find it, an existential crisis—a crisis about our very existence—can leave us scrambling to make sense of everything. And if we can't make sense, we'll often try to make sensory stimulation distract us from the question: *Why are we here?*

We can answer this query best by analogy. Recall the significant books, movies and people you've known. Creative works and acquaintances that mirror our experiences and views grab us and grow meaningful. There may be no single moment when their importance hits us, but gradually they change our hearts. These discrete glimpses of meaningfulness may deepen or fade. But the meaning behind *all* of life? It has to exist—it cannot *not* exist. If we are capable of contemplating it, it already exists as a concept, just waiting for our awareness to make it visible.

Even more certain than such philosophical reasoning is the one way we can fully know life's meaning. And that is to live, *truly* live in everything we do. Only our right action—intentional activity for the greater good of all beings—develops the tools of consciousness that let us perceive the inherent, but hidden, significance in the world. Think of all the positive turning points in your life. Would they have happened without your concrete, purposive deeds and the new understanding they brought you? At such moments you fully comprehended life, because taking new, right action creates new, right associations in our brains that allow us to grasp the world anew. Just as we dedicate energy to create intimacy with a living human being, we must devote our intentions and strength to revealing the significance of life. Both these intentions require sacred acts and create sacred awareness.

DAILY HEALTHY SEX ACTS

- Love life fully, love all life generously, and life will enrich your heart with meaning.

- Think of what holds meaning for you today. Reflect on how this came to be. Now look around. What meaning can you uncover in everyday interfaces with others and objects?

- Focus on one insignificant object, and consider all the associations you have with it. Now love that object and envelop it in your heart's embrace. Does this alter its meaning for you? If so, can you see how your actions can create greater meaning in your life?

"I dote on myself, there is that lot of me and all so luscious."

— Walt Whitman

LUSCIOUSNESS

The very pronunciation of the word *lusciousness* evokes a sensuous quality. Let it roll off your tongue! How much lusciousness do you allow yourself before fears of over-indulgence start to surface? Most people have grown up with a lot of shame and repressive messages that turn them against their inherent potential for luscious sensuousness.

You can imagine a lush garden and how breathtaking it is, but can you imagine having those same feelings for yourself? None of those lush gardens would flourish if its plants were ruled by the attitude that luxuriance is wrong. All those colors, shapes, smells, and textures—if social customs forbade them as shameful, no one would be able to cultivate a luscious garden.

Yet you are allowed to enjoy luscious gardens. And since you clearly have a working concept of lusciousness in your vocabulary, you get to decide for yourself the degree to which you want to embrace a full range of appreciation for your own sensuous spirit, for the lusciousness of your own creation.

DAILY HEALTHY SEX ACTS

- What is your version of personal lusciousness? Ice cream with berries, a sweat-soaked workout shirt, herbal shampoo? Recall into your imagination the moments you felt your natural sensuousness unleashed.

- Now invite those feelings to your everyday activities. What reactions do you get from others? Notice your own reaction to simply asserting your experience.

- Who are the luscious people in your life? Do they know about your luscious preferences? If not, why not? What one luscious thing can you share with them today?

"A marriage is like a long trip in a tiny rowboat; if one passenger starts to rock the boat, the other has to steady it; otherwise they will go to the bottom together."

— David Reuben

31 JANUARY

INTERDEPENDENCE

When two beings depend on each other, an interdependence occurs that's fully natural because, as in all of nature, no single being can thrive alone. In interdependence both parties are mutually reliant, while in dependence, one party leans entirely on the other. A period of dependence may be crucial for children, puppies, kittens and other young to survive, but interdependence is an equally crucial adult developmental task. It's essential not just for a couple but for larger entities as well: for a family or a business, for human society, and for our earth. By tending to your lover, family, neighbors, and the living earth, you're ultimately tending to your own "garden."

Homeostasis, the balancing "wisdom of the body," is key to all healthy interdependent systems, including relationships. It keeps the system's equilibrium, much as healthy bodies keep a proper temperature. Because attachment is so central in our development, we can describe a relationship as though it were a physical body, with vital organs and points of vulnerability. When one of these points is injured—say the "trust organ" or "respect organ"—the entire system might shut down.

Robust systems, relational or physical, correct themselves through both positive and negative feedback. Negative feedback tends to balance systems and positive feedback tends to grow them stronger. When something is wrong in a relational system, negative signals usually grab our attention and call us to reparative action. In a relationship, that's the time to own your part in a problem by admitting your challenges to your partner. But don't forget that it's equally important to build on what's going well, to take time to celebrate moments of joy! For interdependence works only with each member's full participation in the health of the system.

DAILY HEALTHY SEX ACTS

- Take the emotional temperature of your relationship or family today. Are you living in a distressed or sick system? If so, what one action can you take to correct its course?

- When things are going well in your relationship, do you amplify the positive states? How do you do that?

- Are you living in an interdependent system or are you overly dependent? Do you carry your own emotional, psychological, financial, and self-care weight? If you're vulnerable in one of these areas, talk to your partner about it and ask for help in order to keep the ecosystem of your relationship healthy.

February

"Only that day dawns to which we are awake."

— Henry David Thoreau

1 FEBRUARY

AWAKEN

If we metaphorically sleep-walk through life, we miss the abundance, beauty, joy, and wonder life offers. If we sleep-walk through our relationships, we miss the same. Your partner has unique and intricate qualities to show you if you're awake enough to notice. Rise from your apathy for your partner by calling forth memories of times that were filled with play and joy, and bring those attributes into your relationship and into your sex life today.

When you choose to stir that which has been asleep you may at first feel groggy, like an early-morning riser, not knowing exactly how to orient yourself or find your way. Trust that your senses will awaken one by one, because you've chosen to attend to your intention to activate your relationship and sex life.

DAILY HEALTHY SEX ACTS

- Think about your best sexual experiences with your partner and what made your sex life lively when you first met.

- Reawaken your sexuality by sharing those memories and suggesting you try some of those things together again.

- If you're single, choose to awaken your day by paying close attention to every moment. Experience the sunrise, taste every bite of your food, smell the air, notice details about your co-workers or others walking by. Awaken your experience of your sensuality.

"True love is but a humble, low born thing, And hath its food served up in earthenware; It is a thing to walk with, hand in hand, Through the everydayness of this workday world."

— James Russell Lowell

HUMILITY

Humility is an important but often overlooked relational quality. It's commonly confused with self-deprecation or servility, but referring to its derivation from the Latin *humus*, meaning earth, reminds us that to be humble is to be *grounded*. It's human nature to project ourselves into the world with great force and purpose, but this stirring up of energy can dislocate our true self. When, in seeking power and pride, we present a false image of *how we want to be* rather than *who we are*, we receive back a false reflection from the world, which only incites us to more posturing.

To be humble enough to receive from others, we must first receive within. This act of self-love gives ourselves not just an appropriate amount of power and pride but, more importantly, lets us receive others' love. This is a tricky distinction. We try so hard to replace negative internal messages with positive messages, but unless we humbly receive them, we will continue to believe, and struggle desperately to disprove, the old ones.

One aspect of humility is knowing there are infinite things we'll never know. We have been so wrong in our self-assumptions, motives and beliefs. And if we can be wrong once, it's very likely we're still wrong in other as-yet-undiscerned ways. Our coping mechanisms may have served to protect us through childhood, but in adult relationships any self-defense will block the light of intimacy. Healthy, enlightened life constantly corrects itself. Respect for truth makes humility possible and gives us the ability to touch the authenticity of our actual inner earth, our groundedness. To share how we perceive rather than what we believe invites in the truth that we are still growing, still finding more about ourselves each day. What we will discover tomorrow requires the humility of self-renewal.

DAILY HEALTHY SEX ACTS

- We receive our experience, including thoughts and knowledge. Receive with humility and gratitude. Today, try saying, "This thought came to me," rather than "I think this." The transparency to share your mental process as you experience it with another is an act of humility.

- Move from the narcissism that secretly says, "That's not me" to silently affirming, "I am that" with every situation that presents itself today. We truly contain all positive and negative potencies within us, so why point the finger? When we identify with others, we cease to be reactive and our ensuing humility illuminates us.

"If one person is in love and the other not, the cooler one is likely to say, "We would have something better between us if you would look at me rather than at your image of me."

— Robert A. Johnson

3 FEBRUARY

PROJECTION

Projection arises when we unleash our hidden fantasies or fears onto another and then react to this altered image as though it's reality. Like a film director, we cast other people as villains, heroes or romantic leads, often embellishing their roles with details from our own repressed traumas. The saying "If you spot it, you got it" describes our situation perfectly. A man irritates us to no end, so we point our finger at him—forgetting to acknowledge these very same negative traits in ourselves. If our sexual needs are being neglected by a partner who is too mechanistic, for instance, there's a high degree of probability that at some point we initiated this with our own behavior. Likewise, our critique of a lover that is "not adventurous enough" may really reflect our own conservativeness. Conversely, we may become unduly enamored of someone who merely seems to mirror the positive qualities in ourselves that we are not yet able to own.

We mistakenly believe we can read others' minds or predict the future, forgetting that the easiest and most reliable path to clarity is simply to ask our friends and lovers to express their truth. Learning to take people at their word shows respect and maturity. Instead of creating chaos and misunderstanding as projection does, it encourages authenticity and autonomy. If we truly want to experience all kinds of intimacy in life, we have to set aside our projections and be willing to encounter the unexpected. Projection robs us of surprise and growth, so every time our minds begin to weave the predictable narrative, we can just cut it short. We can insist on real information gleaned from genuine encounters in the present moment.

DAILY HEALTHY SEX ACTS

- One way to reel in your projections is to examine the conversations you have with people *in your mind*. Today, note these fantasies, and know this is the script *you're writing for them*, not their words.

- Shake up the Etch-a-Sketch of your thinking! Get out of the *PEA brain* of Projections, Expectations, and Assumptions. When you find your mind lost in a stream of irrelevant, imagined thoughts, simply focus on your breathing and bring yourself back to the present moment.

- Ask rather than assume. Be prepared to incorporate new information based on genuine, free responses from actual human interaction.

> *"The outer conditions of a person's life will always be found to reflect their inner beliefs."*
>
> — James Allen

CORE BELIEFS

Many of us who grew up under a barrage of unending negative messages from our caregivers end up agreeing with them that we're worthless. These feelings of profound inadequacy inevitably bleed into feelings of sexual inadequacy, and a sense of failure crowds out any esteem in our self-concept. Over time, the relentless humiliation and degradation come to seem justified and deserved, and become negative core beliefs about ourselves—a negative self-structure.

Desperate to find any light inside, we struggle against any number of problematic behaviors, some of which turn into addictions that appear to confirm those negative core beliefs. When low self-esteem prevails, a false self may develop to hide behaviors we think just prove our disgracefulness, so we can function—or at least "get by." Or, for others of us, this negative self-structure leads us not to cover up but to create a grandiose, distorted self-importance. Either way, we're left empty and alone, self-rejecting at our core.

Core beliefs, however, are not etched in stone. Like any living thing, even hurtful beliefs can flower into something positive and affirming through our desire to change and through right action. Begin by asking yourself why your most negative core belief is actually a distortion. In other words, why is your belief *not* true? Think about your unique abilities and all the things you know to be honorable about yourself. Be on the lookout for shame, which can keep you in the isolated world of negativity, and notice whenever it rears its ugly head. This is a fight that only you can fight. It's an inside job that requires a commitment to knowing the truth about who you are—even before you believe it.

DAILY HEALTHY SEX ACTS

- Make a list of the qualities you value most about yourself.

- Turn each quality into an affirmative statement in the present such as, "I am a good, worthy, and valuable person."

- Create fifteen customized affirmations and speak one a day for fifteen days, then repeat. Keep this going for one month and watch your negative beliefs dissolve into the nothingness that they are.

"Even if our efforts of attention seem for years to be producing no result, one day a light that is in exact proportion to them will flood the soul."

— Simone Weil

5 FEBRUARY

FAITH

It's a leap of faith to trust someone, and if that sours we tend to regret our faith. We've all asked life for something and experienced disappointment. But it's crucial to recognize when past disappointment seems to spell out inevitable doom and disaster, because holding onto disappointment through resentment and fear makes it a self-fulfilling prophecy. Whenever you doubt your partner's attitudes and motives, take a leap of faith and assume the best, secure that you will be guided at the right time toward the next right action you need to take. Because the only way we can synthesize past experience is with right action. We do the right action with an open hand and with the knowledge and belief that the solutions to our problems are out there. Life is an invitation: We invite the right path for us, the right solutions for us, the right partners for us.

To cultivate healthy sex, we practice what we learn and perceive with intentionality and dedication—regardless of the results we are getting just now. We do so with the faith that eventually a psychologically mature eroticism will emerge. Faith demands that we let go of impatiently measuring results, yet faith requires full participation. You can't make the miracle happen by yourself, but you must show up to take the next right action. Have faith that there is a heart-affirming reason for all hurt and rejection, and do not let sorrow keep you from partaking of life and love with an open heart and mind.

DAILY HEALTHY SEX ACTS

- How have you handled disappointments? Standing or seated, notice your bodily posture and energy. Now carefully summon the biggest disappointments in your life while observing the energy flow in your body. Release any energy blocks to restore your bodily posture to its starting state.

- Summon your greatest breakthroughs and achievements. Notice the effect of these thoughts and feelings on your body. Take a leap of faith and let your body return to this exalted state often throughout the day.

- If a journey of a thousand miles begins with a single step, what single right action can you take right now to move closer to your heart's desire?

"Tell me whom you love and I will tell you who you are."

— Arsène Houssaye

It's not often that we ponder precisely what we find sexually attractive in another. Usually, human beings are stirred by that mysterious force we call "chemistry" when it comes to sex and love. And yet, learning what characteristics make up sexual attraction for us is a necessary part of adult sexuality, albeit one we find challenging. Think about what attracts you to another person, whether a friend, lover, teacher, dentist, or medical doctor. We have to feel some sense of attraction in order to trust those around us. What qualities of attraction move you toward someone?

Attraction is a law of nature that makes entire processes and systems come together to birth something new. What attributes do you possess that you think others find attractive—your intelligence, sense of humor, physical appearance, or something else? When you're open and feeling attractive, you'll attract what and whom you need in your life in order to birth something in you. Whether that something is literally a child or the creation of a new business, the inspiration for a work of art, or to be the best you can be, something new and beautiful will be birthed when you're in a state of attraction.

DAILY HEALTHY SEX ACTS

- Take time today to write about what you find attractive in a partner and what you find attractive in yourself.

- What is the most powerful sense of attraction you've ever felt? Was it to a person, a sunset, a piece of jewelry, or something else? What were the alchemical components to that moment?

- Make a commitment to yourself to change your unattractive qualities in order to deepen your self-esteem and to attract the kind of partner or energy you'd like to have in your life.

"While your friend holds you affectionately by both your hands, you are safe, for you can watch both his."

— Ambrose Bierce

7 FEBRUARY

SEXUAL SAFETY

In the animal kingdom, birds, bees and beasts instinctively know how to reproduce and rear young. They even know to digest specific herbs, shells, bones, and barks to cure disease or rid themselves of parasites, without any veterinarian's prescription. But human beings must be initiated into sexual life and taught how to keep ourselves safe and healthy. As young people, we learn the mechanics of sexual intercourse mainly by description (often provoking considerable surprise!) We must also *study* safety. In fact, the evolving social complexity of our species distances us increasingly from our natural instincts. Ironically, our reliance on experienced others for survival rules creates a novel risk, since caregivers may teach the negative, fearful thinking or self-destructive tendencies *they* learned, and thus lay the groundwork for children's retraumatization as adults.

Such harm occurs so often that many people don't feel safe in safety. It isn't familiar. What's familiar is having the rug pulled out from under them. Their experience demonstrates why transparency, recovery, and accountability are so important. Only once we've learned how to be safe with ourselves—once we're not unconsciously trying to kill ourselves—can we be, and feel, safe with others. For example, some may see unprotected sex as symbolic of intimacy, freedom, and honesty. But in reality it can be a cold, disconnecting act to ignore personal safety and peace of mind. If someone sees sex as only something that happens between body parts, then, sure, anything less than bare skin can't satisfy. But when we learn to value our entire body and well-being, healthy sex includes caring for our safety and the safety of others. More explosively intimate than a part touching a part is a heart touching a heart. This sacred vulnerability necessitates the safety of sober love.

DAILY HEALTHY SEX ACTS

- How safe is your sex? Can you distinguish healthy risks from flirting with disaster? On a piece of paper, draw two columns marked "SAFE" and "UNSAFE," and list your actual and potential sexual and romantic activities in the column that fits.

- *Fire Drill Kits* are healthy tools to use when triggered. These include phone numbers of your therapist, sponsor, or supportive friends; self-regulating exercises to restore emotional sobriety; and inspirational readings to remind you of your integrity. Assemble a fire drill kit today and keep it close.

"Sex ran in him like the sea."

— John Masefield

We're awestruck by the virility of nature unimpeded, as in the ocean or a raging river. If we understood virility as that living, natural power, we would all love to feel so forceful, hearty, and virile! When you think of virile people, even fictional characters, you probably see this quality as inherent in them, independent of external factors. Since true virility doesn't depend on an outside source, sexual potency doesn't get depleted.

But many sexual dysfunctions, and often sexual addiction, spring from a wounded virility. Some upbringing can be sexually minimizing, even castrating or sterilizing. Negative body image—the exaggerated sense of our physical imperfection—is common, as is pubescent anxiety over sexual aptitude. Later overcompensation for such wounds can themselves inhibit virility, as we see in the person who bluffs and blunders through endless sexual situations to hide emotional blocks. If someone uses sex to stimulate—or to simulate—a sense of virility, s/he will lose that sense of power at the moment of orgasm and have to build it up again.

Without strong role models or encouragement by caregivers, peers, or society itself, our free-flowing, natural virility becomes stunted. Our culture recognizes virility only in the limited, stereotypical domain of "strong and silent" heterosexual men. But in nature, virility flowers free of such bias. With acceptance and support, men and women of all orientations, genetic make-ups, and physiological abilities may enjoy their natural, wholesome virility.

You can encourage your partner's virility as a healthy act of sex. The first step is just knowing that each of us is truly virile. That's our native state. By inviting the flow of your respective energies, holding space for your intention, and containing the raw intensity in a secure and sober way, we tap into the restorative power of virility.

DAILY HEALTHY SEX ACTS

- How do you judge sexual virility in others, and how does this match your current perception of your own erotic self?

- Experience your virility right now. Take deep, strong breaths and feel the force of your livingness. Run your hands along your body, like a flowing river feeding all it touches. Invest this—your real, untamed current of energy—in everything you do today.

- Affirm your virility and that of your beloved. Drop the verbal and mental accusations of weakness in yourself and others. Know that there is bountiful vitality behind all you perceive. Choose to know life.

"A discovery is said to be an accident meeting a prepared mind."

— Albert Szent-Gyorgyi

9 FEBRUARY

DISCOVERY

Preparing to meet your lover can lead to discovery in your sex life. Preparation is wholly different from prediction. Rigidly engaging in rote sexual acts will almost always lead to a loss of desire, but preparation means deliberately taking action for whatever possibilities you may create together. If you're genuinely curious about your lover, you will have prepared yourself by considering what s/he likes, what turns her or him on, and what you need in order to be fully present for an unpredictable sexual encounter. For some, preparation has to do with grooming, bathing, buying flowers, wearing sensual clothing, or choosing the right music, setting, or other agreed-upon rituals.

Talking about sex with your partner and learning his or her preferences is one thing. Readying yourself to put what you learned into action is another! When preparations are afoot, there's a container for discovery and surprises, for novel experiences, for "eureka" or "aha" moments to burst forth. When you stop controlling or making love "by the book," and instead start preparing, you free your body, mind and soul, thereby making a space for spontaneity, joy, play, laughter, and—discovery.

DAILY HEALTHY SEX ACTS

- What preparations do you need to make before your next sexual encounter with your partner?

- Put into action what you know about what turns your lover on.

- Take a risk by setting aside what you "usually" do and prepare to discover something new about yourself and your lover.

> *"The true adventurer goes forth aimless and uncalculating to meet and greet unknown fate."*
>
> — O. Henry

In Greek and Roman mythology the Fates were three goddesses who presided over the birth and life of all humans. Each person's destiny was conceptualized as a thread spun, measured and cut by the Fates. The events and course of one's life were beyond human control, set by a supernatural force.

Similar to fate, destiny can be seen as both a great possibility and as our inevitable death. When viewed as possibility, life seems dynamic and filled with potential, and we are here to realize what's best in ourselves. Even if we think of destiny as death, we can see it symbolically and learn that some things in our lives must die or be discarded to be reborn, challenging us to cede control.

What are your deepest fears about life? Do they impede attainment of your needs and desires? Stepping into the unknown conjures fear if we believe our fate is sealed. Even more frightening, however, may be the belief that it is not. Think about which belief you hold. *If your fate is sealed*, there's nothing to lose, so live life with abandon! *But if you don't believe in fate,* you are the master of your life. Your daily choices set your course. But don't worry, if nothing is preordained, you can shift your karma based on better choices you make. *Either way,* spring into the void of the future today and see what awaits you!

DAILY HEALTHY SEX ACTS

- Do you believe in fate or in destiny? If neither, what do you believe about your life's course? Does anyone know what you believe?

- Make a list of your unrealized hopes and dreams. What obstacles have been in your way?

- Share your beliefs and dreams with a loved one.

"The only way love can last a lifetime is if it's unconditional. The truth is this: love is not determined by the one being loved but rather by the one choosing to love."

— Stephen Kendrick

CHOICE

Being honest with yourself about what you need and desire in a mate is one of the greatest gifts you can give yourself. So *choosing* your partner is an act of self-esteem. Settling for whoever comes your way or criticizing your partner for his or her nature are both acts of emotional violence. By being in reality about the person to whom you're relating, you are making a conscious decision to choose that person—warts and all.

Once you make that choice, you're no longer a victim, but an informed participant. When you stop feeling like your mate is doing something "to you," then, and only then, can you love.

When you make the choice to be in your relationship, you get a whole lot of other choices, too. For example, instead of complaining that your partner isn't romantic or sexy enough, consider how romantic or sexy you can make yourself. Actually taking that responsibility not only empowers you, it makes a space for your partner to move toward you in ways you might find surprising. When you choose your partner and take responsibility for your sexuality, you recognize that, ultimately, only *you* can make yourself happy.

If you've chosen your partner, and that person breaks vows you both agreed to, don't deny your situation. Ask yourself if you can heal from the pain in order to choose your partner again, or if it's time for you to go. Choosing after a betrayal can take time; be honest with yourself about what you need to be happy and whole.

DAILY HEALTHY SEX ACTS

- Have you chosen your partner or are you waiting to be rescued? Do you blame and shame your partner or do you accept all aspects of the choice you have made?

- Do you need to adjust how you're viewing things, or is it time to end the love relationship? Be careful about blaming and shaming yourself and the other. If you made a bad choice or no longer want to be in your committed relationship, stop torturing your partner and yourself, and move on.

"And once a boy has suffered rejection, he will find rejection where it does not exist—or, worse, draw it forth from people simply by expecting it."

— John Steinbeck

REJECTION

There's a saying that life's rejection is God's protection. It means that every experience is good for us and leads to our true life purpose, even if we can't recognize it at the time. Realize once and for all: We've all felt that sting of rejection! Yet the place where each holds that hurt is one of the biggest secrets we keep. So what's the gift just under the pain we hide to save face?

That gift is our true self. By masking our pain to save face, we actually lose our true face. Feel your rejection. Let the nobility of your honest emotions support you, and resist the temptation to withdraw and nurse your wounds in the darkness of dissociation and denial. The real, living world will nurse you to spiritual health if you let it. Sadly, we often mistake the object of our desire for that whole world, thinking only that object can save us. Trust that if you're feeling the smart of rejection, your ego has mistaken a short-term goal (like dating a particular person or landing a certain job) for your larger life purpose. Short-term goals are great, but if you focus on each bend in your road, you miss the view. Take heart, for even your inability to handle rejection just now must help you fulfill your true purpose or it wouldn't happen.

Sex and romance are prime areas where we experience rejection. But most often, this means we're preoccupied with getting what we want, on taking rather than giving. Open your heart, give unconditionally, and allow life's inevitable rejections to lead you, with sure steps, to the realization of your most secretly treasured dreams.

DAILY HEALTHY SEX ACTS

- Do you realize that everything that happens supports your spiritual growth, and that your sexuality is part of your spiritual growth? Consider those who reject your emerging sexuality. What gifts do they, unwittingly, bring to your life process?

- Think of your last memorable rejection. Write what was spoken as a short script. Appreciate the difficulty of disengaging your ego from its seeming frustration. Now, pretend you are the playwright of this scene, drawing from your life experience to create both parts. How does this scene help each character develop? Let the truth of this answer remain true for you. Today, let it ring.

"We're all a little weird. And life is a little weird. And when we find someone whose weirdness is compatible with ours, we join up with them and fall into mutually satisfying weirdness—and call it love—true love."

— Robert Fulghum

13 FEBRUARY

TRUE LOVE

Popular media constantly promise that *true love* carries infinite restorative power by joining separate people into an abiding unity. But if we define *love* as an unconditional force that unites, isn't it redundant to add the word *true* to it? How could love not be true, if it's really such a powerful uniting principle? So the term *true love* reveals that there's a lot of false love out there.

Many loves proclaim to be a uniting force, but turn out to be a disconnecting one. It's a fact of human nature that, due to their own past trauma and hurt, people aren't always as they present themselves. The notion of *true love* expresses a paradox: It creates an expectation for an idealized love superior to... every other love experience one has had so far. When the question, "Is this a *true love?*" comes up in a relationship, you can bet it's more like one of you is saying, "I hurt. What's worked for me hasn't really worked, and I need it to work this time. In truth, I am not yet able to integrate my experience."

To experience true love—the unifying power of genuine relationship—we need first to truly love all of life. The degree to which we can integrate an unconditional, unifying love for all of life corresponds to the degree to which we can experience true love.

DAILY HEALTHY SEX ACTS

- Let's talk true love fantasies. What are yours? Do you dress a certain way, talk a certain way? Try on some of the characteristics of your true love fantasies for size. How would they fit and feel in real life?

- Love the world wholly and unconditionally just for today. See each moment of your life as leading up to this point. Send love backward to every step of your past. Send love forward to every part of your future. For you are the true, uniting principle of your love life.

"How happy the lover,
How easy his chain,
How pleasing his pain!
How sweet to discover
He sighs not in vain."
— John Dryden

Life takes on meaning only through reciprocal interaction with the world. To a fishmonger, all things reek of the sea; to a teacher, life is a lesson. What we do is what we know, and how we interact is what returns our way. Reciprocity symbolizes inner and outer worlds matching up in synchronized harmony. The art of existence is to give and receive, see and be seen, and the quality of love as echo and mirror assures us that we have a genuine presence. But those who grew up with a caregiver who was physically or emotionally absent may feel more than this normal desire for reciprocity. They may experience a compulsive urge to accomplish the one, elusive thing they imagine will finally get those absent ones—or anyone—to connect with them.

FEBRUARY 14

RECIPROCITY

If someone in your life doesn't reciprocate, there are two reasons. First, if your right-sized need for validation was denied in childhood, you will involuntarily recreate the same circumstances to correct it. Know that you get second chances so that *you may change the art of your interaction*, not so that others might finally treat you with the loving respect you deserve (and you do deserve loving respect). And there's another reason for unrequited regard; you must be able to receive, to be emotionally available. How many times do you deny or minimize others' genuine kindness? Life is a mirror that reflects your actions—including your thoughts—right back at you. People reciprocate exactly in proportion to how you treat yourself internally. Show yourself love. You have so much love to give yourself—enough to reverberate for eternity. Let yourself live in your own loving.

DAILY HEALTHY SEX ACTS

- Reciprocate your beloved's love on as many levels as you can—in actions, words, body language, vocal tone, and spiritual blessing.

- Think of those you attract to your life. What within you might they be reciprocating? Often when we work on our issues and surrender selfishness, people who don't reciprocate our truer selves ultimately leave our lives.

- Be an echo of an echo today. While it's healthy to have an original presence, it's a useful practice to be able to reflect others. Today, focus on your capacity to reciprocate in all your interactions.

"It's not love's going hurts my days
But that it went in little ways."

— Edna St. Vincent Millay

15 FEBRUARY

NEGLECT

Neglect is more harmful than once thought, especially for young children. It comes in the form of disregarding or ignoring a child's needs, whether emotional, physical, or psychological. Being neglected can wreak terrible damage on children's sense of themselves, and therefore on their self-worth and esteem. These under-valued children may carry the baton of neglect into the rest of their lives. Many of us struggled from the supposedly "benign" neglect by our caregivers, which left us feeling shameful about our appearance, bodies, morals, or intelligence. We may heal ourselves from these wounds. But making such a fundamental change in the way we see—or don't see—our true beings requires stopping and taking an inventory of the self-disregard we still tolerate in our lives.

Survey your life: Take a look at your home, car, work environment, wardrobe, relationships, and spiritual state, and see what parts of yourself you may be neglecting. What has become shabby in your surroundings? In your appearance? In your work? Do you settle for neglectful, cavalier relationships with friends or your partner? If you show indifference to yourself, you can expect nothing more from potential lovers, friends, or bosses.

If you're neglecting your primary relationship then that "garden" won't flourish and grow either. So often we assume that once we're in a committed relationship it will sail on automatic pilot seamlessly into the future. Since no one ever put attention or care into them, persons neglected as children may have particular difficulty grasping that living relationships, like living beings, require tending, hard work, and love. Promise yourself to care for your relationship, and for yourself, and put those vows into practice.

DAILY HEALTHY SEX ACTS

- Take a moment to look at your life and consider your most deeply desired vision for the coming year.

- Do the persons and things in your life reflect that vision or are you tolerating scraps?

- Remove all tattered or shabby things in your life and stop neglecting yourself.

"Before you begin on the journey of revenge, dig two graves."

— Confucius

Almost 4,000 years ago, Hammurabi's Code declared, "An eye for an eye, and a tooth for a tooth." While originally designed to *restrict* punishment to fit the crime, this primitive law may be taken to extremes. That's because our limited human vantage point obscures all but the obvious outlines of an event— especially one that hurt us. So most of us find justification for playing God or meting out karmic retribution, whether subtly as passive-aggressiveness or blatantly as abuse. In the midst of our pain, anyone seems an enemy, even loved ones. *The ones we love.*

When normal conflicts with a caregiver occur within the context of a secure, warm attachment, the child remains connected to the loving relationship, and thereby learns the healthy process of integrating simultaneous feelings of love and hate. But in emotionally insecure households, incidents of rage or hate shred the flimsy connection, and the child desires revenge—one traumatic result of being unconnected to any larger context of caring. Later, those who were never taught—by love—how to accept and resolve conflicting emotions may find historical patterns frequently triggered, and re-experience the anger and sense of wrong experienced throughout childhood.

Demanding retribution for injustice might be fair, but violent payback never brings peace. The means must equal the end. The only antidote for revenge is self-love. How can we possibly invite love, compassion, and awareness when the fires of vengeance consume us? We must learn to place trust in ourselves, rather than depending so much on other people that their slightest betrayal destroys us. Thoughts or deeds of revenge always signal that we've made someone or something else our Higher Power. But there's nobody and nothing out there that can ever make us whole. Peace of mind, and true justice, is an inside job.

DAILY HEALTHY SEX ACTS

- Have you ever had revenge sex to get back at an ex-lover? Rebound sex is revenge sex that involves an innocent bystander and creates a crazy web of karma. How has retaliation affected your relationships?

- Do you trust yourself today? Recall the last time you became overwhelmed with rage and vengefulness. Can you allow yourself to feel rage without revenge fantasies? Acknowledge the vengeful, unforgiving side of yourself. We can only heal what we can handle.

- Whenever people, institutions or doctrines invoke feelings of revenge in you, wish them well. Their emotional growth is your growth.

"The ultimate lesson all of us have to learn is unconditional love, which includes not only others but ourselves as well."

— Elisabeth Kübler-Ross

17 FEBRUARY

SELF-LOVE

Our capacity for self-love filters our experience of the world. Self-love includes and integrates all our elements—admirable or not; so self-love lets us view the world's elements—admirable or not—as a unified whole, too. Conversely, though, to lack self-love shatters our perceptions of ourselves and of the world, and provokes seemingly irresolvable ethical dilemmas.

It's perfectly okay and human to have defects of character. We all experience moments when we clearly realize our dysfunctionality. In the 12-step model this valuable realization is called *powerlessness*. The proper response to it is to cultivate self-love for these moments: If we can't stand ourselves, our powerlessness to love ourselves must be met with self-love. Paradoxically, we develop self-love by loving ourselves for not being able to love ourselves! If failure dispirits us, the remedy isn't success. It's developing self-love, because without it, any success will be short-lived. To comprehend and accept our brokenness and to show self-love anyway engenders more recovery than any affirmation or meditation. Moments of shame when we can show self-love, grow self-love. That's when we're acting like the light of consciousness that illuminates all it touches, regardless of merit.

Self-love is also the means by which we recognize ourselves in any person whom we would judge or blame. We know what it's like to feel unforgiven, unfed, misunderstood. When our rage and blame arise against others, the first thing we practice, even then, is *self-love, so we may love others*. Self-love sustains itself while it supports us and others, because the more self-love we practice, the more we love others, and the more we model healthy self-love, the more we are able truly to love ourselves.

DAILY HEALTHY SEX ACTS

- While making love with an understanding partner, allow each other the time and space, through meditation or affirmation, to find your own levels of self-love that support your being present with each other.

- Today, try to resolve all conflict with self-love. Whenever you lose your center, your cool—whether you get stressed, annoyed, enraged, disappointed, afraid, confused, ashamed, or overcome by any of the myriad character defects of human beings—summon self-love.

"Out upon it, I have lov'd
Three whole days together;
And am like to love three more,
If it prove fair weather."

— John Suckling

As much as we enjoy new experiences to delight our senses, secretly we all seek constancy—to be constant in our affections, perceptions and intentions. Constancy is not monotony, an endlessly dull routine to be easily dismissed. Is there a more maddening ache than what comes when we abandon our own ambitions? Maybe it's as simple as a broken promise to exercise, or as complex as an alcoholic's broken resolve to refuse an offered drink, the sex addict's acting out despite deciding to stay put for the night, or the love addict's leaving twenty messages instead of the single one s/he intended. Our inconstancy to ourselves makes us our own worst enemy and creates tremendous inner conflict.

CONSTANCY

Think of the times you've been betrayed. Now imagine that pain inflicted on yourself by your own hand every time you betray your principles and best interests. A plant needs constant light and water to blossom; so do you need constant care to bloom. It's only through constancy that you learn to love and trust yourself and others.

It's said that the only constant is change. But this truth need not be a fatalistic decree against stability—we can work this adage to our advantage. Whenever we feel down, depressed, and doomed to failure, we can remember when we felt perfectly fine in similar circumstances. At the times we fume over our weight, age, looks, or worth, we would do well to remember that we had the same weight, age, looks, and worth days earlier but recognized them with a positive outlook. We go through—*and get through*—recurring behaviors and interactions. To cope with our own imperfect constancy in all these endless cycles, we may look beyond our sense of self-betrayal, invoke the faith to affirm our nobler nature, and recommit—constantly—to ever-greater constancy.

DAILY HEALTHY SEX ACTS

- Consider whether your actions regularly contradict your aims. Can you stick to a plan, or do you repeatedly rescind your original intentions on a whim? How can you invite constancy into your experience?

- Notice whether those closest to you keep their word. When should you overlook the less-than-reliable promises of loved ones in order to acknowledge their greater virtues? And when would it be better to call them on their fickle behavior, or steer clear of them entirely?

"You may be very, very intense in your sexuality—but once sexuality is fulfilled, it is finished, the intensity gone."

— Osho

19 FEBRUARY

INTENSITY

Sex and love addicts confuse intensity with intimacy and are always looking for the next high. They change people like they change their clothes, for the reward of novelty. Their fantasy of the perfect lover who will fulfill every desire intensifies—like that of a vampire seeking blood—with each passing conquest.

Constantly dissatisfied intensity-seeking in sex and love is fueled by internal emptiness from early childhood. Imagine being emotionally abandoned by a stressed or depressed mother who, unable to attune to her infant's needs, leaves it to fight for its life. Since mother/infant attunement is necessary for babies' physical and emotional growth, a child who doesn't get the neural and affective regulation needed to feel secure grows up empty, numb, afraid, and lonely.

As an adult the intensity-seeker has little skill at genuine intimate connection, although she or he is driven to use people and sex to try to feel better. But the desired intensity ultimately dulls the senses, leaving him or her hungering always for more. Tragically, the locus of emotional control is in a lover's—often a stranger's—hands; life is good or bad depending on whether she or he is wanted, rejected, abandoned, or needed. Intense sex becomes the only criterion of whether life is happy or sad.

Intensity-seeking is an enslavement of our own perpetuation. When we step out of the delirium of always seeking someone new, and meet the same old sad and lonely child within, our healing journey begins. Exhausting ourselves with novelty is a defense against our deepest pain, one that we cannot outrun. But once we stop and feel our losses, we can begin our healing journey and be the authentic, joyous person we were born to be.

DAILY HEALTHY SEX ACTS

- How connected are you to your childhood trauma? Have you ever investigated the wounds of your past?

- Do you drag your past into your present? If you're an intensity-seeker, the answer is most likely "yes."

- Take time to journal and ask yourself whether you have difficulty with sex and love. If so, get some help today.

> *"Love in its essence is spiritual fire."*
>
> — Emanuel Swedenborg

SPIRITUAL LOVE

To experience spiritual love, demonstrate a loving spirit. One definition of *spirit* is the uniting intentional energy behind any activity. We have probably all felt caught up in a group mood of jubilation—"team spirit"—at least once. We may have also felt times of grace, where social expression flows effortlessly. During such exalted instances, it's futile and counter-productive to analyze every single element to find the end-all source of exaltation; the whole of the experience is greater than the sum of its parts.

What we accomplish on our own either succeeds or fails; we feel good or bad. Because we're human we perceive these feelings dualistically. A spiritual experience—the experience *of a greater spirit*—transcends duality and transports humankind out of our black-or-white, bifurcated perception. As a consequence it lifts us out of our isolation. Spiritual love brings us in touch with our larger selves, which always include others.

Unquestionably, we do not create most of our experience. We bear witness. Who among us could write this script? There are infinitely many belief systems, but the concept of spirit— whether energy, blind force, religious deity, mindstuff, or mystery—may reconcile them all. Everything has a spirit, especially love.

Bring awareness to the spirit of your loving. Sexual energy, when directed toward conscious healing or uplifting divine union, can relieve and transform. Do you limit your sexual experience to physical sensation? Why, when mentality and emotionality are so integral to your being? Bring the spirit of all facets of your personality to your sex and love life. Your thoughts and feelings have weight, sound, and appearance. Caress your lover with your mind through erotic intentions. Let your spirituality vibrate and ripple, and know that the flow of sexual union is of *a greater spirit*.

DAILY HEALTHY SEX ACTS

- What is your concept of spirit? Is it compatible with your sex and love life? Imagine you are such a spirit today, and send love to all: family, friends, community, world...

- What blessings do you bring to your partnership? Let your lover know the true meaning of your passion. Before making love, share the loving spiritual intentions of your hearts. Touch the spirit of your truths.

- See your lover through your god eyes. Let your mind rise to the height of spiritual awareness. Every glance, sound, sigh, touch, embrace is a sign and gift of the greater spirit of your union. Caress *greater spirit* today.

"Only when we know our own darkness well can we be present with the darkness of others. Compassion becomes real when we recognize our shared humanity."

— Pema Chödrön

COMPASSION

To have compassion for others in their full array of suffering evokes compassion for our own unknown suffering. To open our hearts to the brunt and breadth of all life bestows the gift of self-knowledge. Conversely, those who are most stuck in their past can't realize their own past trauma—they can't be present for it. Codependent, they try to get others to empathize so they can realize a bit of their own truth. In fact, they're right: Sometimes just compassionately repeating someone's story of trauma lets them see and hear it for the first time. Especially when their pain is walled off by dissociation, they've only been able to acknowledge it with emotional distance or intellectual fragmentation, as it always felt too distressing to look at with emotional and intellectual awareness. To have room and strength in our hearts for others creates a shared security.

We all know we should have compassion, but it's easier said than done. It takes a truly sober and stable heart to be emotionally present, to learn a reliable process for healing trauma head-on without minimizing or self-medicating. Compassion also requires that we let go of any residual shame and programming. Unhealthy, trauma-bonded relationships are fueled by feelings of empathy for one's suffering partner. Similarly, the manufactured intimacy of casual sex promises amazing breakthroughs of erotic compassion but, like a drunken frenzy, the shared experience of emotional connectedness rarely survives daybreak. Authentic erotic compassion can take place only in the vulnerability of genuine sexual and romantic feelings, in attuning to another's internal experience within the context of true intimacy. Real compassion manifests only for compassion's sake.

DAILY HEALTHY SEX ACTS

- Today, show compassion for yourself. Look in the mirror, and feel for whatever you're going through now. Remember where you've come from and the major challenges and triumphs of your past. Then, allow compassion to flow fully within your being. Feel this healing energy as a spark quickening your spirit.

- Seek out current event stories by reading or watching the news, and practice feeling compassion for all parties. Whenever you would cast blame, remember that everyone has a back-story which, if known, would surely evoke your compassion. Today, grant all people a moment of your grace.

> *"You must concentrate upon and consecrate yourself wholly to each day, as though a fire were raging through your hair."*
>
> — Taisen Deshimaru

PRESENCE

Every mental absence represents a moment of life unlived. Habitual lack of presence has many faces: inhibition, negligence, preoccupation, delusion, disguise, or dissociation. We all know people who seem absent—who check out—and it's easy to understand their behavior as having a historical basis. But the principle of projection expressed in the adage, "Takes one to know one," tells us that, since we perceive only what we ourselves exhibit, the inattention we note in others reflects our own unexcused absences. But there's a saving twist to the projection principle: By projecting deeper to perceive the divine presence of every moment, we make our own inner potential fully present. As life presents itself on many levels, so we may be present for life on many levels.

We can all envision how we want to be and the quality of relating we'd like. So what's stopping us? We might have certain blocks about the idea of being present, of showing up. People may hesitate to reveal true selves when past experiences didn't go as planned. Always to function in full presence might seem to require too much effort, as if we only had a limited amount of energy at our disposal. And it will surely deplete us until we install a new working concept: Anything we want to become—to express in presence—we must first perceive. The fact that certain higher concepts exist in the world instructs us that higher truths are to be found within us as well. It is said that "nothing is ever manifested in an effect that is not in the cause." Perhaps the truest desire is to be fully present, to recognize the livingness of the world in all we see, to know that everything reflects a higher order sparkling with connection and meaning.

DAILY HEALTHY SEX ACTS

- Everything you perceive is your presence. Today, look deeply into every moment and perceive divine presence. Recognize each circumstance as having a particular bearing on your soul. Over time, this practice will bring you presence of mind and make manifest your own catalytic presence.

- Strengthen your sexual presence with your beloved. Let your interactions be intentional. Rouse yourself from sleepwalking, from taking relationship for granted. Slow down, look deeply into your lover's eyes, and let yourself be seen. Affirm your feelings with affectionate compliments and pause, letting your lover linger on your words as your find real ways to present your truth.

"How can I tell the signals and the signs
      by which one heart another heart divines?
How can I tell the many thousand ways
      by which it keeps the secret it betrays? "
                          — Henry Wadsworth Longfellow

23 FEBRUARY

SIGNS

Have you ever asked yourself if you saw the signs leading up to a breakup—your lover's signs or even your own? Just as we see signs of our potential and purpose in life, we also see signs that guide us toward healthy relationship. But we want to make sure that these signs are a mutually understood language, not a private fantasy or an unspoken code of expected behavior. People sometimes get "sign-phobic" because of past experiences of being misunderstood, having their actions misinterpreted, or failing to understand or correctly interpret signs from others.

Our whole culture is actually built on signs. When we learn to read, we are learning signs. Reading is a joy, but it's easy to forget that, at first, learning to read was a struggle. It's the same way with signs in relationships. We get tired of struggling as adults and resist working through the confusion and shame that can surface as we learn to read another's signs. But it's imperative to remain centered in reality through open conversation, and it's important not to over-interpret everything as a sign, which can be crazy-making. Stimulate your body/mind and bond by creating personal signs just between you and your partner, and build a mutual language. It's healthy and healing for lovers to clearly state, "This sign is a romantic gesture, and it's a symbol of the way I feel."

DAILY HEALTHY SEX ACTS

- Examine yourself in the mirror for signs of what's on your mind. How do you show—*sign*al—when you are tired? Hungry? Upset? Disconnected? Aroused?

- Observe people's body language today. Can you read what they might be thinking or feeling?

- If you have a chance, let someone know you see his or her joy: "I see you smiling."

> *"It's the way of the lay, not the size of the prize."*
>
> — Sol Yurick

ENDOWMENT

Welcome to the Goldilocks complex: This one's too big, the next one's too small. Typically the competitive nature of Western civilization equates bigger with better. Be it penis, breast, brain, or bank account, we want it all supersized. Judging our body parts is one area where this mentality plays out especially painfully. The highly contagious dis-ease of never feeling good enough in comparison sparks a tremendous psychological dissatisfaction.

But in actuality, some physically large attributes can leave no sensory impression, while small attributes can cause a tremendous reverberation. Why is this? There is a physiological reality that erogenous stimulation requires direct contact on the body's pleasure zones. And yet, anyone who has engaged in astral sex play knows how the body can be brought to an orgasmic state without any physical touch whatsoever. In fact, so much of what we consider physical experience is in fact psychological. While some obsess on precise scales for the many attributes of endowment (penile length and girth, mammary shape and size, body parts' texture and flexibility), we each situate ourselves within a scale that only we perceive.

Perhaps the most important sexual tool is consciousness. If we think we are "not enough" or "too much," we surely are. Similarly, when you give a gift, create artwork, or perform any task with the thought that it's "not enough" or "too much," it surely will be. Instead, feel the intrinsic pleasure of being able to bring yourself to pleasure. Cherish and share this. For internal success—success according to our own scale—it's vital for you to feel *just right* about yourself.

DAILY HEALTHY SEX ACTS

- Through creative visualization, you can stretch the scale of your perceptions. Start by imagining your various body parts as smaller and then larger. Come to peace with yourself in the beautiful combinations of being that are possible.

- Imagine inhabiting the bodies of others—all the shapes, sizes, colors, styles of those around you. How would you find yourself if this were the body into which you were born? Accept and appreciate the diversity of all body types today, especially your own.

"Whenever you're in conflict with someone, there is one factor that can make the difference between damaging your relationship and deepening it. That factor is attitude."

— William James

25 FEBRUARY

ATTITUDE

Do you want to be right or happy? Of course, you want both! But in the heat of conflict, your healthy values of self-protection and self-expression can easily eclipse your equally healthy values of empathy and relatedness. With the attitude of intentionality and mindful practice, though, you can develop the habit of keeping all your values active and in alignment.

Typically we "read" the attitudes of others we know by a mixture of intuition, relational history and projection. When we judge another's attitude, we almost always lose sight of our own. Criticizing others' attitudes as unseemly usually results in hypocrisy, such as when someone snarls, "You need a better attitude!" in a way that suggests the offended party would do well to practice what s/he preaches. In fact, the shame endured from such moral condemnation—especially if it echoes such criticism in childhood—may make any attitudinal correction extremely difficult. So it's crucial, albeit challenging, to maintain a loving attitude and solid centeredness while considering the seeming negative attitudes of others.

Our attitude requires constant calibration. The means *are* the end, since the way you treat yourself corresponds exactly to the attitude you will cultivate in yourself. This is why it's imperative to be gentle and kind with yourself (and thus others), but this doesn't need a grand gesture. Adjusting your attitude doesn't require switching between two extremes, like depression to elation or anger to absolution. An attitude shift might need just a slight smile or a tiny pause before reacting. For even in a triggered state of resentment, *acting* a little more loving is *becoming* a little more loving.

DAILY HEALTHY SEX ACTS

- We've all experienced times when our intention to have good sex or a romantic date somehow blew up in our face. Make it a healthy habit to observe your own attitude.

- Like many qualities, your attitude involves multiple levels—mental, emotional, psychological, spiritual. You might have the right mental attitude, but your emotional expression might leave the wrong impression. Today, notice how you balance communication through your body, tone, and words.

- It's been said that people can hear on the phone if you're smiling. Today, pick one healthy attitude (like patience or tolerance) and practice it even when no one's looking.

"No creature can learn that which his heart has no shape to hold."

— Cormac McCarthy

SEXUAL CONFUSION

It's perfectly healthy to be sexually confused. Confusion abounds in relationships—about appropriate boundaries, whether sex is satisfying, and reading a lover's intentions. In fact, the wonderment of why we're attracted to certain people and how others are attracted to us is infinitely confusing. Healthy confusion inspires healthy curiosity.

But when sexual confusion paralyzes our capacity for erotic relationship, it requires attention. Sexual confusion caused by repression or negative conditioning often feels empty or triggers our anger. Fear of asking questions about sex—or denial that we have any questions—can block our sensual maturation. Our first step is to overcome our emptiness, anger, and blockage by allowing room for questions—a step which sounds simple but is very hard if early programming never let us even admit we had questions.

Difficulty asking questions is one of the best reasons to seek out competent, and perhaps professional, points of view. We each work only with the information we've been given, so it's hard enough to find our psychological blocks, much less to learn how to let the light shine through them. One function of any professional is to relay the most up-to-date information, which gives us access to many points of view through one person. Free 12-step meetings like Codependency Anonymous (CoDA), Sex and Love Addicts Anonymous (S. L. A. A.), and Recovering Couples Anonymous (RCA) as well as numerous therapeutic or spiritual support groups also function as sources for diverse viewpoints, and may shed light on issues we couldn't even have known we had. Sexual confusion doesn't just go away. The only way to find freedom from confusing feelings is to process them, which—as signaled by the word—invites us into the process of asking, and answering, our self.

DAILY HEALTHY SEX ACTS

- Say aloud in a safe space: "I'm sexually confused." Notice any shame, resistance, denial, or other feelings as you contemplate the mere possibility of sexual confusion.

- Reach out to another today to resolve one question that's caused you sexual confusion. Call a trusted friend, 12-step phone meeting, or a professional, and share honestly the level of anxiety or inner struggle it takes to bring light into this part of your life.

"Communication leads to community, that is, to understanding, intimacy and mutual valuing."

— Rollo May

27 FEBRUARY

COMMUNICATION

When we think of communication we usually think of speaking or writing. But some 65% of all communication is non-verbal: We exchange information and connect through myriad forms—gesture, facial expression, tone of voice, touch, and eye contact. In its most basic form, communication is a transactional verbal exchange that's purely functional. But at its best, it's an elegant array of signals transmitted between two beings in concert with one another. The prime example of such unspoken yet unmistakable messaging occurs between the mother and fetus who's about to be born. A symbiotic communication informs and encodes the baby's nervous system based on the mother's experience. Unconsciously, she conveys bodily signals of joy or of stress to her child, stamping him or her with her psyche.

Like that of the mother and infant, the dance of love and mating takes place on the stage of wild, non-verbal communication. A neurochemical cascade signals our percolating mutual chemistry and ignites our system so that our hearts beat quicker, our bodies heat up, and our arousal systems are in gear. This "hot" form of communication needs no words. Similarly, sorrow or pain breathes emotions just as wordlessly: Our hearts weigh heavily and our souls grow cold and dark when sitting with someone who is troubled. Thus feeling deeply with the one we love is also empathic communication, a language that needs no words.

Communication is the sum total of our tone, attitude, body language, and energy. No one really gets away with lying because the human instrument is so perfectly attuned to knowing what's true and what isn't. When you communicate clearly with all of your heart and soul, you will listen differently and the right words will follow, leaving less possibility for misunderstanding and doubt.

DAILY HEALTHY SEX ACTS

- Pay attention to the non-verbal cues you get from people during the day. Respond to what feels true to you. Don't accommodate based on just the words you're hearing. Trust your gut.

- Practice *active listening*. Make a point of listening with curiosity and without defensiveness or mentally preparing your rebuttal. Listen and repeat back what you hear.

- Consider how honest you are when communicating. Do your words line up with what you're really feeling? If not, align your words with your truth and speak from that place.

> *"If I reach for the world with hearts in my palms then surely its love will flow through my arms."*
>
> — Jay Woodman

FLOW

Love seems to promise entrance into a flow state in which activity is effortless. In that moment of flowing accomplishment, we love all—each gender, age, race, class, creed or appearance. We see ourselves in the world, and the world in us. In this enlightened synchronizing of inner and outer experience, we experience external life as an unforced stream of beneficent events. But in fact, it's only by tapping into our inner flow that we can transcend outer boundaries.

To enter this fluid state of mind, many turn to drugs—both illicit drugs like cocaine and internal neurochemical ones like dopamine. Some use free-flowing alcohol to break into that divine state. Others crave wild currents of sex and love to receive from the outside what they can't access on the inside. For there's nothing as alienating as being trapped in our heads, our judgments, our paranoia and mental distortions, unable to return to our earlier garden of earthly delights. We often project our inner exile outward onto partners as the authors of our own emotional blocks.

Yet like traffic snarls around construction zones, some blockages result from tremendous inner work which demolishes negative self-concepts and builds new insights. Sharing each stage of the restoration with a trusted other invites empathy and the intuitive wisdom that can restore our natural flow. Recall the times you've been *in the zone*—that space beyond effort where you're connected to the oceanic swell of true power. This space is not removed from the world; it's born of connection to the world, because a loving other showed you this space. To re-enter the promised land within, reach beyond your borders to join with the world, for that's where love flows.

DAILY HEALTHY SEX ACTS

- When have you felt the flow of being *in the zone* in life and during sex? Often dance, music, math, cooking or similar activities invite your inner flow. Recall the sensations, and let them live in you more often.

- Let your being flow with others. Notice when you feel stuck and disconnected and breathe deeply into the feelings. Reach out.

- What does it take for you to flow with your partner's energy—in conversation, in work, and in bed? Today, suspend self-will and allow your lives to flow together.

"If we hope to live not just from moment to moment, but in true consciousness of our existence, then our greatest need and most difficult achievement is to find meaning in our lives. It is well known how many have lost the will to live, and have stopped trying, because such meaning has evaded them."

— Bruno Bettelheim

29 FEBRUARY

PURPOSE

Innumerable self-help formulas and religious doctrines proclaim the purpose of life. Certain philosophies fix sexual desire at the lowest rung of human goals, stigmatizing sexuality through shame. They conjure an image of carnal man acting out with depraved lust, his only aim to satiate every selfish desire. Who hasn't measured his or her weakness for gratification against this sex-crazed creature of dogmatic imagination? Yet surely there is a higher purpose to sex beyond repressing it.

Individual consciousness endows us with tools to discover the true purpose of our sexuality. Others promise to reveal the purpose of life, but our truest calling is wholly personal. If you ever have one of those "aha" moments that rouse you from apathy, take note! When your breath feels like a dragon in your belly, stimulated yet serene, and you know exactly what you're doing—these are the symptoms of true purpose.

That purpose cannot be tied to external circumstance or even persons. We often locate our *raison d'être* in other people, usually lovers or children. The empty nest syndrome when children move out, leaving a parent feeling useless, signals a purpose tied to circumstances. True purpose doesn't place power outside of yourself, but it also doesn't reinforce the ego. One fact about true purpose is that there's always a greater purpose behind it. When we knowingly seek and serve that as-yet unknown greater purpose, we begin to transform from within. Then all we do vibrates for this truth, including sex, which becomes satisfying on a level beyond any fantasy. We are as virgins until the awakening of true purpose.

DAILY HEALTHY SEX ACTS

- To find your true purpose, take a leap of faith. Quickly, without thinking, write down your greater purpose now! Then, all day, fulfill this purpose.

- Is your greater purpose tied to material conditions? Finishing a project is worthwhile, but it's hardly your purpose in life. What's the greater purpose *behind* that project? And what's the purpose behind *that* purpose? Keep asking until you can't help but spring into action.

- Invite greater significance into your love-making. Give words to your intentions, and share your purpose with your lover using action phrases: "I'm rubbing your shoulders to soothe your beautiful body." "I'm moving closer to connect with you."

March

"Go out looking for one thing, and that's all you'll ever find."

— Robert Flaherty

1 MARCH

INTENTION

Our intentions filter our perception of the world, so set them with care! For example, love addicts project their unsolicited romantic intentions onto others who may not at all reciprocate their feelings, and sex addicts sexualize even the most non-sexual situations through the lenses of their narrow intention.

In contrast, setting a healthy intention means formulating—and following—a conscious, realistic aim and plan. How often have you resolved to make a change only to find your will-power wane and your resolution vaporize? To intend requires that you pursue an effective course of action related to an attainable purpose. Your intention can be as simple as respecting your relationship or as complicated as manifesting a treasured ideal in your life. The challenge is to keep your attention on your intention and to take small actions every day to realize it.

When it comes to love relationships, we rarely set intentions beyond the vows of marriage. We seem to fall into a stupor thinking that we'll never have to reevaluate our goals or dreams with our partners. Many are afraid to talk to their partners about how they and their intentions have changed over time, even when it's obvious. Human beings are dynamic, novelty-seeking creatures and live in a world that never stays the same so, naturally, you and your life will change, whether you set new intentions or not. Make the experiment and evoke your courage to envision the life you'd like to have, now. Talk to your partner about your latest hopes, and dare to set bold intentions together and separately. Find ways to attend to your intentions and watch them manifest into the adventurous life you desire. Go big!

DAILY HEALTHY SEX ACTS

- Set an intention for yourself and for your relationship today. Share these with your partner.

- What one thing can you do in order to keep your attention on your intention?

- Take the smallest action towards your intention for thirty days, and notice what happens.

> *"You know quite well, deep within you, that there is only a single magic, a single power, a single salvation... and that is called loving."*
>
> — Herman Hesse

If you want love, wealth, or an elusive accomplishment, repeat this magic phrase: *O bada bakarrik elə ki senp.* That's what we all want from magic, right? *Oh, if only it were that simple!* We talk rationally about the miracle of everyday life, but what we secretly desire is *real* magic power. The mere idea conjures fantasies fulfilled, but the stark reality... *of reality...* dashes those childish dreams. When romantics seek to *keep the magic* in a relationship, we know this is often an immature search for constant stimulation and validation rather than the mature work of intimacy.

MAGIC

But compared with rational, linear thought, the idea of magic offers an *other* way of thinking, *if* we can integrate it without being swept away by it. For to imagine magic embodies *the other*—the enchantment of human relationship that takes us outside ourselves. When you engage in a sexual act, you vibrate, radiate, and intend it to reverberate beyond the body parts—beyond that sublime moment's thrill—to sustain an open heart. We all long to tap into the mysterious force of love. Our sexuality is already an enthralling, meaningful energy, but to invest imagined magical powers into sexual relationships can tip the scales toward toward crazy-making. Instead of being present to the emergent magic that arises during sex, some go so far as to practice sex magic, harnessing the chaos of orgasm to sigil spells and effect some visualized attainment.

But when we attempt to bind the universe through magic, we often become bound ourselves by ill-considered ambition. We supplant life's infinite magic with our hyperfocused expectations. So much of what we take for granted would seem like magic to past generations, or even to us at past stages of our lives. The future will take more magic. And with loving practice, by planting the seeds of healthy communion and community, we can help make that magic real.

DAILY HEALTHY SEX ACTS

- Our inner being, like a magic mirror, reveals itself in every outer moment. Today, perform daring acts of self-love with a flourish, like a magician onstage!

- We magically summon others to mind just by our thoughts. And our parents, caretakers, teachers, friends and lovers enfold us in the magic of their own mentality. Imagine that!

- What magic can you bring to your relationship? Remember, magic represents an-*other* way of thinking. With permission to free yourself of inhibition and fear, what emerges, from unknown depths of your being, to share in love?

"She wanted to hand over, to yield, to let herself float down the unchartered beautiful fertile musky swamp of life, where creativity and eroticism and deep intelligence dwell."

— Rebecca Wells

3 MARCH

FERTILITY

Sometimes within a relationship, issues of fertility can cause a fissure in intimacy. It can be devastating when a couple becomes fixated on having a baby but cannot achieve their goal. Communication and joy may be smothered both inside and outside the bedroom. The desire to become a parent is a deep human need that almost all of us experience at one point or another. It touches our innate longing for immortality, our desire to pass on our legacy to another generation.

But while the traditional definition of fertility applies to a woman's ability to bear children, the concept of fertility expands beyond gender, age or circumstance. It can express the inner bloom of creativity and imagination that resides within us all, and does not depend on a lover.

Embracing our own fertility means cultivating our feminine energies of reception, of absorbing experience, and of transmuting it into new forms. Our sexuality is one of our greatest fertile powers, and we can harness it to express a rainbow of facets beyond the literal manifestations of reproduction. We can be fertilized by ideas shared with co-workers or performance partners; we can become impregnated with images, sounds, smells and feelings; we can become spiritually fruitful through meditation and quiet, energy-engendering solitude. Fertility applies to every kind of birth, from the blossoming of the first flowers of spring to the conception of a new business. It is all around us, both in nature and in the realm of human affairs. Fertility can never elude us if we are open and actively engaged in the beauty and eroticism of our everyday lives.

DAILY HEALTHY SEX ACTS

- How do you embrace your innate fertility and that of others? Today, give voice to the real process of your own fertility—from the impregnation of your imagination to the germination of your ideas.

- Our environment is always fertile. Look around and perceive the vast fecundity of the universe, always creating and developing vital aspects of life. Whenever you feel depleted or dried up, recharge your spirit with the realization of life's eternal fertility.

- Let life touch you deeply today. Let erotic love enter your world and take root.

"Your vision will become clear only when you can look into your own heart. Who looks outside, dreams; who looks inside, awakes."

— Carl Gustav Jung

VISION

When we are able to look beyond appearances and to behold that which we truly are, we recognize that our essence is interwoven with the divine and that we exist as one of its expressions. The ability to become on the outside that which we behold on the inside comes from our gift of following a master life vision—for imagining and planning our future with wisdom. The capacity to improvise and improve a mental vision of our future potentiality makes human beings unique in the natural world. And in this very human manifestation we each show up as unique beings who long to merge with the infinite and with another human being. Each of us has our own path, which each of us must discover.

When a couple holds one vision for what they want in their lives as partners, they commit to a conscious relationship. But too many allow life to "happen to them," then are frantic when a problem shows up. In effect, a lack of vision leaves life up to chance, while having a vision requires a co-creative process that makes manifest a desired outcome. If your vision for your life is clear, you will manifest your desires. For example, if you don't have a partner but visualize what you want in a partner, it's likely that such a person will show up in your life.

But be careful of simplistic ideas about holding a vision. To make it manifest, you must do your own personal work, and then be patient. Time does not work in the spiritual dimension the way it works in the human dimension. Plant your seeds, hold a vision for abundance, then let go and let your God!

DAILY HEALTHY SEX ACTS

- What is your vision for your life? Take time throughout this week to sit quietly with your attention on that question. Jot down any thoughts, feelings, sensations, or images that come to you. Don't rush the process.

- What is your vision for your love and sex life? Do you prefer a short-term liaison or do you seek a more substantial connection? What would it look like? What are the terms of engagement?

- If you're not in a love relationship, hold a vision for what you want in a relationship. Know your preferences, then keep your attention on your intention.

"Sex and beauty are inseparable, like life and consciousness. And the intelligence which goes with sex and beauty, and arises out of sex and beauty, is intuition."

— D. H. Lawrence

5 MARCH

INTUITION

Think about all the times you've "known" something without actually "knowing it" through conscious thought or reason. At those times you experienced an implicit way of knowing—one that's felt and understood through signals in the body—rather than an explicit knowing dependent on your five senses. Implicit knowing, or intuition, has been called a sixth sense separate from sight, smell, touch, taste, or hearing. Knowing something instinctually rather than consciously is more than knowing facts; it's insight. When you trust what you know implicitly you are relying on your emotionally and physically unified self: your body/mind. Openness to, and trust in, the awareness of your body/mind creates new connections of understanding.

When it's time to make big decisions, especially to decide if we're with the right person, we tend to look at objective data and make mental lists of "pros" and "cons." Take a chance. Jettison your list, and sit quietly instead. Set your intention for an answer to your dilemma, then stop reasoning about it. Pay attention to dreams and thoughts that drift in and out of consciousness when you're taking a walk or working out or after love-making. Intuition bursts from the deepest part of the body/mind, but cannot be forced. Expect the unexpected, but take a wait-and-see attitude about any outcome.

Holding the paradox of intention-setting and outcome-letting is a practice that requires self-awareness. Don't let your "knowing" mind rule with its judgments and solutions. Instead, just notice those thoughts as background noise, stay in your body, and see what emerges. Intuition is the process of letting truth come into view. It's elusive and, like a shy child, will run away if you try to capture or grasp it. Let go, let God, and trust your body/mind's connection to the divine.

DAILY HEALTHY SEX ACTS

- The next time you think about someone, and soon see or hear from that person, consider that your intuition may have been at play. Don't devalue this way of knowing by ascribing all such meetings to chance.

- Notice recurring images, thoughts or songs that pop into your head. Respect your intuition when it tells you to take a different route, grab a jacket, or call a friend.

- Use your intuition to make a minor decision. Keep trying this exercise until you come to trust your intuitive self with bigger decisions.

> *"Agape doesn't love somebody because they're worthy. Agape makes them worthy by the strength and power of its love. Agape doesn't love somebody because they're beautiful. Agape loves in such a way that it makes them beautiful."*
>
> — Rob Bell

AGAPE

Agape is the Greek word that connotes love of humanity, fondness among family, or abiding affection for an-other. Agape is our own true nature, the essence of who we are as human beings. It is the deep devotion we feel for the planet, the goddess, God, Atman, Allah, or Brahman. No matter how we try to capture the essence of Agape, it is ultimately inexplicable, indefinable, and deeply personal, because it can be known only through our direct experience. But however difficult to define, the concept of love has been pondered since the beginnings of humanity. Every culture has its word, or words, for this emotion.

Take time now to think about what stage of love you're in, either with yourself, in your relationship, or in relationship to the world. Is your love a new love or a more mature love? What components inherent in the relationship let you know that you are loving well and well loved? Agape is a more mature love: love of humankind, love of oneself. If you fall deeply in love with yourself as a mature adult and recognize your true nature as being one of love, then you will experience Agape—the love that can never be taken away from you.

DAILY HEALTHY SEX ACTS

- Look in the mirror and into your eyes. Repeat the affirmation, "I love who you are" three times. Note how you feel when you are finished.

- Make contact with a loved one today, look into his or her eyes and say, "I love who you are." Observe how saying this up close makes you feel.

- Meet the world today from a place of Agape. Notice what you receive in return or how you perceive the world. Create your own word for this transcendent and ineffable experience.

"And this is one of the major questions of our lives: how we keep boundaries, what permission we have to cross boundaries, and how we do so."

— A. B. Yehoshua

7 MARCH

BOUNDARIES

Dysfunctional families use boundaries to punish, intimidate, and control, imposing rigid rules and regulations on their members and often crushing their souls. Members of those families usually end up emotionally cut off from their hearts, unyielding, and angry at life. Chaotic families, on the other hand, exercise no boundaries, invading one another's emotional, physical, and psychic spaces and leaving no room for individuality. In both cases, each individual's wants, needs, and rights are violated, whether by being forcibly opposed or utterly ignored. Members of such families rarely feel safe or cared for, so they don't develop a solid sense of their own identity.

Healthy boundaries are physical, emotional, and psychological constructs we create and maintain in order to feel that each person's own identity is safe in the world. While they may be flexible, boundaries help us set limits so we can be in functional relationships that enrich, support, and inspire us. When we respect ourselves and set good psychic and physical boundaries with others, we give ourselves a protected space that lets our unique abilities and characteristics bloom into our full potential. This form of self-care, in turn, invites us to love an equally unique other in safe and functional ways.

DAILY HEALTHY SEX ACTS

- Think about each person in your life with whom you need to set boundaries. Is it your boss, family member or friend? What have you been avoiding saying to set those boundaries? What is the best way to say it? When is the best time to say it?

- Are you tolerating something in your relationship that you resent because you don't want to upset your partner? If so, act today by telling the truth with an open heart.

- Be willing to listen to your partner's need for boundaries and to be flexible when necessary. Good boundaries make good lovers!

"The love that lasts the longest is the love that is never returned."

— William Somerset Maugham

Unrequited love ranks as one of the most painful experiences in life. It brings to the surface a deep sense of inadequacy and failure; it can even make us want to die. While we usually feel unrequited love for another person, we can also suffer from a job we didn't get, a house we couldn't afford, or a friendship that never soared. Learning to comfort ourselves in the face of disappointment is one of the great tests of self-love.

UNREQUITED LOVE

Sometimes we need to delve into our past to heal this discouraging pattern. Perhaps we've unconsciously aimed our affections at a cold, unresponsive party because it recreates trauma from our childhood. Or we may simply never have experienced reciprocity in any of our primal relationships, and therefore have no clue how to find it now. The pain of unreturned affection can be akin to masochism; we may even relish the sting and wallow in it, unable to admit the part we play by chasing unavailable partners.

Part of the misery of unrequited love stems from the impossible conditions we've placed upon the object of our desire. Perhaps that person didn't cherish our attentions or compliment us as we had dreamed. In failing to fulfill our private schemes, the person becomes a source of obsession for us, a symbol for all we lack in our lives.

But this situation gifts us with something, too: the chance to practice giving without expectations. We can admire warmly, appreciate the other person's excellent qualities, acknowledge our attraction, and then accept the reality that those feelings are not mutual, and move on to seek a successful love. And if we can't move on, we can get help. After all, we each deserve an enduring, nurturing love that is returned in equal measure.

DAILY HEALTHY SEX ACTS

- Visualize anyone who spurned your affection or failed to appreciate you—friends, co-workers, groups, and all your unrequited loves. Let any unresolved longing come to your awareness.

- Now remember similar feelings from your childhood. Was it belonging that was denied you? Did a group of friends ignore you? Was a parent inattentive? If you ever felt invisible or devalued as a child, how do you make yourself seen and valued today?

- If you're longing after someone who doesn't reciprocate your feelings, ask yourself what you get from revisiting over and over the feeling state of unrequited love.

"Ultimately spiritual awareness unfolds when you're flexible, when you're spontaneous, when you're detached, when you're easy on yourself and easy on others."

— Deepak Chopra

9 MARCH

AWARENESS

Some say awareness is our original state, in which we are unbound by a limited sense of self. This inclusive consciousness clues us in to the nature of all life, for our very existence endures only as a result of our awareness, as does our joy and love. When we can see life as a unified whole, rather than through the narrow, distorted filter of past trauma, we can see ourselves exactly as we are—just as only a clean mirror reflects honestly. Awareness, then, lets us make informed and wise choices in life, including with whom we choose to be in active relationship. Likewise, awareness of our body, mind, and spirit leads us toward our desire to be sexual.

Awareness during sex, though, does not mean judging or comparing either ourselves or our partner, but alertness to our shared experience. In fact, anxiety and ego prove to be the enemies of eroticism since, whether we're judging *ourselves or our partner*, we're acting from a need to prove to ourselves that we're good enough. Focusing only on ourselves or only on our lover—whether in criticism or idolatry—destroys eroticism, which requires sexual connection. Observe your scene, including your own pleasure and your partner's. Bear witness with full attentiveness to the sensations in your body and heed the signs of ecstasy emanating from your partner. Recognize and focus your attention on the way both your bodies move, taking your cues from your interactions rather than from self-consciousness in your own head. Practice conscious, connected awareness.

When you become cognizant of the special ways your lover responds to your style of love-making and how you respond to your partner's, you've obtained a special knowledge that no one else possesses. You are now conscious and informed in your awareness of who both of you are sexually, bringing you closer to true eroticism.

DAILY HEALTHY SEX ACTS

- How aware are you of yourself? Take a moment today to be interested in your stream of consciousness so you can experience your essential existence.

- Wipe the grime of the past away by releasing old thoughts and judgments about your sexuality. Invite in a new script about who you are as an aware, erotic being.

- Pay rapt attention to every move your lover makes during sex. Bear witness to the sights, sounds, tastes, and physical feelings of your experience together without trying to "make" anything happen.

> *"That which so delighted my eye made my heart sink to the depths of the earth."*
>
> — Richard Wagner

POLARITY

Human consciousness flips back and forth between extremes like a pendulum. Feelings of contentment and possibility give way to frustration and hopelessness in a taunting game of emotional roulette. We're the best, we're the worst. Psychological inflation cedes to deflation in an endless loop contaminating whatever it inspects— our talents, appearance, relationships, or experiences. But those are feelings, right? Mercurial, unpredictable, irrepressible feelings. We'd have as much luck controlling the ocean's currents. But thoughts! Our thoughts are more Apollonian, more structured compared to our freewheeling, Dionysian emotions. Yet even our much-vaunted reason sharpens itself through trenchant internal debate.

In fact, the egoic need to judge and rate everything that happens to us seems always to summon this seesawing effect. That's because evaluating rather than experiencing life is a learned coping mechanism, which develops our ability to differentiate but blocks us from perceiving the unifying truth behind all outer seeming events, and from feeling part of it.

To deduce from this polarity of inner experience that the world really pivots on opposites would be a mistake, as if for every dollar made, there'll be a dollar lost; for every moment in love there'll be a moment alone. For reality isn't perfectly balanced, unless behind the curtain of death there are compensatory experiences we can't know. Real experiences in this world aren't quantitative, they're qualitative. If we're wealthy, we may not feel wealthy enough. If we're in love, popular, successful, talented, we may still feel their opposites. This paradox stems from the ego's habit of grasping reality only in personal terms, which brings us the unending, upsetting duality of polarity. But we can find a comforting flipside even to this disquieting routine, if we recall that our perceiving any reality ensures we'll eventually perceive its opposite—in this case, an ultimate, reconciling unity.

DAILY HEALTHY SEX ACTS

- Look under the surface to perceive the unity in every situation. Unity is rarely announced with the blaring trumpet call of a revelation; it starts out as simple and subtle as a fine thread.

- To begin any committed relationship inevitably brings its end—whether by choice, circumstance or death. Knowing this, why embark on any? One answer is so we may open our heart to contain all of life. Today, reconcile any oppositions by surrendering to this higher purpose.

"How people treat you is their karma;
how you react is yours."

— Wayne Dyer

11 MARCH

KARMA

Do you ever feel misunderstood? Perhaps your parents or partner don't always understand your actions or intentions. Count your blessings! People might ignore your virtue or genius, but they also ignore how selfish, envious, manipulative, and objectifying you are at unseen times, thankfully. The next time you feel misunderstood, consider it karma for all the times you're lucky you were.

It's easy to get upset when life doesn't go our way. But if life actually went the way of our spinning thoughts and conflicting motives we would really be a wreck! Karma is the cumulative impact of our actions returned to us, and helps us develop this complex tool called human consciousness. The concept of karma might evoke being judged by some omniscient, omnipotent entity, but that's not karma, that's punishment trauma from childhood. A moment's contemplation convinces that our actions ripple in us psychologically, neurobiologically, sociologically. We carry the weight and chatter of them to others through our body language and the way we perceive and perform. In this manner, we are the judge, jury and *executor* of our karma.

The word *karma* derives from the Sanskrit word for action. We can't change the actions of cause and effect, but we may cause new effects at any time. When we bounce a ball against a wall with a certain force and at a certain angle, it will inevitably bounce back in a matching reaction. This is cause and effect. However, we may run forward and catch the ball, and this new, corrective action demonstrates how we might affect our karma. But how may we become more aware of the force and angle of our habitual actions? How may we know what actions to take and their karmic results? One way to change karma is to face it.

DAILY HEALTHY SEX ACTS

- Examine your actions. List five actions you took today, and the energy and intentions you gave them. Were your actions, energy, and intention aligned? Realize that energy and intentions count as karmic actions.

- You can always invite right action into your life. You might share daily challenges with a trusted ally, therapist or sponsor and request direction. You might sleep on a problem and let intuition guide you, rather than simply react. You might follow a spiritual path through study or attendance. Today, pick one problem in your life, and practice the tools to help you realize the next right action.

"No sooner met but they looked, no sooner looked but they loved, no sooner loved but they sighed, no sooner sighed but they asked one another the reason."

— William Shakespeare

SIGHS

Love is a relief. It's a relief finally to find someone who matches our inner vision. We might not even have realized how lonely we were, or how nervous. We all have unknown stress—from not belonging, not sharing others' feelings or interests, fearing that we'll never deeply connect with another. To connect even for a moment on some level brings relief to swallowed stress, so we sigh. Art and poetry usually depict the lover's sigh as a swoon, but it may just as easily signify sadness, regret, dismay, boredom, or futility. Where there's a sigh, there's a provocation.

People who sigh during sex or in romantic embrace might seem to be in their own solitary experience. The slightest touch can release repressed tension that may be deeper than that of the current circumstance. Certain people, whether healers or seducers, have the ability to play people like a piano, touching more than skin—touching this life tension and releasing a cacophony of erotic sighs.

What is it to exhale, and to accompany this exhale with a song? A sigh feels like it comes from the gut or the heart. It's an intimate sound, a communication in a way, as if words were superfluous. Is it possible to sigh without feeling safe? Sighing signifies trust—a psychological seed that may sprout into articulation of ideas and thoughts, but is not yet at that stage. A sigh can be a way we express that we feel safe enough to share feelings or perhaps just within ourselves. It's a space that we may create a lot of space around.

DAILY HEALTHY SEX ACTS

- Listen today to the sighs and wordless sounds people make. Can you respond to the ringing trust that a sigh engenders? Notice the prosody of ensuing dialogue and try to elongate your emotional connections.

- Give a good sigh. Practice expressing unknown, inexpressible feeling through sighs. At what point does it feel forced or annoying, and when do you feel comfortable and safe enough to share these subterranean feelings through the direct language of the heart? Today, discover right-sized sighing to free your inner song.

"What laughter is to childhood, sex is to adolescence."

— Martha Beck

13 MARCH

PUBERTY

Puberty is a rite of passage ordained by nature. Transition from childhood to adulthood sends surges of hormones that overwhelm the body and brain, catapulting our sweet children into unrestrained pseudo-adults. Gone are the cuddly yet bold girls and boys who seem safe in their own skin. Enter the angst-riddled, gangly teen who's unsure of his or her every move but whose body seeks sexual arousal.

Menstruation, and erections, and orgasm, oh my! Physiological changes shock teenagers as they leave childhood behind, their bodies morphing into new and unrecognizable things. Without proper education and preparation, ill-timed periods and erections can be a humiliating source of shame. Our first sexual experiences can color our sexuality for a lifetime. Cultural myths, peer pressure, pornography, and, unfortunately, sexual abuse are powerful, if improper, educators. Puberty marks the physical sexual maturity rendering us capable of reproduction. Yet, as we know, it takes a long time to achieve psychological and emotional sexual maturity.

Sexual exploration is a natural part of adolescence and pushes us toward individuation. It lets our personality and sense of self emerge in new, exciting, and complex ways at a time when the liberation of adulthood looms. But if our sexuality is tampered with, we can be left with a shame-based sexuality that impacts our adult relationships.

Without proper stewardship, puberty can be painful, confusing, and traumatizing. The adolescent brain undergoes major reconstruction, breaking down and reorganizing at higher levels of complexity, leaving teens unable to sort out the range of experiences coming their way. If we talk to our pre-teens in appropriate detail about love and sex and the wisdom of waiting on them; if we make sure they know sexual abuse is not their fault and should be reported immediately, we can usher them into lifelong healthy sexuality.

DAILY HEALTHY SEX ACTS

- What was puberty like for you? Did you know what was in store for you?

- How did you learn about menstruation, erections, and masturbation?

- If you have a pre-teen at home and you haven't talked about sex with him or her, now's the time to do so. Don't wait for her or him to get misinformation from the media or classmates.

"You don't need to justify your love, you don't need to explain your love, you just need to practice your love."

— Don Miguel Ruiz

PRACTICE

Making our lives better always involves practice. Our habits are like the grooves on an old-fashioned phonographic record, and only practice of new, healthy habits can *cut new grooves* in our brains. Researchers continue to uncover the phenomenal neuroplasticity or adaptability of the human brain, which has the capacity to alter and evolve throughout our lifespan. Every consistent focus of our attention eventually becomes hard-wired into our neural pathways, so getting good grooves comes with devoted practice.

Engaging in practice with others provides major support. Researchers discovered that "mirror neurons" fire both when we perform some activity *and when we observe another performing that activity*. This discovery suggests that, by mere observation, our brains may imitate not just others' acts but their mental states as well. However it works, working with a support team provides expertise to guide our practice and empathy to keep us going.

Physical therapy can hurt, but must be repeated many times to recover a bodily function. No one expects physical therapy to be fun. In fact, people know that such practice involves a greatly delayed gratification. But physical therapy patients want to walk or use their hands again, so they persevere through physical and mental discomfort, leaning emotionally on their support team of therapists, family, friends and other patients to relearn lost functions.

The practice required to recover from unhealthy patterns of behavior can be as intense as physical therapy and requires the identical commitment. Often people seeking healthy new behaviors wonder why they don't get better once they understand their issues. But just as in physical therapy, comprehending why your leg got hurt and what's needed for healing will not by itself make your leg better. You actually have to complete each daily practice.

DAILY HEALTHY SEX ACTS

- Whatever you desire, it will require practice to get there. Conceive a practice plan. If you need help, ask for support.

- We all want greater intimacy. We all want healthy self-esteem, serene moods, and robust health. Practice for a few minutes today to deepen your breathing, to smile, to affirm your inner beauty, and to reach out to loved ones with affection, regardless of results. Select one, or all, of these actions and practice *every day* for the next month!

*"To honor and accept one's own shadow costs nothing and is immediately—
and embarrassingly—ever present. To honor and accept one's own shadow is
a profound spiritual discipline. It is whole-making and thus holy and the
most important experience of a lifetime."*

— Robert A. Johnson

15 MARCH

SHADOW

Sunlight shines on us and casts our shadow on the earth. In the same way, the inner light of consciousness shines in each of us, and casts an inner shadow wherever we're not transparent. Any act, thought or feeling we perceive as "not right" casts a shadow. So it's true that "if you spot it, you got it." Thus we all know at some level that "pulling a geographic" is ineffective—we can't run away from our problems because we're their source.

Still, most of us stay blind to our shadow, which we readily project onto others—partners, parents, strangers on the street, media personalities. We all project our most negative *and positive* traits outward, even though to others they're "as plain as the nose on your face." Trouble is, we can't see our own nose without a mirror. Life is that mirror. If we look into our life, we can develop personal and relational consciousness.

Look at the character defects in others that aggravate you the most. The shadow in you amplifies them in your personal drama, like the proverbial butterfly's wings whose fluttering creates a hurricane on the other side of the world. If you deceive, rage or manipulate a little, your shadow will allow you *to hide out* among people who deceive, rage or manipulate a lot. Does your partner frustrate you with sexual or emotional unresponsiveness? You can bet that you habitually dismiss your own unresponsiveness elsewhere. Recalibrate your outward expression, receive a proportioned response. Change yourself, change this world. No other way.

DAILY HEALTHY SEX ACTS

- The shadow is a gift for those who know how to shadow-play. To enlighten yourself on where your shadows lie, notice the ways others work your nerves and locate the feeling of this shadow in your own actions. (And to see where you secretly shine, discern the behaviors you most admire in others.)

- Wholeness and transparency are not achieved by escaping or expunging one's nature, only by embracing and integrating all aspects of livingness—good and bad. Today, whenever blaming another overshadows your thoughts, tell yourself in truth, "I've done that, too," and remember when you have. Then forgive both of you.

> *"There are two basic motivating forces: fear and love. When we are afraid, we pull back from life. When we are in love, we open to all that life has to offer with passion, excitement, and acceptance."*
>
> — John Lennon

FEAR

It's been said that people operate out of fear or out of faith. Operating out of fear of our worst-case scenario as a way to hedge our bets against getting hurt is both illusory and costly. Fear keeps our lives small; anxious thoughts consume the mind and crab our experience. Worry, a kissing cousin of fear, fills even a peaceful present with its self-fulfilled painful imaginings. Where is your attention? Is it on what you can't get, what doesn't "ever" work out for you, or other lack and limitation? If so, the very experiences you're afraid of are likely the experiences you invite into your life and consciousness.

To live in faith means that we can leap into the unknown and risk not knowing exactly what the outcome will be, especially in our relationships. Typically, if we follow our gut instincts, that leap of faith pays off, because we have chosen an attitude of possibility instead of fear. You may notice that your fear system registers threat whenever you take a risk, leaving you more anxious than usual. Learning to tolerate that anxiety so it doesn't paralyze your actions is the first step towards shaking off the rule of fear. See if you can move in counter-intuitive ways by feeling the fear and taking a (reasonable) risk anyway.

Next, consider where you limit yourself sexually out of fear. Ask yourself, "What's the worst thing I can imagine about expressing my sexual preferences to my partner?" Is it that you'll be rejected, humiliated, or abandoned? Is that a realistic fear or one you're dragging around with you from your past? Part of being a sexual adult is taking full ownership of who you are sexually, what you like and dislike, and communicating that to a healthy partner who won't shame or leave you. Take a leap of faith today with someone you trust, feel the fear, and do it anyway!

DAILY HEALTHY SEX ACTS

- Identify three things that scare you (even though you know they're actually safe). Take a leap of faith and try one of those things this week.

- Identify one thing about your sexual preference or style that you worry about telling your partner. Ask yourself what the likeliest—the most realistic—outcome would be if you shared this information.

*"Love is seeing God in the person next to us,
and meditation is seeing God within us."*

— Sri Sri Ravi Shankar

17 MARCH

MEDITATION

The word *meditate* stems from the Latin root *meditari*, meaning "to ponder." Every one of us employs tools of meditation when we concentrate on a subject or mull over a situation. More formal meditative practices may involve ceremonial postures, repeating a mantra, emptying the mind, or focusing on an idea. But with the right intent, any act can be meditative, including sexual connection. Because honest meditation isn't ever about escape from reality. In healthy meditation we learn to tolerate our original inner peace, which most of us cannot easily recapture. For many of us, stopping the clock and releasing all worry is frightening, but with practice we can learn to feel safe within our own minds and, likewise, within peaceful, loving relationships.

All healthy rituals ebb and flow with us. Each day we raise water from the well, but today we may sip while tomorrow we gulp it all down. There will be times we can't be bothered to sit still, and sublime other times that rock us to our core. We can't control the effect of every ritual, but to attain any result we have to show up, whether to a formal practice or an informal meditation—such as reading these daily reflections. Even when nothing seems to sink in, the mere act of participation signals a noble inclination of our subconscious, our higher self, which already knows the meaning of these words before they're written.

Studies have shown that longtime practitioners of meditation display enhanced neural coordination. Concentration literally trains the brain. It's possible that if we sit in reflection enough times, certain realizations might spontaneously dawn on us. Ancient civilizations silently observed animals, oceans, skies and stars in meditative efforts that brought stunning insights beyond the capacity of habitual consciousness. Your personal awareness may similarly transform you through an always-available, even if momentary, act of meditation.

DAILY HEALTHY SEX ACTS

- Slow down. Take three deep breaths. After you finish reading the rest of these words, take a moment to close your eyes and center yourself in space. Notice physical sensations, and let go. Observe emotional sensations, and let go. Summon love from the depths of your body, and float in this eternal splendor. Return when ready. It's your quality of life, it's your call. Make room in your life for your inner life.

> *"The moods of love are like the wind, and none knows whence or why they rise."*
>
> — Coventry Patmore

MOOD

Here's a common enough phrase: "I'm not in the mood." Whether it's a defense against social events or sexual intimacy, we all know how much mood plays a part in forward momentum. The "I'm not in the mood" excuse might be based on avoidance, which can in turn be based on past trauma or resentment or even confusion. So "I'm not in the mood" is truly a catchphrase for "I am dealing with some personal issues around this subject that I haven't brought to light yet."

A wise saying tells us that only once we actually commit to taking an action does the universe give us the energy to do it. So when we feel this lack of *right mood*, it's because we're not fully committed to *right action*. Children similarly often don't want to go outside to play or participate in healthy activities, but once they start they don't want to stop. So as adults, if we let our so-called moods derail activities that are sensible, reasonable, and healthy for us, it's likely that there are underlying issues we should seek to understand. To help us, we might acquire a mood vocabulary to deepen our comprehension. Instead of being "not in the mood," we might really be craving security or quiet or solitude or warmth. By coming to know our moods we can learn to regulate them so our moods are not our masters.

DAILY HEALTHY SEX ACTS

- What do you have to do today that you know would benefit you but that you do not feel like doing? Is it exercise, cleaning, homework, reaching out, or something else?

- Get yourself settled in to where you would start this activity. Notice your mood. Talk to the part of you that resists, that does not want to get with the program. Give yourself a hug, take yourself by the hand, and gently lead the way. Stay present with your mood and repeat these loving gestures as needed.

*"The love that gushes for all is the real elixir of life—
the fountain of bodily longevity."*

— Josiah Gilbert Holland

19 MARCH

HEALTH

Most of us understand the value of physical health, and have received helpful programming so we know to seek treatment for medical emergencies like broken bones or chronic pain. But although physical health includes *sexual health,* for many people it's embarrassing even to have sexuality, much less to care for it or share information about it. What makes people put up with unsatisfactory sexual functioning? Perhaps some people have grown up to believe that focusing on sexual issues will worsen them, create bigger problems, or lead to preoccupation—a superstition that would feel ridiculous if it were about any other health issue. An all-too-common response to this belief is not to think about sexual problems at all.

Traumatic or genetic issues might permanently affect sexual health. It might not be possible for everyone to reach an optimal state of sexual health, but we can each attain our personal potential for sexual health, given our circumstances. Even people with chronic physical health issues deserve sexual expression and healthy solutions can be sought. If a sexual act doesn't feel right, we can develop a process to discern the underlying issue and either set it right or get help. What would it look like if sexual dysfunction, addiction, or trauma manifested as an actual medical condition with noticeable bodily symptoms? Truthfully any sexual problems, whether physical or psychological, are health problems. As a society we have much work to do in order to restore the concept of sexual health to its own state of health.

DAILY HEALTHY SEX ACTS

- Restoring your sexual health might include examining your sexual history, as you would review your medical history for a physician. 12-step programs often require a sexual inventory as part of the healing process. An online search will guide you to complete your own version of a sexual inventory.

- We can express deep sexual energy with a partner without getting physical. If your partner has health issues or is ill, you can still radiate erotic energy toward their inner being. Affirm sexual health regardless of the external circumstances.

- For medical problems, you find the right specialist. What sexual issues recur in your life today, and where would it be most sensible to go for help?

"And on her lover's arm she leant,
And round her waist she felt it fold,
And far across the hills they went
In that new world which is the old."
— Alfred Tennyson

We've all fallen down the rabbit hole of stubbornly foul moods that make the whole outside world seem similarly savage, disconnected and disharmonious. Whenever you're stuck in such an internal split, you can bet that's how you're going to perceive the world. It takes a real mental transmutation—sometimes with the help of another's wise words, or a stroke of good fortune—for the world to shine again.

RENEWAL

Health-wise, we want to be able to renew our lives without always depending on others or on fluctuating circumstances as a catalyst. Addictive and/or anorectic patterns are reinforced by a dependence on external stimulation, while sober and recovered feelings and mental states rely on inner fitness (even if facilitated by "personal trainers" such as health professionals and healthy programs). Conscious acts by which we renew ourselves—like meditation and mindfulness—counterbalance self-limiting, dependent patterns. They restore inner integrity which, with time, naturally bestows good health and grace, and ultimately lets you and all you relate to feel renewed.

DAILY HEALTHY SEX ACTS

- Renew your vows today—to yourself, to your partner, to your God or gods.

- Renew the energy and intention of your engagement in your relationship, your job, or any other relationship you're in that has become rote. Find ways to breathe new life into your surroundings so that you can begin anew with each passing day.

- Right now, imagine everything you do and see as if it were for the first time: These are the first words you've ever read in your new home or at your new job, surrounded by new people you've just met for the first time. Now's your chance to make a first impression. What pathway of your unlived life is opening for you here?

"I am only one, but still I am one. I cannot do everything, but still I can do something. And because I cannot do everything, I will not refuse to do the something that I can do."

— Edward Everett Hale

21 MARCH

RESPONSIBILITY

When you see the word *responsibility,* how do you respond? For many, the term does not have the happiest of associations. The word so often represents an external, authoritarian mandate rather than an inner call to action. So how do we embrace responsibility when it conjures up some herculean list of chores or a repressive sermon?

One helpful interpretation defines "response-ability" as the *ability* to *respond.* So, being responsible may very well require responding "no" when others' requests are just demands or ultimatums masked as collaboration. Clearly, responsibility is not the same as ironclad duty. But how can we show responsibility to ourselves?

We can respond to ourselves only insofar as we are aware of our true needs and desires, and practice self-care responsibly. Self-care differs hugely from selfishness. Some people spend entire lives seeking security through isolation, caring only for their wounded self or the secretive self that wants to take them down—the internal saboteur. But we also all have an innermost Self who aspires to realize our genuine, and generous, vision for the future.

Perhaps ultimate responsibility means actively seeking, and then fulfilling, our unique potential. That hidden calling is revealed wherever we feel exalted and whenever we find our powerful, honest voice to speak it. Certainly, the human desire to conform—to obscure our distinctiveness—makes self-revelation, and thus self-responsibility, difficult. But we can invite responsibility into our lives, just as we can invite in eroticism or joy. And when we act responsibly for ourselves, we let others act responsibly for themselves. Through the practice of mindful acts, such as showing up on a regular basis, we prepare ourselves to be graced by responsibility in relationships with ourselves, then with our loves, and finally with our lives.

DAILY HEALTHY SEX ACTS

- How much time do you spend each day being responsible to yourself? List your obligations to yourself, such as practicing self-care, establishing personal security, or exploring your potential.

- The concept of *responsibility assumption* states that everything perceivable is part of us and mirrors our karmic actions—that is, that all external phenomena are but outer symbols of our inner reality. Consequently, all visible change starts invisibly from within.

> *"Ring the bells that still can ring.*
> *Forget your perfect offering.*
> *There is a crack in everything.*
> *That's how the light gets in."*
>
> — Leonard Cohen

PERFECTION

Picture the perfect life, the perfect family, the perfect relationship, the perfect recovery, and you've drawn a seductive and sometimes deadly delusion. We all know couples who don't dare voice their reality, or authentically state fears and negativity, afraid it will spoil the illusion of perfection. As if anyone else really cares whether they're perfect! The relationships people care about are the meaningful ones they share. Those seemingly flawless relationships can feel disengaged and sterile. Outsiders might smile and say, "Oh, that's nice." But there's no personal meaning.

Our society celebrates the perfect score, the record-breakers, the famous. Other societies have different perfection paradigms—their ideal beauty, their worthiest royalty or shamans. Clearly, "perfection" is relative, and not only geographically but temporally: The "perfect" grades or "perfect" game that appears ideal at one moment might be revealed as misinformed learning or mediocre effort the next moment.

We can apply this relativity of perfection to our own accomplishments and struggles. We don't have to let the dominant narrative define us. Societal standards can be a blessing, guiding us to excellence, or a burden that crushes individuality. Indeed, the quest for perfection has led to wonderful achievements. The art is to seek excellence while avoiding submission to perfectionism. Healthy perfection relies on humanity and humility. It invites meaning and connection. If life goes wrong, the antidote is not to make it "better," and certainly, not "perfect," but to make it fuller of meaning. Every failure to meet expectations has value because relationships are a self-renewing process. This isn't the win-lose mentality of power over people, it's power *with* people. Here, progress *is* perfection.

DAILY HEALTHY SEX ACTS

- Look for the places where you try to present the illusion of perfection. Let others in! Take a chance today, and share your real truth as you really feel it. This might be as simple as saying, "I don't know how to share my real truth with you." And just that much can be perfect for the moment.

- Keep a progress chart. Every day, as you take steps towards healthy intimacy, no matter how insignificant they seem, write them down in a private notebook. "Today I looked my neighbor in the eyes and said hello." Whenever in self-doubt, refer to your words and re-affirm the progress of your perfectly personal path.

"To obtain a vision of Beauty and Divinity, each man should begin by making himself beautiful and divine."

— Plotinus

23 MARCH

DIVINE EXPRESSION

There's a concept that all life, all experience, all thought and all action is an expression of the divine. We're born on the backs of successive ages of heartache and sorrow, joy and love, grief and pathos, distortion and error striving for success. One hint about the definition of success is that "succession" is derived from the same root. Success, then, is a continuous pattern—an integrated and inclusive sequence. Every encounter is a divine part of the overall pattern leading ultimately to an experience of the whole, to the overview which is the true success. This truth calls us to honor all the darkness as well as the light in human experience.

When we think of divinity we think of the truest, highest beauty, right? God or the gods have an ease, a certain luxury, command, gravitas, a dignified sparkle. And our capacity for creative, divine expression shares that same energy, facility and grace. When we're at our best, we know we have the flow; we strike the mark; our wit hits. And when we say just the right phrase we see it affect people: They nod or shudder, their defenses crumple a tiny bit, it hits their heart. We have spiritually connected through our own connection to the true spirit of our intention. More and more, you will realize that this divine expression is within your grasp at every moment, for you wouldn't be able to recognize and express divinity creatively if it weren't already within you.

DAILY HEALTHY SEX ACTS

- Bring your divinity and highest ideals into your body and voice today. How does your voice sound? What words do you choose? You know those scenes in movies where a character practices in front of the mirror? DO that!

- Consider the ways that you separate your spirituality and your sexuality. What would it be like to find divine expression in sex, and what would that look like for you?

"I believe that if an individual is not on the path to transcending his society and seeing in what way it furthers or impedes the development of human potential, he cannot enter into intimate contact with his humanity."

— Erich Fromm

Society is greater than the sum of its individual parts. It takes on a life of its own, sweeping us up into the status quo and warning us not to stray from social acceptability lest we wish to be ostracized. Anyone who sticks out in either a positive or negative way is suspect, and may become the target of ridicule and rejection. This "herd mentality," while meant to protect us, often also strips us of authenticity, originality, and spontaneity.

When it comes to sex, our collective societal consciousness has undergone centuries of sexual trauma. Inhumane sexual power politics have plagued humanity since the start of civilization. Present society is still emerging from the dungeons of gender inequality, sex trafficking, child sexual abuse, prejudicial laws against LGBT, domestic violence and marital rape, just to name a few enormities. It's only in the 21st century that most of these issues have been honored with national discussion. Clearly, we have a lot of healing to do.

Fear and conformity still dominate most of us. And yet, we see a slow blossoming of enlightenment as, one by one, courageous people come forward to speak their truths and tell their stories. As we enter honest dialogue about our private experiences, we begin to form a more accurate picture of all of society, instead of being sucked into a caricature that reflects the opinions of only an elite minority. Rather than allow the government, the media, or our families to tell us what we should care about, how we should feel, or how we should express our sexuality, we can take back our power and tell them what's important to us. Then, at long last, society will have to reflect us, the people, and not the other way around.

DAILY HEALTHY SEX ACTS

- Is your sexual nature in step with society? How have societal standards impacted your sexual education and experiences?

- Imagine you were born into a utopian society where everyone's healthy, safe sexuality was nurtured into full bloom, and their deepest emotional and erotic identity acknowledged and appreciated. How does this feel? Today, live that socio-sexual ideal.

- How do you contribute to a sexually just society? Throughout the day, notice whether you're part of the problem or the solution. Affirm your own and others' healthy sexuality in mind, word, and deed.

"I do not trust people who don't love themselves and yet tell me, 'I love you.' There is an African saying which is: Be careful when a naked person offers you a shirt."

— Maya Angelou

25 MARCH

AVAILABILITY

When we dote on friends and lovers who don't love us back, although it's counter-intuitive, *we are the ones who are emotionally unavailable*. It's easy to blame the love-avoidant, whose selfishness is obvious: they don't return messages; don't show up when they say; don't communicate any change of plans; and even in person they're evasive and non-committal. But love addicts or codependents appear as the very picture of availability, weighing every possible impact of their actions on the love object.

But that's precisely the problem—human relatedness has become objectified. They aren't interacting with a real person; they're pinning their hopes on a fantasy. In a tragic paradox, the more they seek to make everything right, the less right it becomes. Forced emotional intimacy, which includes compulsive disclosure, is the hallmark of love addiction and codependency. To be truly available means to tolerate another's unique reality without trying to force closeness, and even to accept rejection while still affirming loving-kindness.

People-pleasing prevents availability because to be genuinely available to others we must first be available to ourselves by practicing authenticity and self-care. When our mind clamors for our attention with endless mental chatter, it's often a sign that we're not available within. If you are held hostage by your mental and emotional states, you will probably find yourself held hostage by others' drama, and you may be holding others hostage as well. Outer states reflect inner states. When you can find peace in the moment as it unfolds, you become available to your greater self.

Become available to your own thoughts and emotions, and ask what they want from you. Gently avail yourself within, and you will gradually lose patience for unavailable people and attract those who are truly present.

DAILY HEALTHY SEX ACTS

- What does it mean to you to be available? Some people confuse availability with servitude—having to fulfill another's every material, emotional and sexual need, any time of day or night. When are you available to others? When are you *un*-available?

- Be available to yourself today. Be present with your thoughts and feelings. Everything will work out, and is unfolding exactly as need be. As you self-soothe with self-love, enlarge the circle by inviting others into your inner availability.

"Be not angry that you cannot make others as you wish them to be, since you cannot make yourself as you wish to be."

— Thomas à Kempis

CODEPENDENCE

Codependence is borne of dysfunctional, often traumatic childhood experiences that negate the child's independent identity. Abusive parenting patterns linger in the child's unconscious and may be re-experienced throughout life with intense emotional pain. These patterns also produce difficult adult relationships because the codependent remains immature, thwarted in self-knowledge and thus in discovering what's personally meaningful. When the self has been subordinated, self-love is incomprehensible. Yet self-love is an essential building block of mature, respectful relationships.

Having self-love means we treat ourselves with warmth and understanding when we make mistakes. The more self-compassionate we are, the more optimistic, motivated, and happy we are, and *who* we are in the world affects *how* we are in the world. Setting boundaries signals to others that we care about ourselves, and is another step towards countering codependence. Without functional physical and internal boundaries, we let people walk all over us—a continual abuse that keeps us perennial victims always mourning what's been "done to me."

Growing up in a dysfunctional family distorts reality. Often the brightest kids clearly see the "elephant in the living room" and refuse to ignore it, making them "problem children." Living as an adult tolerating someone who is harming you, emotionally or physically, is not living in reality. Trying to change that someone into an idealized version of who you'd like that person to be is a zero-sum game, while owning your reality and expressing it bespeaks mental health.

To recover from codependence, you have to re-parent yourself by taking care of your adult needs because no one else will—that window closed long ago. Start today by expressing your thoughts, feelings, and concerns to others in a moderate fashion, neither overly emotional nor emotionally cut off.

DAILY HEALTHY SEX ACTS

- Make a list of all the ways you were victimized or abused as a child.

- Make a list of all the ways you've been a victimizer or abuser as an adult.

- How do these lists inform your relationship choices? Share them with a trusted other and process your feelings.

"There are seasons in the life of a couple that function, I think, a little like a night watch. One stands guard, often for a long time, providing the serenity in which the other can work at something. Usually that something is sinewy and full of spines. One goes inside the dark place while the other one stays outside, holding up the moon."

— Marlena De Blasi

27 MARCH

SERENITY

No matter your circumstances, you have the ability to stay serene. Whenever you notice that you are losing your serenity, you have found a fantastic guidepost that shows you how you lose yourself through your addiction to discontent, anger, anxiety, shame, drama, or chaos. These psychic habits are the key factors that rob you of your rightful serenity. For lack of serenity is not just a signal of reactivity; it's also a reinforcement, a doubling down that creates constant ripples of reactivity pulling you even further from your serenity.

Sex and attraction are perfect playing fields to mark the depth and constancy of your serenity. Your ability to be present for the sex act no matter what happens—especially with the combustible neurochemical energies flooding your system from arousal to satisfaction—involves a heroic temperance of emotional and neurobiological regulation. Whether giving, receiving, anticipating, or fulfilling, you're always poised to let go, to go for the gold. So sex always brings up, and always frustrates, desire. And keeping your serenity within all of that, focusing on serenity as a relational practice with a loved one, can help build the healthy emotional muscles that maintain your serenity in daily life.

DAILY HEALTHY SEX ACTS

- Today, work to expand your ability to maintain serenity. You might try to hear it as a tone that you can hum. As you shift your focus from task to task, preserve this harmonic sense of peace. When *monkey mind* or *whirlwind world* disrupt the flow: Stop. Summon Serenity. Hum. And Start Again.

- Now try this in bed with your lover during foreplay. Let each other pause long enough to recapture respective connections to inner serenity.

> *"Love makes your soul crawl out from its hiding place."*
> — Zora Neale Hurston

ISOLATION

From birth onward, we need others to survive and flourish. But past hurts may leave us, like a wounded animal, crawling up into a ball and isolating. Abuse especially creates isolation. With no one to turn to, the abused child learns self-comforting through auto-regulation, which often leads to addictions using sex, drugs, or constant distraction to self-soothe. Abused children reach adulthood ill-equipped to meet their true needs because they have no idea what those are.

Addiction is a disease of isolation, sequestering our souls from ourselves, from others, and from reality. When you think, "No one knows what I'm doing," "I can change my behaviors by myself," "No one is hurt by what I'm doing," or "I'm not hurting myself," you're living in isolation. These distorted thoughts stem from the compartmentalization you learned as a child: Always live in secrecy; never tell about the pain, loneliness, and sadness. In a classic Catch-22, the better you build the double life, the further you sink into isolation, thickening the walls of denial. Without even knowing it, you come to believe your own tall tales justifying, minimizing, and intellectualizing the personal hell you have to construct.

If we are to be instruments of giving, we must come out of the dark by taking the painful action of admitting there's a problem. When you tell one other human being your deepest, darkest, most shameful secret, you have begun the process of emerging from isolation. Like a mole living underground, you may need to let your eyes adjust to the sunlight of truth as you take one step at a time to banish shame and reclaim your soul. Every time you ask for help, stop trying to change others, create support networks, and exercise humility by admitting your mistakes, you are coming out of isolation and becoming a whole person.

DAILY HEALTHY SEX ACTS

- How do you isolate yourself from your relationship or from getting into a romantic relationship? Is it by spending hours in front of the television, Internet pornography, drinking alone, or gaming?

- Who knows about these isolating behaviors?

- Make a commitment to yourself to tell one person about your secrets today. Ask for help.

"Remember that wherever your heart is, there you will find your treasure. You've got to find the treasure so that everything you have learned along the way can make sense."

— Paulo Coelho

VALUES

What does it mean to have values? It's one of the most misunderstood concepts, probably since values have usually been forced upon us as children through lecturing and preaching, rather than allowed to be discovered. As children we naturally learn the magic of play, the delights of taste, the warm glow of love, but we are rarely afforded the same opportunity to unearth the sacred vitality of our personal values in an organic manner.

Truthfully, values derive from our being able to assign personal importance to aspects of our life. Knowing our values, in other words, is the art of *valuation*—the ability to *assess the worth* of our choices and desires. That's why it's important to live in harmony with our values, because our values are what we actually treasure in life.

If we're not living up to certain values, perhaps they're not really ours to begin with. Or, just as likely, there is conflict within our value system that is paralyzing our ability to qualify experiences. The power we have as adults to establish genuine, personal values provides one of the great joys of life. Let your true values ring throughout life and guide your every action—especially behind closed doors where no one's watching, whether in the secret privacy of your bedroom or of your own value-able heart.

DAILY HEALTHY SEX ACTS

- Take a few minutes today and write down any of your values that come to mind. Then ask yourself if these are truly *your* values and, if so, what you are doing to live up to them.

- Share your values. This makes us feels vulnerable, so it's common for many people to "share their values" chiefly by doling out advice. If you realize that your values are about you and not about anyone else, you can let those you trust know what's authentically important to you.

"You can't promise how you'll feel. But you can promise to cultivate a virtue, such as the virtue of love."

— Phillip Cary

PROMISES

It's said you can only love someone to the extent that you love yourself, and it's the same with trust. If we constantly make vows—"I'm going to do this, I'm not going to do that"—but fail to follow through, our untrustworthiness will spill out into our lives. We will fail to live up to our potential—*our promise*—in a desired area, and will attract others' broken promises. A crucial step toward breaking this pattern is to acknowledge and, if possible, to share the grief we have experienced in childhood and youth from being let down.

So it can be healing, especially during sex, to make promises and keep them immediately as a method of cutting new grooves into our psychological patterns: "I promise to touch your knee," and to do so. Develop awareness of what it sounds like and what it feels like to promise something and then to do it. As superficial as this elementary practice may sound, it lays the foundation of a new blueprint which can be extended to grander, more *abstract* promises.

The early development of abstract thought often begins when a child first grasps that Mommy or Daddy, although currently not seen, *is somewhere else.* Non-localized space and time are abstract concepts, utilizing the pre-frontal cortex of the brain. But when our nervous system gets triggered by fear or hurt, our capacity for advanced thought is hijacked by our lower brain, built for emergency response. To follow through on a promise means we are operating from a functioning higher brain. Promise-keeping is less a moral issue than a question of whether we are neurophysiologically capable of holding a wished-for promise in mind until its fulfillment.

DAILY HEALTHY SEX ACTS

- What aspects of your reality failed to fulfill their promise? Consider whether or not you keep your own promises in these areas.

- Evaluate the key promises made and broken by you and others throughout your life. How realistic were your expectations, considering the capacity of each person who promised?

- Right now, make a promise aloud to do something simple (for example, to speak a phrase or nod your head) and *do it!* Today, before you take any action, first promise to do it and then do so. Notice thoughts and feelings that arise as you retrain your brain.

> *"Nothing limits intelligence more than ignorance; nothing fosters ignorance more than one's own opinions; nothing strengthens opinions more than refusing to look at reality."*
>
> — Sheri S. Tepper

31 MARCH

REALITY

Reconciling our inner and outer reality is one of the great projects in life. For, more often than not, we impose a hierarchal imbalance between inner and outer reality, usually deeming external fact as superior to internal truth. Yet such inequality can enslave us in pain. Deliverance from this bondage requires owning and expressing our personal truth. But what if we can't recognize that private truth anymore?

Sharing what we know of our inward reality can save us from this hurt because there's no other place where reality gets more distorted than in isolation. As the apparent originators of our own thoughts, we believe we can control our ideas, our lives, and ourselves. But we constantly fear what might happen if anyone saw behind our facade to our internal reality. That's the psychological place where we try to keep parts of our real selves secret.

To gently bring ourselves to a place where we can let our reality become more transparent requires letting people see into us. Therapy, 12-step meetings, and journaling can help develop the transparency such intimate honesty requires. This new sincerity opens the door to the place where we can learn, grow, and connect with others sexually and romantically in a state of integrated reality, without any disparity between what we think and feel and what we present. We certainly can't attain this level of connection through faking it. Real transformation and real success comes from the inside out, transforming each of us at our core. We can only accomplish it by transporting the core of our personal reality toward the light.

DAILY HEALTHY SEX ACTS

- Take a few moments and quickly write down what's real for you. Try to express yourself instinctively without judgment or hesitation.

- Pick one or two aspects of your inner reality that have never been expressed out loud, and safely share them with a trustworthy acquaintance today.

April

> *"It is as hard to see one's self as to look backwards without turning around."*
>
> — Henry David Thoreau

1 APRIL

SELF-AWARENESS

A chief characteristic ennobling us above beasts is our capacity to contemplate and interpret our own actions, emotions and desires. This supremely human self-awareness is both an art and a privilege. Throughout the day as we encounter disturbances within our core, we can cultivate the power to step back and evaluate the deepest origin of our feelings. Our decision to pause and reflect proves that we have evolved beyond impulse, reactivity, and knee-jerk habit. Self-awareness signifies emotional maturity and plays an integral role in a healthy love life. Sharing insights with a partner, we take responsibility for our anger, sadness or dissatisfaction through honest dialogue instead of blindly acting on animal-like instincts.

Self-awareness takes hands-on practice, however. The patterns of thinking that provoke our deepest questions rarely provide the answers. Zen Buddhists recognize and celebrate this by meeting a query with an absurd reply—a response intended to induce a shift in consciousness that disrupts worn-out mental routes. When self-reflection fails to lead to epiphany, we can practice *contrary action*, an "outside-in approach" that adopts new behavior to prime new awareness.

Becoming self-aware, then, entails a subtle paradox: accept ourselves but strive to improve. As we work to fulfill our potential, we will encounter hopelessness. So it's crucial to mark our progress. One evidence of growth is that *we notice* triggered feelings we ignored before, when we focused on whatever grabbed our attention. Also, we find that problematic behaviors and triggered feelings don't last as long; we still hit the same notes, but we more quickly change our tune. Finally, our compassion for ourselves and others grows, allowing us to reach out for support when triggered. Although our problems do not disappear, expanding self-awareness lets us experience the world differently, and finds us seeking solutions based on *quality* rather than quantity.

DAILY HEALTHY SEX ACTS

- How has your self-awareness evolved beyond key stages in your past? How might your life be different if you could have addressed past problems with your current awareness?

- Consider your goals. Where will your self-awareness need to grow to meet them? Today, visualize in detail your ideal job, dream date, or other desire. Pay special attention to the quality of self-awareness you have for each aim. Live in that awareness today.

- Share your expanding inner world with your lover *in the same way*—surprised, curious, amazed—that self-awareness finds you.

"The universe is like a mirror. Say a kind word into a mirror, and it will say the same back to you. Curse into the mirror, and the image curses back. The Creator doesn't inflict punishment or stand in judgment of anyone. It is our own actions that rebound into our lives like reflections bouncing back from a cosmic mirror."

— Yehuda Berg

MIRROR

Mirroring is the crucial step in childhood development when the caregiver acknowledges the child's autonomy, reflecting accurately what the child communicates. Children test this mirror, often dressing in outlandish outfits that defy conventional taste. In a secure household, such self-expression doesn't threaten. But in narcissistic environments every little act reflects the value(s) of the parent. When personal autonomy is outlawed, the free flow of consciousness halts and insecurity takes its place. Externally imposed identities alienate individuals from themselves and from an authentic experience of the real world. So our adult relationships often act as mirrors into past programming. But when we break through the mirror, and realize those relationships also reflect the shared experience of an ongoing process, we can own our past programming. Better, we become grateful that the more we're driven to seek out personal truth, the more truth we find.

The concept of *the other* delineates everything *out there* which we're not, including behaviors and beliefs which clash with our self-concept. Our identity develops throughout our life but typically stands firm at skin and the personal self. Yet all we perceive—every person and trait we might name—passes *through* us since, if it did not *enter into* our personal consciousness, it wouldn't exist for us. Our physical bodies certainly do not exhaust our existence. Empathic knowledge lets us experience all races, ages, and genders. And all that enters our awareness is part of who we are. When we step out of the confines of programmed identities to bask in the exquisite otherness of the universe, we come to realize that we share one life. All ripples in this one life reflect what Jung called the central Self—the deepest, truest dwelling of our identity.

DAILY HEALTHY SEX ACTS

- In what ways was your identity pre-defined? Since we each must answer existential questions independently, it's narcissism (familial or cultural) when people claim their assumptions as absolute truths.

- Get out of your head and into direct experience. Today, mirror the world in energy, movement and quality. Let your consciousness flow with the traffic and soar with the airwaves.

- Realize this: You are all colors. All shapes and sexes. All of us. Then consider: How does it feel to be the *other side*—in politics, religion, fashion? Let the expansion of your personal self bring you to your true Self.

"Freedom is not freedom from connection."

— Joss Whedon

3 APRIL

FREEDOM

When we think about freedom, we usually define it as the absence of restriction—beyond the reach of oppression, judgment, inhibition, or pain. But we may more properly view freedom as a positive enactment— a moving toward life and a search to connect out of free will. In fact, the freedom to do and to feel—to love, to experience, to fulfill our potential—is true freedom.

Typically, the call for freedom in a relationship confuses it with autonomy, with having "my space." Yet healthy relationship requires mutual autonomy, allowing respective voices to be heard and authentic selves to grow without either trying to manipulate the other or impose a given outcome. So an agitated demand for relational freedom might actually screen a desire to escape frightening confrontation. It may be a coping mechanism learned in childhood—often through *time-outs*, the forced isolation of children to resolve their issues alone which, of course, they cannot possibly do. When such neglectful emotional exile is the default parenting style, the child may develop a compulsive need for freedom *from* people, leading to love avoidance in relationships. And this enslavement to deadening, detrimental withdrawal patterns out of fear of intimacy is the very antithesis of freedom.

Conversely, we attain the freedom to relate with unconditional love by acknowledging and addressing personal issues, and by building our relationships on trust and trustworthiness. Valuing ourselves and others empowers us with the freedom to care deeply without fear of rejection and disappointment. And the freedom to forgive—perhaps the hardest freedom to capture—consecrates our own impure impulses, permitting the light of awareness to illuminate them and to let us work them out. In these ways, freedom to feel and to act frees us from our habitual self, and frees us to become our best self.

DAILY HEALTHY SEX ACTS

- What does healthy freedom feel like to you? Do you bring this feeling to your relationships, work, and alone time? Or do you wear the chains of personal circumstance and obligation? Today, cast off those chains and invite the triumphant feeling of true freedom into all your interactions and activities.

- Reflect on any desire to escape from life, people, or situations. Now, flip the script and find the freedom to move *toward* them. What would have to happen for you to feel free to express yourself fully while perceiving reality through the lens of unconditional love?

> *"We are aware that we can never meet our own needs at the expense of others. Emotional liberation involves stating clearly what we need in a way that communicates we are equally concerned that the needs of others be fulfilled."*
>
> — Marshall B. Rosenberg

NEEDS

Each of us has needs, whether met or unmet. We would hardly be human if we didn't. There's no shame or weakness in desiring validation and affection. What's truly damaging to our lives—what brings unnecessary pain and deprivation—is either refusing to acknowledge our needs or being unable to voice them to others. The only way we can begin to get our needs met is to enter into a process of transparent communication both with ourselves and with other people, honestly admitting what we require and thus taking responsibility for our own happiness. Not only will such expression help us to satisfy our own needs, it also trains us to appreciate those of others, and affords them the safety and respect of coming forward with preferences of their own. In this way, we affirm that we are neither masters nor followers, but are all co-creators.

In a relationship, we might initially view our needs as conflicting with those of our lover. But it's really only the strategies by which we seek satisfaction that ever conflict. For instance, we may want to gaze deeply into the other's eyes during sex, while the other prefers to avoid eye contact. Our real needs, though, aren't about eye-gazing or not. The real needs are: "I need connection" and "I need independence." And it's perfectly possible, whether we gaze into eyes or not, to meet those respective needs for attachment and liberty. Our desire to feel connected may stem from childhood experience of abandonment; our lover's need for independence may stem from a childhood experience of coercion. If we understand and voice our needs we can honor them both, because we have built empathy rather than resentment. Empowering ourselves and others is a natural byproduct of expressing and exploring our needs openly and directly.

DAILY HEALTHY SEX ACTS

- Common core needs include stimulation, honesty, inclusion, and harmony. List your inner needs and share them with your partner. Ask your partner to reciprocate. The goal here isn't necessarily to meet one another's needs but to express and acknowledge them together.

- How do you voice your needs? Can you affirm a healthy need for appreciation and affection in a strong and sober tone? Or are these natural needs muffled by self-judgments, perhaps in the voices of shaming authority figures from childhood?

- Today, in every interaction, imagine the unmet needs that might exist for others and yourself.

"None of us can help the things life has done to us. They're done before you realize it, and once they're done they make you do other things until at last everything comes between you and what you'd like to be, and you've lost your true self forever."

— Eugene O'Neill

5 APRIL

TRUTH

Why do people miscast reality? Lies are walls, and to lie is to block our light. For there's no deception without self-deception. Somewhere along the way we learned to deny a personal truth. Growing up, we depended on caregivers not just for food and shelter but also for information and ways to interpret life. How helpless we were against the easy-to-ignore intellectual abuse of misinformation or lies! This abuse of truth and trust created in many a "Why not?" attitude: Why not break the rules and act out against our nature? Every so-called pathological liar has been deprived of the integral process of developing truth. Such family-of-origin issues often included *gaslighting*—camouflaging deceit by casting fault on another's perception—named after a *film noir* in which a villain's lies about flickering gaslights make the heroine think she's going insane.

How painful and crazy-making it is to be lied to... even though we've each lied to another ourselves. Those past falsehoods remain with us. And every one of us has broken through denial to realize it, so we know we are still capable of falsity. Even now, we lie by omission, or imply a lie through careful wording that obscures the truth. Or we silence our truth out of fear—still a deception. Probably, we're still trying to find the right way to share it.

Spiritual truth, whatever its shape, is the first model of veracity. When we heal the trauma of intellectual abuse enough to align with the living heart of a spiritual truth, that inner model of sincerity finally enables us to recognize the ring of truth in others. At long last, trust reestablished creates a loving space for our relationships to share wondrous truth as we discover it and as it finds us.

DAILY HEALTHY SEX ACTS

- When you share your truth, are your words secondary to your behavior? Someone in a rage speaks only the truth that he or she is enraged.

- Do you dispute others' versions of reality and thus fail to hear what's true *for them*? You don't have to agree, but today, hear another's truth.

- With whom do you share your truth? When you're stuck on someone who can't receive it, you're stuck in a relationship that's not genuine.

- What's your spiritual truth now? No matter its state, embrace and seek to uncover it throughout your day's events.

"What is straight? A line can be straight, or a street, but the human heart, oh, no, it's curved like a road through mountains."

— Tennessee Williams

SEXUAL ORIENTATION

Exploring sexual orientation can be a wonderful adventure that leads to exciting, unexpected realizations about ourselves and others. Instead of seeing orientation narrowly as a binary of gay versus straight, we can view it as a flowing, creative expression along a spectrum, neither fixed nor inflexible. We can expand our identity by trying different energies and role-playing, even within a committed relationship. If we are single, we can consider dating outside of not just our assumed sexual orientation, but also our established preferences for body size, age, race, or other preconceived categories we've deemed "right" for us.

Unexpected attractions can feel threatening. They may expose our vulnerability to social rejection or frighten us with imagined consequences. In trying to cope with the unknown, we may temporarily shut down, deny our feelings, and label our emotions as "wrong." But if we push further, we can begin to break down some of the cultural conditioning that has informed most of our choices about sexual self-expression.

How can we truly know who we are when society so condemns and hates certain identities, and bolsters these prejudices with legal statutes that deny whole groups of people their basic rights? Increasingly, we are discovering that boxes marked "male" and "female" are too primitive to contain the limitless flowering of human sexuality. In their place, we must cultivate respect and tolerance towards other people's struggles for authenticity, especially in a political climate that privileges conformity. We all must recognize the trauma experienced whenever a given sexual expression is stigmatized, imposing extraordinary obstacles to sexual and relational development. We can gently begin to let go of black-and-white thinking, and open up to the mystery and exhilaration that comes from taking healthy risks.

DAILY HEALTHY SEX ACTS

- Have you ever felt attracted to someone outside your sexual orientation? What would it mean to your identity and your relationships if you were ever to pursue such an attraction?

- Walk in the shoes of other people today. Imagine growing up with a totally different *arousal template* (pattern for what you find attractive.) Let your expanded awareness engender empathy for others.

- Today, show your solidarity as a proud member of the LGBTQA (Lesbian, Gay, Bisexual, Transgender, Questioning, and Allied) community.

"How we spend our days is, of course, how we spend our lives. What we do with this hour, and that one, is what we are doing."

— Annie Dillard

7 APRIL

ACTIONS

"Action!" is the director's call when the stage is perfectly set for the scene to be acted out. But waiting for the perfect scene in everyday life is a zero-sum game. Not waiting for action, but taking action—perfectly prepared for or not—lets you achieve your personal and professional goals. Movement towards something good and desirable wholly engages our life forces. But actions that create healthy and genuine excitement differ from those that just create drama. In fact, especially where sex and love are concerned you must be both active *and* discerning. Seeking and being sought after are action states driven by nature's imperative. But only when your actions follow your intention toward true goals does life unroll all its possibilities.

Like courtship, sexuality requires action. Often one person in a relationship complains that the other never initiates sex. But sex is not initiated only genitally. Sexuality can be transmitted through a gaze or the tone of voice because it's the intention that moves things into action. In addition to sex, engaging your partner in any kind of planned activity, whether it's a date for the theater or a hike in the woods, demonstrates your intention. Through our intention-rich actions, others know that we love them, that we're attracted to them, and that they matter to us. The adage that "actions speak louder than words" rings true. For it's not what you say but *what you do and why you do it* that moves things forward in any relationship.

Reality does not always conform to what you want and need. But wrongly believing that you can just think it into conformity will prove frustrating. If your life lacks something good, accept that reality. And then take intentional action to change it.

DAILY HEALTHY SEX ACTS

- Take an active step toward your partner today. Is it time you initiated sex or made plans for the evening? Is it time to propose deeper connection or is it time to end things?

- Be honest with yourself about the reality of your life. Instead of fighting what is, choose to see the depth of what you have, assess what you need, make genuine intentions, and then take action to create those needed changes.

- What one action can you take today to harmonize with the flow of life? With the other in your relationship?

> *"Arousal leaves us mind-blind."*
>
> — Malcolm Gladwell

AROUSAL

When we think of arousal, we naturally think of sexual arousal. But sex is only one arousal state in the body. Excitement, joy, fear, and anxiety are all states of arousal that can exist on their own or during a sexual encounter. Self-consciousness and anxiety can interfere with sexual arousal, dampening down our lust and robbing us of the heightened promise of sex. Obsessing about sexual arousal and demanding it of ourselves creates other problems.

When our sexual arousal owns us, we do indeed become "mind-blind." Thinking that the object of our arousal will fix all our loneliness, pain, and fears, we're blindly led by our sex organs to people and places we'd never consider when operating from "mind-sight"—our ability to "see" from a place of clarity. When thus overpowered by sexual arousal, we tend to think of arousal as the domain of the genitals, and entirely miss the magic of full-body and sensory arousal. What a joy to leave the collapsed state of compulsively seeking relief through that restricted view of sex, and to celebrate the full-body, heart-centered arousal that comes from genuine joy states!

Today, make the word *arousal* synonymous with *happiness*. Arouse each of your senses by taking a deep breath of morning air, seeing the beauty and abundance that surrounds you, tasting the sweet and savory on your tongue as you eat your first meal of the day, and feeling the skin of your lover's hand or lips as s/he wishes you, "Good morning!"

DAILY HEALTHY SEX ACTS

- Do one thing to arouse your senses in celebration of your sexuality as a source of joy, wholeness, and all that's good about you. Eat a piece of delicious fruit, smile at your neighbor, listen to a favorite piece of music, or give your partner a hand massage.

- Notice the arousal system in your body. When do you get excited, scared, or anxious? What people, places, or conditions create these various arousal states in you? Become familiar with how you can amplify positive arousal states such as joy and how you can regulate negative arousal states such as fear or anxiety.

- Engage your partner in arousing activities through play. Laugh, skip down the street, walk arm in arm, or dance the night away.

*"Someone who will tremble for your touch...
someone whose fingers are a poem."*

— Janet Fitch

9 APRIL

TOUCH

The miraculous healing power of touch should not be underestimated. Who we are and what we do touches people's lives, sometimes quite literally, as molecules are shared and exchanged in every interaction. And not just the physical sensation produced by touch, but the intentions behind the action matter. Loving motives for our touch transfer to the other person and affect them not just physically, but emotionally and spiritually, invigorating all the senses and activating the nervous system. But our harmful touch, through bullying or domestic violence, damages others severely in ways we cannot measure.

A human baby won't develop properly if deprived of loving touch. If human contact is inadequate or unkind, the baby will develop problems ranging from poor psychological health to self-harming behaviors that often lead to addiction. And as we mature into adulthood, touch remains just as integral to our survival as when we were first born.

Sex is the ultimate form of loving touch, as it reaches places that only a lover can. Relationships need loving touch to survive; otherwise, they wither into emotional or sexual anorexia. But don't try to force togetherness, to fix it, to give the right touch or the right pleasure. If you and your partner need to train yourselves consciously to touch each other, try simple acts such as holding hands, hugging, or giving and receiving massages to induce biochemical and psychological connection. Touch is an innate gift that each one of us possesses just because we are alive. Even when we're not feeling our best, at any moment's notice we can become channels of livingness through the miracle of loving, healing touch.

DAILY HEALTHY SEX ACTS

- Today, reach out with loving touch to trusted friends and family. Broaden your circle of intimacy to neighbors and healthy acquaintances. Shake hands, share hugs, and pat backs. Invest your deepest affection—all that you would express—in heartfelt gestures.

- Touch yourself as you ache to be touched. Wherever you're sore or lonely, let your own fingers channel the healing energy of the life you've been given into your amazing, faithful body. Be the touch you desire.

- When you make love, focus on the moment of touch. Let this point of physical contact between you become a dance of your loving intentions.

"Love, love, love—all the wretched cant of it, masking egotism, lust, masochism, fantasy under a mythology of sentimental postures."

— Germaine Greer

SENTIMENTALITY

Originally, the term *sentimentality* simply referred to feelings about a subject. But when the concept became the catchword of the Romantic Movement in the late 1700s, a rationalist backlash against excessive emotional expression gave the term negative connotations that still survive. Although sentimentality means something different to everyone—nostalgic memories, overdone affection, or irrational attachment to beloved objects—today the term usually describes superficial or regressive emotionality.

In Jungian thought, sentimentality masks savagery much the way psychological inflation ("I'm the greatest") stems from and leads to deflation ("I'm the worst") in a pendulum swing of egoistic delusional states. It's the same consciousness that gushes over the adorability of a little child in one moment, but finds it a little monster in the next. That is, sentimentality objectifies people and experiences, making ourselves the sole and inconstant arbiters of their worth. This objectification must be false, since it exists solely in our shifting moods rather than in the other's or object's true value. Thus it enters us into a false, imagined relationship with life. There's a world of difference between *affection* and *affectation*.

When we shackle our sentiments to preconceived ideas about feeling, it's often the result of programmed messages and coerced transference in childhood. The child who finds solace in the pretend companionship of a teddy bear to escape the pain of isolation develops a sentimental feeling that's often encouraged as a substitute for cognizant emotional processes. And the emotional power of others' sentimentality can challenge our autonomy by making our refusing to share someone's supercharged sentiments seem—however unjustifiably—indifferent, uncaring, or contrary. At its worst, sentimentality assumes that someone's private, perhaps random feelings must be universal. That assumption blocks other individuals' mindful empathy and genuine acceptance, and gives real feeling a bad name.

DAILY HEALTHY SEX ACTS

- Consider your most treasured belongings, favorite activities, highly valued hotspots, and prized perceptions of people. If you have sentimental feelings for any of them, you will feel easily threatened, and perhaps angry, whenever others fail to share your opinion.

- Settling for affected, manipulative or superficial feelings might signal a greater fear of real emotion. Today, take deeper breaths and allow your positive sentiments to bring you to your larger unconditional love.

"Reading is like the sex act—done privately, and often in bed."

— Daniel J. Boorstin

11 APRIL

PRIVACY

For partners to feel safely open with each other, it's crucial to clarify standards of privacy between the both of them and between them and the outside world. For perceived privacy violations can trigger anger and hurt as one partner feels the other has trampled his or her boundaries and values. Is it permissible to read each other's letters and emails, to listen to phone messages, to scroll through call logs and text messages?

An invasion of privacy, such as snooping around for information that hasn't been willingly shared, can destroy trust. We all have an inner spy that can stoop to surreptitious means to satisfy idle curiosity or, more commonly, to allay nagging doubt. Distrust and fear can provoke many to act outside their usual integrity. But breaking boundaries in order to feel safe can have the opposite effect on a relationship. On the other hand, if we maintain open communication we can trust in that process to correct any wrongs in our relationship, and resist being tempted to ferret out hidden information. Of course, if one partner breaks the commitment, s/he might reasonably surrender some privacy in order to rebuild trust, perhaps providing access to electronic devices and communications for a time.

Respecting privacy involves more than possessions or words. It's also valuing the sacredness of each person's emotions and inner processes, which s/he may or may not choose to reveal. Similarly, we can't assume the right to air unsolicited opinions and unwanted advice. We often embark on critical dissection of mates, children, family or friends without consideration of their privacy—their personhood. Reflect on how often in your life unflattering information has been publicized rather than kept private, and the resulting hurt. Learn to draw, and respect, the line between healthy, agreed-upon levels of transparency and disrespectful display.

DAILY HEALTHY SEX ACTS

- What were the standards of privacy in your family of origin? How does that programming inform your current relational attitudes?

- Today notice how you protect your own personal privacy and that of others. Where do you need to relax boundaries? Where might you reinforce them? Find the healthy balance between controlling your reputation and compulsive disclosure.

"A final comfort that is small, but not cold: The heart is the only broken instrument that works."

— T. E. Kalem

HEARTBREAK

When we think of heartbreak, we imagine overwhelming distress for which there is no cure. Yet when you choose to live life fully, to see each day as if it's your last and to open your heart, you will not be able to escape the pain in the world. Look into the eyes of the homeless on the street, visit your neighbor who is dying of cancer, turn on the news and hear the atrocities that abound the world over, and life will shatter your heart into a million pieces. This is the risk embedded in loving life and another, and no one can protect you from that. The greatest calling in life is to love deeply, knowing that eventually we either leave or will be left, whether by choice or by death. It's been said that we are here on earth to risk our heart—that our heart was made to be broken.

Trying to outrun your own natural reaction to crushing loss only strengthens it and proves to be a fool's errand. Mood-altering substances or experiences keep the agony at bay temporarily, but ultimately invite it back in spades. But if you can recognize heartbreak as the catalyst for healing unresolved issues, you will find the eye of the storm. While you mourn the personal loss of love or a universal pain, know that your life is changing—growth is taking place and something new is rising from the ashes of your grief. This process can be thought of as a holy fire, as a sacred act between you and your Higher Power, as a time to "let go and let God." The challenge at these times is to dive deeply into the pain, for denial accrues more suffering. In sitting still, transformation begins.

DAILY HEALTHY SEX ACTS

- Take time to see the suffering around you. Don't look away. How does it feel in your heart? How does it change you?

- Visualize sending white healing light through your Higher Power to the Higher Power of someone in need. Let your heart break for that person's pain so you both may suffer a little less. Be generous with your love.

- Choose to see heartbreak as bittersweet. Ending a romance or friendship, while wrenching, can be the beginning of liberation and growth. With whom do you need to end things today? Show empathy to your own self through your actions. Be brave.

"Vanity, revenge, loneliness, boredom, all apply: lust is one of the least of the reasons for promiscuity."

— Mignon McLaughlin

13 APRIL

PROMISCUITY

The word *promiscuous* comes from a Latin root meaning *mixed up*. Unlike *polyamorous*—loving many—*promiscuous* implies indiscriminate, reckless hooking-up that is more akin to a compulsion than to a committed lifestyle choice. Having sex with multiple partners in itself may not be harmful, but when the motivation for this behavior comes from a desire to numb out or escape reality rather than from joy and love, promiscuity becomes a debilitating drug. We can be preoccupied with the constant pursuit of new partners, sometimes to the exclusion of self-care, socializing, and work. We may even risk disease, violence, or unwanted pregnancy.

Of course when discussing promiscuity, it's important to examine the context in which the word is being used, for unfortunately our culture throws around much shaming and name-calling when it comes to sexual habits. No one has the right to dictate to us with whom, with how many, or how often we engage in sex. What matters most is our own feelings about our behavior. Do we feel drained, exhausted and depleted by our hypersexual activity? Does it cause us to neglect other areas of our lives? Are we avoiding being present?

Here it may be wise to slow down our impulses through sober perception—to measure them, caress them. Instead of blindly following desires, we can use them to get to know ourselves and others better by acknowledging attractions without feeling the constant need to act on them. We can hold our impulses with love, see what they are made of, where they come from, what they are trying to tell us, and where they may lead. In this way we can feel that our sexual connections are conscious and examined, rather than random, chaotic, and just plain mixed up.

DAILY HEALTHY SEX ACTS

- How comfortable are you addressing promiscuity in yourself or others? What are the perils of such an examination? What potential opportunities might there be for inviting clarity into what drives a sexual appetite?

- Write a list of promiscuity's pros and cons to better understand it. How many statements can you come up with in support of, and against, hypersexual activity?

- We live on the go, with little time for shared truth. Today, seek meaningful intimacy in all your interactions as a way of embracing another's heart and uniting in self-knowledge.

"I wish I could drink like a lady.
I can take one or two at the most.
Three and I'm under the table.
Four and I'm under the host."

— Dorothy Parker

If we want a lover's touch to reach our deepest self, we have to remove barriers to intimacy. The fact is that certain substances, depending on how and why we turn to them, can prevent true, deep connection with others. Paradoxically, an oft-cited objective for imbibing alcohol in particular is to loosen inhibitions as a *social lubricant*. Indeed, alcohol and drugs seem to calm nerves and soothe social anxiety, so logically their use should make it easier to connect. But the real hangover from them is that distances still remain and inhibitions creep back in. Self-medicating with psychoactive substances cannot permanently cure patterns of reserve. Relying on any external substance to self-soothe creates dependency, a type of materialism that makes the drug—alcohol, gambling, cocaine, food, or sex—into one's Higher Power.

But what constitutes sobriety is different for everyone—there's no one-size-fits-all sobriety. That's why it's healthy to practice *sober-fasting*: abstaining from addictive behaviors or substances to see if they're being used to numb feelings and if they hobble one's mind and interactions. We should also check *emotional sobriety*, the ability to regulate feelings and expression, since some people self-medicate with defense mechanisms just as others do with substances. We've all seen people who did not act sober, who behaved foolishly and irresponsibly, and we've all probably experienced both admiration and annoyance for the fun and the mess they create. To sober up seems to many like making life "so serious," as if seriousness precluded joy, warmth, spontaneity and fun. But there can be a delusional, blind quality to non-sober festivities. To have our eyes open soberly with all our senses and memory intact allows some of the most rewarding, soul-nourishing, and long-lasting pleasures possible.

 DAILY HEALTHY SEX ACTS

- We all need to cultivate warmth and joy from within—to be carefree but not careless. Can you tap into those feelings, or do you place the power of your amusement outside of yourself into substances or habits?

- Can you pinpoint people or subjects that have a sobering effect on you? Specifying what sobers you helps you identify what persons or thoughts you may be escaping through addictive behaviors.

- Is sex an area where you want to sober up? Can you maintain a heartfelt connection to your beloved even when apart, or are sex and love like drugs—do you go into withdrawal if you don't get your fix?

"In our desire to impose form on the world and our lives we have lost the capacity to see the form that is already there; and in that lies not liberation but alienation, the cutting off from things as they really are."

— Colin Gunton

15 APRIL

ALIENATION

Our fast-paced world can have the effect of alienating us from our community, our sense of self and sexuality. Isolated and alone, we can easily lose ourselves in computers, cell phones and television where our sense of vitality and identity become lost or unreal. The human mind exists in relation to other people, so our estrangement from family, friends, and the natural world can feel like we're losing our identity or life is passing us by.

Stop and notice your surroundings today. Take time to recognize that you stand on a living, breathing planet. Notice the warmth of the sunshine on your body as you walk to your car, the feel of the breeze on your neck or the cold, icy air on your face. This mindfulness practice directs you out of the captivity of your thoughts or the material world, and into the present moment and place.

When you can have a sensuous experience with nature and recognize that you and it are one, you will begin to heighten your sensual and sexual pleasures with a partner. Don't let the natural world become foreign to you. Join with Mother Nature and recognize her power and beauty as your own.

DAILY HEALTHY SEX ACTS

- Take time for a silent walk in nature, alone or with your beloved.

- Smell the flowers and notice the beauty surrounding you. If in a romantic relationship, hold hands with your beloved and gaze into one another's eyes.

- Recognize all surrounding beauty as your own. You are the link connecting all that you perceive.

> *"It took me years to figure out that upset was upset, and tumultuousness was not the same thing as passion. Love isn't drama."*
>
> — Deb Caletti

DRAMA

Almost everyone loves exciting "human interest" displays, whether in art, fashion, music, or food. The dramatic flourish piques our thirst for novelty like nothing else. Momentous events like meeting a new person, getting a new job, falling in love, travelling to an exotic land, or adopting a baby create heightened moments that make us feel life is worth living. And let's not forget the play of Mother Nature's dramatic glory in any sunset, the hummingbird in your backyard, or the vast blue sky.

When we're cut off from the magnificence of what sits before us every minute of every day, we tend to create drama through exaggerated, overemotional behavior. If you grew up in a chaotic household where people's needs had to be magnified to garner attention, you may have a propensity to do the same. Sensationalizing every move you make or every wrong incurred against you will get you the attention you may be craving, but it will never fill what's missing inside of you. Often those who are most melodramatic feel empty internally and need constant attention in order to feel valued and loved. And if creating our own drama isn't enough, our tabloid culture is at the ready, giving us a ringside seat to celebrity lives. Like voyeurs, we gawk from out of our own inadequacy, imagining what it would be like to be other persons, to look like them, to be their friend, to have a stake in their life.

But these thoughts are delusional, because real life brings us (and even celebrities!) only fleeting excitement, not a steady string of amazing events keeping us in a forever-heightened state. Like the real drama of a great theatrical play, the ebb and flow of events makes life rich, textured, and varied, and leaves us with genuine curiosity for whatever's next.

DAILY HEALTHY SEX ACTS

- Do you create unnecessary drama in your life? If so, what do you know about why you do that? What can you do to change?

- Do you create drama in your love relationship? Talk to your partner about what underlies this tendency and what you really need.

- Are you someone who dampens down your flair for the dramatic? If so, find a creative expression for the excited and emotional parts of yourself.

> *"Sex, a great and mysterious motive force in human life, has indisputably been a subject of absorbing interest to mankind through the ages."*
>
> — William J. Brennan, Jr.

17 APRIL

SEXUAL FASCINATION

"Sex sells," they say. We know advertisers use subliminal sexual messages to sell products—orgies hidden in ice cubes. That's because erotic imagery affects people's brains first, followed by body parts, like an accident we can't *not* look at. What is it about sex and sexuality that's so provocative? If we weren't repressed on some level, would sex still hold us enthralled? Certainly the world is wounded by sex-negative messages, and part of our cultural fleshly fixation might be trying instinctively to restore sacred sexuality to its rightful place.

Yet true eroticism really does demand a deep connection to stir us inside, to rouse us from sleepwalking through life. So the issue of sexual fascination might not be so much the result of sexualization intruding on society, but more likely is the imposition of societal obligations onto individual erotic integration and genuine interaction. Were we to live more authentic lives, perhaps our errant sexual fascination would be absorbed by our healthy sexual expression.

Surely there's a biological imperative to mate and reproduce. But even beyond that, there's a psychological imperative to sexual fascination. Sexuality is one of the rare, true transformations of ourselves that we've witnessed: We started out with scant consciousness of the subject, but that unawareness transformed with puberty. All of us lived life when sex was the farthest thing from our minds. Try to remember the careless freedom of play, basking in the beingness of others. As adults, responsibilities and obligations can often bind us to a daily grind. For some adults, then, sex might be one of the few interactions that restores their openness and sensory exploration of play. It's not hard to see why sexual preoccupation might take over when people become locked out from experiencing fulfilling lives.

DAILY HEALTHY SEX ACTS

- Consider your fascination with sex. What is the feeling as sexuality suddenly enters a routine day, whether by an erotic image or a sexualized spark?

- Speak from your center. Does your vocal pitch waver throughout the day as circumstances overwhelm? One way to counterbalance the overpowering allure of the sensory world is to operate out of your inner potency. Whenever you find yourself transfixed by anything or anyone, summon personal power and speak from your heart and in your true voice.

"Only in sex the noise sometimes stops. I say 'sometimes.' If you have become habitual in sex also, as husbands and wives become, then it never stops. The whole act becomes automatic and the mind goes on its own. Then sex also is a boredom."

— Osho

HABIT

Our personalities often seem to be amalgams of habitual patterns set from birth. We appear to be comprised of predictable likes and dislikes and to function as creatures of habit. True, order and beauty require some rule and discipline, but a life without variety is just plain drab. Yet altering our typical course even a bit—trying a new diet to improve health or relearning biomechanical movement patterns to ease back pain—challenges us. Transforming unexamined patterns of being requires real dedication—what some call the *willingness factor*. But most people get complacent or lazy, accepting their lot in life and letting their habits become unconscious automatic reactions or regular practices. Over time, though, bad habits can turn into addictions. Breaking an addiction demands a steadfast commitment to breaking habits. Fortunately, when breaking those habits becomes a matter of life and death, we tend to fight for our lives.

Yet it's often valuable to try new behaviors even if our very survival is not at stake. Think about your sex life. If you interact with your partner predictably or feel that your sex life has gotten dull, examine whether you've made your encounters too customary, and if you're willing to make changes. Perhaps, having frequently repeated the identical behavior plus reward, you've conditioned yourself like Pavlov's dogs. So it always works, but—unlike a dog—you feel manipulated and as though your partner isn't meeting your needs. Somewhere along the line you (perhaps both of you) chose to check out and stay in a well-worn groove to save emotional energy. Today, why not shake things up and wake yourself up, out of your stupefying comfort? Take responsibility to break habits in your life and seek new, more life-affirming and fruitful actions.

DAILY HEALTHY SEX ACTS

- How willing are you to take action to create a healthier, more vibrant sex life? What actions do you need to take in order to make that happen?

- What habits do you have that are self-destructive or lazy? What do you get out of tolerating those habits? What do you need to do to change them?

- Today, make yourself accountable to another who will help you break bad habits.

"Nobody has ever measured, even poets, how much a heart can hold."

— Zelda Fitzgerald

19 APRIL

POTENCY

If you really excel at something, you've mastered it by doing it so many times it's become a means of self-expression. Similarly, the true promise of sexual potency is as a vehicle for expressing yourself. So potency isn't just a way to get your fix, to get your rocks off. That type of self-centered sex stems from self-centeredness, not self-expression—and carries many limitations. We actually fulfill our potential through expression, not consumption. In fact, if you consume something, it's gone. Consuming is selfish, an isolated act that reinforces isolation. No one else can possibly participate in the thrill you get from greed, lust, or overindulging. These aren't experiences that are even possible to share from your heart.

We share through communing, through expression. And this is the only way that we can fulfill our potential, because if we aim to fulfill our potential through consumption, we will never be satisfied. But sharing our experience through expression builds a common vibration that gets us in sync with ourselves, with our partners, with our spirits, with our community, with our world, with the whole flow of life... with the vibration of life. Through sharing openly, there really is no end to what we will discover about our personal potential for living and loving.

DAILY HEALTHY SEX ACTS

- Vibrate today: Feel your heart beating, the many vibrations of your body supporting you in every effort. Let life flow from you outward.

- See people in motion outside. When you see a person walking, let your imagination walk with him or her. Inhabit every moment with others, and identify with all these bodies in motion. Feel the potency of literally lifting another's spirit.

- Know that loved ones are lifting your spirit always. Be in your potential today.

> *"My actions are my only true belongings. I cannot escape the consequences of my actions. My actions are the ground upon which I stand."*
>
> — Thích Nhất Hạnh

CONSEQUENCES

Whatever you do becomes a part of your pattern. Whatever you fix your attention upon is your choice for where you want to go next. For some, the thought that their acts have real consequences can be paralyzing. In an effort to escape this paralyzing fear, people often tell themselves, "It doesn't matter," or "I can get away with this." But this message is very much an illusive, destructive mode of addictive thinking. Only being able to self-regulate in order to soothe your paralyzing anxiety—to let go of fear and to trust in the restorative power of your life—can bring healthy consequences.

Sometimes people consider only the external consequences of their deeds: "Will I get caught? Will I get yelled at, fired, left behind?" They might very well get away with their little dramas and escape reprimand or rejection. But in the most important context—the status of their inner spirit—they never get away with anything. And that's the real tragedy: not to care for and value their own being and spirit enough to safeguard against losing inner status. People often shortchange integrity and values to earn a better place in their exterior, visible life, but in the act they lose their place of honor within. You are your own witness, jury, and judge. Only right actions lead to *feeling right*.

DAILY HEALTHY SEX ACTS

- Reclaim your inner place of honor. Write a list of what actions you honor in yourself today. Write another list of the actions in which you've lost your integrity. Now use clear, concise and vivid terms to describe the qualitative differences between these two lists. Underline, memorize, and imprint these differences in your mind, because they mark the qualitative difference in the life you will lead depending on which list you choose as your direction.

- Quickly brainstorm three actions you can take to restore your honor... *to yourself*. This is not about anyone else. You cannot escape the consequences of your past actions, but you can always take a new action to begin to heal. Take right action today.

"Trust thyself: every heart vibrates to that iron string."

— Ralph Waldo Emerson

21 APRIL

SELF-TRUST

The worst betrayal is self-betrayal. We often falsely focus blame on another, for to grasp how we let ourselves down can be devastating. Seriously, we can't trust that we'll be in the same mood or have the same intention from one moment to the next: A promise we make in one mind-state might be upended with the slightest shift in circumstance. How often do we wake up ready to conquer the day, whether by action or interaction, and an hour later, can't even remember that feeling, much less act on it?

Let's be honest: If our thoughts and emotions were personified as a partner, what a shifty, exasperating relationship that would be!

It's said the mind is like a bad neighborhood at night—you don't want to go there alone. Our head sometimes takes us to unhappy or unkind places because of unprocessed trauma. Distorted, uncontrolled thoughts can even lead to addiction, a form of retraumatization. Habituated early to self-abandonment, addicts in recovery always come to realize that they've never been present for their own feelings and needs. Partners of addicts often feel not only that they can't trust the partner to avoid traumatic scenarios, they can't even trust themselves.

How can we establish trust in ourselves? By showing up for ourselves, being accountable to trusted others, sticking to a self-defined regimen of integrity, following through with our words, and loving ourselves when we fail. It's crucial to practice self-empathy, for trust can't be willed into existence. That didn't work when our caregivers tried to impose their will on us, and it won't work internally, either. Only when we can tap into a place of self-trust, with a reliable process of reparation for inevitable mistakes, can we build trust with another person. Because you can't give until you've got.

DAILY HEALTHY SEX ACTS

- Set special time aside to be present with yourself in order to gain your own trust. See if you can stick to a regular schedule of self-care, such as daily meditation or similar acts of self-love.

- When life doesn't go as planned, practice self-empathy by soothing yourself with kind words and thoughts. Speak to yourself as you would to a frightened child or pet. Do this aloud, tapping into the healing power of your own loving voice. The gift of self-trust is worth your full attention and practice, regardless of how uncomfortable it feels right now.

"The only unnatural sex act is that which you cannot perform."
— Alfred Kinsey

SEXUAL POSITIONS

There are endless sexual positions that feel fantastic, and it can be very empowering to own one's sexuality through mastering new ones. However, it can take a long while to feel comfortable in certain poses, and it can feel intimidating to learn in front of an audience (even of one). We often rush to acquire the basic moves of physical intimacy and then assume we're done learning. Just like when starting a new job, it can be embarrassing to repeatedly ask, "Where does this go?"

To learn a new position, it helps to have a partner who's kind, caring and patient enough to instruct us or let us practice. But we don't have to wait for the right sexual mentor to teach us a position. We can take stock ourselves of where we feel comfortable, where we don't, why we don't, and how we might learn to appreciate a certain position. We can share our discomfort. It's important to cultivate enough patience and empathy—with others and ourselves—for when we can try out these positions, having faith that we'll find a way to make them work and feel great.

Shame-inducing associations, such as that we lower our worth by going down on a lover or taking it from behind, limit pleasure. If we can own the faultlessness and vitality of our entire energy field, we gain mobility, openness and expression. As when practicing a yoga pose, we never finish learning sexual positions, but there are "aha!" moments when we grasp the energy of a pose and make it part of the sensual vocabulary we use to express our physical connection to life.

DAILY HEALTHY SEX ACTS

- With your lover, take time to experience a new position today. Breathe into any discomfort. Don't worry about the sex, just experience the feelings in your body and thoughts in your head. Safely and lovingly share your feelings and thoughts, and observe where this level of intimacy takes you.

- If you're single and masturbation is permissible for you, try masturbating on your bed in a new position. The goal isn't to achieve orgasm or to heighten pleasure, but to find a new level of comfort with the full range of your body's pleasure possibilities.

"Try a thing you haven't done three times. Once, to get over the fear of doing it. Twice, to learn how to do it. And a third time to figure out whether you like it or not."

— Virgil Thomson

23 APRIL

CURIOSITY

The desire to learn plays a large part in helping us fulfill our potential in life. Inquisitive exploration of the strange, novel, or rare helps us mature into wisdom and makes us interesting in our own right. When we are eager to find something out, we activate a state of internal arousal that is contagious to those around us. The most probing thinkers of all are usually accomplished men and women to whom we are drawn as teachers or mentors. Great minds are curious, looking to solve life's puzzles or to appreciate the ordinary from new perspectives.

Like great thinkers, good listeners are curious. And curious listeners make good friends and lovers. We all know people who talk endlessly about themselves and never ask about our experiences or how we're doing. Such a person tends to be self-centered, a trait manifested by their making assumptions rather than inquiring, interrupting others rather than hearing, and completing others' sentences because they already "know" what others will say. Their communication style leaves us feeling frustrated and diminished.

But when we listen to others with interest and genuine care, we give them—and ourselves—a great gift. The person being heard without an imposed agenda feels validated, attended to, and liked. The person doing the listening gets the opportunity to practice compassion, empathy, and open-heartedness—skills we all need to hone in order to be better and wiser human beings. Curiosity may have killed the cat, but curiosity with discernment and the real will to connect opens the window to deep love relationships.

 DAILY HEALTHY SEX ACTS

- Get curious today about the simple things in life. Start with anything you see in the natural world. Rather than focusing on what you already know, be inquisitive about what you don't know. Wonder at the blue sky, ask questions about how birds fly.

- How curious are you about the people in your life? What do you really know about them? Do you know your niece's favorite color? Your son's favorite band? Your partner's secret desires?

- Don't assume you know anything about anyone today. Ask questions, then listen with an open mind and heart.

"I will give you the sun and the rain, and if they are not available, I will give you a sun check and a rain check. I will give you all this and more, until I get so exhausted and depleted that the only way I can recover my energy is by becoming infatuated with someone else."

— Elizabeth Gilbert

RAIN CHECKS

Life happens. We all have good reasons for postponing quality time with a spouse, playing hooky from get-togethers with friends, or cancelling dates with a prospective partner. A sickness, an impending deadline, a change of material or emotional circumstances are all common excuses. Certainly, allowing someone into your real, occasionally messy life as it unfolds can be an authentic way of connecting beyond the mask of perfection: If you're not in the mood, inviting others into where you're at can be transformative. But if rain checks are your habitual way of (not) relating to people, you might as well pass out a card that says, "I'm not present" along with your phone number.

For anyone in recovery from sex or love addiction, a rain check during a no-dating period might circumvent the commitment to sexual and emotional sobriety by simply disengaging. It can be a way of keeping sex or love addiction alive, the way Voldemort (He-who-must-not-be-named of the Harry Potter universe) put parts of his soul in other people to stay alive in case his main body was destroyed. If our fix has been to use other people to escape our own reality, then a rain check in recovery is a way of doing just that by distracting the brain with far-off fantasies to avoid fully committing to a new course of action.

Sometimes the only way to become present is to start doing things that are contrary to what we've been doing. When situation after situation just "doesn't feel right," maybe it's time to shine the light on what you're contributing to what feels wrong. There's a saying that the universe doesn't give us energy until we take the next right action, which runs counter to the common misstep of waiting for the "right energy" in order to act.

DAILY HEALTHY SEX ACTS

- Can you fully commit to others, or do you like to have your escape route mapped out? Notice the urge to take any rain checks this week. What are you feeling in your body? What drives your lack of commitment?

- Do it differently. If you cancelled any dates or social activities, take the initiative and make new plans today. Or if you like to have many lovers on hold, let this go for once, and find your way on the merit of your own presence without the false insurance of empty promises.

"Not everything that is faced can be changed.
But nothing can be changed until it is faced."

— James Baldwin

25 APRIL

CONFRONTATION

For some of us, our only model for confrontation comes from our formative teenage years when parental control crushed our needs and desires. In adulthood, confrontation can still feel frightening—so much so that we avoid it at all costs for fear of psychic annihilation. We've learned it's easier and safer to avoid or sneak around a frustrating situation, hoping that if we ignore it, it will go away. But situations rarely go away. In fact, the longer something festers, the worse it gets. Facing up to and dealing with a problem is the only way to rectify it. And that fact in itself challenges us to grow.

Similarly, being confronted by someone can feel unsettling or threatening. It's painful to be met with an argumentative defense or hostile words. However, if we can turn *towards* any intense energy in life and face it boldly, we experience a feeling of satisfaction and confidence afterward. This practice discovers and strengthens our true self.

We usually equate confrontation with facing adversity, but facing love can create an equal amount of disequilibrium. Without a doubt, falling in love is one of the most amazingly beautiful experiences in life. But the will to withstand the confrontation of love—the heat radiating from the blast of neurochemistry designed to create a sustainable attachment—requires fortitude. Telling your boyfriend or girlfriend that you're falling in love can actually feel confrontational, even when adversity doesn't lurk around the edges of your love. Saying "I love you" for the first time while face to face with your lover means that you're dealing with the truth and willing to withstand the excitement of confronting your unknown future together.

DAILY HEALTHY SEX ACTS

- How well do you handle direct confrontation? Do you ever try to communicate by *triangulation*—relaying information through a third party rather than directly to the person concerned?

- The next time someone says something you don't like, make an effort to stand up for yourself by telling him or her that you don't agree with what's being said. Notice how you feel.

- Are you withholding speaking the truth to someone in your life? If so, to whom, and why? Make this the day you'll be honest with that person about your feelings, whether negative or positive.

"The raindrops patter on the basho leaf, but these are not tears of grief; this is only the anguish of him who is listening to them."

— Zen saying

SEXUAL CLIMATE

In healthy climates, sexuality thrives. Romantic and erotic attractions seem to arise as an altogether internal urge, but we often ignore how much the social and environmental climate where we live impacts them. Social climates include neighborhood attitudes, schooled beliefs, peer pressure and media culture, all of which influence sexual development. Each of us knows that certain messages voiced in certain tones may ring in one's consciousness for years. While your inner orientation might attune you toward chosen messages while tuning out others, there's no doubt that living in a climate of acceptance rather than one of repression favors the chance that you will hear and unknowingly assimilate healthy rather than unhealthy messages. There are sexual practices common enough today, such as oral and anal sex, homosexuality, and casual sex, that were taboo in times past. To engage in any sex act in a climate of disapproval lends it an additional layer of danger that can become intertwined with sexual arousal. Fetishes are often the result of a crushing sexual climate, as fetishists are driven to repeat a crucial, but often repressed, stage of their developing sexuality.

Geographical climates also affect sexuality. Certain committed relationships may not survive changes in climate, such as travel or moving to new homes or cities. We may also find marked differences between sensuality in tropical cultures and that in colder climes: Less clothing, bountiful vegetation, open-air exercise, greater resources for shelter and survival will encourage sexuality differently than will conditions that are polar opposites. Of course, human sexuality never strictly follows any stereotypes. Still, when dealing with sexual or relational conflicts, stress, or fatigue, it's wise to weigh the current climate—social and geophysical—in which they occur.

DAILY HEALTHY SEX ACTS

- 12-step programs offer the acronym HALT (Hungry, Angry, Lonely, or Tired) to help check in with one's personal climate. What's your climate today, and how do these factors affect your sexuality?

- Today, try to map out the climate of all your significant sexual relationships. Were any of them marked by cramped quarters, stressful jobs, family crises, health issues, or natural disasters?

- Map out your own internal process—the way you can stay centered through the storms of any climate.

"Be kind whenever possible. It is always possible."

— Dalai Lama

27 APRIL

KINDNESS

Loving-kindness is one of the greatest gifts we can give ourselves and the universe, especially in a world where so much violence takes place daily. Being able to give this gift starts with how we treat ourselves: If we're riddled with internal messages of violence instead of consideration and soft-heartedness, that's what we'll project onto our lives. Habitual self-judgment and self-flagellation indicate a punitive, critical internal structure that hobbles our full potential and displaces the natural kindness characterizing mental and sexual health.

The human animal is wired for both love and war. As gregarious creatures we have a high capacity for attachment to others, but we're also always scanning for danger from them. When our personhood has been distorted by abuse, we can be viciously cruel, and even murderous, to our own kind. Yet when we're raised with loving-kindness, the structures meant for war are more rarely activated. Instead, the reflective part of our brain—our higher self—makes more accurate assessments of ourselves and others, and suggests our most appropriate actions.

"Love your neighbor as you love yourself." In our fast-paced times the practice of sweetness, charity, compassion and understanding requires that we slow down. Take time to meet your neighbor with kindness, notice when you can let go of aggravation so you can be curious and helpful instead of shutting down. Practice benevolence and patience, and scan not for war, but for the violence you perpetrate on yourself (like calling yourself an idiot) or your intolerance of others.

 DAILY HEALTHY SEX ACTS

- What act of kindness do you deserve today, this week, or this month? Are you good-natured about your mistakes or do you take yourself to task brutally? What do you need to do to neutralize the violent voices and make a bigger space for the voices of compassion and kindness?

- Share with a trusted other or your partner the judgments you have of them. Listen to your words and see if those judgments are your projections of yourself. Without reacting, but with kindness and compassion, listen to the other as s/he expresses judgments of you.

> *"Love is a smoke rais'd with the fume of sighs;*
> *Being purg'd, a fire sparkling in a lover's eyes;*
> *Being vex'd, a sea nourish'd with lovers' tears:*
> *What is it else? A madness most discreet,*
> *A choking gall and a preserving sweet."*
>
> — William Shakespeare

MADNESS

It's been remarked that "insanity is doing the same thing over and over and expecting a different result." Unfortunately many of us feel more comfortable with insanity than with the relative calm of emotional sobriety. The debilitating trauma of mental disturbance might be the devil we know, while the devil we don't know might be healthier experiences that threaten our fear-based defense system. If we didn't grow up in a peaceful family, if there were issues that were never resolved, they will resurface until addressed—and love and sex seem to be some of their biggest playing fields.

Of course, facing mental illness in family and caregivers, or in ourselves, brings unique challenges and requires support that is too often lacking. It wasn't so long ago that those suffering serious psychological maladies were locked up in sanatoriums or attics never to be seen, much less served. We must work to overcome the stigma and misunderstandings surrounding mental illness. It's easy to expect too much of people who are, in fact, psychologically sick. If someone had a broken leg, we wouldn't expect her or him to hit the dance floor. But if people experience mental disorders—depression, dementia, ADD, PTSD, or other psychic illness—we often mistakenly expect them to keep pace with our personal, and mostly learned, standards.

Just like physical illness, a mental illness can be temporary or lifelong. The fact is, we all experience lapses of mental well-being in our lives, including emotional blackouts, irrational thoughts, and meltdowns. Understand that *if it's hysterical, it's historical*—we naturally become reactive when past trauma gets triggered. Our ability to reconcile our own inconstancies and our own insanity—temporary or not—directly correlates to our ability to accept the madness of others without being driven mad in turn.

DAILY HEALTHY SEX ACTS

- What does sanity look like to you? List sane behaviors and states such as; showing up on time, following through on intentions, having a peaceful and loving relationship with your beloved, enjoying hot and healthy sex that's physically, emotionally, and spiritually satisfying.

- Recall moments when you've lost it. Are there common themes? Trace triggered outbursts to your past. Have you felt like this before? You deserve better than to lose yourself. If your car broke down, you'd get it fixed rather than pretend it didn't happen. Reach out for help by sharing your truth with trusted others today.

"The time is always right to do what is right."

— Martin Luther King, Jr.

29 APRIL

ACCOUNTABILITY

If you are not accountable, you are not available. Hiding from the responsibility entrusted to you through your unique perspective, your personal *account*, is a way of hiding from life. Whenever you are not available, you cannot experience true and lasting pleasure. You are like scorched earth in a desert: Even when it rains, the water runs off in flash floods and can't sink in to make you more fertile.

Lack of accountability creates compartmentalization—an inner maze of supposedly safe spaces in which to hide. The problem with hiding from accountability is that true erotic opportunity—the chance for the satisfaction that brings real happiness—always knocks on the wrong door while you're holed up in another room. By the time you get there, unbolt the latch, and open your heart, the desired possibility is long gone, while the knock still rings in your ears and throws you to your knees.

Whatever our actions, there is a corresponding effect on our presence in this life. When we tell a lie or fail to deliver on a promise, we switch off our own inner receptors to life. Luckily, setting right any past wrongs does more than assuage guilt. Our new accountability creates availability creates presence creates greater receptivity creates pleasure. When we show up for life, *only then* can we really show up for sex.

DAILY HEALTHY SEX ACTS

- Begin by being accountable to yourself. Admit to yourself any damaging or dishonorable actions you've engaged in that you've minimized or lied about, even by omission.

- Be accountable to your partner. Do the right thing today. Clear up any secrets, deceptions or evasions you've passed off on them or others in your life.

"Two things threaten all our lives: high-tech warfare and industrially driven ecological disaster. Both are a kind of madness; borne of emotional injury. Both are the result of arrests in emotional development. Both are problems of relationship."

— Robin Grille

SOCIAL AWARENESS

Twentieth-century feminists taught that "the personal is political." But world political problems—hunger, poverty, gun violence, climate change, human rights violations—are also personal. The problems of governments, corporations, school boards—all organized groups—stem from the feelings, needs, and, yes, unresolved traumas of the persons composing them. And when we repress our natural compassion by blinding ourselves to the humanity of those we encounter in person or in the news, and choose to see them merely as cogs in a wheel, our objectification rebounds on us and leaves *us* feeling disconnected.

For healthy transformation is possible only through shared humanity. Treating others as persons—*personally*—by imagining how we'd like to be treated in their place humanizes our whole being and invites unexpected breakthroughs. If you remember this the next time you negotiate with a company's Customer Service representative—that is, if you interact *personally* with the corporation's living, human element—you may be surprised at the ease and completeness of the resolution. People, at their core, long for connection even though their tone and actions seem to demand robotic obedience.

And the way we, personally, treat a sexual partner mirrors our relationship to society, and vice versa. We've all been burdened by the traditional construction of sex as pillaging or gratifying in a show of power, punishment and politics. But you and I know this is not the true nature of organic sexuality, but a traumatized response to fear and confusion, of the world disordered. Healthy sex is one of the highest states of shared experiencing. So to touch this experience in ourselves and our beloved, and to bring the healing vibrations of this sharing connection to our own social awareness, creates one small but significant shift in the paradigm toward a healthier and more loving world.

DAILY HEALTHY SEX ACTS

- Today, consider the human elements in current social issues—politicians, pundits, and people affected. What formative personal traumas might be informing each perspective? How would you feel and respond in each of their shoes?

- How do you act in public? If you bully others with your opinions or shrink from the stage, you're hardly putting principles into practice. Social interaction is how we manifest our personal awareness.

- See the world with your god eyes, and show empathy to humankind. Share your truth so it can be received.

"Relationship is a mirror in which you can see yourself, not as you would wish to be, but as you are."

— Jiddu Krishnamurti

May

"Never let go of that fiery sadness called desire."

— Patti Smith

1 MAY

DESIRE

The notion that we must sublimate all worldly desire and passion in order to live a spiritual life is an outdated and limited model of sanctity that serves only to oppress. At its base is the assumption that desire is nothing more than an unending hedonistic quest, devoid of any holiness or meaning. In fact, true desire is a yearning to *know oneself more fully*. Through an integrated approach to desire we combine the senses, consciousness, love, and all of our humanity so that we can approach the fulfillment of our own personal longing for inner peace and freedom.

The vehicle in which we must make this quest is our body. Our body is embedded in our consciousness—not just in the self-image of our mind's eye but also in the neurological structure of our brain. So full acceptance of our body is crucial for attaining deep knowledge of ourselves. By igniting our senses, knowing bodily pleasure, and connecting with our hearts and our grasp of the divine, we begin to set ourselves free of shame, guilt, and the puritanical ideas of our ancestors.

When you wish to become sexually connected to yourself and your partner, meeting in a place of honor is a good starting point. When you're in your sexual integrity, desiring fully and freely invites a kind of honesty, a nervous excitement where there's no rush to cover up desire or push it away. You accept that as part of your adult sexuality, and you recognize it as the engine that arouses you and your partner. Don't be shy. Speak your love, your carnal desire, what you are seeing and would like to see or do with your partner, whether it be loving, lustful, or lascivious. This kind of connection enflames your emotional and physical arousal, allowing you to desire fully and to love deeply and spiritually.

DAILY HEALTHY SEX ACTS

- What does desire mean to you? What do you long for and how do you call forth what you yearn for? Write about these topics and see if you can locate the source of your desire in your body.

- What is your greatest sexual fantasy? Write it out and interpret it as you would a dream. What are the symbols of your desire, and what do they really mean to you? In other words, what are you truly seeking in sex? Share your findings with a trusted other.

"They said that Love would die when Hope was gone.
And Love mourn'd long, and sorrow'd after Hope;
At last she sought out Memory, and they trod
The same old paths where Love had walked with Hope,
And Memory fed the soul of Love with tears."

— Alfred Tennyson

MEMORY

It's been said the thought of a tiger is not a tiger. In the same way, the memory of an event is not reality. This truth can be vexing, especially if you've ever had anyone challenge your version of events. Defending the validity of one's memory can be hard-won but is necessary for sanity and self-esteem. But autonomy is not the same as accuracy. Even the most open-minded of us has a relatively narrow outlook, and every human memory is by its nature flawed: Were we to experience an event in our distant past with our current perception, our perspective on it now would vary widely from our memory of it. So how do we work with the unreliable recollections of our mercurial, volatile process of memory?

Like dreams, memories come to mind bearing meaning for our present situation. But memories may also become neurotic. Have you ever fallen into a lapse, replaying certain emotionally-charged scenarios? The look someone gave you. The tone of their voice. The way they affirmed or denied you. Resentments are the ultimate mental loop, usually reinforcing an inner complex. Euphoric recall, interestingly, is equally a trap by the compulsive mental echo of arousing memories. It takes practice to shake off deeply embedded thoughts, usually through disclosing the stark truth of key memories with a trusted ally.

We must engage past memory to create future change. We must constantly *recall* our intentions. Change is not natural for many of us; *implicit memories* have been imprinted into the very cells of our brains and bodies which, having learned life from a certain angle, always expect those same results. Ironically, it's only through the productively employed process of memory that we can remake our dreams into our desired reality.

DAILY HEALTHY SEX ACTS

- Where does memory get obsessive for you? Write down any recurring resentments, trauma or euphoric recall (such as erotically charged memories.) These aren't always memories with which we'd choose to identify.

- If you interpret your major recurring memories like a dream, what would they signify about you?

- *Procedural memories* are processes that the brain and body learned "by heart," like riding a bike. What new patterns would you like to imprint into your procedural memory?

"Music is the mediator between the spiritual and the sensual life."

— Ludwig van Beethoven

3 MAY

MUSIC

There's nothing like a favorite love song, whose power touches our lives with meaning and immediacy. Its lyrics or melodies might speak to deeply felt histories in a direct way that bypasses the endless discussions we have about relationships. Interestingly, most music seems to concern love and sex (or to have been inspired by love and sex!). In some ways, then, music might function as a secondary sexual education where other forms of instruction have failed, by showing us how to recognize the signs of love, and how to let go when love is unrequited or dies. We all reach moments in our lives when our emotions and mental states defy language. Music mimics guttural sound patterns— the sigh of despair, the moan of ecstasy—that we recognize on an intuitive level. Musicians make sense of all these sounds in our lives, and so turn our pain and blundering patterns into chorales and cadenzas. So goes the poem, *The Mourning Bride:* "Musick has Charms to sooth a savage Breast."

In fact, the right music can be a medicinal cure or therapeutic tool for a lot of sexual or relational difficulties. Mood music accompanying romantic conversations or sexual activity might stimulate a shared rhythm. Certain tempos will inspire couples to take it slow or speed it up. A rousing overture might help lovers get out of their heads when inhibitions overwhelm, and for those who disconnect emotionally, a meaningful melody has the power to bind souls together in place and time. Discussing personal musical tastes and negotiating musical choices with a partner provides the opportunity to invite tolerance and compromise, and to step into another's world for a symphonic spell. It can be sexy to experiment by selecting music that tonally and rhythmically sounds like the kind of sexual intimacy toward which you aspire.

DAILY HEALTHY SEX ACTS

- Select music for desired romantic moods and relational goals. Create a playlist for the many qualities of amorous interaction you'd like to experience, and invite your lover to do the same.

- Every night this week, find time to listen to at least one of your musical selections—whether during dinner, while making love, or simply enjoying the present moment. Pay attention to the feelings in your heart, the thoughts in your head, and the sensations in your body, and hearken to inner harmony.

"People are like stained glass windows: they sparkle and shine when the sun is out, but when the darkness sets in their true beauty is revealed only if there is a light within."

— Elisabeth Kübler-Ross

MAY 4

DIGNITY

Living in dignity means feeling worthy of honor and having a sense of pride. *Dignity*, *honor* and *pride* sound like lofty ideals or old-fashioned aspirations. But as with most commonplaces, closer examination shows their depth. Dignity is not self-centered entitlement or arrogance. It's our true center, what we respect in ourselves, and all the good we value in others—all that's solid and stable and merits love.

Without dignity we settle for scraps. Sometimes wholly unawares, we choose people who hurt, denigrate, or betray us, and we play the victim in a nightmare of our own making. Negative self-talk and feelings of loneliness urge us to say or do things we don't feel good about, date someone even though it doesn't feel right, or take a job even though it isn't a true fit. Stepping out of what feels good, right, and true compromises our integrity in a flash, just as disrespecting ourselves throws any shred of dignity right out the window. When our dignity gives way to enslavement by self-destructive behavioral patterns, we lose self-respect because we let that self fade and become someone we no longer recognize. We need to go through a painstaking process of self-examination in order to rebuild a sturdy self and to win back our dignity.

Simple acts such as wearing clean clothes, surrounding ourselves with good people, tending to our surroundings, eating healthfully, and doing good deeds are everyday ways of experiencing dignity. For dignity never requires lavishness or pomp; it is quiet and steady. When we honor all that is good in us and give it pride of place in our life, our imperfections and undesired traits fall away. Dignity is our divine right, and we strengthen it by acting in accord with our true selves.

DAILY HEALTHY SEX ACTS

- Do you live in recognition of the strong, dignified parts of yourself or the weaker, petty sides?

- Open your mind to possibilities and consider that most people want the best for everyone. Make it a choice not to criticize anyone or anything you encounter today. Honor the good inherent in all, and watch in wonder as your own dignity grows.

"Sex is always about emotions. Good sex is about free emotions; bad sex is about blocked emotions."

— Deepak Chopra

5 MAY

EMOTION

Our emotions well up from our circumstances, mood *du jour*, or relationships, and are accompanied by feelings. Emotions and feelings are not synonyms: Feelings are our subjective reactions—positive or negative, strong or mild, pleasant or unpleasant—to basic emotions such as joy, anger, love, and hate. There's no telling when emotions will show up, but the visceral energy they pour into our bodies demands that we mobilize them by expressing our feelings. Such expression is at the heart of creation—to burst forward and give birth.

Unfortunately, many of us have ingested long-standing internal messages that tell us to swallow our feelings, not to "bother" others with them, to keep a poker face. This repression shuts down vitality states in the body, leaving us feeling empty or dead at the core, unable to reveal our soul's song or to experience life's delights and despairs—and, therefore, unable to connect in love.

The rushing emotions of artists expressing themselves in song, painting, music, poetry, or dance have created masterpieces. Don't be quick to chase your feelings away, reject them, or wallow in them unreflectively. Instead, invite them in, notice them, declare them, and recognize that the emotional energy underneath these feelings is your soul's unique song, your humanity, and your life force. When you observe a feeling and dive into its root, you will find an emotion in the body at its core. The inherent wisdom of your body is the "true north" of your compass, pointing you in the direction of deep insight into your reality and, quite possibly, into the nature of life.

DAILY HEALTHY SEX ACTS

- When you experience a pleasant, unpleasant, or neutral feeling, name it as such and surrender to it. Notice it. Don't chase it away or try to change it.

- Emotions are the music of your soul. Share them with your partner today. Let them see all of you.

- Express your emotions in your love-making through feelings, words of poetry and love, or guttural sounds. Breathe, don't hold back; trust that creation is bursting forth from you.

> *"The eyes flirt most. There are so many ways to use them."*
>
> — Anna Held

Flirting is what the elusive, heartbreakingly lovely butterfly does as it lands on flower after flower, only to flutter off towards a new object of affection. If you've ever had a butterfly alight on your arm, you might have felt a compulsion to capture it. The fleetingness of such a visitation might cause anxiety. But it doesn't have to. It can just be appreciated in the moment as pure grace. Similarly, flirting requires a certain detachment, an acceptance of beauty around us that we cannot necessarily possess or control. If we accept its playful energy without lamenting any deeper intrigue, it can be fun for everyone involved. However, when compulsive flirting becomes a tool for manipulation, unwanted advances, or avoiding emotional honesty, we can get caught in the net of the butterfly collector who destroys life by attempting to possess it.

On the path towards sexual intimacy, flirting is a healthy initial stage, and there are as many ways to flirt as there are people. Some draw us in with Sphinx-like silence, and surprise us as we find ourselves pursuing *them*. Some shower us with sexual heat, moving into our personal space and radiating seductive energy until we boil with desire. Others dazzle us with humor or intelligence, somehow knowing exactly how to flatter us or comfort us with just the right amount of tenderness. If you are new to flirting, you might experiment until you find your own unique style. Someone out there will truly "get" it, and it's a wonderful feeling to connect with another on a special wavelength; to be acknowledged as attractive; to be admired and appreciated.

DAILY HEALTHY SEX ACTS

- Recall your last flirtation. Was it with a stranger or a friend? Was it for fun, or to convey real feelings? What did you seek, and find?

- How do you telegraph romantic or sexual interest? Today, practice flirting in the mirror or in writing, and notice your level of comfort. Switch roles, and receive your own flirting. How do you respond? When you play these roles, notice the traits you admire. Do you seek them in others?

- Today, flirt with your beloved. Bring a smile to your lover's lips, a spark to your lover's eyes. Can you separate flirting from playing mind games, losing your mind, or masking yourself? Your intention here is simply to please your partner and you.

"Life for both sexes—and I looked at them, shouldering their way along the pavement—is arduous, difficult, a perpetual struggle. It calls for gigantic courage and strength. More than anything, perhaps, creatures of illusion as we are, it calls for confidence in oneself. Without self-confidence we are as babes in the cradle."

— Virginia Woolf

7 MAY

CONFIDENCE

Liberation comes in many forms, one of which is self-confidence: security in your own abilities, qualities, and accomplishments. Feeling the freedom to take risks for your most daring dreams certainly requires confidence in yourself, and that self-confidence grows out of self-compassion. When critical voices echo in the mind, the self-forgiving person can lovingly shoo them away so they don't take up permanent residence.

But we can't, and need not, make it alone. Practicing the self-compassion to forgive our foibles is crucial, but having the equal courage to rely on others completes our foundation of confidence. During times of profound emotional pain we all depend on our beloved to show up for us in a way that's firm and steadfast. We need the soothing knowledge that the person we love most in the world will be present to care for us. Confidence in relationships builds when we make ourselves vulnerable enough to receive, for when we receive we have the fortifying experience of being loved. And when a loved one is in need we must call upon our own self-assurance to stand strong for our beloved, even when we do not feel up to the task.

The friends and family members we confidently rely on, and who rely on us, become our confidants. We confide our deepest, darkest, most shameful truths to them because we trust they will hold them in a safe place. One of the strongest antidotes to feeling alone in the world is knowing that there is someone who values you, whom you fully trust, and in whom you can confide. Paradoxically, people who enjoy the emotional liberation of self-confidence attained it by opening themselves to rely on their confidants.

DAILY HEALTHY SEX ACTS

- Whom do you rely on most in your life? Do you trust them implicitly? If not, why not? Should you be relying on them?

- If you don't feel that your partner can be steadfast for you in times of need, talk to him or her and express your concerns. Find out what's missing so you can both feel more secure.

- How trustworthy a confidant are you? Do you keep secrets or do you gossip? What impedes you from keeping your word?

> "When we are able to see our own greed, jealousy, spite, hatred, and so on, then these can be turned to positive account because in such destructive emotions is stored much life, and when we have this energy at our disposal, it can be turned to positive ends."

— Marie-Louise von Franz

NEGATIVITY

All the qualities we treasure in life—happiness, success, freedom, beauty, love—could never exist without their polar opposites. To define a trait, we must differentiate it, just as to separate wheat we must know chaff. Yet despite their interdependence, we habitually interpret "negative" traits as *inferior to* positive ones. As long as we impose a hierarchal judgment on qualities, we will experience similar bifurcations in our life—rich versus poor, men versus women—which limit us. So it's important to integrate our own negativities, keeping in mind that to acknowledge is not the same as to indulge.

The lotus flower symbolizes enlightenment because it springs, gorgeously pristine, from muck. The danger of valuing only *positive thinking* is that it can mask denial of equally valid negative states. Are you strong enough to bear witness to your own negativity without being thrown off center? When we fixate on our treasured states and deny the reality and necessity of negativity, our negativity about negativity—our immature interpretation of it—destabilizes us. Much of our early programming focuses on teaching us what's positive and negative in our character and behavior. This gives us social standards, but often creates lasting mental distortions. Innate, legitimate emotional states such as sorrow, frustration, and anger become tainted by a judgment as "negative" that can block their potential to illuminate and transform.

When we judge the so-called negativity of others, we usually violate boundaries through unsolicited advice, verbal abuse, or emotional hostage-taking. Better to see the world—even the negative parts—through another's eyes, to help us tap into our true god eyes. Then we see the situation more fully, which creates empathy. And empathy holds the skeleton key to unlock the valuable kernel of truth in any negativity we honestly experience in others or our self.

DAILY HEALTHY SEX ACTS

- While it's healthy to explore negative self-truths, it's unhealthy simply to dump our troubles. Do you know the difference between examining your problems with trusted others versus indulging in a "pity party?"

- Do you turn a blind eye to negativity in your experiences or personality? Summon one memory of your own negativity and simply sit with it, as you would with a sick friend. Recall the sounds, smells, feelings, and circumstances. Unpack the event to gain greater understanding, and illuminate your negativity by your loving attention.

"Caresses, expressions of one sort or another, are necessary to the life of the affections as leaves are to the life of a tree. If they are wholly restrained, love will die at the roots."

— Nathaniel Hawthorne

9 MAY

CARESSING

Think of a warm, summer breeze caressing your body, and the softness you're left with as it passes over you. This caress feels like the unrestrained affection we are called to bestow on one another when in love. Caresses aren't just simple hugs, but moments of lushness and calm that can be demonstrated in small gestures or tokens of fondness for another.

A caress received upon reuniting with your partner after a long day at work may be just the medicine you need to feel more deeply connected. Simply rubbing your partner's shoulders can lead to gentle kissing of the neck, ears and lips, becoming a communication all of its own. Other times you and your lover may encounter each other intensely by looking into each other's eyes, and feel each open to the other. This deliberate little act can move an exhausted body into a state of vitality, gratitude, and even joy.

Without affection in the form of touch, patting, and stroking, an infant will fail to thrive and may even die. This need persists in adulthood, since caresses remain an essential form of communication between one nervous system and another. When you are upset or need comfort, the quickest way to calm down is for someone who cares about you to touch you gently. If you were touch-deprived as a child, emotionally closing off may be your default mode. If so, start slowly by caressing your partner and asking for caresses. This delicate form of touch will teach you the importance of being responsible for what you want and need, and exactly how to communicate it.

DAILY HEALTHY SEX ACTS

- Ask your lover for a gentle, stroking massage. What does that feel like? Do you relax or tense up? If you tense up, ask your lover to alter his/her touch until it feels right to you.

- Don't forget to breathe. We could even say that breathing is an internal caress, filling the vital organs with essential energy for life. Pay attention to your breath today and whether you're filling up your lungs deeply or breathing shallowly.

- Stroke your partner's face while looking into his or her eyes. What do you see? How does this make you feel?

"Where love rules, there is no will to power; and where power predominates, there love is lacking. The one is the shadow of the other."

— Carl Gustav Jung

POWER

All's fair, they say, in love and war. If we equate the two, "winning" in love probably means exerting the most personal power: being the one who breaks up first or who has the upper hand in arguments. Certainly, personal power is a driving force in our lives. We're all familiar with power-grabbing partners who force the other into an inferior position, whether consensually through domination-and-submission sex play or covertly through emotionally and intellectually abusive behavior. There are also boundary breakers who get off on coercing lovers to commit acts outside their level of comfort, values, or even safety. And of course, the ultimate fantasy of having every need satisfied by a doting lover can be especially seductive when we're unfulfilled in key areas of our lives. But when this kind of win-lose thinking plays out in our relationships, it's a signal to surrender to a *Higher Power* because human power trips inhibit intimacy.

We often enact the power struggles that we grew up with and which may have programmed us internally. So it's important to observe how the power plays of our past show up in our present. Power-playing is a self-fulfilling prophecy: Those who solely seek power will be enslaved by it. What we all desire is the responsibility that goes with power—having power to make sense of our own lives by integrating seemingly incongruent experiences into a holistic, honest understanding of ourselves. When people replay childhood power trips, though, they're caught in a psychological block—a dissociation in which the brain short-circuits like a power strip flooded with so much power it trips the circuit. Shifting our paradigm from *power over others* to *power with others* allows us an organic, self-renewing source of strength. We may not be able to dictate our every wish, but we can always tap into our true power.

DAILY HEALTHY SEX ACTS

- What were the power dynamics you experienced growing up? Was there room for the healthy expression of personal power—of yours and of others—in your family and friendships?

- One way to diffuse a power trip is through transparency: openly admitting your own motives, such as wanting to change others and the world. Is there any situation you're involved in that would improve if you were to reveal your intentions?

- Today, empower yourself to tap into the true source of your power.

"Beyond the beauty, the sex, the titillation, the surface, there is a human being. And that has to emerge."

— Jeanne Moreau

11 MAY

SEXUALIZATION

There can be no doubt that we live in a highly sexualized society. Everywhere we turn, sex is being used to sell something—food, a travel destination, a work of art. It's a highly effective but corroding strategy that influences us even when we're not aware of it. Because human sexuality and body parts are being appropriated to peddle every imaginable commodity, it soon becomes difficult to disentangle ourselves from this sort of thinking in our personal relationships. We begin to fixate on the sexiness, body shape or attractive mannerisms of others to the exclusion of all their other qualities. We fetishize the turn or size of a person's facial features, muscles, or genitals, separating these from their spirit.

People can sexualize even ordinary events like making a new friend or being introduced to new colleagues. This hyper-aroused state is also a very disconnected one; it cuts us off from forming real bonds to others that are rooted in a heart connection and the acceptance of human fallibility. We crave human contact, yet find ourselves isolated and alienated even when surrounded by other people. This is the direct result of sexualization: It leaves us lonely.

Worst of all, when we compare and criticize our own appearance in the mirror, we reduce our core worth down to a number on a scale. To heal from this collective mental illness doesn't mean we won't still appreciate the sexual attractiveness of another person. It just means that we are also willing to accept that other components of a person—their sense of humor, imagination, empathy, creativity and willingness to show up for us in life—are just as valuable and can be equally treasured.

DAILY HEALTHY SEX ACTS

- Do you sexualize people of a specific body type, age, hair color, or other trait? Do you ignore other people to focus solely on those who attract you? Today, notice your tendencies toward sexualization.

- Imagine being sexualized by someone you don't want checking you out. How might this impact your presence and interactions? Have you felt this way before? If so, when was your earliest experience of unwanted sexual attention?

- One of the signs of sex addiction is compulsive sexualization—seeing every personal encounter only as a possible hook-up. Are you or anyone you know so sexually fixated that it interferes with forming healthy relationships? If so, what can you do about it?

> *"Never give up, for that is just the place and time that the tide will turn."*
>
> — Harriet Beecher Stowe

QUITTING

To recover our natural capacity for healthy relationships, we learn we have to show up *as is*. This can feel clumsy and uncomfortable. But it's way easier than showing up out of obligation, weighing our self down with what we imagine others expect. It's these internalized pressures that distance us from genuine connectedness and personal truth.

In fact, the external problems we perceive are mirrors of our inner lives. Would that we could truly escape them! That's why when people *pull a geographic*—run from relationships, jobs, homes—the problems follow. Worse, they compound: There's the original trauma plus the additional trauma of cutting off all ties, including healthy ones. Even suicide—the ultimate quitting—may not end our troubles! As Hamlet asks, "For in that sleep of death, what dreams may come?" The thought of suicide symbolizes our deep need for internal transformation. If we remember this symbolism when suicidal ideation strikes, we'll remember it's telling us to transform our self from within.

Know that, when it seems the worst pain is yet to come, the worst pain is already behind us. We've experienced untold emotional and physical hurt, from the vulnerability of our birth to the public stumblings and private agonies of childhood. All current confusion, fear and helplessness are the mere shadows of yesteryears' suffering. In order that we not stay trapped in our present perceptions, we must remind ourselves that whenever we feel *hysterical*, it's *historical*. We don't get to escape historical trauma just as we can't ever really quit any internal event. But as we process past trauma, we find the way to see through momentary distortions and to wield the compassion, understanding, and courage never to quit, but to preserve—in every circumstance—our own spirit.

DAILY HEALTHY SEX ACTS

- It's said the moment you're ready to quit is the moment before a miracle happens. Are you a quitter? How do you handle the stress of imagined failure or impending success?

- Quitting is different than a conscious, informed choice to end something. How do you know when it's time to move on? Consider past decisions to quit a job, hobby, or committed relationship. Did any internal conflict continue?

- Today, show up *as is*. Invite others to show up as themselves, without obligation or expectation. Breathe life into stagnant, accustomed roles, and touch our shared humanity to discover unimagined possibilities.

"To him she seemed so beautiful, so seductive, so different from ordinary people, that he could not understand why no one was as disturbed as he by the clicking of her heels on the paving stones, why no one else's heart was wild with the breeze stirred by the sighs of her veils, why everyone did not go mad with the movements of her braid, the flight of her hands, the gold of her laughter. He had not missed a single one of her gestures, not one of the indications of her character, but he did not dare approach her for fear of destroying the spell."

— Gabriel García Márquez

13 MAY

OBSESSION

Obsession can by itself destroy the ordered life we have worked hard to build, like a black hole sucking in all time, emotion, thought, and energy. *Obsession* originally meant a *blockade* or *siege*, but in the 1600s came to signify *haunting* by an evil spirit. Fixation on a certain person, goal or object may begin innocently enough, but it can become our sole focus to the exclusion of all other healthy activities and interests. Such is the cunning, debilitating stranglehold that obsession can have on us.

Life-long obsessions have their roots in childhood. When caregivers obsess about our behavior or neglect us, instilling in us a drive to grasp for something we did not receive, our carried shame can fester like an untended wound until it consumes us. As adults, the subconscious yearning to resolve our unmet needs can make us latch frantically onto another for safety, and can manifest as an obsessive relationship. Obsessions sometimes extend beyond human interactions into work or everyday habits like hand-washing. Whatever their nature, obsessions can leave us isolated, disconnected and disturbed.

Yet we tend to idolize as "genius" someone's "one-track mind": A musician may become fixated on mastering an instrument; an athlete may zero in on achieving a world record; a businessperson may seek victory over competitors at all costs. But we need to recognize that, regardless of whether an obsession is self-improving or self-destructive, it can wreck the equilibrium of all our human powers—intellectual, physical, artistic, moral, emotional—that together sustain a happy, healthy life. Drive, dedication, and discipline are valuable tools for achieving a goal, but what makes us human is our ability to balance many goals at once.

DAILY HEALTHY SEX ACTS

- Practice the 3-second rule when gripped by romantic or sexual obsession: 1. Acknowledge you're in an obsessed state; 2. Recognize that you don't have permission to objectify this person; 3. Say a prayer to respect his or her privacy, turning your attention to the present moment. Repeat as needed.

- How do you tell the difference between a *healthy* and an *unhealthy* obsession? Today, disclose one obsession—a hobby, romantic interest, recurring subject of gossip—with three people you respect, focusing on any confusion or discomfort you feel about your focus.

"The word patience means the willingness to stay where we are and live the situation out to the full in the belief that something hidden there will manifest itself to us."

— Henri J. M. Nouwen

Patience mustn't be confused with avoidance or compliance. If you're being "patient" about getting your bills paid off or about getting an illness treated, it's probably not wise to wait idly for further revelation before taking action.

When we talk about patience as a relational skill, though, we're talking about non-reactivity or emotional sobriety. Does impatience ever make anything better? To respond to a stressful situation with your own stress just creates more stress, just as responding to a hostile dog in any way except with patience only agitates it further. The secret reason why patience is considered a virtue and why this quality is vital for love and sex is that the practice of patience actually soothes the nervous system. You take deeper breaths, your brain gets more oxygen, and a host of other physiological effects benefits you.

Obsessive-compulsive traits are properly defined as both obsessive; needing to do something all the time, and compulsive; needing to do it right now. But anything we seek that's truly valuable is worth our waiting for, and will wait for us. And if it really can't wait, maybe it's not right for us at all, or is not meant to be just now. The surest emotional recovery is not situational—having what you desire—but developmental—learning how to live with the desire. To strengthen our inner quality of patience, rather than chasing the specific situation we think we want, we develop our capacity to be in right relationship to any life situation.

DAILY HEALTHY SEX ACTS

- Practice *pausing* today. Count, "1..., 2..., 3..." before taking any action, whether it's stepping into the shower, exiting the front door, or starting the car ignition.

- Take a "media fast" today. Turn off all social media for the day. Leave your phone in your pocket and notice the world around you. What do you see? Pause a while... *Now what do you really see?*

"Oh, tell me whence Love cometh!
  Love comes uncall'd, unsent.
Oh, tell me where Love goeth!
  That was not Love that went."

— J. W. Ebsworth

15 MAY

DELUSION

If you've ever held onto a thought that contradicted what everyone else agreed was reality, you may have been engaged in your own personal delusion. Such idiosyncratic belief is especially common in cases of unrequited love, when one person feels it and the other does not. The lover lives in the delusion that the beloved returns the sentiments, or fantasizes that the other will surely do so eventually. This delusional thinking, taken to its limits, can devolve into stalking behaviors. While serious delusions evidence serious mental disorder, plenty of us entertain minor false imaginings that preserve and perpetuate stories we've created to shield us from the realities of our lives.

"Delusions of grandeur," a phrase we've all heard, means a false impression of one's own importance. This type of self-aggrandizement is born out of profound insecurity and a sense of inadequacy. But being right-sized in your own estimation brings self-confidence, contentment, and accurate perception. It lets you choose well when dating and seeking the right mate. So it's useful to examine your delusions and fantasies consciously, since they reveal your desires, your search for meaning, your questions about your identity and sexuality. For while sex and love can bring joy and pleasure, you must stay in reality about *you*, about what you're really looking for and whether the person you're with can actually meet your needs. There's nothing wrong with dreaming the dream or longing for the perfect mate. The challenge is to *look at your own truth first*, and then to look at the truth of who stands before you, beyond the obvious, into his or her essence, to see whether he or she is, indeed, gazing back.

DAILY HEALTHY SEX ACTS

- Remember the stories you made up as a child about your prince or princess coming into your life. What was the basic theme of each story? Were you being rescued, introduced, or finding one another in some magical way?

- If you've held on to delusional threads of that story, let them go. Write about your past fantasies, then look inside yourself for the truth of what you were hoping for.

- Are you in reality about your love choices? If not, share with a trusted friend and think about what you need to do to find your way to truth.

> *"The Eskimos had fifty-two names for snow because it was important to them: there ought to be as many for love."*
>
> — Margaret Atwood

The simplest phrase in the world, "I love you," offers a myriad of distinctive meanings from "I'm enjoying the sex" to "I intend to marry you." We conceive of love as a feeling, but once love is expressed through language it becomes an idea as well. Language itself creates a new form of love.

Certainly, both verbal and nonverbal communication are essential for sexual intimacy. However, feeling love and *saying* you feel love are separate processes. In a relationship, stating your love is one of many big moments setting the stage for *the next stage*. What does it mean to say the "I." word, to come to a place where you can both avow feelings of love? Just as a loving emotion may be mingled with confusion, fear, and shame, our thinking process can be similarly convoluted. Language is important as it represents the end result of our internal processes—emotional and mental—and what we're willing to bring into being. This is one reason it is said that whatever words we choose to use are only the tip of the iceberg.

Still, language reveals us. To demonstrate, if the simple statement, "I love you," were charted out as a mathematical equation, it might include so many operations evaluating interpersonal and cultural influences that it might take up several classroom blackboards! Even a sample shorthand formula might look like this:

$$\text{Mentality} \{(\text{Need for Romance} + \text{Security}) > (\text{Fear of Rejection})^{100}\}$$
$$- \text{Memory} \{(\text{Declaring love led to intimacy last time}) \div (\text{That relationship ended terribly})^3\}$$
$$\times \text{Anxiety} (\text{Will she/he reciprocate?})^{10} \sqrt{} \{(\text{is this bad timing?}) + \text{Intuition} (\text{I'm getting a good vibe})\}$$
$$\times (\text{Courage} + \text{Nerve} \pm \text{Recklessness}) = \text{"I love you."}$$

This illustration shows that the language of love can be as complicated as language will permit.

DAILY HEALTHY SEX ACTS

- Does your language authentically convey your inner feelings and thoughts? Do you enjoy using language to communicate? What influences do you think shaped your love (or lack of love) for language?

- Get what you're really thinking down on paper in a daily journal. As you find the truest words to express your private self, you will hone the core language skills needed to navigate your public life.

- Tell someone, "I love you" today, and reveal the true meaning of your feelings in the distinctive language of your love.

"A lover's eyes will gaze an eagle blind.
A lover's ear will hear the lowest sound."
— William Shakespeare

SENSUALITY

What does it mean to live a sensual life? To practice sensuality in our relationships? Although sensuality produces and refines physical eroticism, it is an entire way of being that extends far beyond carnal pleasures of the flesh. It engages our hearing, our sight, our senses of smell and taste, and our experience of touch to create a richer, more rewarding erotic existence. Sensuous engagement occurs when inhaling the heady perfume of a rose or enjoying a friend's smile. It means becoming sensitized to the seasons, the gentle mist in the air, the vibrant colors of a sunset. It's these attunements to the natural world's treasures that inspire our sexual expression. If we are not sensual when we are alone, how can we hope to be sensual with a partner? Do we, in private reverence, nourish our bodies with delicious food, exotic baths, oils and healing massage? Or do we compartmentalize sensuality, believing it exists only when we are making love?

When we do engage with a partner, we can build profound communion and synchronous revelations especially through the power of touch. Human touch holds untold possibilities, much more than as a means of arousal. Like sensuality, it can be a world unto itself. Exploring the uncharted realms of pressure, temperature, pain, direction, timing, tension and equilibrium, we can take our love-making to unimaginable new levels. Such mindful sensuality can also help us experience— sense—qualities of a partner we wouldn't ordinarily notice or cherish, like a characteristic facial expression, a particular odor, or the way he or she holds our hand. In this way, sensuality grounds us in the details that make each of us, whether in private or partnered, unique.

DAILY HEALTHY SEX ACTS

- Trace the outline of your lover's body with your eyes, your fingers, and your tongue. Transmute any imperfections and perceive the innate, sensual artistry of his or her being. Guide your lover to your body in kind.

- Ironically, our senses become heightened both by fear and by security. Today, feel safe enough to engage your senses fully. Allow your eyes to drink in details, your ears to hear the music of the spheres.

"Life isn't one damn thing after another.
It's the same damn thing again and again."
— Edna St. Vincent Millay

PATTERNS

Our entire understanding of the world is built on the patterns we perceive. From mathematics to neurobiology, observable patterns define our field of awareness. Over some fixed patterns we have no control: Planets orbit the sun; electrons orbit atoms' nuclei; newborns instinctively breathe, suckle and cry; animals domesticated for generations still follow automatic patterns of behavior. Despite this, we know that certain patterns can be reset. Dogs might be programmed innately to bark or chase cats but with daily training, new behaviors can replace instinctive scripts.

The entire field of psychology focuses on discovering and retraining patterns, and recovery from destructive patterns of behavior is more possible than ever. Even informally, when people share stories they often repeat the same details over and over as they process them into their looping procedural memory, making the explicit literally implicit in their brains.

It's been said that life is a spiral slowly progressing upward and looping back down in repetitive patterns. We may feel dejected to find old patterns repeating, but they do so each time at a higher level of consciousness. Recovering addicts in particular report the eternal reappearance of deep-set psychological patterns. But while the patterns might feel the same, the fact that the recovering addict is sooner and more keenly aware of them represents a tremendous advance. Ever-increasing attentiveness forms part of the new pattern of recovery, and finally creates new behavior. The very fact that our lives are built on so many patterns reveals a larger pattern to our lives.

DAILY HEALTHY SEX ACTS

- Today, observe patterns in the world around you—the weave of your clothes, the hum of traffic, the rhythm of your breath. Recognize how patterns impact your consciousness at every level.

- Pay attention to mental and emotional patterns as well. As you mentally loop through habitual thoughts, verbalize this typically unnoticed routine. Or bring awareness to one emotion—happiness, curiosity, or fear—and note any pattern to its reappearance throughout the day.

- You can train your brain to reset its patterns. Pick a simple goal such as exercising, deep breathing, or feeling your feelings, and spend just ten minutes a day in gentle practice in order to repattern.

"Sexiness is a state of mind."

— Halle Berry

SEXINESS

At some point in a long-term relationship, desire drops off and we worry that we're no longer attracted to our mate or that we're no longer attractive. That's natural, because no one ever told us that it's our responsibility to figure out what makes *us* feel sexy. So people often cave in to the forces of age by letting themselves off the hook regarding healthy eating or exercising regularly. We get complacent in our committed relationships, assuming that our partner will forgive our laziness because s/he loves us. Indeed, that is a paradoxical benefit of "growing older" with someone: We're loved no matter what and we accept that looks and bodies change with time. But holding the opposite end of that paradox means that *we have to challenge ourselves* to do what makes us feel sexy, for the sake of our own vitality as well as for attracting our partner. If you've let yourself gain extra pounds or have stopped tending to your skin, hair, and muscle tone, then ask yourself, "Why?"

Sexual energy is a creative force in our lives and contributes to the well-being of all—meaning that when you're vitally engaged and living a full life, others around you feel it and can be inspired to do the same. Take charge of your sexual feelings and set an example for younger generations! Ignite your sexuality by taking an inventory of where you've gotten lazy. Look at the changes you have to make and challenge your partner to join you in finding ways that make them feel sexy, too.

DAILY HEALTHY SEX ACTS

- Commit to feeling sexy by doing one thing today that relaxes you or that moves you to tend to your body.

- Ask your partner about the things and actions that make them feel sexy and if they're willing to engage in a process of change with you.

- After you try those activities, notice how you feel. Make a list of activities that make you feel sexy and commit to doing them on a regular basis.

"We always deceive ourselves twice about the people we love—first to their advantage, then to their disadvantage."

— Albert Camus

JUDGMENT

Judgments can create a wedge in relationships through our own insecurities, and keep us from loving more deeply or at all. Judging can prevent us from exploring our own intimate and sexual limitations because it's easier to diminish the other person than to look at ourselves. In the electric flash of a single thought, we can turn the reality of another to rubble. But hidden in the debris are our own silenced truths. Cultural and familial programming creates false standards that hijack our focus and block us from our greater humanity.

One of the greatest truths we can realize is that everything perceivable is in process. When we judge ourselves and others, we are judging works unfinished. "He's not worthy." "She isn't good enough." "They're on the wrong side." All we think, we convey nonverbally, and our negative judgments only reinforce our prejudiced, narrow-minded positions in a relentless loop. We can't change people, but we can change our judgments through risking intimacy. Each performance, project, gesture expresses the reality of the person who creates it, and the reality of each of us is irrefutably, ipso facto, beyond reproach.

Constant judging is akin to saying "I hurt. I need help." But we rarely offer love and empathy to those who judge. Often, we judge them in turn. Yes, sticking to our principles and perceptions is valuable. But our own false judgment, which hinders rather than helps someone's process, is a wholly learned form of psychological abuse. No one should play the role of Higher Power for another. Only when people seek our expertise may we serve the spirit of the wisdom with which we've each been tasked. Ask permission before offering unsolicited advice, and know that internal negative judgments make us lose our connection with true life.

DAILY HEALTHY SEX ACTS

- What recurring judgments do you make about others and about yourself? How are your judgments different from objective evaluations? Whose voice from your past is really speaking through you?

- Know that your judging mind is a product of your past. Today, recognize your judgments for what they are, and let self-love fill the void gnawed out by carried shame. Love yourself and others. See how intimacy creates new reality.

"You are so weak. Give up to grace. The ocean takes care of each wave 'til it gets to shore. You need more help than you know."

— Rumi

21 MAY

GRACE

When we think of grace, we typically conjure images of ballerinas making the impossible look simple and elegant as they glide through space. Or perhaps we marvel at the divinely beautiful movements of basketball stars as they float upward to sink basket after perfect basket. In fact, we consider most graceful talents as otherworldly gifts from above.

The word *grace* holds a myriad of meanings across cultures. Zeus's three beautiful daughters were called the Graces, who personified and bestowed charm, joy and beauty. In Greek mythology in general, the gods were endowed with superhuman powers but when they misbehaved or flouted the laws of nature, they were thought to have fallen from grace. The concept of grace is also deeply embedded in Christian ideas of salvation and blessings. Even in business dealings, when we grant someone a grace period we give him or her extra time to fulfill an obligation. When we hold people in our good graces, we regard them with favor. But like the Greek gods, when modern-day heroes such as sports figures or powerful politicians are caught breaking the law, they are demoted from icons to mere mortals and forfeit their position of hallowed exaltation.

All these uses of the term *grace* derive from the Latin *gratia*, meaning pleasing or grateful. We rightfully equate grace with thankfulness, as when we say grace before or after meals. To surrender to grace is a cultivated act of courage by which we give up worry, fear, and doubt and choose to live in gratitude. When we live in gratitude we make space in our lives for goodwill to flow. Life then takes on a quality of ease without obstructions or drama. When grace is the norm, joy and happiness permeate all our relationships.

DAILY HEALTHY SEX ACTS

- Keep a gratitude list for one month: Each day, list five things you're grateful for. What happens when you acknowledge the abundance in your life?

- How grateful are you for your relationships? How often do you share your gratitude with the people in your life? Small appreciations go a long way.

- Pay attention to your physical grace today. Do you hold your head high and glide through your day? Do you slog through it with heaviness in your body? Or are you somewhere in between? What changes in your diet, exercise or mood might help you move with greater grace?

"Affirmation of life is the spiritual act by which man ceases to live unreflectively and begins to devote himself to his life with reverence in order to raise it to its true value."

— Albert Schweitzer

AFFIRMATIONS

What we affirm to ourselves becomes our reality, because it's what we're *choosing* to see. Is the glass half empty or is it half full? When we affirm that it's half empty, we see lack and limitation in our life; when we see it as half full, we see a life of possibility. And when we see the glass of equal parts water and air as completely full, we affirm a life of abundance. Do you affirm yourself daily? Are you willing to take a leap and state in the *affirmative* what you choose to see in yourself, even when those affirmations hit the most shameful places inside you? If you can't affirm in yourself what you choose and what you love, you won't be able to receive love from your beloved.

Once you become more comfortable affirming yourself, you can begin to affirm your partner. Look past your petty preferences ("I don't like his haircut" or "I don't like that dress on her") and see that person with loving and understanding—with your god eyes. Affirm your partner's beauty, sexuality, body, and soul. Melt into a sensuality of recognition for who your partner really is. In this way your affirmations about what you love in yourself and in your partner actually create a reality that's genuinely open to and supportive of the richest possibilities.

 DAILY HEALTHY SEX ACTS

- Make a list of the qualities you want to embody, then turn that list into personal affirmations you speak daily—into "I am" statements made in the here-and-now: "I am beautiful, whole and complete just as I am."

- Ask your partner to make his or her own list, then share your lists with one another.

- Take turns affirming each other using the lists you've made for yourselves.

"Love has no uttermost, as the stars have no number and the sea no rest."

— Eleanor Farjeon

23 MAY

SURPRISE

Perhaps the biggest surprise in life is just how much depth there is to people. We don't know how profound we are, nor the extent of our capacity to love. We've yet to plumb the depths of our souls, our potency, being, and consciousness. We may think we know, but if we simply pay attention we'll be constantly surprised.

When we try to "spice up" a relationship with boudoir lingerie, romantic getaways, new sexual positions or sex toys, we're using just the material manifestations of what's perhaps the greatest thrill of all—a partner's capacity for anticipation and consideration. Studies show that small, unpredictable acts of kindness—like unsolicited shoulder rubs or affectionate smiles—do more to maintain relational happiness over the long run than the most exotic and generous, but obligatory, gestures or gifts.

Of course, it's meaningful and wonderful if the person you love cares enough to go to any effort. But we don't have to wait for anybody else to gift our hearts with spontaneous acts of caring. Each of us is more than capable of allowing our own creative impulses to rejuvenate our lives. We may receive unfiltered ecstasy in any moment just by letting go of preconceptions, by becoming more fully present.

Healthy relationships have a healthy dose of competition, which can create novelty. Just as when you run in a race next to someone, there's surprise because that person has a heartbeat that's beating like yours—here's where your heartbeat is, and look, here's where another's heartbeat is. Healthy competition might empower you to pick up your pace. The surprise of life, of livingness, gives our existence color, vigor, and immeasurable depth when we tap into it.

DAILY HEALTHY SEX ACTS

- People from a background where sudden changes were unsafe may develop a pattern of avoiding spontaneity. Does this describe you or anyone you know? What safe procedures might resolve any fear of change to allow for healthy sexual surprises? Do you know the difference between spontaneity and impulsivity?

- Focus on your erotic impulses today. Sometimes you've got to give to get, so if you long for affection or attention, turn it around and receive satisfaction by giving your lover those experiences. Let your own bodily sensations guide you in reaching out to touch another.

- Today, listen for the heartbeats of everyone you encounter. How does this level of sensitivity break through your routine preconceptions?

"Love is a friendship set to music."

— Joseph Campbell

Movies, TV, and magazines typically portray romantic love as the only significant kind of relationship. Yet deep, grounded friendships often last longer than any other kind of connection. New friends bring zest to our lives by igniting or reigniting interests. They can make us laugh and question ourselves in fun and interesting ways, inspiring a sense of play that arises from the delight of getting to know someone. Over time, the new friend becomes a close friend and, if we're lucky, a best friend and an old friend.

MAY 24

FRIENDSHIP

One of the greatest riches in life is having an old friend, a person you know and who knows you better than anyone. Sharing a history with someone is invaluable because, together, you remember joyous occasions, raucous nights, broken hearts, and the pain you endured when you struggled against one another or together against adversity. A close friend will reliably support you, sympathize with you, help you, and travel the globe with you literally and metaphorically. Good friends confide in one another and hold up a mirror so we can see who we are and who we can become. But it's important to remember that friendships, like gardens, need care. Tending to your friendships sustains and grows them; your labors let you reap the fruit of steadfastness, companionship, or a shoulder to cry on.

Building a love relationship founded on friendship sets the stage for a dependable union over time. When you fall in love with your best friend, you are connected throughout your life through a special bond. As two spirits mingle in friendship and love, there's a feeling of security that supersedes all the petty problems in life. Like family members, you won't always agree, but you will rarely be lonely when you base your love on friendship.

DAILY HEALTHY SEX ACTS

- Take stock of your friendships. How many male and how many female friends do you have?

- How do you define friendship, and what are your criteria for friendship? What qualities do you need in an acquaintance, friend, or best friend? Are your friends really friends?

- How good a friend are you? How can you become a better friend in all of your relationships?

"There are two important points: The first is that both gender and sexuality are learned forms of social practice, and the second is that looking to 'natural differences' between women and men for lessons about sexual conduct is an error."

— John Gagnon

25 MAY

GENDER

"Love is blind," they say. So why do we focus on gender? We look at every new acquaintance through preconceived notions based on that person's being male or female. Most of us were taught from childhood to attribute gentleness to girls and forcefulness to boys. Worse, we learned to reject parts of us we deem contrary to our gender roles, and some of us may now also repress others' gender-bending. Even if we are open-minded, when a female shows no desire to procreate or when a male shows no inclination towards sports or war—when there stands a soul who refuses to conform—we are faced with the absurdity of our gender parameters. Trapped in the narrow dichotomy of pink versus blue, we ignore the rainbow of human expression. This censorship of ourselves and others denies the flowing balance between our left and right brain, between action and receptivity, between yang and yin, and leaves us internally and externally imbalanced.

In certain cultural symbolism, masculinity implies active and superior functions, and femininity, passive and inferior functions. But take note: Symbolism isn't reality. Transposing gender symbolism onto real people causes problems in civilizations and souls.

Although *gender identity*—what gender you identify with—is entirely separate from *sexual orientation*—what gender you desire—many confuse the two. This confusion brings pain and exclusion especially to gender-variant youth and adults—and to the free flowering of all our own inner energies. Healthy gender identity grows from the ability to embrace and express our entire range of energies without falling victim to external gender politics. When we can finally value all our traits without labeling them by gender, we'll end the oppressive, inaccurate bifurcation of humankind.

DAILY HEALTHY SEX ACTS

- Even supporters of gender and transgender equality can let deep-rooted gender bias distort their daily interactions. Today, imagine everyone you see as the opposite gender from what you perceive. If you have children, notice how differently you might treat them.

- Write two lists: your *masculine* and your *feminine* traits. Then ask yourself what makes each trait "masculine" or "feminine." Next, perceive each trait as oppositely "gendered"—masculine as feminine, and vice versa. Affirm each quality within yourself.

- Do what you can to make this world safe and welcoming for all varied gender identities, starting at home.

"Sexual addicts are hostages of their own preoccupation. Every passerby, every relationship, and every introduction to someone passes through the sexually obsessive filter."

— Patrick Carnes

SEXUAL ADDICTION

Sex is a normal, healthy urge. But for the sex addict, it becomes perverted into a coping tool to medicate trauma, tension or discomfort. Over time, the sex addict's symptoms worsen; he or she becomes habituated to current behaviors and takes greater risks to recapture the initial euphoria that could numb the psychic pain. It's a devastating disease that treats other people as objects—like pills or powders—to be consumed, hoarded, discarded. It can lead to a loss of employment, loss of friends and family, other addictions, or even arrest and public humiliation. The abuse of sex—not sex itself—becomes a weapon of self-destruction. Despite much progress and new information, sex addiction is still shrouded by stigma and shame that make it difficult for those suffering to receive the help they need.

During the healing process, we compare sex to the element of fire. Fire can destroy life, or it can support life by cooking our food, keeping us warm, and comforting us in the darkness. Just as we must learn to separate its dangers from its gifts, the sex addict must learn how to separate unhealthy from healthy sex. That's no easy task, especially for someone who grew up in a family that did not teach healthy love. It is a slow process of facing one's primal, never-met needs for non-sexual nurturing, intimacy, friendship and community, and of delving into the painful early traumas that the destructive sexual behaviors disguised, often for years. Usually a period of total abstinence—a "fast"—is required to cleanse the addict's psyche of old, damaging behaviors and to prepare him or her for new experiences. The journey to recovering one's sexual self as something good and whole can be long and arduous. Human resilience is remarkable, however, and healing is possible.

DAILY HEALTHY SEX ACTS

- What did you think when you first heard the term *sex addict*? Has your view of sex addiction changed?

- To broaden your understanding of sex addiction, you might read a book on it, attend an open 12-step meeting in one of the "S" programs (Sex Addicts Anonymous, Sex and Love Addicts Anonymous, Sexual Compulsives Anonymous). You can always call the intake line of sex addiction treatment centers and ask questions.

- Do you or someone you know have a problem with sex addiction? What's stopping you from healing this area of your life? Today, address these issues with trusted others.

> *"Sometimes, reaching out and taking someone's hand is the beginning of a journey. At other times, it is allowing another to take yours."*
>
> — Vera Nazarian

27 MAY

HOLDING HANDS

Do not use force and do not seek power; just interlace your fingers and see what happens. Holding hands for the first time can be a monumental experience when done consciously. Do you remember your first moment holding hands with your lover? That simple act can kindle passion like nothing else. The anticipation borne of flesh touching flesh charges your system to excite your heartbeat and to imagine a life in connectedness. When we pause and fully appreciate the ordinary act of holding hands, the familiar becomes a journey to extraordinary possibilities.

We safeguard children by holding their hands to shepherd them across a street, to play with them, or to reassure them that all is well. The feeling of being held, of knowing that we're anchored to someone, creates security and grounds us to the core of our being. Sometimes we miss out on the natural joy of holding hands because we're caught up in the complexity of what it means. In many cultures around the world, girls hold hands with girls, boys hold hands with boys, adults of the same sex hold hands with each other as a gesture of friendship, love, and community. In those cultures people seem less hung up on the sexual connotation of handholding and more focused on how it connects them.

When we drop self-consciousness and move into the present, pretension falls away and makes a space for authenticity. In that moment, the simplest gestures, like holding someone's hand, can be the beginning of something wondrous. Don't miss the opportunity today to make contact with someone you love. Take your mother's hand when you walk down the street with her, your father's when you sit next to him at lunch, your teenager's when you sense s/he's in need, and your lover's—just because.

DAILY HEALTHY SEX ACTS

- How many people's hands can you hold today?

- Next time you hold someone's hand, notice the feeling in your palm, the way your fingers interlace, and the energy between you and that person.

- Don't be stingy! Hold hands, walk down the street and swing them with glee!

"There is no pornography without a secrecy."

— D. H. Lawrence

Pornography excites the brain, in part, because it gives us license to have unabashed sex. Like art, it's a personal taste: For some, porn is exhilarating and enjoyable with a partner, but for others, it embodies exploitation of the vulnerable. It's even difficult to determine exactly what is pornographic. In fact, when a Supreme Court Justice was asked how to define pornography he replied, "I know it when I see it."

PORNOGRAPHY

Pornography is a form of free speech. But the question remains: is it sexually liberating, or a form of sexual repression/oppression? The answer is that it differs from person to person. For some, porn is a window to sexual variety; an invitation to express their most carnal self, while others find it mirrors their personal trauma. When porn is additive to your sex life in ways that you find fulfilling, then you know it's right for you. Watching porn may also be very informative about different positions and possibilities you may want to try with a partner. You may also discover that you're not alone in the full range of your desires.

If you find yourself watching it compulsively, or feeling demoralized afterward, it may be a way of avoiding the present and having a relationship with a real person in real time. The performance aspect of porn reminds us that sex in porn isn't real sex. It usually lacks foreplay and embodied connection with another. Since we're rarely watching authentic sex between two consenting adults, pornography perpetuates cultural myths about women and men: Women are interchangeable sex objects without their own unique needs, and men have permanently erect, impossibly large penises.

It's important to remember what's true for you. Be careful not to compare yourself and your partner to images. If you watch pornography, make sure it's additive to your experience and your psyche, not degrading or debilitating to your sexuality or to your self.

DAILY HEALTHY SEX ACTS

- Do you know the difference between pornographic and relational sex? What's the difference for you?

- What do you like about pornography? What do you dislike about pornography?

- Find out what really turns your lover on, then have an honest conversation about the "dos" and "don'ts" of your sex life.

"The three hardest tasks in the world are neither physical feats nor intellectual achievements, but moral acts: to return love for hate, to include the excluded, and to say, 'I was wrong.'"

— Sydney J. Harris

29 MAY

MORALITY

How do we each write our own moral code? Any morality we cherish must truly express our most authentic core self. That can occur only when our actions are fully aligned with our values, and this union is one of the building blocks of self-esteem. Our morality must be applicable and upheld under all circumstances, otherwise it's merely what we call "relative" ethics. If we value honesty, for instance, we cannot pick and choose when, where and with whom we are honest. Without consistency and commitment, we will never experience the thrill of transformation in our personal lives.

But sometimes we find major discrepancies between our internal idea of a moral life and the way we actually live. Whenever we do, it's an excellent idea to write out our thoughts and feelings about those behaviors, as nothing heals more powerfully than awareness. If we look at the Golden Rule, "Treat others as you would be treated," we notice that we often fail to adhere to this principle in our primary relationships. Nowhere is moral shortcoming more prevalent than in the intersection between our espoused morality and the way we engage romantic and sexual partners. In truth, how we function sexually is a microcosm of the way that we are in the world. We might ask ourselves, "Are we being selfish, considerate, or dismissive? Are we minimizing, compliant or controlling?" Sex is the ultimate laboratory where we can actually try out new ways of relating to ourselves and our lover, being conscious and mindful of how we impact another person. It takes great humility to open a genuine exploration of our lived—not just stated—morality. But to live by the dictates of our own internal compass brings equally great joy, serenity, and self-respect.

DAILY HEALTHY SEX ACTS

- Today, observe your moral code in action. Do you practice what you preach? For example, perhaps you believe people should be more loving. Are you able to become more loving?

- The saying, "Progress, not perfection" is a moral value we all may embrace. What does it mean to be *good enough*, and how do you practice this?

- Sometimes recovering our integrity in the present involves a *moral inventory* of past wrongdoing. How are you accountable today for the actions of your past? Whether moral, immoral, or amoral, can you see *your part* clearly in the major circumstances of your life?

"An aphrodisiac will disappear, delusional, like permanence or wealth—a shimmering, as if love were a ghost."

— Lauren Lipton

APHRODISIACS

Aphrodite, the Greek goddess of love and beauty, is the namesake of *aphrodisiac*. For centuries people have believed in the erotic power of specific wines, food, potions, herbs, oils, and lotions. Paracelsus was first to publicize the "doctrine of signatures"—a popular concept accepted by ancient medical philosophers like Galen and Dioscorides that the gods marked flora and fauna with special visual "signatures" to reveal their true purpose. Thus certain foods (like oysters, asparagus or even rhinoceros horn) that resemble human genitalia were thought to have aphrodisiac properties.

While none of these substances have been scientifically proven to increase potency and desire, certain healthy foods can be fun to play with and might be a way to introduce novelty into your sex life. Moreover, delicious chocolates, oysters, or strawberries and cream can have the effect of making you feel sexy. But remember, no material can substitute for the love and connection you and your partner have. There's no magic potion that can ignite your sexuality like your heartfelt connection.

DAILY HEALTHY SEX ACTS

- Today, focus on the shape, texture, aroma, and taste of your food. How does each bite make you feel?

- What are common aphrodisiacs for you? What turns you on? Is it chocolate, ice cubes, sensuous edible oils, or something else?

- Suggest to your partner that each bring one aphrodisiac to bed next time you plan to have sex. Surprise one another and keep an open mind—you never know when you might learn something new about yourself and your lover.

"Caring about others, running the risk of feeling, and leaving an impact on people, brings happiness."

— Harold Kushner

31 MAY

IMPACT

We influence our planet and one another through our words and actions. The lasting impact of our actions on others or our surroundings can be monumental or minuscule, known to us or not. A profound statement of shared meaning or a mere smile from a stranger may equally shift the way we perceive our self or our life. Think about your day yesterday. Who affected you? A co-worker who made you laugh? An angry customer on the phone? Either left you with a residual feeling.

Imagine the impact great thinkers have had on local and global cultures. Then think about the impact terrorists have had in those same societies. Good or bad, these actions have woven themselves into the fiber of our psychic landscapes, changing and shaping us in ways we may not have asked for. When Aristotle, Walt Whitman, Dorothy Parker, Yogananda or other great ones walked the earth, they struggled with their own existential issues that later became philosophical issues for us all to grapple with. The gifts of their minds and the risks they took speaking and recording them reverberate through every generation, bringing each to the same questions but often from a more evolved vantage point.

In Buddhism, the Eightfold Path contains ethical conduct, two elements of which are right speech and right action. It's not necessary to practice Buddhism to value paying attention to what we say and do, and to acknowledge how much our words and acts touch everything and everyone with whom we come in contact. Like most creatures of habit, we can easily forget to reflect on the importance of right speech and right action, and end up hurting the Earth or offending our partners through our lack of awareness. Wake up today to the impact you have on your world!

DAILY HEALTHY SEX ACTS

- When we respect ourselves and others, we are perceived as attractive. Take action today to impact your love relationship in a way that makes you feel good about your commitment to your lover.

- Do you need to apologize to anyone for any negative impact you've had on him or her? If so, what is the best way to do that? Whose assistance do you need in order to make sure you're actually honoring the person you hurt rather than just assuaging your guilt?

June

"Coition is a slight attack of apoplexy. For man gushes forth from man, and is separated by being torn apart with a kind of blow."

— Democritus

1 JUNE

INDIVIDUALITY

Becoming an individual is the natural but challenging process of growing into adulthood. The adolescent begins to separate from his or her family of origin, striking out to answer the life-long question, "Who am I?" A healthy family system supports youngsters' desire to stretch wings by staying flexible and open to their shifting attitudes, opinions, and ideas which may differ from those of the family. A rigid, unhealthy system fights against any changing landscape of the family, shaming or forcing their teen to live under its closed rules, and thus sets the stage for rebellion. Persons who never individuate from their family of origin are likely to stay enmeshed with them, either in rage and self-destruction in the form of addiction, or in codependence.

No matter how or whether we individuate, we take our identity from family roles and values that may or may not serve us in adulthood. Keeping the valuable parts and discarding the rest require a conscious investigation into the family ethos. Those who don't individuate tend to drag their parents', grandparents' and, yes, even great-grandparents' codependent issues into their own current relationships. Understanding that what worked for one generation won't necessarily work for the next is crucial to individuation.

When we enter a love relationship we often unconsciously arrive with ancestral baggage, acting out forbearers' trauma unknowingly. These habitual patterns may be so deeply ingrained in us that we cannot even see them. We quickly learn, however, that we can push our partner's buttons and they can do the same to us. Committing to putting yourself and your spirituality first is a tall order, especially if you've been conditioned to put others before you. But becoming an individual demands that we search our soul deeply, and tolerate emotional growing pains.

DAILY HEALTHY SEX ACTS

- Do you know who your grandparents and great-grandparents were? How did they live? What did they struggle with? What did they hand down to your parents and to you?

- What problematic behaviors and family traits do you bring to your current relationship? Have these issues ruined past relationships?

- What actions do you need to take to get out of the family web of codependence and become your own person?

> *"Life in Lubbock, Texas, taught me two things: One is that God loves you and you're going to burn in hell. The other is that sex is the most awful, filthy thing on earth and you should save it for someone you love."*
>
> — Butch Hancock

CONDITIONING

Early childhood conditioning is essential for our growth, but hanging onto it in adulthood is like a butterfly clinging to its cocoon. It is our individual responsibility to question received beliefs and discard those that no longer serve us. Trouble is, we identify so strongly with so-called personal points of view—all of which were given us at some time by another—that we often don't know how *not to identify* with them. Some people turn to drugs and alcohol in an attempt to mitigate early influences and experience new thought. But inebriating one's sensitive brain only mirrors the original trauma of being overpowered by extrinsic programming.

We are conditioned by caregivers, teachers, neighbors, peers, media, politicians, spiritual leaders, and our entire culture. Some overtly attempt to control our thinking, committing psychological abuse comparable to brainwashing. Other influences parrot groupthink programming thoughtlessly, like a radio left blaring. Although we are genetically programmed to tune out overly painful messages, if the bombardment is constant enough it becomes ingrained in our memory.

Negative conditioning makes harmful thoughts feel safe and insecurities seem secure. Even if we learn to recognize these distortions in our thinking, long-term negative conditioning can give them such a sense of familiarity that we feel disloyal negating them. The feeling of not being good enough can become especially habitual if one's conditioning equated worthiness with rigidly idealized behavior, particularly in regard to sexuality and relationships. But there's no rationale for keeping tuned in to a program that no longer addresses our true needs. It's up to us to change the channel of our customary thinking. No one else can possibly find the new frequency attuned to our individual truth.

DAILY HEALTHY SEX ACTS

- What conditioning did you receive as a child from caregivers, community, and culture? Do these messages still support your self-image, relationships, and dreams? Counter negative programming and shine the light on all your *stinkin' thinkin'*.

- The tragedy of negative conditioning is that life usually meets our expectations, which, in this case, are our most negative ones. If you happen to catch yourself in toxic patterns—the result of past conditioning—start with empathy for your own authentic, love-growing self.

"High on a throne, with all the splendor and pomp his gold can command, man is yet poor and desolate, if love passes him by. And if it stays, the poorest hovel is radiant with warmth, with life and color. Thus love has the magic power to make of a beggar a king. Yes, love is free; it can dwell in no other atmosphere."

— Emma Goldman

3 JUNE

FREE LOVE

The most recent "free love" movement, while echoing earlier ones, was energized by the 1960s social revolution and sought to separate the State from all matters related to marriage, sex, and birth control. Its salient point was that sex, sexuality, and love relationships should be entered into freely, without politics or the law governing our choices.

But when we talk about free love on an interpersonal level, we must examine the inner recesses of our intentions more closely. Consider that using love to enslave or to hold onto another is a sure indicator of low self-esteem. Trying to change someone so s/he fits your ideal, or coercing someone into staying with you—especially when you're compromising your own integrity—signals that you're not operating from a grounded place of self-love. Demanding constant, unquestioning validation from another human being can be the equivalent of holding him/her an emotional hostage. In truth, you don't really want that person; instead, you want that person to fill in a missing part of yourself.

Take a moment to think about love as a freeing power. The adage, "If you love something, set it free," is sound. When you surrender your demands for love, you will recognize that the only real love is free and, remarkably, will return to you exponentially. It takes courage to take your personal need out of the equation so you can give your love generously and without expectations. When you live in the reality of who you are and what you really want, you likewise honor your partner and all your other relationships. In this space of free love you, too, will be loved for who you are and not for any other reason.

DAILY HEALTHY SEX ACTS

- Do you currently have someone in your life who isn't right for you, but whom you keep around because you don't want to feel lonely? If so, take a risk today and set her or him free from your half-hearted relationship.

- Practice loving-kindness to all you meet. Give away your love through a smile or simple gesture, and free yourself from trying to control all outcomes in your life.

"In the silence of night I have often wished for just a few words of love from one man, rather than the applause of thousands of people."

— Judy Garland

PILLOW-TALK

Ideally, we share more than skin in bed; we also share our truth. The way we connect after love-making through lighthearted and tender pillow-talk complements the eroticism of love relationships. This gentle, honest and affectionate way of relating may include cooing, cuddling and caresses. It's adult play. When lovers feel completely unabashed, basking in one another's presence with adoration and appreciation, they often revert to a childlike state.

Children, before they learn to talk, murmur and babble. This preverbal stage is a vulnerable one. A toddler's experimental babbling shows that s/he feels safe and that trust has been engendered. It's through this trust that the child takes the emotional opportunity to grow, because it's through babbling that the development of vocal muscles allowing language occurs. Similarly, it's possible in adulthood that pillow-talk builds the relational vocabulary—the actual expressive skills for deeper, more meaningful conversations with a partner.

Pillow-talk develops *couple consciousness*, which blends the consciousness of each person as an individual with the collective consciousness of the couple as a unique entity. Like individuals, every healthy relationship progresses through certain stages. The more we invite pillow-talk through shared trust and appreciation, the more our relationship nurtures its own meaningful and distinctive language. The bond of this authentic, private language fulfills the lovers deeply, and inspires those outside the relationship as well.

DAILY HEALTHY SEX ACTS

- Setting a sacred space for pillow-talk requires a relaxed approach. Impossible to impose, such moments of heartfelt connection grace us. Observe your body language and emotional energy. Are you inviting and receptive, or negating and dismissive? To create pillow-talk, build trust with your partner by showing appreciation and affection.

- Pay attention to sounds and feelings after interactions with anyone in public—your social intercourse. Whether two hearts come together for sexual intimacy, casual friendship, or ordinary dealings, there's always an opportunity for the mutual sharing of true selves. Today, let the language of all your relationships develop through gentle expression and warm regard.

"Every life is noted and is cherished, and nothing loved is ever lost or perished."
— Madeleine L'Engle

5 JUNE

CHERISHING

A significant predictor of love's endurance is how we cherish one another. Relationships require attention, dedication, and communication as we work through outer and inner issues. But an absence of mutual cherishing makes love feel more like a convenient living arrangement or a self-help project than an amorous embrace. Similarly, eroticism offers infinite opportunities to cherish one another. The sex act can involve giving and receiving, mutual pleasuring, even tolerating as an act of caring. But cherishing elevates sex above all these ways. Just as we cherish our best traits, prized possessions, and breakthrough accomplishments, it's essential to cherish the sexual energy we share. Cherishing real human beings, though, requires a willingness to see the beauty in their imperfection and to adore them all the same.

The same is true about valuing life. Every moment offers an occasion for cherishing, even if it's the silver lining in every cloud. And to bear witness to the sober reality of our proverbial rain, of our pain, doesn't discount the simultaneous certainty of our blessings under the sun. Life is filled with little disappointments and conflicts, and romantic interactions can easily become tainted with resignation and buried resentment. But that's why expressing true feelings and needs is so crucial to love's survival.

For cherishing requires a clean slate. It's only with a trusting, open heart that we see clearly. Overlays of secret agendas and manipulative stratagems lose us in the murky world of shadow projections. Cherishing is the clear outpouring of unconditional love, and it's only through this perception of sharing souls that equality is ever possible. There isn't a fixed amount of love, such that cherishing another depletes us of personal power. That's not how love and blessings work. If anything, when it comes to affection and appreciation, to give endlessly makes it possible endlessly to receive.

DAILY HEALTHY SEX ACTS

- Practice the physicality of cherishing. Great works of art portray lovers trembling before one another, hands to heart in deeply felt surrender. Search for paintings and photographs that express the cherishing of which you're capable. Practice the poses and, as they say, "act as if until."

- Today, cherish your life, your love.

"Of all the girls that are so smart,
There's none like pretty Sally;
She is the darling of my heart,
And lives in our alley."

— Henry Carey

DISCRIMINATION

When our walls of prejudice block others' light, we might seek out unconscious, subversive, or even illicit means to integrate those we deem inferior. How many of us have fantasized about or fooled around with people we would never take home to our parents? Is that reluctance based on the people or our prejudice? To judge and divide sets us in a prison of our own making. So it's vital for human beings to recognize the light in everyone.

But to discriminate *wisely* we need to see our own and another's natures. Just because we want to open our hearts, eyes and minds to honor all life doesn't mean we should open our arms, homes, and wallets. Mother Teresa could transmute all personalities to share her unconditional love, but most of us will strive to balance our dual capacities for charity and self-care.

Valid discrimination requires self-knowledge. The term *trauma bonding* explains the attraction between couples who share similar or counterbalancing psychological damage. Romeo and Juliet's impulsive affair, usually cited as the epitome of true love, is more a tale of trauma bonding. We can only perceive in others the qualities we have perceived in ourselves, and what we haven't *worked through* will be *worked out* on others. Many profess attraction to rebel types over supposedly nice types, but to someone else the nice one might not seem so nice and the rebel might seem quite conformist. But willfully to choose "bad" over "good" people, things, or behavior is a personal delusion—the result of repressed desire meeting unexamined conditioning. Illuminating *how* we discriminate helps us define deeper values that may guide us to seek what's truly good for us.

DAILY HEALTHY SEX ACTS

- Show unconditional love today for all you encounter, but protect your personal boundaries. Recall the difference between unconditional and indiscriminating, and that you might hold untrustworthy persons in your heart while keeping them at arm's length.

- What attracts you to others? Define your "arousal template," all the factors you find sexually stimulating.

- Often, sex and love addicts in recovery struggle to tolerate intimacy with a healthy partner, which differs from their familiar arousal template. How does your present discriminating taste serve your sexual health?

"Adopt the pace of nature; her secret is patience."
— Ralph Waldo Emerson

7 JUNE

PACE

Ponder the quality of your sexual experiences and what natural pace feels good for you, from the gentle blossoming of a flower to the sweeping excitement of a lightning storm. Are you turned on by a sense of caring when it's slow, or athleticism when it's fast? Your interpretation of rhythm and speed might be very different from your partner's. Verbal communication about how the pace of sex actually feels can be a sexy addition to your love-making. Typically, men travel more quickly from arousal to orgasm than do women, but this rate fluctuates depending on energy, mood, and other influences. A slower pace may calm anxiety and allow for deeper sensual and emotional connection. Slowing down during sex keeps the entire body stimulated, rather than fostering the excited frenzy that aims for the dopamine surge in the brain. Watch yourself when you have thoughts that it's taking too long or going too fast. When people are nervous they tend to speak and move faster, so it can be a sign of confidence and mastery to take one's time.

So often sex is treated as a solitary act, compartmentalized in time, that starts the minute we get naked and ends at the moment of orgasm. But sexual energy builds with the flow of everyday life, just as affection is built during the week. We may pace ourselves in our relationships, too. So much of our habitual consciousness becomes wrapped up figuring out sex, love and relating, that we don't invite enough of *not knowing*, of mystery. What emotions do we experience after we walk away from a moment with a lover? How does it feel to hold and sleep on any relational concern, and what are our thoughts when we wake? Great relationships and great sex aren't always created by facing everything front-on. Sometimes it's the sideways glances that build a healthy relationship. Sometimes it's the nourishing afterglow we remember later that defines hot sex.

DAILY HEALTHY SEX ACTS

- Check in with your partner about the pace of your love-making. Ask intimate questions and share your responses regarding the way you both love to have sex. Let your communication be sexy, and demonstrate while discussing through sexual play.

- We may choose to connect not just for personal pleasure but to have a vibrational consequence, a reverberating effect on our capacity for sexual love. What kind of pace are we moving at if we are sharing in one of the most profound sexual and emotional experiences of our lives?

> *"One should always talk well about oneself!*
> *The word spreads around and in the end, no*
> *one remembers where it started."*
>
> — Jean Cocteau

The way we talk to ourselves filters how we experience life. Even more, habitual self-talk causally impacts— creates—our reality. The story we tell ourselves over and over in time becomes our life story. Self-talk is self-fulfilling prophecy, and in many cases it's a self-perpetuating prophecy. From the moment babies are born they start to experience the world in tone, sound, pace, vibration. We all know that the way a person speaks can communicate more than what s/he's actually saying, and children are highly receptive to such nonverbal communication. All that we are gets expressed. Even the act of faking who we are conveys our personal reality. So from birth we steep in this stew of historical influences that contribute to the way that we think. These thought patterns can easily become synchronous with our life patterns. That's why the most efficient and effective way of taking the wheel of our own lives is by practicing self-talk the way we would want to receive it. We bring awareness to where we shame ourselves, criticize ourselves, feed ourselves distorted messages. If we were more conscious, we would not want to have such messages on the ticker tape of our minds.

Just as much as we want to manifest positive attributes in our external life, we need to do so in our inner life, and that's the place we start. What are you thinking *right now* about yourself? In what kind of voice do you want to receive love and healthy sexual intimacy? We don't have to strain our ears to hear loving validation from an external voice all the time; we can start to practice positive self-talk in tone, sound, pace and vibration that stimulates and satisfies us. This is how we create our own music.

DAILY HEALTHY SEX ACTS

- Practice right now to find the pitch and pace and syllables and words you love to hear. Delight your own senses, and self-romance. When you find a positive statement worth repeating, experiment with different tones and rhythms.

- How can you get through to yourself? It's time to put all other messages of self-talk to sleep. Pick several positive self-talk statements that you *recognize* as true, but from conditioning you may have difficulty *realizing* as true. Let these messages sink in to your inner ears with loving sensual playfulness. Gently bring your awareness back to these exercises throughout the day.

"Soul meets soul on lovers' lips."
　　　　　　　— Percy Bysshe Shelley

9 JUNE

KISSING

Lips touching lips as a sign of love between humans, interestingly, has no known origin. In fact, there are debates about whether kissing is an innate or learned behavior. Other mammals besides humans smooch and some rub noses as a greeting of affection, comfort, or social connection. On a practical level, when our faces are close together we exchange scents and biological information telegraphing whether we are making a good mate selection. Ultimately, however, people kiss because it feels good. Our lips are comprised of erectile tissue and, like our tongues, are filled with nerve endings. Kissing is erotic and activates arousal and pleasure centers in unique and exciting ways.

And for that reason, kissing is one of the most intimate things two people can do with each other. To kiss deeply and slowly is to surrender to closeness between yourself and your lover. Inevitably, caressing and fondling follow kissing— but don't let your arousal rush you away from the moment. Slow your kiss and taste your partner's lips, feel the scent and heat of your lover's breath, and give yourself over to the sensations that arise in the moment.

When kissing, we automatically close our eyes. Lost in our own personal reverie, we take a trip to Venus with our lover as co-pilot. Kissing awakens the body and signals to your partner that you're aroused. In this state of surrender, the scents of your bodies mingle, and your embrace enhances the act of kissing, creating further arousal. Linger in the kiss and let the union of your lips be the moment of meeting, love-making, and contacting the divine within each of you. Kissing is sensuality in action and, during intercourse, invites high levels of eroticism.

DAILY HEALTHY SEX ACTS

- How do you feel about kissing? Do you have hang-ups about kissing that you need to address?

- What's your style of kissing? Do you vary length or pressure? What's your preference?

- When was the last time you slowed down and kissed your partner? Do you kiss during sex? If not, why not?

"People will ask you the question 'how is life treating you?' But my question is 'how are you treating life?'"

— Rasheed Ogunlaru

TREATMENT

We can't learn this enough: The way we treat ourselves mirrors the way we treat others. But how do we hold this truth in our heart and mind as a daily practice? There's an inherent dilemma in envisioning a better relationship while simultaneously accepting our lover in the present. At what point does setting our sights on sexual growth impede current intimacy through expectations, instead of enhancing it through awareness? Dissatisfaction with the status quo can be a healthy impetus for self-improvement, but chronic discontent can block real change.

Understand that the recovery of sexual and emotional health is as challenging as you can imagine. If it was always impossible for you to let go and cede control, or, conversely, to express your truth and stand up to someone who broke boundaries, you now have to learn and practice untested skills. So it's essential to treat ourselves with all the love and understanding we longed for, because working through our issues instead of dancing around them is tough.

And when the going gets tough, the tough get treatment. Therapeutic treatment offers a place to set aside the way we habitually interact. Through *empathic attunement*, a therapist tracks his or her own bodily based feelings as a road map to the inner world of the client, just as a mother attunes to her child in order to make the child's implicit feelings explicitly understood. Similarly, the 12-step programs' slogan, "You have to give it away to keep it," describes the sponsor relationship whereby members strengthen their own recovery by helping others recover. Whenever we treat others with empathy, holding their hearts in ours, we attune to their struggles and hopes. And through this process, healing arrives in our own hearts.

DAILY HEALTHY SEX ACTS

- Do you treat others as you want to be treated? If not, why not? Today, pretend that you are the soul inside everyone you meet, and show everyone appreciation. You'll find you're showing appreciation to yourself as well. Treat life like a mirror, and see how your inner experience reflects your treatment of others.

- Act *as if*. If you haven't got it in your heart to be your best self around others, act *as if* you do—in other words, "fake it until you make it." Treat yourself to your best self, by connecting to the world through your heart in empathic attunement.

"Love doesn't just sit there, like a stone, it has to be made, like bread; re-made all the time, made new."

— Ursula Le Guin

11 JUNE

PARTNERSHIP

Today more couples than ever identify themselves as "life partners." This term underscores the fact that your significant other shares a certain proportion, or part, of your life. She or he is not your whole life, otherwise your bond might be called *wholenership* rather than *partnership!* In relationship, we share part of our lives, we share part of our day, and we each do our part.

Intimate sharing is reciprocal, appropriate and measured. To know and be known doesn't mean sharing everything there is to know. In fact, too much information can overwhelm a relationship just as easily as not enough sharing can distance you emotionally. True partnership is both *quantitative* and *qualitative*—it involves *real time* spent together in a *healthy way*.

You might already have experienced unhealthy models of "being part of" a relationship, perhaps in your family of origin. Sometimes parents didn't do their part, or they didn't allow anyone else's part. What was your model for being part of something, for being in a partnership? What is your ideal of partnership today? How do you communicate these innermost relational values?

DAILY HEALTHY SEX ACTS

- Spend a few minutes today writing as a way to explore these issues. Jot down responses to these questions: How often do you communicate with your partner? *How* do you communicate? What percentage of your time feels like enough in a partnership? Do both partners have room for other important relationships?

- Discuss with your significant other what it means for each to do his or her part.

"Something amazing happens when we surrender and just love. We melt into another world, a realm of power already within us. The world changes when we change. The world softens when we soften. The world loves us when we choose to love the world."

— Marianne Williamson

SURRENDER

To surrender is to relinquish our reserve of personal power in order to realize a Higher Power. Historically, our violent culture has viewed the noble act of surrender as weak, cowardly behavior that compromises integrity and abandons one to the whims of an uncaring adversary. This is Higher Power recast as personal threat—a position that's entrenched in a childhood marked by abuse or neglect. Those least able to surrender to the greater good are always the ones who have endured the most psychic or physical trauma, and continually surrender to their own fear.

The notion of a Higher Power may feel threatening to anyone impacted by power games growing up, but it's actually a simple truth. Our homes, streets, schools, society all spring from a power greater than any of us alone. It's ironic that the human species is, in infancy, completely surrendered to caregivers for survival, but in adulthood is unmatched by any other species for denying other powers.

That same willfulness tells us we're the ones who have to make life happen, that we'll only be sexually satisfied if we control the situation. Yet giving up control during sex is crucial to great sex—the same way giving up control in relationships leads to great love. Our lack of trust in community keeps us stuck, but intimacy expands consciousness, and occurs especially within sex because we feel another person's breath, heartbeat, heat. Shared pleasure is a surrendered moment, it's not "me making this happen, look what I did." Sexual intimacy is the result of power *with* others, not *over* others—even in BDSM relationships where the consensual surrender to shared power makes such exploration possible. When we surrender power we get to witness true power. And only such surrender makes it possible to experience the power OF love.

DAILY HEALTHY SEX ACTS

- Today, let go of your agenda. We're much more powerful than we can ever plan. Look beyond your program and find your real potential.

- Does life have you "crying uncle?" What do you need to surrender to move into your potential? Is it a behavior or habit, a personality trait or defense mechanism that no longer serves you?

- You don't have to know how to surrender. Simply attune yourself to the reality around you—and you've surrendered to the moment.

- Surrender your need for control during sex. Let sexual surrender activate your erotic touch.

"When late I attempted your pity to move,
Why seemed you so deaf to my prayers?
Perhaps it was right to dissemble your love.
But–why did you kick me downstairs? "

— J. P. Kemble

13 JUNE

SEPARATION

The path to intimacy is often paved with separations. Whether a partner wants space for a night or to part formally for weeks—or longer—asserting independence sometimes supports personal psychological health, upon which the health of any relationship depends. Most separations originate from an individual's wish to gain better perspective, which implies that at least one partner has been codependent, controlling or compliant. So it's imperative to avoid assumptions or mind-reading during this time.

We also know that autonomy is crucial for genuine love. So why does a partner's desire to assess the relationship without our participation feel so threatening? Perhaps it's because we all experienced the pain of false judgment in childhood, when a beloved parent or teacher wrongly accused us or failed to recognize extenuating circumstances. Even if we've buried that painful memory, we emerged with wounded trust. It's no wonder that separation from a lover would trigger these issues.

Another legitimate reason for separating comes when aspects of the relationship need to change. If separated lovers reunite without change, well, nothing has changed and they'll probably face the same problems again. But how can partners change a relationship when they're apart? One healthy way is for each partner to examine his or her *thoughts about the other* during the separation: Is there much projection, expectation, or assumption? Awareness of these thinking habits will reveal where the healing must come. For if we give up on transforming personal patterns, if we demand to be exactly loved as is, without course-correcting, we've not only given up on the relationship with the partner; we've given up on our inner relationship with our self. In contrast, any time we learn how to discuss our boundaries, needs, and thoughts openly, we create a healthy atmosphere, without which genuine eroticism is unreachable.

DAILY HEALTHY SEX ACTS

- Recall any moments of separation from your current or past partners, whether it involved sleeping on the couch or taking a time out in the love relationship. What feelings came up for you, and how were they resolved?

- Today, reach out to your partner by affirming your mutual autonomy to make personal decisions that advance your individual psychological health. Share your thoughts about your contribution to the relationship, and show support for what's working.

"I wish that people who are conventionally supposed to love each other would say to each other, when they fight, 'Please—a little less love, and a little more common decency.'"

— Kurt Vonnegut, Jr.

DECENCY

Common decency may be the most crucial attribute needed for social harmony, yet it seems less common than ever. Decency implies simply being good citizens and neighbors who modulate our behaviors to conform to agreed-upon standards, including modesty, propriety, and peaceable behavior. Modern life has stretched the bounds of what's considered decent and has opened a dialogue about unchaining us from puritanical judgmentalism. Traditionalists regularly complain that any cultural development deconstructing convention in service of rightful inclusion and self-expression "rips at the very fabric of decency." But even more open-minded persons acknowledge that we now have fewer agreed-upon standards of behavior, that people must make their own decisions about decorum, and that such a self-guided compass may create a society where "anything goes, anytime," which is hardly a recipe for good citizenry or being a good neighbor.

In relationship we must ask ourselves if we're honoring our mutual contracts with our partner. Are we decent in our emotional and sexual treatment of each other? Do we tend fairly to the household, finances, children, and ourselves? Out of insecurity, do we flaunt our sexuality or money indecently to get attention? Do we ignore our children indecently because what we want is more important than their banal demands (like carpooling, help with homework, or attending another sporting event)? Knowing where to draw the line between what's decent and what isn't shows maturity, compassion, stability, and right living. When decency is "common" in our lives, our children learn—and we recall—what is required for a reasonable standard of life, and we leave a legacy of harmony.

DAILY HEALTHY SEX ACTS

- How do you define the word *decency*? Do you adhere to its qualities as you've defined it? If not, why not?

- Is there a difference between your own code of decency and that of the culture at large? If so, how do you feel when you behave according to your own sense of decency?

- Do you practice decent behavior in your love relationship? Does your partner share the same view of decency and hold to those values?

"Some Cupid kills with arrows, some with traps."

— William Shakespeare

MANIPULATION

Manipulation is a word that wears two faces. On one side, it describes the skillful ability to operate a machine, work a craft, or make a lover's body quiver with pleasure. On the other side, it denotes a dark desire to control others through deception, coercion and exploitation. This selfish skill takes over when a lover won't conform to our expectations.

Instead of accepting our partner as he or she is and trusting the wisdom of his or her choices, we decide we won't take "no" for an answer, and begin to pull the marionette strings. Perhaps we use guilt subtly, in order to ensure our lover won't hang out with anyone else over the weekend. Maybe we may make false promises in order to lure the object of our desire into our premeditated schemes. Or we use the threat of anger to make sure nobody disobeys our wishes. Manipulation is the beginning of a cycle of abuse, and it must be nipped in the bud if any real intimacy is to be achieved.

Being on the receiving end of such behavior is often too painful to acknowledge: How could a loved one act with such blatant disregard for integrity, for our self? Yet when it comes to passion, we have all experienced moral weakness. Love brings out the best and the worst in us in equal measures.

Our only path out is to embrace wholehearted honesty. To show a lover that we are vulnerable provides the antidote to our own manipulative instincts. Being transparent, even when we're full of fear, increases our self-esteem, whereas manipulation destroys it. Gradually we learn that there is no separation between ourselves and others: to honor another's autonomy is to honor our own.

DAILY HEALTHY SEX ACTS

- Write an inventory of the different ways people have manipulated you throughout your life. Have you confronted these codependent behaviors? Have you used any of these manipulation strategies yourself?

- Today, notice how you go about getting your way, which usually involves how you spend time and resources with others. Is your process open-hearted, or are you coercing your partner and exploiting weaknesses?

- Reveal your motives. You have every right to explore your needs and to express your truth. Manipulating people instead to get your way is only a sign of your insecurity, because it obstructs the real power of your inner life and your own voice.

"The enemy of a love is never outside, it's not a man or woman, it's what we lack in ourselves."

— Anaïs Nin

BLAME

In our weakest moments or when we're operating out of the worst parts of ourselves, we have a tendency to blame our partners for our every discontent. When we fault someone else out of our own anger, we're doing our best *not* to confront ourselves. To avoid getting pulled in to this process, take a look at your complaints, and then turn them back around on yourself. Take stock of your own shortcomings and start to focus on what you can do differently to change aspects of your relationship that make you unhappy.

If there are issues in your relationship that you need to talk about with your partner, but s/he refuses to talk about them or remains unwilling to accept any responsibility for these difficulties, simply take note of that. Ask yourself, "What part of the problem belongs to me, and what part depends on him/her?" Remember that, ultimately, the relationship game is about *you* making yourself okay.

DAILY HEALTHY SEX ACTS

- Try for one entire day to take responsibility for *all* that happens in your emotional life. If someone cuts you off in traffic, or doesn't say hello, or fails to deliver on a promised action—just for today, explore staying out of the blame game. Instead tell yourself, "I am the only one responsible for my reactions."

- What happens if you just smile despite disappointments, and let everyone off the hook—including you? We're all doing the best we can with what we've got, and perhaps if we all receive love and kindness instead of shaming and guilt-tripping, we might do better.

"Romantic love is mental illness. But it's a pleasurable one. It's a drug. It distorts reality, and that's the point of it. It would be impossible to fall in love with someone that you really saw."

— Fran Lebowitz

17 JUNE

ROMANTIC LOVE

The ideal of romantic love began as a ritualized social construct during the Age of Chivalry, idolizing human feelings at a level previously reserved for religious worship. Chivalric romance—by definition—would never be sexually consummated; it served instead as a culturally acceptable way for those in the favored classes to project incredible distortions, exaggerations, and deep existential yearnings onto another human being. Unfortunately, today's version of romantic love is often just as unrealistic—a heightened feeling state marked by intense expectations and endlessly exploitable by films, books, products and services. In short, modern romantic love exemplifies mental intoxication by a "love drug." We medicate our boredom, alienation and hopelessness by feeding on the neurochemicals that flood our brains whenever we encounter a likely object.

Romantic love is short-lived, however. So we're soon off to find a new source of validation, not realizing that it's normal for relationships to become more mundane and practical over time. Or we may default to enmeshment or avoidance—templates of interaction learned in childhood—becoming controlling, manipulative and jealous as we try desperately to reanimate the initial spark. Feeling abandoned and rejected, we might deeply resent the change we assume originates in our partner, not grasping that the fleeting nature of romantic love makes it unsustainable.

We can integrate the desire for romantic love into healthy relationship, however. We can meet the need for excitement and novelty by nurturing shared hobbies, taking ourselves out on dates, or finding particular symbols, objects or experiences that delight us both. We can come up with our own private language for our specific romance. Creativity and sharing can help close the gap between initial heady romance and mature healthy love.

DAILY HEALTHY SEX ACTS

- Everyone secretly loves to romance and be romanced, but the attendant expectation, enmeshment and letdown sour it for many. What is your attitude toward romance?

- How do you romance your lover? This is different than seduction, stimulation, or coercion. Write down examples of when you've been romantic in the past.

- Romance your partner today. Make a loving gesture of appreciation with the intention of arousing your lover's passion and soul.

"The only reason we don't open our hearts and minds to other people is that they trigger confusion in us that we don't feel brave enough or sane enough to deal with. To the degree that we look clearly and compassionately at ourselves, we feel confident and fearless about looking into someone else's eyes."

— Pema Chödrön

TRIGGERS

We all have emotional triggers. When provoked to fear, rage, or lust, we react, losing our usual awareness and becoming gripped by the object of our attention, scanning for and countering every possible threat. Triggers can be as obvious as a car's honking horn leading to a blind flash of road rage, or as subtle as the turn of someone's head raising past memories and present-day projections. In these reactive states, higher brain functions get hijacked by survival instincts of our lower brain, triggering a fight, flight or freeze response. Triggered emotions can feel negative or positive, so arguments as well as attraction can set the brain and body on high alert and create a rush. But even when pleasant, reactivity undermines autonomy.

People with serious physical or emotional trauma may experience triggers as an unconscious defense mechanism, looking like the "knee-jerk" responses of a "hair-trigger" personality. "If it's hysterical, it's historical" is a fundamental 12-step insight: Emotional triggers usually stem from unprocessed trauma that clouds our perspective, so our memories instead of our good sense inform our present-day interpretations.

The more we're in confrontation with others, the more we get triggered. Triggers destroy creative thinking about options, giving the illusion that there's only one way to respond. If we become aware of what triggers us, we can take responsibility for our reactions rather than blowing up, blaming the world, or throwing caution to the wind and indulging self-gratification. Developing awareness and recognition of emotional triggers can be tricky, because shame often blocks us from recognizing our sensitive spots and makes us dismiss them in an effort to conform. But everyone's inner life is different, and we each have unique triggers. Once we stop denying our personal truth, we start to regulate emotional reactivity.

DAILY HEALTHY SEX ACTS

- What are your emotional triggers? Common ones include interactions with certain people, holidays and anniversaries of significant events. List your triggers and memorize them.

- The next time you're triggered, name it aloud: "Someone honked at me, and I feel triggered." Say it over and over, until you release a deep breath.

- Respond if it's appropriate, but first try to recover emotional sobriety. This is one of the toughest life adjustments to make, so be loving with yourself through the whole process.

"Someday, after mastering the winds, tides and gravity, we shall harness for God the energies of sexual love. Then, for the second time in history, we shall have discovered fire!"

— Teilhard de Chardin

19 JUNE

SEXUAL ENERGY

A lot of people use sex to feel better about their sexual energy—the life-making energy that we give and receive from the world. But we can feel better about our sexual energy all the time; it's not a matter of whether we're having sex or not. In fact, it's hard to define exactly where sex starts and ends. Does it start the moment you take your clothes off? The moment you perform one of your favorite sex acts? At penetration—is that sex? Does it end at climax? We all have a sexual energy within that interacts with our world. To exist is to touch life and to experience the glow of that interaction.

Many people experience deprivation when it comes to healthy sexual energy. Even if people are sexually active, they can still experience deprivation because they're often thinking "I want sex now—the way I want it." Whether or not one is in fact having sex does not determine one's sexual energy, just as if one is an honest person, one is honest even when not actually in the act of telling the truth. One's status as "honest" gets to coast on one's general actions and doesn't need constant proof. There are times where one is graced and can actually tell the truth in words, while at other times one is graced by the knowing that one is truthful. Try to see sex in these terms: There are times when we are graced with relational sex with another, and there are other times where we may feel content and fulfilled knowing that we are healthy sexual people.

DAILY HEALTHY SEX ACTS

- What would it be like to think you just had the greatest sex right now? What is that energy like for you? Carry yourself with the real result of this thought in your body and emotions today.

- Cultivate this feeling of both healthy and abundant sexual energy all the time. Sex comes in many colors, shapes, and sizes and at many levels. Know that—regardless of past or present circumstances—the deepest part of you is a healthy sexual being.

"I have said to you to speak the truth is a painful thing. To be forced to tell lies is much worse."

— Oscar Wilde

DISCLOSURE

Keeping secrets from, or telling lies to, your partner can be an enormous burden that will ultimately get in the way of your sexual intimacy. A guilty conscience is not sexy, but making yourself vulnerable is.

Exposing your true self means facing your shortcomings and any accompanying shame you feel about your actions. Speaking the truth about things that make you feel bad about yourself can be scary or painful, but is essential if you want to build your relationship on honesty. Living a life of secrets and lies doesn't allow love and sexuality to flourish but, instead, suffocates them.

Take time today to think about what an act of courage it would be for you to disclose any secrets and lies you're holding that separate you from your partner. Are you ready to face yourself and stand up as an adult? Keep current with your partner by banishing secrets and lies from your relationship, and experience what it's like to live in honesty every day.

DAILY HEALTHY SEX ACTS

- Today, disclose just one secret you've been keeping from, or one lie you've been telling to, your partner. Let honesty be your goal, and don't expect reciprocity. Do it from your heart because you want to be truly known, and want the other to know you.

- Drop your defenses. Notice how tight your body gets and how you may have a tendency to become self-righteous about what you've done. Ask yourself if your actions are in your best interest or the best interest of your coupleship. If not, tell the truth today.

- Stay present. If you get anxious out of fear, you may find yourself backpedaling. Stop, take a breath, and then be honest. Don't lie to yourself by telling yourself, "What s/he doesn't know won't hurt him/her." Lies in the present hurt more than the action in the past you're covering up.

"The practice of peace and reconciliation is one of the most vital and artistic of human actions."

— Thích Nhất Hạnh

21 JUNE

RECONCILIATION

True reconciliation happens only when the parties involved take responsibility for changing themselves instead of each other. Even if it took two to tango, making up is an inside job. Our capacity to forgive those who have wronged us mirrors our ability to reconcile different aspects of our identity and history. Reconciling past trauma with present healing transforms us so deeply that acceptance and non-reactivity become possible.

Reconciliation requires us to reach beyond judging the other. If we can see every difficulty as touching some aspect of our soul, we will realize that our problem with someone else's behavior may reveal a self-doubt we have yet to resolve. Another advantage of choosing to see all that happens as if from God—however we understand God—is that this lets us stop playing God. Whenever we fixate on our judgment of anyone, we're playing God. Of course, separating from people who hurt us is healthy, but we can learn to open our hearts to them even when we no longer open the door to them.

Our very nature designs us for reconciliation. We integrate constantly fluctuating dualities of happy/unhappy, sure/unsure, healthy/ill. Our genes blend two ancestral lineages, maternal and paternal, into a chain of inherited traits and lived histories that unconsciously inform our lives from before our birth, regardless of the make-up of the family that raises us. Everywhere, we can see the damage done when entire peoples stay in endless conflict. Looking at all these calls to inward and outward reconciliation teaches us the lessons of humility and compromise. Splitting from others based on a false theory of self-preservation rarely results in peace of mind, for we're still at war with our thoughts and nature.

DAILY HEALTHY SEX ACTS

- Make peace in your heart with those you've cut out of your life. Right now, send loving energy and forgiveness to all phantoms of your past, and allow yourself to be forgiven in this act.

- List the positive traits of those you're estranged from: ex-lovers, former friends, difficult relatives. Today, show appreciation of these very people in thought and word—without inviting them back in your life.

- Is it time to reconcile with someone? Talk it over with three trusted friends whose conciliatory actions you admire. Provided there's no harm to anyone—especially yourself—make the call to repair what's broken in your relationship.

"Lovers, of course, are notoriously frantic epistemologists, second only to paranoiacs (and analysts) as readers of signs and wonders."

— Adam Phillips

LOVE MESSAGES

Many people have lost the power of their words to communicate personal and meaningful messages. Education trains us to convey facts—often at the cost of valuing our unique perspectives. When we communicate, are we merely conforming? Do we placate with catchphrases, condemn with sentences, or seduce with a silver tongue? For people robbed of the pleasure of authentic speech, communication must seem like a doctor's appointment as they're poked and prodded for readable symptoms. But the real aim of language is to love another through our words, to connect our hearts to those who listen.

Our world whirs with instant messaging, texting and sexting. Never has a culture exposed us so constantly to so many words and ideas. Sentiments slip through our fingers as we're delighted, provoked, bored, or repelled, but rarely can we hold them long enough to be truly impacted. That's where love comes in as the uniting principle which joins people as well as experiences. We must reclaim our words as powerful tools whose power derives from perfect alignment with our truth. That way, whoever reads or hears our words will hear that truth.

Writing with truth requires self-knowledge, as we can write only from our thoughts and being. Done with awareness, we communicate more than just our words because, in unseen ways, writers and readers are connected. A person might write an entirely appropriate love letter, but any hidden compulsion or anxiety may trigger an unconscious reaction in the reader beyond what's written. What happens to the affection that sped a love letter after love is gone? Do magical words lose their luster, revealing in retrospect only mistaken projections and manipulations? We read people as much as we read paper, which is why a true heart truly shared is worth more than words.

DAILY HEALTHY SEX ACTS

- Believe what people reveal about themselves, on purpose or not. If someone spends all her or his words attacking others at a party or on a dating site, take note.

- What is your communication style? Love addicts often loop, repeat, overshare, and jam unneeded words into a sentence. Predictably, love avoidants play language like hide-and-seek. Today, find your own meaning first, then say what you mean, simply.

- Write a letter you'd love to receive, with all the adoring truths you yearn to hear. Let it inspire you to convey loving thoughts and feelings to others who deserve them.

"One moves from an innocent wholeness, in which the inner world and the outer world are united, to a separation and differentiation between the inner and outer worlds with an accompanying sense of life's duality, and then, hopefully, at last to satori or enlightenment—a conscious reconciliation of the inner and outer once again in harmonious wholeness."

— Robert A. Johnson

23 JUNE

DIFFERENTIATION

Human beings have a paradoxical need to be affiliated with others while simultaneously maintaining a sense of independence. Knowing who we are in a relationship means, in part, that we give a partner the space and respect to do the same. We call this process *differentiation*: the ability not to overreact to our partner's upset and to operate autonomously even though our partner may want things his or her way. The challenge is to hearken to our partner's needs and requests while tolerating the tension inherent in every healthy relationship. We all have to learn to live with the give-and-take that accompanies being with someone and loving that person deeply. Differentiation demands that we know our own patterns and are willing to work with and on them—to combat our self-centeredness or shame rather than to be an emotional victim or perpetrator.

Seeking differentiation in a love relationship reminds us that the first step towards intimacy is intimacy with ourselves. To love *ourselves with another* requires that we grow up, because only then can the real work of intimacy begin. Your partner can love and support you, but you have to change your fundamental patterned responses that don't work. Creating a healthy relationship means you nurture your differentiated self while connecting closely with the one you love to create a healthy interdependency. Choosing this balance gives you space for an honest exploration of sexuality with each other to the depth of your hearts and spirits, because part of differentiation is speaking your truth. Intimacy reveals new ways to know your partner, share your struggles, request your needs be met, stay open to change, and keep dreams alive.

DAILY HEALTHY SEX ACTS

- Inventory your relationship behaviors to determine whether you're taking a more differentiated or a more codependent stance.

- Check your inventory to see if you're on the side of mature love—supporting your partner's potential, which may mean his or her starting a job requiring travel, returning to school, or taking an exciting trip with friends. Perhaps you fall more on the immature side of love—restricting options for you both by being possessive, engaging in power plays, pitying yourself, or controlling the relationship and your partner. Once you locate your love, take it in the direction you both want it to go.

"To set up what you like against what you don't like—this is the disease of the mind."

— Jianzhi Sengcan

PREFERENCE

On a deep level, our souls yearn for connection with all souls. There are people we think we prefer and others we don't, but half the time that's a lie: We tell ourselves the fairy tale of our hatreds out of fear, but we revisit that tale as it suits us. Deep down, we'd love to love and be loved by all.

We also have personal preferences in material objects and acts—clothes, flavors, habits. These partialities result from inborn tendencies or from affirmative encounters we had when expressing preferences brought us positive experiences and taught us to share our truth gently and without fear. But when we let preferences dictate our lives and associations, we disconnect from the vast diversity of life and humanity.

Unfortunately, psychological or spiritual abuse perpetuates trauma through misinformation, distorted thinking and discriminatory beliefs. Such abuse creates a neurotic, reactive mindset that uses personal preferences as an inner armor against intimacy and connectedness. This learned trauma lies at the root of xenophobia, the fear of foreign experiences.

No one's preferences are inherently better than another's, although learning from those we respect can shape our perspectives and our preferences in turn. It's important in all relationships to compare and contrast—to enjoy the similarities and respect the differences. Indeed, true connection is possible only through an open mind that allows others their boundaries and what works for them without jumping to the warped conclusion that *their* choices and values violate *ours*. There is nothing like love to show one the world from another's eyes, and this exposure can transmute negative judgments. Transmutation doesn't necessarily transform the lead of negativity into the gold of positivity, but it can let one see into lead so deeply one sees the gold.

DAILY HEALTHY SEX ACTS

- What do you secretly like about the people you don't like? When you flash on their image, is there any quality that might be attractive in anyone else? Our preferences don't have to be all-or-nothing. Today, look for, and love, the value in the grey areas.

- Take a chance and explore your preferences. If you favor certain flavors, textures or looks and ignore others, try to experiment beyond your bias. Notice what exactly you find disagreeable in anything you dislike. Imagine a treasured lover bringing each new sample to you as a shared experience.

"Much of our highly valued cultural heritage has been acquired at the cost of sexuality."

— Sigmund Freud

25 JUNE

CULTURE

Our culture presents one of the biggest hurdles—ergo, advantages—to self-transformation. When we think of culture, usually we think of the world beyond our individuality: society, media, community. But there is a personal culture, as well: our thinking, feeling, behavior, beliefs and daily routines. Compare your inner values and acts with those of the external culture. How does your interior culture match or relate to the social culture? The truth is, we're entrenched in a larger culture that symbiotically mirrors how we act upon ourselves, making it doubly hard to transform into how we want to be in the world.

The word *culture* originally signified "tilling the land," underscoring its relatedness to cultivation. Like living culture added to milk to make yogurt, human culture grows *us*. We might tell ourselves that we see behind the curtain of our culture, but whenever we engage in activities counter to our true values we are conditioning ourselves culturally. Once you've experienced something, you can't *un*-experience it. Based on this truth, Buddhist precepts of right action include abstaining from toxicity in media and personal communications. Although we might claim the ability to resist the overt conditioning of tabloids, "reality" TV, porn, and similar exploitative cultural expressions, every exposure carries an undeniable effect. So if it doesn't reflect your values, if it doesn't show you the life you truly want to live, then don't participate in that cultural experience.

When it comes to the culture of loving relationships, it's easy to fall into routines that fail to nourish shared hearts. Carefully considering our home culture helps us make little healthy shifts here and there that cumulatively grow our relationship, in the same way that conscientious efforts of individuals sharing their truth gradually shapes the greater culture.

DAILY HEALTHY SEX ACTS

- List the words that describe your personal culture and the culture of your loving relationships. How can you shift your own culture?

- Are you engaging in activities that you admire? If you're putting up with toxic scenarios, try taking a break for one week, and seek healthier cultural experiences instead.

- Cultivate your relationship by gently shifting how you interact with your partner. Today, speak in pleasing tones, move with your most impassioned style through the room. Light the fire of your eroticism by expanding the culture of your love.

> *"I beg you to have patience with everything unresolved in your heart and try to love the questions themselves."*
>
> — Rainer Maria Rilke

QUESTIONING

The process of questioning, like any activity, requires moderation to be healthy. Without moderation, questioning can turn self-devouring, where the question itself becomes a means of avoidance and dissociation. Questions can be manipulative, as if asking enough questions might almost resemble caring. Questions can be used to distract from the real issues, from really being seen and experiencing real intimacy. There are also those questions that are really statements, serving only to confirm fears, doubts, justifications and assumptions. Such leading questions create their own reality.

How you respond to questioning can also reveal various defenses and deep-rooted patterns. This might mirror your schooling or upbringing: Were questions asked and answered in a healthy way? Or did you practice counterfeit ways of asking and answering? If you learned the art of *in*authentic communication very young, and practiced it and honed it in adolescence, should you be surprised that it would seep into every relationship?

The reason we ask and answer any question is to invite truth to come into consciousness—truth that is beyond our grasp at the moment. It is an act of faith, a way of surrendering oneself to the fact that we're human and don't have many answers, but we may receive them. True responses to true questions are more than intellectual information; they bring a shift in consciousness.

DAILY HEALTHY SEX ACTS

- Today, take a moment to consider the right wording for your unresolved questions. Observe whether your questioning stems from and leads to intimacy or distancing.

- The next time you are asked a question, rather than spout statistics or disconnected info, pause and repeat the question out loud, and bring it within yourself to find your own answer.

- Is it possible to let any answers emerge to the important unasked questions from yourself and others in your life?

"The most important trip you may ever take in life is meeting people halfway."

— Henry Boye

27 JUNE

COMPROMISE

The heart of compromise is the willingness of all parties to sacrifice reciprocally and equally for the greater good of a relationship. Reconciling conflicting needs for the sake of unity can't work if just one person does it. A coerced compromise, when one partner deceives or overpowers the other without allowing room for shared truths, usually results in an empty agreement that's soon undermined by unilateral acting out.

Compromise demands open-hearted listening, being present for another's reality, and sharing personal truth without superiority, selfishness or resentment. In that way, true compromise invites light, healing, and relational harmony. We all carry this reconciliation pattern within us—the ability to intuit and value others' needs. But we must actively cultivate the habit of compromise, based on openness to new ways and readiness to question old ones, so we can strengthen our good instincts.

When trivial disagreements blow up into impossible obstacles, there's usually a defense mechanism gone awry. Simple differences of opinion may come to represent a parent's lack of care or the undependability of life itself. Especially where lovers are concerned, small details can become extreme sticking points, while tiffs in a more impersonal context might be resolved easily. Sometimes what we seek to gain through "winning" a conflict is not worth what we're refusing to sacrifice. And true compromise often involves sacrifice: As on the path between Scylla and Charybdis, the monsters of Greek mythology who lie on either side of a narrow strait to devour sailors and ships, either way you go there will be losses. Through life experience we gradually learn to differentiate between the ideals, values and principles which can, and those which cannot, be compromised.

DAILY HEALTHY SEX ACTS

- Are you involved in any conflict at present? Consider the degree to which you perpetuate reactive patterns learned in your past. Find it in your heart to compromise for the greater good. If necessary, write out a "pros and cons" list of what's lost and what's gained by your actions.

- Today, endeavor to practice the art of compromise. Look deeply into others, and perhaps allow every person a little more space for himself or herself, while embracing your own true center. Ask yourself, "What is the greater good for all concerned in this matter?"

"I like to see oral sex and manual sex and intercourse as foreplay for my vibrator sex."

— Betty Dodson

SEX TOYS

What are toys but models of reality that entertain by teaching skills and revealing who we are through how we interact? In youth, toys are like training wheels: They impart developmental skills—especially the skills of relationship. We learn how to share our toys through a challenging and continuing process of valuation, boundary-setting, self-expression, and mutuality.

So as adults, to introduce toys into sexual play can teach intimate sharing with a partner and invite greater sexual realities and experiences. To do so the focus needs to be on the energy, intimacy and feeling between the lovers, not on the thing—the toy. For with the slightest shift in intention, sex becomes materialistic, fetishistic, objectifying, or even exploitative. It's healthy to be skilled in many styles of sexual relating, so objectified sex is not always negative. But it's very easy for a toy to take on depersonalized energy as a focal point—to become, rather than an opportunity for inner exploration, an externalized symbol for the relationship that displaces authentic connection. That would turn a sexual tool with the potential for play and expansion into something dead and mechanistic that blocks true feeling.

For certain physically challenged individuals, sex toys offer otherwise unattainable erotic pleasure. Particularly for those whose physicality prevents certain sexual acts or even access to their own genitalia, sex toys can be a saving grace. Controlling or codependency can resurface when the sex toys come out, providing a structured way to observe—perhaps to change—interaction, and to let trust flow within a partnership. Of course, it's imperative to be in touch with what we're sensing, thinking, experiencing and projecting, and to feel safe enough to voice our truth. Such intimate sharing is a key part of any sex play.

DAILY HEALTHY SEX ACTS

- What's your familiarity with—and personal feelings toward—sex toys? For some, they're the domain of adult bookstores with seedy associations; for others, vibrators, anal beads, nipple clamps and the like provide a valuable extension of healthy sexual play.

- If you'd like to introduce toys into your sex life, start by researching online or discussing it with someone reputable in the know. Some sex toys are more safe and effective than others.

- Share your desires with your lover. Always seek to stay in touch with both of your respective emotional feelings at the center of heightened physical feelings.

"Thoughts lead on to purposes; purposes go forth in action; actions form habits; habits decide character; and character fixes our destiny."

— Tryon Edwards

29 JUNE

CHARACTER

The term *character* encompasses all the distinct emotional, intellectual, and moral qualities that each of us possesses. This unique blend of internal strengths and weaknesses makes us stand out as individuals. Desirable characteristics such as humor, empathy, generosity, and wit seem to emanate effortlessly from a person, and charm others. When we think about "the life of the party," we imagine a charismatic and fascinating individual, an icon of attraction, a larger-than-life character everyone wants to be around.

But when we display undesirable characteristics that alienate friends and family—harshness, selfishness and thoughtlessness—our character is revealed as glaringly defective. Immediately or eventually, people fall out of our lives. A dark cloud of loneliness is cast upon us. When we let the quality of self-centeredness rule, we become enslaved to our characteristic isolation. If we wish to live in community and in intimate relationships, we must scrutinize how our character traits of poor attitude, negative beliefs, or careless actions hurt others.

Making a commitment to change our character is a monumental undertaking that can feel overwhelming. But it helps if we keep in mind that on the flip side of every problematic characteristic lives a positive one. Passion can be the flip side of rage; compassion, the flip side of self-loathing; and vulnerability, the flip side of sarcasm. Begin today to practice new, healthy qualities as a way to open your heart. Then watch yourself unfold into the precious being you were always meant to be with the genuine character you were meant to have.

DAILY HEALTHY SEX ACTS

- Make a list of your positive character traits. Did someone teach you these virtues? If so, who? Or did you have to learn them yourself? Either way, how do you use them now to give back to the world?

- Make a list of your negative characteristics. When did you learn to defend yourself in these ways? How did they protect you? Do they still serve you? Talk to a fair witness about the negative traits you'd like to release. Pay attention to your tendencies, and practice new characteristic ways of being.

> *"A successful marriage requires falling in love*
> *many times, always with the same person."*
>
> — Mignon McLaughlin

MARRIAGE

Marriage is a publicly recognized union between two people. When two persons, no matter their sexual orientation, openly unite their lives out of mutual respect, love, and adoration for each other, they enter into a marriage. Whether or not the coupling is acknowledged by law, joining lives with vows of commitment to share the future defines marriage. Choosing a lover who understands you deeply, whom you cherish as your best friend, and whom you connect with sexually is a good guideline for marriage.

But advertisements and movies depict marriage differently, as a fairy-tale paradise trip—the proverbial "happily ever after" at the end of the story. Clearly, this is not the case. Too many people jump into marriage without recognizing the demands of sustaining a heartfelt connection over an extended time. Deep relationships are messy business. The amount of self-confrontation and emotional maintenance they require can become incredibly uncomfortable. Calm and maturation take place only when we stay willing to examine ourselves, give our partner the benefit of the doubt, and hold the vision we are both trying to achieve. Giving up control and surrendering to the greater good of the relationship is an ongoing, and a tough, practice.

Marriage is an endangered species. Fewer than half the couples that marry make it, and fewer people are marrying today. Consider the purpose of marriage for you. It takes a rare kind of devotion to yourself and to your beloved—truly through thick and thin, in sickness and in health—to endure the rocky road. Marriage can, in fact, be a happily-ever-after story, but only if it's also a story of two partners growing and forming themselves in the space and freedom each gives the other throughout their life together.

DAILY HEALTHY SEX ACTS

- Sit with your beloved, and have each write the other a letter expressing dreams and fears for the relationship. When finished, seal each in an envelope, exchange them, and agree to hold them—unread—until your relationship gets rocky and you both agree to read them.

- If you are considering marriage, write down the most meaningful reasons for which you want this union and why you want it with your beloved.

- If you're already married, revisit your vows. Have you upheld them? Should they be rewritten? With your partner, evaluate the state of your marriage and where you may need to course-correct.

"Do you want to meet the love of your life? Look in the mirror."

— Byron Katie

July

"To identify with others is to see something of yourself in them and to see something of them in yourself—even if the only thing you identify with is the desire to be free from suffering."

— Melanie Joy

1 JULY

IDENTIFICATION

It's been frequently noted that to tell anyone, "I love you," we need first be able to declare the "I." And only when we develop a personal identity may we respond personally to life. So identification with another and with life is an art that starts with identifying ourselves. But there's a risk to thinking of all that happens only in terms of ourselves. Solipsism, the antique philosophy affirming that the universe is knowable solely through the knower's unique perspective, may become unhealthy if it justifies personalizing everything to the point of self-absorption.

Someone with a preoccupied attachment style filters the world through a distorted, unmeasured egocentrism. Such a person sees a partner's independent preferences in décor, friends, or movies as a threat to the relationship. Because enmeshment was the parenting style, autonomy was never encouraged or even permitted.

In fact, most people tend to identify themselves rather narcissistically through narrow personal preferences and patriotic allegiances. It seems bizarrely superficial to build an identity based on our taste for certain flavors, clothes, or locales. Doesn't it make better sense to affirm our true selves by identifying with the universal experiences of others beyond our range of sheltered familiarity? Humanity is not one-size-fits-all, and any definition of ourselves or of others which applies stereotypical experiences broadly must miss the richness of genuine human relatedness.

Participation in support groups or community events lets us identify with people we never thought of as similar. By letting down our guard, we begin to uncover shared humanity. Like checking a side-view mirror, observing those we usually disregard can expose our own psychological blind spots. When we identify with others' trials and tribulations, we often discover unexpected truths for ourselves that might never have been brought to light.

DAILY HEALTHY SEX ACTS

- Today, use "I" statements in all your communications. Focus only on your knowable feelings and thoughts, instead of assuming you know what's true for anyone else.

- Stop the judgments. They only serve to isolate you. Identify with everyone you encounter on their terms, not your interpretations of them, by listening carefully to their words as if each moment held special meaning.

> *"Your heart and my heart are very, very old friends."*
>
> — Hāfez

FAMILIARITY

We've all heard that "familiarity breeds contempt," implying that deep acquaintance leads to boredom and disrespect. This saying is often cited as an excuse for a wandering eye. But when familiarizing ourselves with a person engenders disregard, you can bet it's not intimacy that's the cause. On the contrary, disenchantment in a longstanding relationship results either when we encounter an entirely *un*familiar, inassimilable aspect of the person, or when we relapse to very familiar patterns that have always limited our ability to relate.

To be completely honest, what many of us fear is not our familiarity with someone else, but *the other party's familiarity with us*. We're afraid they'll discover or guess an inexplicable scenario in our history or a secret fantasy of ours which will make them reject us. How can we make our particular truths understandable, so they're as comprehensible to them as to us? Our own acquaintance with how we think and feel—with our internal process—will always sustain our capacity for true familiarity with others.

We develop this capacity for familiarity with humankind through hands-on experience—learning others' stories through direct interaction or even through literature and movies. Similarly, in sexual relationships our touch finds familiar places and responses that create a soothing recognition. But if we do nothing to broaden our inner awareness, it's easy to invite familiar early programming, which may include an unhealthy taste for conflict and discomfort, into a new and promising relationship. To familiarize ourselves consciously with our past conditioning lets us engage in new ways of sharing through mental, emotional and sexual exploration. The healthy novelty such sharing continuously creates may give our age a new adage: "Genuine familiarity breeds content."

DAILY HEALTHY SEX ACTS

- Today, recognize the enjoyable familiarity you feel for everyone in your life. Summon the warm glow of comfortable connectedness, and share it with new, unfamiliar faces.

- When you sense conflict or discomfort, familiarize yourself with your own internal programming. To begin, simply internally narrate what's happening as it's happening: "I'm triggered," "I'm trying to hide a mistake," "I'm feeling this way towards this person."

"We lay there without moving. But under us all moved, and moved us, gently, up and down, and from side to side."

— Samuel Beckett

3 JULY

MOVEMENT

Sex is like a dance whose movements follow physical laws of speed, force, weight, and space but meld together to create a seemingly indefinable experience. If we analyze these movements, we find that their qualities can be expressed on a polarized scale, such as fast/slow, light/heavy, strong/soft. Proportions of these qualities may fluctuate between lovers given changing moods, while other qualities remain fixed to the personality, physicality and history of each person. But all movement, at its core, is vibration, whether emotional, mental, psychological or spiritual.

How many times have you experienced incompatibility in movement styles with lovers? We feel and express our feelings in different ways due to the different measuring scales taught by our life experiences. To help synchronize your sexual movements, try this: Rather than passing judgment on incompatibilities, such as, "You're too rough/fragile, robotic/clingy, or passive/intense," try to express literally what you are feeling. This can be as simple as sharing, "I am feeling this moment as gentle," or, "There is pressure on this part of my body." Simply narrating the play-by-play of what's happening, when it's happening, and how it's happening will help partners get on the same page and create a springboard for more attuned sexual experimentation and experience.

DAILY HEALTHY SEX ACTS

- How do you move through the day? Be aware of your physical expression today. Do you grace and glide, slump and stumble, jitter and bug?

- How does your physicality inform your sexuality? Imagine your ideal dance of sexual expression, and try to bring the energy of that movement to your daily routine. Let yourself move and be moved by life!

"She liked that word: we. It sounded warm and open, like a hug."

— Lauren Oliver

HUGGING

Hugs are comfort and connection in action. When we hold another in our arms we express emotion through our bodies instead of with words, whose power to convey feelings often falls short. Holding our lover or our loved ones tight can feel as though we want to draw their essence right into our very being. The desire to hold another tight—sometimes too tight— is a natural outpouring of love. In fact, young children have been known to squeeze small pets to death because they love them so much! We've all had the experience of wanting to squeeze or, metaphorically, "eat up" a deliciously cute baby, puppy, or kitten. Something about the young and vulnerable makes our system come alive in a way that has us both wanting to protect and consume them.

The body has a wisdom and language all its own. Hugging is a way to shift our internal state when we're feeling out of sorts, and the best person to help us do that is our beloved. Notice the synchrony of your breath, heartbeats, and the natural rise and fall of your bodies as you hold a long hug together. When stressed, your best regulator is your partner. Another benefit of hugging is that it can presage sexual engagement. A long, languid hug in the morning when you breathe together can create high arousal that either leads you to sex in the moment or builds excitement for later. Either way, allow for ease and let the awareness of time melt away as you fold into your lover's body. If you're watching the clock, you're out of the present moment and your energy will diminish, as will your partner's. Stay relaxed; let your two-ness meld into oneness and hug until you're both ready to let go.

DAILY HEALTHY SEX ACTS

- Practice hugging every morning upon waking. Notice the warmth and softness of your partner's body.

- Hug at the end of every day after your lover comes home. Notice the length of time you hug. A minute-long hug is a long hug!

- Tolerate your anxiety around hugging. Notice whether you're standing on your own two feet or whether you're leaning on your partner. Track the tension in your body and hold the hug until you feel yourself and your partner relax.

> *"Celibacy goes deeper than the flesh."*
> — F. Scott Fitzgerald

5 JULY

CELIBACY

Swearing off certain foods like sugar or flour may sharpen your awareness of how much you crave them and under what circumstances. In the same way, a palate-cleanser of conscious celibacy can be an equally mindful practice, even if done for only a month, or two, or three. For however long it's kept, celibacy can be an act of reclaiming one's sexuality which, for most people, developed in stages of life or situations that were stressful.

Probably your sexuality evolved without much mentorship or helpful intervention—unlike, say, your eating habits. Most people had constant supervision of their eating habits as children. And just as well, since at the crucial age where peer pressure is so strong, most teenagers might have elected a diet of junk food—pure instant gratification with little redeeming health benefits. Similarly, in the absence of intelligent sexual guidance, instant gratification might characterize most people's current sexual diet.

A period of sexual fasting can lead to surprising realizations: about how much of one's sexual activity is using other people to make oneself feel better right now; and about how feeling better right now really means not feeling stressed out by facing one's reality. Sex, especially if it's become compulsive, can be about using pleasurable feelings to hide from real feelings. This disconnection from genuine emotions may result in a barely noticeable but growing neediness for ever more pleasurable feelings. So for some people, celibacy might even be a long-term way to practice a certain inner vision of true connectedness—the idea of closing one's eyes to really see.

DAILY HEALTHY SEX ACTS

- Consider taking a one-month vow of celibacy—no sex, no porn, no masturbation. How would this impact your life? Would this even be possible for you, and if not, why not?

- Write out a pros & cons list. What are the pros for abstaining from sexual activity for a month, and what are the cons?

> *"There is need of variety in sex, but not in love."*
>
> — Theodore Reik

If you've ever been in a long-term relationship, invariably there came a time when the sex began to seem stale. You wondered how you grew so dissatisfied and disconnected and you may have blamed your boredom on your partner. Perhaps you felt stuck in your job, or the family you worked so hard to raise suddenly felt more like a source of chores than a blessing. At this point, it's important to stop playing the blame game. A sense of variety, whether sexual, occupational or social, comes from embracing a state of mental and spiritual renewal. Truthfully, we can experience novelty in each fresh second. But when lack of freshness dampens our whole disposition, it springs from our inability to give expression to unpredictable and unprecedented internal states of genuine feeling, emotion and perception.

Once you take responsibility for your own happiness and excitement, you can find a thousand ways to spice up your sex life. Variety doesn't just mean introducing whips or whipped cream to your foreplay. Certainly there's a lot of pulp advice about reigniting your love life. But we don't always have to vary sexual positions, props, or places. In fact, such theatrics only provide short-term solutions at best. To invite true novelty, each of us can experiment to vary our emotional perceptions and responses. Try to find one thing about your partner that you never knew before. You may think you need to join a threesome, when just starting a genuine conversation and learning something new can satisfy a deep-seated need for discovery and adventure. Let real life in, let people have a lasting impact on you. Relationships don't exist in a vacuum. If we want our sex lives to be spontaneous, sensual, varied and exciting, we need to develop these qualities on our own.

 DAILY HEALTHY SEX ACTS

- Today, engage your senses. Hear the beauty of all voices, and let their vibrations arouse your feelings. Imagine sounds, scents, and sights sweetly caressing your nervous system, sparking your ability to appreciate variety.

- If you have conversations in your head with your lover or others, flip the script! Defy your own expectations. Let people lovingly surprise you.

- Introduce a new emotion into your love-making. Focus on your awe, relief, sympathy, or joy for your partner. All these emotional states are real and within you. Give your inner world healthy expression—and hold on for the sensory ride!

"Your sacred space is where you can find yourself over and over again."

— Joseph Campbell

7 JULY

SACRED SPACE

For many in our society, televisions or computers have replaced spiritual shrines. People create sacred space in their environments for hobbies and habits, while beloved treasures like healthy love and sex must often clamor for any attention. Where is the special location set aside for exploring feelings? The vision-for-life room? The arrangement of our homes literally makes room for similar arrangement in our lives. Think of the place of honor that alcoholics set aside for glassware and mini-bars. Similarly, sex addicts often create a sacred space in their homes for porn and sexual materials at the expense of sacred space for entertaining friends and family. Do you grant your truest ideals sacred space around them, and if not, why not?

What is the nature of your sacred space in this exact moment as you read these words? How can you create a greater circle around yourself to preserve your own sacred space throughout the day? While all space may become sanctified, most of us know that we do not always live at our full potential for consciousness. So a self-determined sacred space can work like a mirror to reflect and magnify our fledgling attempts at mindfulness. The more defined our sacred space in time and place—the more charged with holiness—the more successful our attempts to embody our healthiest values.

DAILY HEALTHY SEX ACTS

- Notice your environment. Where do you spend your time? What can you do to preserve and consecrate your everyday space so it reflects your highest personal values?

- The atmosphere of a bedroom is a shared sacred space designed by the preferences of both partners. Just as you have made your relationship reflect the shared value of remaining in relation to each other, how can you transform your space together to celebrate your respective values?

- If your physical space is limited, consider temporary transformations for a room to use for meditation or lovemaking. Drape a beautiful piece of cloth over your television set or change your bedspread. Revitalize the ordinary by adding flowers, a simple candle, or covering lamps with colorful pieces of fabric for impromptu mood lighting. Let your imagination run wild.

"Love must be strong enough to find certainty within itself.
It then ceases to be moved and becomes the mover."

— Herman Hesse

There's something sexy about people who possess strength and with whom we can be strong in turn— who can bear our strength. So often we mete out just enough strength to handle the immediate situation, sensing but never achieving the true range of our power. Brute strength on the battlefield or in sports certainly thrills, but exercising the muscles of relational skills provides the subtler joy of speaking in our true voice with the gentle strength of our soul. For it takes great fortitude to communicate honestly, soberly, deeply about sexual needs, since many cultures malign and ridicule individual truth.

Striving to become our best selves as we face each day requires strength—a daily surrender, and healing from each night's kiss of oblivion. Relationship— facing this imperfect, meaningful life with another—challenges us constantly to let go of selfish needs and expectations. For the more we grasp, the less we gain. Our might lies not in conquering the world but in conquering ourselves.

In this society where sexual messages are so warped and the meaning of love is so lost, we need to be peaceful warriors championing relational and sexual health. It takes great force to do so, since it depends on a knowledge of our self apart from the powerful group mindset. And it takes strength to balance ourselves—not to reinforce our ego unduly but to operate in the spirit of our vision and to be causal in our choices. Strength means sticking to our true self, and may be measured by how much we appreciate every distinctive true quality of our beloved. When this differentiation leads to real individuation, we reach our purest desire—to love all we experience fearlessly and with strength.

 DAILY HEALTHY SEX ACTS

- Are you strong in yourself? List your unwavering strengths, and realize how they originated.

- Some people confuse strength with rigidity or false pride. Self-perceptions of personal power can be the self-deceptive result of early established defenses. True strength connects our true self to life. Today, ask several people to share what they consider your strengths to be. Let their responses guide how you exercise personal power this week.

- What next right step do you need to take for self-actualization? Be strong, and let the polished stone of your past efforts speak through you as you risk taking this step.

"Once, I got naked and danced around your bedroom, awkward and safe. You did the same. We held each other without hesitation and flailed lovely. This was vulnerability foreplay."

— Miles Walser

9 JULY

FOREPLAY

Foreplay is the precursor to the play of sex. Overlooking or rushing it from anxiety about its intimacy can make a couple's sex life fall flat. Foreplay may include all five senses, starting with the most obvious sense of sight. It's true that the eyes are the windows of the soul: Gazing into one another's eyes deepens and enhances your soulful connection. As you make eye contact with your partner, talk about what stimulates you visually—a color, a piece of clothing, or the way s/he moves toward you. Find out what's visually arousing to you both so you can incorporate these simple additions into your foreplay.

One of the most powerful aphrodisiacs is the sounds our lover makes during sex. Pleasurable moans and groans heighten the sexual experience. When we surrender to the moment, these resonant tones beckon harmony, signaling sexual pleasure to us and letting us know that we are in concert. Other essential parts of foreplay are taste and smell. Whether kissing and licking or enjoying sensual foods, the mouth is an integral player in foreplay. Likewise, the natural odor of your partner can be very arousing, as can scents you pick and choose together. Body oils, perfumes and colognes and the smell of the heat between you can be a source of high arousal.

Finally, touch is a major element of erotica. The feel of our lover's hand, the sensation of our bodies touching, caressing, or brushing against one another sends a clear message that we're wanted. Take time to slow your pace and concentrate on touching and being touched. Curb your eagerness to move on to the next thing and instead use a beginner's mind, so that you're giving and receiving with presence and gratitude.

DAILY HEALTHY SEX ACTS

- What aspects of foreplay do you like the most? Which do you like the least?

- If you were to design the perfect prelude to intercourse, what would it look, smell, feel and taste like? How long would it take? What elements would it include?

- Design the ideal foreplay scenario with your lover, and commit to playing it out.

> *"Perversity is the human thirst for self-torture."*
>
> — Edgar Allan Poe

PERVERSITY

The word *perverse* stems from the Latin phrase "facing the wrong way." It describes unconventional or even deviant behaviors or outlooks. Sometimes it refers to acts that are deeply corrupt and inappropriate, and can also be thought of as a disruption of balance.

For those seeking the addictive thrill of rule-breaking, perversity can feel like liberation—a chance to articulate a dark side unacknowledged by mainstream society. And this need not always be a bad thing. For instance, expressing perversity in artistic mediums creates a channel for collective trauma or curiosity to reach cathartic, healing communication. But it's crucial to differentiate between what's taboo due to social inhibition and what's taboo because it causes real harm to others. For instance, in the past homosexuality was labeled a perversion like bestiality and pedophilia. But unlike those, homosexuality presumes mature consent. Polygamy may seem like another wrongfully tagged perversion worth defending as, on the surface, no one appears to be coerced. But within a culture of ingrained gender inequality, polygamy violates human rights. Judgments about perversity therefore cannot be pronounced outside the societal context. They are irrevocably linked to the mores of the era and location, and change as ideas evolve.

If we become gripped by obsession or break our own codes of healthy conduct, we become perversions of our true selves. Without a stable psychological core, healthy sexual experimentation can mushroom into debilitating, time-consuming fixations and fetishes that, like drug addiction, bring more pain than pleasure. On the flip side, justice becomes perverted when those who deviate from society's behavioral standards are cruelly and unusually punished. We must navigate the extremes of perversity and sanctimony, for regardless of traditional societal judgments, it's now up to each of us individually to learn to face the right way.

DAILY HEALTHY SEX ACTS

- Have you ever indulged a fantasy or performed an act you consider perverse? If so, recall the surrounding details: What were you feeling? What drove the behavior? How was this situation resolved?

- Do you have secrets you will take to the grave? Recall every perversion you're too ashamed to share. Know you're not alone: Phrases like "take to the grave" exist because many feel this way. Summon unconditional love for damaged parts of you which haven't been integrated.

- If it feels safe, address any unhealthy perversion in your life, whether past or present. What would turn it in the right direction?

"When I say 'I will be true to you' I am drawing
a quiet space beyond the reach of other desires."
— Jeanette Winterson

11 JULY

FIDELITY

Often we think of fidelity as being true to another person, locating the object of our commitment outside our self. But perhaps the true meaning of fidelity is a devotion *to* our self. Consider that being faithful to a person, cause, or belief means to commit to one's own integrity and values. Honoring one's own principles is in fact the only way to remain loyal to another, for when we break our vows to someone, we disavow ourselves. As in musical recording, where fidelity is the pristine replication of the original, being true to another means upholding our original intention. But our ideas about fidelity may have been tarnished by the role models we grew up with, who may have conveyed a poor representation of real fidelity.

Constancy in a relationship requires discipline. If there's an agreement to stay faithful from the beginning, discipline will sustain us over life's rocky crags—but only if fidelity remains our guiding principle. All living relationships require fidelity. Think about the steadfast commitment it takes just to keep a simple houseplant alive—one must water it regularly to sustain its bloom. Likewise, getting a new pet, beginning a new acquaintance, nourishing an old friendship, or committing to a love relationship all require reliable efforts to thrive and grow.

Being faithful to all living beings we've made commitments to sets an example for the younger people in our lives, modeling what genuine fidelity looks like. Without good role models we can't see all of the components that go into fidelity—all the sacrifices we make for the greater benefits of staying true to ourselves. Fidelity is a costly, but valuable, virtue that demands we give up some things in order to have some things worth much more: integrity with others and our self.

DAILY HEALTHY SEX ACTS

- Do you practice fidelity in all your relationships?

- Have you been unfaithful to the commitments you've made? Today, make a list of how you can rectify what is out of alignment with your self, and take action on each item, one by one.

- Is there someone in your life who needs your help? If so, make a gesture today to be faithful to that relationship.

"I thought when love for you died, I should die.
It's dead. Alone, most strangely, I live on."

— Rupert Brooke

No one knows the hurt of heartbreak until they've experienced it. The gnashing pain of saying "good-bye" to a lover—when we know the relationship isn't working, when we have to leave in order to grow into our potential, when we've been so terribly betrayed that we can't hold a vision for healing, or when someone dies—is beyond comprehension until we live through it. Loss is so devastating that many people hold onto pain, resentment, or anger as a perverse way to stay in relationship with the one we've said "good-bye" to. Sometimes it even feels righteous to stay in anger, hurt, or upset—almost as though we can right the wrong if we dig in our heels. Yet over time, this stance leaves us embittered and stuck, hanging on for dear life so as not to feel the awful feelings of sorrow. Worse, that mental clinging precludes our moving on.

Grief, on the other hand, is an essential step in our progress forward. Grieving requires the ego and the recriminations to get out of the way so that we can become vulnerable and fully feel the loss of what once was. Without the full-bodied sensation of our grief and loss, we can never get past them. Letting go and grieving is a cleansing and healing process for all: we tear open our emotional prison and energetically release ourselves, and our former beloved, to move on.

DAILY HEALTHY SEX ACTS

- If you're holding on to an old wound and haven't let yourself feel the loss, take time today to write about what keeps you invested.

- Free yourself for a good cry over your primary losses.

- Have a small ceremony to commemorate the anniversary of the loss of a loved one, whether it was a relational loss or literal loss. Light a candle in his or her name to free them, throw a rock into the ocean to symbolize an aspect of the relationship that needs to be let go, or plant some flowers so that your grief can blossom into something new.

"Love taught him shame, and shame with love
at strife soon taught the sweet civilities of life."

— John Dryden

13 JULY

SHAME

Shame is a communicable dis-ease passed down through generations. The physiological signs of shame seem universal across cultures with varying practices and beliefs: lowered head, downcast eyes, tingling red face. Social shaming is employed to ensure expected behaviors, and healthy shame is necessary to keep society intact because we must know when we are behaving in shameless ways. However, shame can also be a form of emotional abuse. It's deeply embedded in the human nervous system—we feel it in our gut—and it is one of the earliest emotions that children display. The word *shame* probably derives from a root word meaning "to cover," and when we feel we've done wrong or even just look foolish, we want to run for cover!

So there is healthy, socially shared shame and toxic or "carried" private shame. Healthy shame clearly reveals the errors of wrongdoing and guides us to self-correct. For minor infractions, we can gently laugh, and playfully remedy the situation—such as letting someone off the elevator before we rush on.

But carried shame is self-punishing and has no basis in our actions. It often uses negative self-talk such as, "I am the worst!" This wholly learned behavior results from shame-inducing parents, teachers, bullies, and even fictional characters who informed our worldview. Toxic shame is the natural result of such programming, and therefore we do not have to be ashamed of this shame, because *it's not ours*. The truth is you have a reason for existing—your own natural grace. The sooner you look beyond the curtain of this shame, the sooner you will see what attracts you to move towards life in fulfillment of your true purpose.

DAILY HEALTHY SEX ACTS

- Healthy shame can include shame over living in a civilization built on war, slavery, and other injustices. It can also include feeling out of one's integrity through cheating or stealing. Can you feel empathic shame, and can our shared shame guide you to right action, such as making amends or reparation?

- Which is more prominent in your thoughts, the shame of not being enough or the shame of being at all? Feel your shame to free your shame. Recovery from sexual/romantic dysfunction or addiction means fulfilling your true purpose, not conforming to the status quo. You have a right to be, you were meant to be, so today let yourself simply exist without apology or agenda.

> *"The only normal people are the ones you don't know very well."*
>
> — Alfred Adler

While few of us want to be considered abnormal, being *normal* suggests that we follow a predictable, entrenched pattern. You might have the same morning routine, the same way of thinking about certain subjects, and the same type of response when you're triggered, all of which have become the *norm* for you. Whenever one of these patterns gets disrupted, it feels, well, abnormal. Even when people talk about negative habits they'd like to replace, they're really talking about changing their normal—meaning their invariable pattern. To seek self-improvement, you must be ready to step outside your norm.

We know from experience how deeply ingrained these repetitive patterns are, and the profound effort that any psychological makeover requires. The first step to replacing your current version of normalcy always begins with clear intention backed by awareness. Of course, there are cultural norms beyond the capacity of any single individual to change. The tool of *mind mapping,* meaning holding the other in mind, will deepen your understanding of any social behavior that might appear abnormal, including the sometimes incomprehensible behavior of friends and lovers. How were they raised? What are their immediate needs? Viewed in the context of their life experiences, you might come to tolerate and/or appreciate new versions of normality.

DAILY HEALTHY SEX ACTS

- Try new things, or try things a new way today

- Walk backwards when you enter and exit your bedroom. Sleep on the other side of the bed.

- Attempt your habitual activities in different areas. Rearrange the furniture and the photos. Notice the feelings that come up for you and your ability to handle novelty.

- Now, ask what you really want to create in your life. STOP stopping yourself.

"There is hardly anyone whose sexual life, if it were broadcast, would not fill the world at large with surprise and horror."

— William Somerset Maugham

15 JULY

SEXUAL STIGMA

A *stigma* is a mark of disgrace. Its Latin plural, *stigmata*, refers to Christ's crucifixion wounds, suggesting that there may be a spiritual value to being disgraced by society.

Two problems attend any psychobiological issue, particularly sexual dysfunction: the inherent problem, and the problem about the problem—the stigma. What a tragic irony that the mere shame of having a problem can prevent its solution! *Internalized* stigmas about arousal issues, rapid ejaculation, sex addiction, jealousy, negative body image or other difficulties can compound the inherent problem by keeping the sufferer from relating them to a partner. Stigmas not only block our ability to enjoy sex, they block our ability to function freely in the world.

There are personal wounds and there are societal wounds. Sexuality and sexual activity have always been prime targets of stigmatization. Cultures the world over—even ours—intimidate and persecute vilified segments of the population. Great strides have been made healing social stigmas surrounding homosexuality, divorce, mixed-race couples and unwed mothers. But damage has been done. And not just to denigrated individuals, but to the society that has traumatized them. Social acceptance of a previously stigmatized class is not the same as reparation. It's said that in the repair stage, a verbally-abused child needs to hear any positive statement of encouragement ten times a day in order to heal each injury. Similarly, to counter the debilitation caused by social and internal stigmas, we need to show ten times the love and empathy we think it will take—just to begin.

DAILY HEALTHY SEX ACTS

- Reflect on how sexual and social stigmas touch your personal life. What direct or indirect wounds do you bear as a result of such judgment? Take one positive step to liberate your sexual and psychological health from undeserved stigma.

- How are you triggered by sexual stigmas? If specific sexual phrases, ideas or images ever paralyze you, investigate the root cause. Recall all previous experiences of your sexual paralysis, until you locate the source of your stigmatized feelings.

- Envision a world without prejudice and repression, where the only message we've all ever received is to love and accept one another. Show ten times as much love and compassion to others today.

> *"When two people decide to get a divorce, it isn't a sign that they 'don't understand' one another, but a sign that they have, at last, begun to."*

> — Helen Rowland

The word *divorce* can summon up a world of pain. It represents the dissolution of a cherished dream most of us nurture: the longing for endless love. Having sworn an oath of eternal loyalty, it can truly feel like death to concede that a marriage has failed. Often there is much blame, resentment and grief, and these unwieldy emotions can seem insurmountable. We are filled with self-doubt and hopelessness. How did things come to this? What could we have done differently? Are people meant to be monogamous for life, or is that a fantasy that doesn't work in practice? These misgivings keep us up at night. Even if the divorce is not our own, it threatens our faith in society's established institutions and the possibility of long-term romantic fulfillment. In some circles, there is stigma and shame attached to ending a marriage. In others there is indifference and cynicism. Whatever the situation, divorce is a significant life event and must be worked through.

Is there a healthy way to navigate this loss? Absolutely! First, remember that we are all doing the very best we can at any given point. We're all only human. So to forgive ourselves and others unconditionally for mistakes is the most liberating, life-affirming action we can take. Then, know that divorce may end one type of relationship, but it can also mark new beginnings—the beginning of independence, friendship, or a renewed passion for a forgotten career or craft. It may signal a new adventure in sexual expression that's free from expectations, routine and ceremony. Each of us has the right to take steps to improve our life, and while divorce can challenge us, it may also empower us. To let life unfold without judgment is a grand exercise in embracing the present moment.

DAILY HEALTHY SEX ACTS

- Reflect on how divorce has impacted your life. What feelings come up for you, and what are the feelings beneath those feelings?

- Do you have any judgments about divorce? Make two lists: one to describe people who are married, the other to describe people who are divorced. Do these lists describe the same kind of people to you, or not? If not, why not?

- Today, summon love and forgiveness for everyone whose lives are touched by divorce. Show empathy where needed. Affirm people's power to make decisions that are right for them, and their ability to heal.

> *"Sex is full of lies. The body tries to tell the truth. But, it's usually too battered with rules to be heard, and bound with pretenses so it can hardly move. We cripple ourselves with lies."*
>
> — Jim Morrison

17 JULY

PRETENSION

Almost every movie ever made, including pornography, depicts love-making in a pretentious manner. Cue the music, the close-ups, the frozen poses of unadulterated passion. There are many reasons why we might want to be pretentious—to pretend—during sex. We all want the most flattering lighting and angles for our bodies to look good; we shift to hide a physical flaw or an awkward feeling. Such pretense is understandable. But all those false moves stifle subjective, autonomous experience. Pretension is always an act of objectification requiring conformity to some programmed ideal; intimacy requires only connection.

"Do you want to save your face or save your ass?" is a common saying in recovery. To save our butts requires honesty and mindfulness in everything we do. Saving face is only a short-term solution at best, and often leads to greater shame down the road. Simulating orgasms or feigning romantic interest are ways of saving face by circumventing truthful confrontation, yet the emotional disconnection these avoidance tactics provoke will surface in one way or another. When we accept and communicate our true thoughts and feelings as we experience them, we begin to release shame about them and to understand how these inner states enter our consciousness. But if we recognize only the content that's socially acceptable, while denying recurring mental and emotional patterns, we're pretending *to ourselves*. We all know that hypnotic, trance-like state of dissociation from reality, and we know we thrive only when we're in touch with our most authentic individuality. Covering up reality with posturing, however seemingly innocuous, creates psychological disturbances that over time will pull the rug of our pretensions out from under us. For life needs us to show up in our lives, to be present, vulnerable and real for ourselves and for others.

DAILY HEALTHY SEX ACTS

- Where do you put on an act? Ask yourself what you're trying to hide through pretension. Intimacy requires revealing the truth about who you are and how you experience life. Today, disclose vulnerabilities to others by shining the light on your reality or simply acknowledging the ongoing process of your becoming self-aware.

- For those who habitually enmesh, vent, attack, or who dwell on negativity, it can actually be healthy to communicate with a lighter touch, with diplomacy. Can you draw the line between brutal honesty and sugarcoating to the point of pretension?

"Little drops of water, little grains of sand,
Make the mighty ocean and the pleasant land.
Thus the little minutes, humble though they be,
Make the mighty ages of eternity."

— Julia Abigail Fletcher Carney

TIME

When we feel that something's going to happen, we often say that the seed has been planted. This horticultural metaphor fits almost every moment, because seeds need to develop in their own time and with the right conditions. But people experience both objective, quantitative time and subjective, qualitative time, and often it seems that never the twain shall meet.

We all know people who profess—or have done so ourselves—that there's never enough time to return phone calls, attend events, meditate, develop intimacy. But we also know there's plenty of actual minutes and hours. It's qualitative, psychological time that taxes our attention. Without having learned to process feelings and events fully, our days get crowded with instant replays and future projections. Whatever time we do have becomes overwhelmed by our psychological content. The time it takes a person to travel from point A to point B is easily scheduled. But the journey from point A to point B in our minds is harder to measure.

The more we try to force time, the more of an egotistical obstacle we create and the more psychological time everything ultimately takes. This couldn't be truer in relationships, which take time to blossom. Nothing speeds the process of building trust and true caring, except to show up with love and willingness... one day at a time. And when we engage in sexual activity, taking time to arouse ourselves and our partner fully makes the difference between getting each other off or turning each other on. When sex is more of a masturbatory act, synchronicity doesn't matter. But if sex is a union, if the principle erotic goal includes love—which is unity—it becomes crucial that both parties are present, and devote a certain measure of psychological time.

DAILY HEALTHY SEX ACTS

- Do you make time for what's important to you? Often people wait until they finally "feel ready," then find that their priorities have shifted. Don't let time waste you. Engage in what engages you.

- The experience of time depends on our perception. Is there a difference whether you have minutes to perform a task, or eternity? Breathe deeply to release today's pressures, and take your precious time, regardless of the time it takes.

- Do you need to speed up or slow down in your love life? Remember, the objective of a relationship is to relate, so synchronize your timing for connection.

"Sexiness wears thin after a while and beauty fades, but to be married to a man who makes you laugh every day, ah, now that's a real treat."

— Joanne Woodward

19 JULY

LAUGHTER

Laughter is a spontaneous, full-bodied expression of amusement that transports us into a state of joy. The body heaves in mirth, releasing sounds and movements that universally communicate our attunement with the entertainment. Whether induced by a lover, comedic movie, good friend, or ironic observation, laughter activates our sense of well-being. Laughter and play are the best medicine for the doldrums, so if you can't remember your last hearty belly laugh, you may be depriving yourself of an essential source of vitality.

When we think about sex we rarely think about evoking play states accompanied with laughter. Sex is usually portrayed as ravenous, serious, or carnal but hardly ever as fun or funny. Yet when you allow your soul's full expression in sex without self-consciousness, you may find yourself goofing around in ways that get you and your partner laughing. This playing requires a secure sense of self so that a partner's levity doesn't feel condescending or uncaring. Insecure couples have difficulty expanding their ideas about what mood sex should be in. Such restriction makes hilarity off-limits because it impinges on their ideas of attractiveness and what sex is supposed to look like.

When children dive into play states they engage in outrageous ways of being by imitating creatures, evoking imaginary characters, or pretending they're superheroes—the sky's the limit. Adults remain more bound by social constraints and ideals of sex appeal, and tie their self-esteem to their ideas of what "sexy" looks like. In order to have fun during sex—to have fun sex—we have to risk letting go of social roles and moving into a genuine sexual play state with our mates. If your play is consensual and you can suspend your self-judgment, the sky can be the limit for you, too—plus you'll have some laughs.

DAILY HEALTHY SEX ACTS

- With a friend, lover, or social group, agree to laugh out loud even when you don't feel like it. Start laughing and engage your body by stamping your feet and shaking your arms. Don't stop until it has become infectious and everyone is having a good belly laugh. Repeat as needed!

- Start your next sexual encounter with a consensual play state—light tickling or having a pillow fight can move energy and invite fun. Better yet, come up with your own ideas of what makes you feel light-hearted and connected to your partner.

> "A chicken and an egg are lying in bed. The chicken is smoking a cigarette with a satisfied smile on its face and the egg is frowning and looking put out. The egg mutters to no one in particular, 'I guess we answered that question.'"

> — Author unknown

RAPID & DELAYED ORGASM

Rapid orgasm in men, more commonly called premature ejaculation, is usually born of anxiety. Its counterpart in women is delayed orgasm. Many men feel pressured to "get it up" at a moment's notice and perform on cue, as if all men should be aroused and stimulated the exact same way. Women, likewise, can feel pressure to orgasm even when they're not aroused or don't feel the need to orgasm in order to enjoy sexual pleasure. Anxiety during sex serves to dampen stimulation, making men and women alike struggle with getting an erection, lubricating, or coming to orgasm. In a Catch-22, anxiety initially adds to sexual stimulation because overall physiological arousal is activated by anticipating sex. Sex can be exciting enough, but when anxiety about performance enters the body/mind, some men have difficulty stopping ejaculation. With women, the opposite occurs; too much anxiety creates pelvic tension and shallow breathing, delaying orgasm.

Our cultural ideas of men as more active and women as more passive in the sexual arena intensify anxiety for both. Men who struggle with rapid orgasm often feel that they better be "off to the races," performing at a high speed with a hard erection, in order to measure up as a lover. Women can bring messages of inadequacy to the sexual encounter, comparing their bodies to younger ones or pornographic imagery. When partners who are emotionally enmeshed get together, a contagion of anxiety can permeate their sex life, leaving it limp, frustrating, and dreadful.

The best remedy for anxiety during sex is *slow down and notice*. When we attend to the pleasurable sensations in our own body, sex can become a mindfulness practice. By dropping expectations about how we "should" be or our partner's needs, and by allowing ourselves truly to feel, self-consciousness evaporates.

DAILY HEALTHY SEX ACTS

- Take time to think about how much anxiety you bring into your sex life. How can you slow down? What conversations would let you take care of what's best for you in regards to touch, rhythm, and pace during sex?

- Pay attention to how closely you track your partner during sex. Is your attention focused on getting it right for him or her? Are you trying to keep up an image of looking good?

- Are you in your head or in your body during sex? Pay attention and try to breathe into your body.

"It dances today my heart, like a peacock it dances.

It sports a mosaic of passions like a peacock's tail,

It soars to the sky with delight, it quests, O wildly,

It dances today, my heart, like a peacock it dances."

— Rabindranath Tagore

21 JULY

DANCING

In the animal world, dancing is part of the mating process. Among humans, dancing can be a mating ritual, as well as personal exploration, social assimilation, and cultural ceremony. Ancient dance rites had many functions—they relayed myths, taught customs, invoked gods, and made magic. Similarly today's dancing has a cultural component, nonverbally imparting social trends and emerging consciousness. In group dancing, individuals couple, couples swap, threesomes become moresomes, and singletons find their way within the multitude. Consciously and unconsciously, we integrate our dance rhythms to represent a shared humanity. Is there any more egalitarian place in modern times than the dance floor?

As nonverbal communication, dance affirms that musical harmony beats at the core of our inner and outer lives. So dance can be a political as well as a personal act. The advent of modern dance presented the radical belief that human life, in all its pedestrian banality and routine, is a worthy ballet. Plodding through the day, stumbling into work, rushing to drop off the kids, sitting immobile for extended time in cars, in front of computers, at the dinner table—these can easily make us forget the eternal dance of our existence. But we all dance our life story, because we express personal reality through our movements all the time. Choosing to express our feelings and ideas freely through the motions of dance brings conscious order and choice to our lives. Sometimes it's only in the ecstasy of unrepressed movement that we may enter the stillness of our authentic selves. In such sacred moments, the world seems to be in step. This is why the idea of finding love across the dance floor endures—symbolizing that, when we know the true rhythm of our heart, we know the other.

DAILY HEALTHY SEX ACTS

- How does it feel to dance with your partner? How do you dance— touching or not? Synchronized or individually expressive? Does the room disappear, or do you calibrate to other dancers?

- Pick one problem and work it out with dance therapy. Focus on every aspect of the issue from its emergence to your struggles with each person or entity involved, and express your emotions in movement. Let the innate wisdom of your body lead you to new perceptions and possibilities.

- Let today be a dance. Samba in the shower, tango through traffic, gogo as you go. Track your feelings and share your joy.

"Researchers have found that even more than IQ, your emotional awareness and abilities to handle feelings will determine your success and happiness in all walks of life, including family relationships."

— John Gottman

EMOTIONAL INTELLIGENCE

Most societies, it seems, prize thinking at the expense of feeling. Our schools test and foster academic intelligence but leave emotional and relational powers ignored and immature. We learn that crying jags and angry outbursts are unacceptable, so we conform to the regulated moods of others. That means that our deepest feelings of fear, rage and shame, and other prickly, unpopular emotional realities "burst out" only in their most primitive, unschooled states rather than being accepted, integrated, and learned from. And that's a loss, because every emotion can teach us about ourselves and can impel self-transformation.

Emotional intelligence allows us to recognize emotional states in ourselves and others. Thus we become more adept at empathy, which is the master key to resolving conflict. Empathic interaction has been shown actually to grow children's brains, establishing neural pathways in response to mutual communication. People whose emotional intelligence is undeveloped or repressed often turn to addictive behaviors to self-soothe from frightening feelings, or they dump their dramas codependently, hoping others will comb out their tangled moods.

Healthy interaction seems to involve three stages: initial good relations; then inevitable rupture from rejection or misunderstanding; and finally repair. The repair stage is the most constructive step and creates true intimacy. Emotional intelligence is needed to repair what goes wrong in human relationships. Without internal assessment and empathic dialogue, the repair stage gets short shrift and conflicts get swept under the rug rather than resolved, until they burst out again.

Since we constantly communicate nonverbally, any unvoiced struggles in relationships sneak out in subversive ways. Too bad we've been taught to hide how we truly feel, mostly from ourselves. For only when we communicate with the authenticity engendered by emotional intelligence can the ensuing attunement with our beloved lead to real love.

DAILY HEALTHY SEX ACTS

- Take time to repair any recent disruption in your relationship, even if seemingly insignificant. First, get clear with your feelings by identifying them in writing. What core needs drove your emotions? When you're ready, ask to share your truth with your partner, and be prepared to receive his or her truth in turn. Repair doesn't result from finding a solution, it's achieved through mutual understanding.

"Listening is an attitude of the heart, a genuine desire to be with another which both attracts and heals."

— J. Isham

23 JULY

LISTENING

Great conversation requires great listening. When we give people our full attention, noting and responding to what they are saying, they sense that they matter to us. Making an effort to center oneself and to be alert to the nuances of what the other is trying to communicate is a body/mind event: Implicit cues from our own bodies during a conversation give us information that our intelligence alone can't grasp. These visceral reactions are a form of listening, just as discerning the meaning of the spoken word is. When we're willing to be quiet rather than worry we'll have nothing clever to say, feelings are evoked, meaning is made, metaphors emerge, and a new vista is reached in true conversation between two.

Recall a conversation in which the other person constantly interrupted you or, worse, completed your sentences. It probably felt self-centered rather than mutual because the interrupter looked only for patterns that supported what she or he already "knew." Not connection, but rather the anxiety to be right or to feel superior drove that conversation. In fact, it was hardly a conversation at all since it really included only the person who already decided its outcome! This type of exchange may have left you feeling frustrated and alone.

Listening during sex is no different. If you constantly anticipate your lover's next breath or move, or have decided you already know what she or he is going to "say" with her or his body, then you're not really listening. Likewise, if you're planning what to say or how to act sexually, your own experience will be stilted and unimaginative. Activate your senses. Heed the cues coming from your body and your partner's. Listening to this non-verbal communication may take you to new heights and harmonies.

DAILY HEALTHY SEX ACTS

- Are you an interrupter? If so, what do know about that habit? Has anyone ever confronted you about it? Notice your anxiety the next time you interrupt in a conversation.

- What does it feel like in your body to be listened to? What are you doing when you're listening well to others? How does your body feel?

- With your beloved, take turns listening without talking. Repeat back to him or her what you heard to check for accuracy.

> *"The fickleness of the woman I love is only equaled by the infernal constancy of the women who love me."*
>
> — George Bernard Shaw

ATTACHMENT

Human beings are wired for attachment; we need other human beings from the time we're infants in order to grow, flourish, and meet our full potential. Seeking attachment is one of the primary activities of people the world over. In other words, the "boy meets girl," "boy meets boy," or "girl meets girl" story is probably the most talked-about subject on the planet!

And why's that? Because through attachment to another, we learn to stand on our own two feet and safely traverse the terrain of life, knowing that someone out there "has our back." What a wonderful feeling to know that you're known and loved, and that you matter to one safe person in the world! And yet, we human beings are funny creatures—we want to be deeply attached *and* completely free at the same time.

Examine how much you seek love and adoration. Then consider whether receiving that kind of attention actually brings you relief or annoyance. Learning to tolerate the intimacy that attachment demands is part of healthy loving and eroticism. Pay attention to what happens in your body when your desire for attachment is in fact met by someone you're dating or by your partner. Some will feel soothed while others will feel "smothered."

DAILY HEALTHY SEX ACTS

- Notice your attachment needs today. Do you ask for comfort and soothing or do you retreat and handle things on your own?

- Notice your reactions when your partner wants to get emotionally close or when s/he expresses a need.

- Make a concerted effort to do what's counterintuitive, such as giving your partner a hug even if you don't feel like it. Recognize and tolerate your discomfort and breathe into the hug so as to expand your attachment system.

"Narcissus does not fall in love with his reflection
because it is beautiful, but because it is his."

— W. H. Auden

25 JULY

NARCISSISM

Narcissism is simply the inability to recognize others for who they are, as unique individuals in their own right, who exist separate from the narcissist. A narcissist is capable of responding only to people who perfectly reflect the narcissist—the identical psychological content expressed in the same style. Their allergic reaction to "the other" makes real relating impossible, and results in much reactive isolation.

People often confuse narcissism with vanity. But unlike the self-admiration of the vain, true narcissists possess surprisingly low self-esteem. Healthy interest from and about others was rarely modeled in their early lives. Missing that experience led to a lack of healthy differentiation—the ability to maintain and express one's own identity while simultaneously allowing others to maintain and express theirs. This ability marks a true relationship; it is not a piecemeal, fragmented or compartmentalized relation in which one can endure others only in small doses. In vibrant relationships, the parties may have different values, but can accept each other as separate, distinct, and equally worthy persons.

As in the Greek myth about Narcissus, who fell so in love with his own reflection in a pool that, trying to cling to it, he eventually died, narcissists simply cannot see beyond their own image. This difficulty surfaces especially in love and sex. It's ironic that with a narcissist, the most physically intimate act can sometimes leave a lover feeling the most shut-out and unseen.

DAILY HEALTHY SEX ACTS

- What would it be like to experience just one day without pursuing your personal agenda? What would it be like to bask in the exquisite otherness of the universe and others as if exploring new terrain?

- Let go of familiar feelings and goals, and embrace the unknown world beyond the wall of your perception.

"Anxiety is love's greatest killer. It makes one feel as you might when a drowning man holds on to you. You want to save him, but you know he will strangle you with his panic."

— Anaïs Nin

Sometimes we're not even aware of anxiety as our own, busy as we are projecting it outward onto external problems and people. Like an unexpectedly discovered bruise on our bodies, our inner psychological states can surprise us by revealing a trauma we never noticed—anxiety and tension. Other times, an audible sigh announces the sudden realization that we were stressed. Knowing this, we can take steps to release all tension, known and unknown.

Childhood anxiety is buried especially deep. Without a secure attachment to caregivers, a child cannot acquire emotional tools to regulate anxiety. Forceful instances of conflict, enmeshment, or neglect shock a child's nervous system and induce a fight/flight/freeze response. With repetition, associated triggers become embedded into the child's procedural bodily memory, so that the sight of a fist, the tone of a voice, the shrug of a shoulder, or the most innocuous-seeming gesture provokes powerful unconscious anxiety. And this process stretches into adulthood unless the memory is released or reprogrammed. Even the conscious awareness that a specific trigger creates anxiety does not completely eradicate its affect because the reaction happens on a cellular level.

Your first day at a new job may be fraught with anxiety, bringing nervous energy, shallow breathing, and a higher-pitched voice. But after you've gotten the work down cold, you won't even remember the tasks that paralyzed you at the start. A new procedural memory has supplanted your previously dominant anxiety-activation process. Such pattern replacement manifests in all practiced endeavors, especially love and sex, which are typically loaded with unconscious associations and triggers. A devoted practice of loving intentions and shared intimacy with a caring partner does much to counteract relational anxiety, allowing access to lower erotic vibrations as breathing becomes more connected to the body, the voice to the heart.

DAILY HEALTHY SEX ACTS

- Notice your anxiety levels throughout the day. Become familiar with your triggers—sounds, looks, movements—and trace them to their source in your deepest past. Release or reprogram the troubling memory by making new associations. For example, remind yourself the street "where [your ex-lover] works" is now the street "I take to yoga class."

- Next time you're trying something new sexually, be willing to tolerate anxiety in order to grow and change. Recognize anxiety as a natural part of your sexuality and invite it as a welcome, temporary guest.

"When we treat people merely as they are, they will remain as they are. When we treat them as if they were what they should be, they will become what they should be."

— Thomas S. Monson

27 JULY

RESPECT

Respect can be an arena for key issues to play out. Lack of respect will be keenly felt by anyone who grew up with an insecure attachment to caregivers, whether in chaotic households or with neglectful or domineering parents. If the personal integrity of such a person is (or is perceived to be) wounded, this often results either in an unending quest for respect or a constant evaluation of whether others are worthy of respect. We've probably all heard parents, teachers, friends or lovers at one time or another declare, "You need to show some respect!" It's the oddest demand, because there's never been a moment when that admonition is followed by respect toward that person!

Would that we could simply demand respect to receive it! But no. To earn respect, we need to show people the way to respecting us. When we were kids we didn't respect anything, until someone lovingly showed us the way to honor persons, ideals, customs, ourselves. If we're not willing to take on that responsibility for others, how can we expect them to have already learned any respect for us? If you have a deal-breaker that bars you from developing close friendships or romantic relationships with someone who doesn't respect your hobbies or interests, recall that at one time *you* didn't even share those interests! It's possible to develop reverence and love for any subject if someone brings it to us in the right way. We could come to admire and even love any person someone brought us to understand. We've done as much for ourselves: We grew to understand ourselves, and everything that we respect in life. So when we invite people into our interests, and into ourselves, we're showing, and earning, respect.

DAILY HEALTHY SEX ACTS

- Seeking respect can be a sign of trying to manage one's reputation rather than examining personal behavior. What qualities would you like others to respect in you? How can you lovingly show them the way you respect any given quality in yourself, and share the special meaning it has for you?

- Empathy also engenders respect. It's easier to empathize when we recognize similarities, shared values or respective truths. Affirm your respect for others today. Listen, and let them know the loving qualities you see in them.

> *"Jealousy, that dragon which slays love under the pretense of keeping it alive."*
>
> — Havelock Ellis

Jealousy, that insatiable emerald-eyed monster, is a universal human flaw that has been explored in some of the most poignant works of art ever created. Who can forget Antonio Salieri's suffering in the face of Mozart's unrivaled genius in the film *Amadeus*? Or Othello's murderous rage as he obsesses over his sweet Desdemona's imagined infidelities? Sexual jealousy in particular is one of the most powerful forces in the psyche. Daily we see people on the news who have succumbed to its power and engage in violent, destructive behaviors. These spectacles remind us of the dark side of love—the possessiveness and desire for vengeance that can haunt us if we don't work through our issues before getting involved with others.

At the root of jealousy lies a fundamental belief in *scarcity*. We are riddled with deep, primal fears—that we won't get our needs met; that we'll be abandoned; that we are, at our core, unlovable. Jealousy is frequently hysterical, which means it's historical: It's an emotionally charged state embedded in the defenselessness and deprivations of childhood. Confronting these deep-seated fears can be terrifying, but it's the only way to heal the traumas that drive our disturbance. As we open instead to the principle of *abundance*, we can begin to share our heart with others in an open, flowing fashion, finally understanding that love is not a limited commodity to be hoarded. On the contrary, love is as common and renewable as air and water. It is all around us and inside us, like our breath, and native as our heartbeat and pulse. Once we fathom the infiniteness of love, we can begin to let go and relax, allowing others to choose us from a place of authentic affection rather than coercion.

DAILY HEALTHY SEX ACTS

- Recall the last time you felt jealous. What was the situation, and how did you respond to your own jealousy? Did you feel shame or justification? How does this memory sit with you now?

- Whenever you feel jealous, try simply to admit the reality of your feelings without shame: "I feel jealous." Pinpoint exactly what's threatening your peace. Seek the fear behind your jealousy—losing face? not being enough? Where did that fear originate?

- Send love to yourself in the past. Wish yourself well. Send love to yourself in the present as you face your deeper truth, rewiring the ways you learned to relate.

"Men are not punished for their sins, but by them."

— Elbert Hubbard

29 JULY

SIN

The word *sin* derives from a Sanskrit root meaning "missing the mark." This useful definition steers clear of judgmentalism and offers the metaphor of an archer aiming to hit the bull's-eye. Those who rail against so-called "sins of the flesh" are more like hecklers in the stands at the archery competition rather than trustworthy judges. It can be a very hurtful and confusing experience to be threatened with punishment and rejection if we don't toe a certain moral line. Luckily, as we move towards adulthood we can throw off the shackles of other people's imposed values and learn to develop our own. We can find mentors and powers greater than ourselves whom we trust, and allow them to help us hit the mark. Sometimes we will fail and make mistakes, but that, too, is part of the process of growing up. We can examine our sexuality in light of whether it is hurtful to others, or us, rather than whether it is socially approved.

Another relieving idea to recall is that actions considered "sins" at one time may be perfectly acceptable in another. All of us have engaged in or considered a sexual act that another era deemed a vice. As a society we're always in the process of redefining behavioral standards. Thanks to those who spoke their truth against sex-negativity in schools, laws, and customs, many parts of the world hold certain sexual freedoms as natural, though they were seen as unnatural in the past. Being a conscientious objector to unjust laws is a vital act, because without such activism we would be stuck in the dark ages that criminalized genuine love while protecting domestic violence and sex crimes. Still, as a society, we've much to learn to hit the mark of healthy sexual education, protection and recovery.

DAILY HEALTHY SEX ACTS

- When did you first hear about sin as it relates to sexuality? Recall any specific programming you may have picked up. Do those messages serve you today?

- How do you invite healthy sexuality, and where do you miss the mark? Who might best help you reach your goal?

- Take a stand against the sins of sexual violence and the sins of intellectual abuse, such as sex-negative propaganda that fuels oppressive laws. Today, invite healthy sex into public discourse through your moral marksmanship by writing letters or essays on subjects that concern you.

> *"Barn's burnt down—now I can see the moon."*
>
> — Mizuta Masahide

To have a heart full of reverence for all that exists is the secret principle of acceptance. And acceptance is an infinite loop: If you revere life, you can accept reality; and only when you accept reality can you revere life. You must jump right in to this acceptance loop, but it's not that hard. In fact, it's impossible to take your deepest breath and refuse life in that same moment. Acceptance is objective empathy—the belief that everything that is, deserves to exist or would never have come into being. So even before our choice, discrimination, and intention come into play, we must practice acceptance. A first step is to acknowledge that there are no good people and there are no bad people; there are only people whose experiences taught them to cope the best they can.

But acceptance doesn't mean approval, advocacy, indulgence, or submission. We don't let the universe toss us into the tide of another's creed or being which may be hateful and damaging to us. Acceptance simply ushers into our awareness what already exists. And by affirming the livingness of others, we spring to life.

The result of acceptance is connection to your world, which allows a connection to the very center of your most secret self. This linkage frees your ability for deeper experience and feeling. It invites your self-awareness to help you enter into a co-regulated partnership with another that may contain preference patterns and arousal templates different from your own. Acceptance is a precursor to the most potent intimacy, and acts as a lightning rod for sexual ignition, because the cosmically connected, overflowing energy in your body is evident to attuned others. Through the widening empathy engendered by ever-greater acceptance, you overflow to feel your lover feeling your own overflowing body.

DAILY HEALTHY SEX ACTS

- Who accepts you unconditionally? Do you yourself? Think of all the moments when someone's acceptance affected your life. We may not approve of everyone, but we can accept and love people unconditionally as others have loved us despite our faults.

- Accept yourself. Accept your life. Accept your feelings and fate. Today, walk in the world with loving acceptance of all you perceive. Know that there is a greater meaning beyond the superficial veil of existence, and that acceptance for all that is, despite our biases and inherited narratives, is the key to greater perception of that meaning.

"If there is light in the soul, there will be beauty in the person. If there is beauty in the person, there will be harmony in the house. If there is harmony in the house, there will be order in the nation. If there is order in the nation, there will be peace in the world."

— Chinese proverb

31 JULY

HARMONY

When we think of harmony, we think of musical composition and the lyrical way musical notes combine simultaneously to produce chords and seriatim to create progressions. We also find kinetic harmony in the graceful choreography of dance, with its balance of lightness and strength, movement and stance, speed and deliberateness. The beauty that emerges from propagating something pleasing and whole delights our senses and lifts our spirits. When we are in harmony with nature, we know there's an agreement that has been met and a joining that has taken place, bringing not only health but also peace. Moreover, when life is harmonious there is consistency, a quality human beings long for perhaps as much as love.

Just as music and dance are by-products of individuals' expression, so, too, is the coupling between two people who form a partnership. Like a *pas de deux* or a barbershop quartet whose every member sings a specific part, it's essential to dance your own steps and sing your own song in the relationship. If one part dominates the other, the beauties of each get lost. In relationship, we strive to hold on to our individuality while dancing and singing with our partner.

Like music and dance, copulation is an intricate form of natural harmony. When the passionate meeting between two creates a third energy, the pattern of the entire universe is replicated. Controlling your partner or holding back your own essence halts the unfolding of the balanced, pitch-perfect harmony of your divine union. By being mindful of your part, you can set an intention to weave something beautiful, then enjoy with delight the music and dance you have made manifest.

DAILY HEALTHY SEX ACTS

- Practice walking meditation today by staying present and noticing harmony in all aspects of life. What do you see? What surprises you?

- In moments of discord or upset in your relationship, make a concerted— that is, a concert-like—effort to harmonize. What adjustments do you need to make? What are your perceptions of your partner? Share those perceptions in a way that supports harmony.

- Next time you make love, add music to the experience and experiment with the rhythm and how it brings your body, mind, and soul into harmony with one another.

August

"The truest form of love is how you behave toward someone, not how you feel about them."

— Steve Hall

1 AUGUST

DEMONSTRATION

Our constitutional freedoms of expression give us the right literally to take to the streets—to *demonstrate*—when some concern moves us passionately. When we "walk the walk," we get on our feet and prove our desire to make change happen by showing people around us that we mean business. Similarly, when you're recovering from an addiction you have to take concrete, visible actions to earn back the trust of friends and family members. And when you're living in a love relationship you also have to actively participate in the relationship. How many times have we heard the phrase, "walk the walk" and taken it for granted? Love isn't just what we say, love is what we do.

For example, cooking a meal for someone is an act of love—an outpouring of creativity, talent and energy that takes time and effort. A delicious meal is the physical manifestation of the cook's heart, a way of physically showing how much you mean to him or her. Your appreciation might be expressed by sensuous moans as you savor the tastes, texture, and symphony of the delicious morsels. Your verbal demonstrations reflect your own gratitude that someone went to the trouble to give to you so generously.

Ravenously devouring your lover clearly demonstrates your desire to merge, to create a mystical third, and to reach Nirvana. But on a daily basis, demonstration of love can come in the most mundane acts like appearing at your lover's bedside with a morning cup of coffee or tea, or running an errand for them because you know they can't tend to it. Every demonstration counts. Don't get lazy or take your partner for granted, walk your walk.

DAILY HEALTHY SEX ACTS

- Demonstrate your love for someone today with a small gesture.

- Demonstrate without getting "brownie points:" do something nice *anonymously* for a co-worker, neighbor, or other friendly acquaintance.

- Make a grand display for your partner that you're sincerely connected to—have fun with it!

> *"You can kiss your family and friends good-bye and put miles between you, but at the same time you carry them with you in your heart, your mind, your stomach, because you do not just live in a world but a world lives in you."*
>
> — Frederick Buechner

The very term *relationship* summons different associations for everyone, and rightly, for there's no ideal or standard one. We often transfer expectations from familial relationships or past romances into a new one, only to find that our partner plays by different rules. So we must learn to bind ourselves together in new, shared ways while keeping healthy, and highly personal, boundaries.

People often prioritize their primary romance, as if their life exists only when reflected in another's infatuated eyes. But we are in relationship with every person in this world, even if some relationships are hidden from us. Saying we "choose to enter into a relationship" disregards the fact that no human can create relationship. Think about it: We didn't consciously manifest any of the social acquaintances in our lives. This precise power is beyond us. And it's also beyond our power to end a relationship, although we may quit an intimate pact. But calling that process "ending a relationship" elicits much egotistical confusion. It's liberating to leave unhealthy people, but we can't ever truly leave relationships. Every lover we left behind lives on in us. We summon their memories and sometimes even speak to them in our heart. Even past hurt cannot blot out interrelatedness. In truth, our spirits flow into one another.

Some relationships have been so damaged by past trauma that the very concept of them—the simple idea of "father" or "friend"—makes one recoil in fear of pain. But we possess the potential for every healthy relationship conceivable, regardless of the people in our lives. We can repair the most damaged personal relationship with anyone—with or without that person's involvement. We're connected to others by invisible strings. We choose to pluck certain strings to make music, but even the untouched, possible notes reverberate in the sometimes syncopated rhythm of our song.

DAILY HEALTHY SEX ACTS

- What happens if you drop the title of *sister, neighbor, lover*? Defining relationships by roles creates impossible expectations. Today, connect with the actual *self* of each person. If you sense your own true inner self, then surely you can relate.

- Heal your relationships. Allow yourself a healthy relationship to the concept of *mother, father, teacher, friend*. Let yourself be a *lover*, a *parent*, a *child*, a *leader*, a *follower*, a *kind stranger*. Only connect.

"They say all lovers swear more performance than they are able, and yet reserve an ability that they never perform."

— William Shakespeare

3 AUGUST

SELF-EXPRESSION

Everything we do is self-expression, because our nonverbal cues actually communicate more than spoken words ever could. A picture is truly worth a thousand words, and we perpetually express a picture of our inner lives—known and unknown. There's no way NOT to express our inner reality. Thus the *ways* we express are as significant as the *words* we express.

Verbal expression always represents a decision about what we choose to bring into public view. In the case of someone who barely speaks, his or her words carry more weight since they are not diluted by over-explanation. Similarly, you're with yourself all the time so you fully understand the meaning of your words, but those who become your *audience*—your listeners—hear only little snippets of your constant inner conversation. The truth is that shared, meaningful language is based on trust that is built. The more you nurture an accurate mutual understanding of verbal expression with others, the more you develop a special bond of comprehension that lets you finish each others' sentences and "hear" even non-verbal cues. The gift of that cultivated mutual understanding is that you can really see who you and others are, and really understand what you're creating in your shared lives.

DAILY HEALTHY SEX ACTS

- What non-verbal, creative expression do you wish you could participate in? Painting and cooking are two such examples. What would you like to express?

- Practice aligning your verbal and nonverbal expression privately. Recall an emotionally charged event in your life, and narrate what happened while observing and feeling the feelings as they happened.

- What are three positive statements that express the way you feel about each of your significant relationships? Let them know how you feel—*in the exact way that you feel it.*

"Plan for the future because that's where you are going to spend the rest of your life."

— Mark Twain

PLANNED SEX

It's not always possible to be emotionally present for other people. In fact, it's challenging to be present even for ourselves at every moment. When planning sex with a partner for a future time, we inevitably confront our own fluctuating moods before our "appointment." Even spontaneous sex can require negotiating or waiting for another's moods—a delay over which we have no control. So since both parties' desire waxes and wanes, planned sex is a practice just like meditation. For example, sometimes we don't feel like meditating but we recall its value and train ourselves to practice it—and usually receive its benefits despite not having been in the mood. Similarly, by showing up for each other and keeping a sexual commitment, sex becomes even more profound over time. When we make plans and honor them, we discover our ability to show up for ourselves and others in the moments we've agreed to.

We can also plan time for conscious communication to preclude accidental argument. If we're upset about something, we might request a discussion at a later date rather than interrupt current activity for a confrontation. Rather than walking around "meaning to say something" or introducing a tough topic with, "Oh, by the way...," why not make a plan to sit down for shared truth? Life decisions deserve more consideration than happens casually on the run, and our relationships merit determinations made by choice, not chance.

While there's no guarantee fate won't throw a curve ball into our love lives, we can insure ourselves emotionally by dedicating special times for affection, sexual connection, and communication on important issues. Planning proves we know the importance of our love and how much it impacts us. Planning prevents our constantly dropping hot potatoes in each others' world. Life does that enough.

DAILY HEALTHY SEX ACTS

- Make a date to connect with your beloved for sex or intimate talk. Notice the anticipatory feelings arising, and prioritize your commitment as a weekly ritual.

- The next time you feel upset enough to confront a friend or associate, schedule a sit-down meeting for a later time, and follow through even if your feelings have settled.

- Today, plan one moment for self-care: Set your alarm, regulate any moodiness or scheduling conflicts, and stick to your plan.

"In all the world, there is no heart for me like yours.
In all the world, there is no love for you like mine."

— Maya Angelou

5 AUGUST

PRECIOUSNESS

You're more precious than you know. What makes a gemstone so priceless? Rarity—whether from short natural supply, craftsmanship, or nostalgic or symbolic meaning—makes certain gems, stones and jewels precious. Thus the value of a stone depends on its existence, its form, and its context. Similarly, at birth you were given many valuable gifts, starting with your precious life that makes all of your experiences possible. Your form is another precious gift. This work of art, your exquisite physical body, possesses built-in processes and systems more detailed and astounding than will ever be fully known. Science cannot make a more perfect body. And you've been gifted with context—a living story that, through your precious awareness, will take you on more adventures than any fiction writer could ever conceive. No one sees the world as you do. You alone synthesize all your experiences, and no one else has your particular vantage point. You may recall times filled with worries, fears and struggles, but you're here now, so you've prevailed. Through all your ups and downs, the worth of your existence has never altered. In a world where everything changes, your preciousness holds the key to your immutable, true nature.

Affirm the preciousness of all living things, and hold that assessment itself as a value more precious than any other way of perceiving. To dismiss preciousness is to devalue yourself and your experience. When we can see ourselves and our lives as precious, we can also think this way about others. We get glimpses of the worthiness of our lovers, our children, and our friends that are too easy to lose sight of. The more we invite a practice of affirming preciousness, the more we recognize our own significant value.

DAILY HEALTHY SEX ACTS

- List everything you find precious. Notice your feelings and thoughts when writing this list. Is there anything to prevent you from affirming your own preciousness?

- To feel *terminally unique* is to possess the inflated sense that you're so special, no one could possibly understand you. It's a tactic to isolate yourself and alienate others. How can you value your unique experience and still relate to the world?

- Today, attune yourself to the preciousness of each moment. Cherish your life, your body, and your consciousness. Share your true heart's treasure.

"If a person loves only one other person and is indifferent to the rest of his fellow men, his love is not love but a symbiotic attachment, or an enlarged egotism."

— Erich Fromm

PHILIA

The ancient Greeks named kind-hearted love *Philia*. It's the love we feel for friends, family, and community, as well as for lovers we truly like. Platonic yet emotional, *Philia* lights up our hearts when we meet an old friend and inspires us to make new ones.

People sometimes throw over Philia for the more exciting Eros (erotic love) or the spiritually superior Agape (unconditional love). When some people fall in love, they forget friends and family and abandon community allegiances in a seductive regression. After their isolating fixation inevitably ends, they seem to come out of hiding, exclaiming, "What was I thinking?" as they start to lean on friends and family again. But we don't have to exile any form of love to enjoy another, as if we possessed a finite quantity, or a single quality, of love to offer the world.

Indeed, we should question the limiting love that sees the couple as "us against the world." In childhood it's normal for feelings of powerlessness and disappointment with caregivers to turn into temporary feelings of rage, rejection, and hatred. But when elicited too repeatedly, such splitting from caregivers to protect autonomy proves traumatic for the child, who still depends on them for survival. When our capacity for Philia has been wounded, we create petty conflicts and readily feel persecuted.

As adults who no longer need those flawed caregivers, we can and must allow ourselves to experience deep loves: for ourselves, for a partner, for family, for friends, and for community. Regardless of the circumstances of our upbringing, let us cultivate Philia so that, along with Eros and Agape, we can weave ourselves with all the strands of love to others and to our world.

DAILY HEALTHY SEX ACTS

- What feelings do you have toward family, friends and community? Expand your capacity for Philia—regardless of whether those in your life deserve it.

- Consider the degree to which you balance romantic and platonic relationships, and whether you favor one over the other. Integrate your love experience with your life experience.

- Do you rely on certain relationships to absorb the stress of conflicted relationships, past or present? Care for those wounds, and then show up for others with kind and courteous love in your heart, as a person among people.

> "What others say and do is a projection of their own reality, their own dream. When you are immune to the opinions and actions of others, you won't be the victim of needless suffering."
>
> — Don Miguel Ruiz

7 AUGUST

INVULNERABILITY

Vulnerability is often framed as weakness in our culture, partly due to the ethos of rugged individualism that is the hallmark of capitalist economies. The expression of feelings and of need, especially for males, invites derogatory name-calling and sets the stage for shame and the subsequent construction of defenses against emotion. When a person is repeatedly criticized, made the butt of jokes, or bullied, the core of who she or he is becomes shame-based, blocking all natural openness. Like a moat around a castle, shame sequesters our ability to be vulnerable and renders us incapable of expressing self-compassion or empathy for others. Thus it primes a lifetime pattern of cutting off emotions and connections and hiding behind defensive walls.

True and healthy *invulnerability*, on the other hand, is a state of equanimity—an internal place of self-compassionate strength that keeps us invincible in the face of gossip, offensive actions, or the fleeting opinions of others. By accepting both the good and the bad in life—but not judging our worth by our fortune—we become invulnerable to the slings and arrows that others may fling.

When we think of an invulnerable object like a battleship or a bridge, we imagine it as so well constructed internally that an outside attack couldn't hurt or damage it. Likewise, when we are secure and confident, our core can't be wounded or injured from an external assault because we protect it from the inside out.

Emotional vulnerability ensures the softness in our hearts that lets us feel for ourselves and others. Healthy invulnerability, ironically, grows out of this vulnerability, and lets us walk boldly through the world with strong internal boundaries, immune to the projections of others. Like yin and yang, vulnerability and invulnerability live together in an essential balance.

DAILY HEALTHY SEX ACTS

- Make a list of the ways you are "invulnerable" that are problematic, and a list of the ways you are "invulnerable" that are a source of strength.

- What is your preferred way of being invulnerable?

- If you discover that you use invulnerability as a defense against feelings, consider dropping those defenses so that you can become more vulnerable in healthy ways.

> *"You can discover more about a person in an hour of play than in a year of conversation."*
>
> — Plato

PLAY

People of all ages need playtime. Interacting just for the enjoyment of companionship builds trust and affection. Sadly, it's easy to sacrifice play to obligations. People who lack quality playtime sometimes try to bring this energy into their lives through sexual acting out. It's not hard to see why sexual activity and play often get mixed up. The goal of play is to experience delight in collaboration with another, and dating and many expressions of sex and love involve simple, joyful play. But it's important to find nonsexual ways to renew your spirits by playing with loved ones and friends. We can turn to our childhood to see what worked for us in the past, how we were able to release ourselves in healthy recreation, and what exchanges were most satisfying to us.

Play can be learned at any time of life. Not all of us grew up in circumstances where healthy play was possible. For some, "play" triggers vicious competitiveness or narcissistic power trips. Sometimes play masks unprocessed trauma or cruelty, often exposed through mockery: "Can't you take a joke? — It's all in fun." Growing up we all encountered other children who were a nightmare to play with, many of whom emerged into adulthood with the same difficult personalities. But as we age, we develop greater autonomy and discrimination in picking our playmates. Secret motives may lurk underneath all social play, but if the parties are healthy, the primary intention isn't to score a deal, show off, or humiliate someone. Healthy play is an intimate but nonsexual way of sharing ourselves through validating and building on our common experiences and the pleasures of fellowship.

DAILY HEALTHY SEX ACTS

- Say "Yes!" to all invitations to healthy activities this week. When you attend, let go of ulterior motives and try to recapture (or finally capture) the simple spirit of friendly play.

- Plan one hour of play today. What would be a fun and invigorating activity? Whom would you like to invite to play?

- Informed by past disappointments, we often don't trust ourselves to get close to new friends. Cultivate a sense of play in all your relationships and daily interactions!

"Anyone who is in love is making love the whole time, even when they're not. When two bodies meet, it is just the cup overflowing. They can stay together for hours, even days. They begin the dance one day and finish it the next, or—such is the pleasure they experience—they may never finish it."

— Paulo Coelho

9 AUGUST

MAKING LOVE

Love is an unseen intrinsic force that flows to and from all living beings. Its tremendous power and potential, like that of the wind or the sun, may be underestimated until we harness it to action. When our physical bodies become the vessel for expressing this infectious energy, we call it "making love." The primary difference between making love and having sex hinges on our holistic involvement. Engaging in wild, hot sex with no strings attached can be liberating and exhilarating, but it stays purely on the physical plane. By contrast, when we make love, we engage with a partner not only physically but emotionally, mentally, and spiritually, transcending the limits of personal identity to participate in a transformative sanctifying act. We are practicing emotion in motion. Evoking the passion of Eros and Venus through multiple vibrational frequencies stimulates and activates all our *chakras*—our body's energy centers. We touch the hem of enlightenment.

Sexual expression does not always have to be physical, either. Erotic energy may radiate from the depths of our being and into the core of our partner, and this can be expressed through something as simple as nursing him or her back to health. Sexuality is extremely sensitive and intuitive; a single whisper, wink, or caress can ripple throughout our day. To make love, therefore, does not necessarily require the uniting of bodies. It is a perpetual state of deep understanding and bonding, of connecting. It is a celebration of everything it means to be human.

DAILY HEALTHY SEX ACTS

- Make love, not war! Do your actions, words and thoughts reflect the warm glow of your loving nature, or the bloodlust of your warring nature? Remember, remember, always try to remember—world peace starts within.

- How does your *love*-making measure up to the other styles of sex in your skill-set? If you aren't filled with love, then you're not making love, are you? How can you tap into true feelings of love and share them?

- Today, make love to your visible or as-yet-invisible soulful mate with every vibrating fiber of your being. Use your imagination to attain a new erotic plateau.

> *"Divine is Love and scorneth worldly pelf,*
> *And can be bought with nothing but with self.*
>
> — Sir Walter Raleigh

WORTH

Love is free. If love costs, the expense is due to an attendant trait other than love. Ambition will cost you. Envy, fear, revenge and greed all have a price. Honestly, we all possess most positive and negative attributes to varying degrees. A transcript of your thinking during an hour with your lover will reveal many considerations beyond love: "Is my partner attractive / entertaining / wealthy / powerful / popular enough?" These neurotic measures of worth are ingrained habits from early programming and, who knows, perhaps even earlier. For the human tendency to appraise others for selfish reasons is entrenched. Love is the only antidote. Love is a freeing agent, it unites and releases. Love identifies with all it touches, obliterating the erroneous and painful sense of separateness that leads us to compare and despair.

Trading flesh for finances bespeaks an age-old sexual attitude that still dominates certain cultures. It's no wonder we struggle to find the worth of sexual love separate from egoistical concerns. When we put a price on sex we objectify all involved—seller and buyer alike. It's hard to ignore how much our partner is worth materially. Of course, this assessment differs from appreciating a partner's worth. Calculating worth and appreciating worth seem to involve similar processes, but the results diverge widely: One oppresses and the other exalts. Even giving your lover high marks on your mental checklist is a form of objectification, creating a power dynamic wherein your lover's value depends on the conceit of your current opinion. But appreciating another's worth is an intimate act that involves sharing personal truth with open-handed regard. Developing the habit of giving love freely requires practice, but you must know by now you're worth it.

 DAILY HEALTHY SEX ACTS

- Take a moment and consider all the ways you rate the worth of your current or most recent lover. Is s/he worthy because of his/her looks, status, or talents? Release yourself from using others to feel better.

- Endow yourself with worth. Know that even in your weakest area, there are those who find you worthy. Take a leap of faith and let this be true for you.

- Share your internal process of feeling attracted. Is it the way your lover walks through a room? Say it as you see it. Don't delay, don't attribute the precious worth of these moments to the career, the education, the thing.

"Real sex is as much about reciprocity as it is exploration and if you need a reason to resent a man later on, just consider the guy who doesn't believe in cunnilingus."

— Roberto Hogue

11 AUGUST

ORAL SEX

When did you learn about oral sex? Its initial discovery can be shocking because so much grooming pressure dictates that you have to cover up and keep yourself very clean "down there." During the oral stage of early childhood, most children are repeatedly admonished not to put objects in their mouths. Because of such programming, mouths and genitalia carry a lot of psychic weight. At different times in history, oral sex has been exalted, condemned, and even used as punishment. How do you feel right now, just reading about it?

We can liberate ourselves from the unhealthy shame, avoidance and fear that inhibit developing a pleasurable oral sex technique.

People like oral sex many different ways; there's no standard whatsoever and there are myriad subtleties in performing fellatio, cunnilingus, and anilingus. Do you know how to groom yourself for oral sex or share grooming tips with your lover? For some, giving but not receiving oral sex can trigger personal issues. Can you remain aroused while giving oral sex? Some people have the attitude of "tit for tat," counting the number of times like dealing cards. But oral sex doesn't mean one of you is "on hold" while indulging the other. Many couples develop a shared dynamic, mirroring a partner's energy and actions while performing simultaneous oral sex in the sixty-nine position. Since you are solely responsible for your experience, it's healthy to be able to communicate what feels good and what could feel better. Such conversation can trigger feelings of shame, but only through truthful sharing can we fulfill intimacy—even when everything feels great. When you truly connect with your own erotic feelings and sensations, giving pleasure will begin to feel like receiving pleasure.

DAILY HEALTHY SEX ACTS

- Do you consider oral sex... *sex?* Does your partner? Have you ever talked about how you like to give and receive? Do you even know yourself? Explore your oral sex arousal template in writing.

- It's often challenging to express how we feel, especially if oral sex is painful, not that pleasurable, or poorly timed. Risk talking about oral sex today with your beloved.

- When a lover pleases his or her partner with oral sex without expecting anything in return, it may evoke tsunamis of affection and appreciation! How might oral sex be received by your lover today?

"I cannot love as I have loved,
And yet I know not why;
It is the one great woe of life
To feel all feeling die."

— Philip James Bailey

Apathy might overtake any one of us unexpectedly, but usually someone significant said or did something hurtful. That uncontested fact gets swallowed and, like a parasite, this sense of fault will slowly drain the body and brain unless the originating source of friction is examined, confronted and healed.

The fact that humans lose interest in people, in hobbies, in life may also indicate unhealthy patterns in feeling states and perceptions rather than any single cause. We all know the experience of sitting in bed feeling exhilarated one day and lackluster the very next. The issue is not whether we need to find a more fulfilling bed.

To practice healthy behavior and pursue heartfelt goals, we sometimes have to blind ourselves to momentary hindrances such as boredom, resistance, and disenchantment, which can all be forms of self-sabotage. In the same way, when going on vacation and experiencing tedious stretches between destinations, we can't walk down the airport terminal thinking, "Oh, no! If this is what the rest of the trip is like it's going to be terrible." We've seen the brochure; we know we're going to reach that sandy beach.

All relationships hit rough patches, and sometimes problems seem permanent. There's a knack to knowing whether we're still engaged in a healthy process that's going to pay off, or when it's really dried up and we should move on. Tolerating this conundrum ("Is it me or is it her/him?") long enough to answer it is a sign of maturity. If we lead rich lives and take responsibility for feeling whole, fulfilled, and interested, we have less need to seek constant external stimulation, and may instead bask in our self-generated feelings of love and connection.

DAILY HEALTHY SEX ACTS

- How do you communicate your inner experience? One extreme might be to cover up any negativity and pretend everything is okay, and the other extreme might be to blame others for all that's disagreeable. Can you acknowledge these two extremes while sticking to your middle ground? Share openly and honestly today. Let others in.

- When have you recently lost interest in something or someone? Using free-flow writing, explore the mental process that triggered you to lose interest. What exactly was unhealthy for you? Did you really give it a chance, or did you ignore warning signs that could have been transformed through healthy deliberation?

"A person does not have to be behind bars to be a prisoner.
People can be prisoners of their own concepts and ideas.
They can be slaves to their own selves."

— Maharaji

13 AUGUST

INHIBITION

Restraint can be an act of self-preservation and dignity, even an essential part of valor. Caution in the face of danger is prudent and wise; it takes courage to hold back an action, emotion, or thought that could inflame a situation. Such discipline can be especially challenging when personally offended, and requires us to inhibit impulses that drive our bodies to retaliate to the offense. In those moments, keeping our cool allows for the possibility of holding and waiting, giving us time to assess the situation. The capacity to restrain impulses so we can think clearly and use good judgment demonstrates our ability to self-regulate. For example, knowing when to speak and when to listen is a necessary skill for maintaining a harmonious and intimate relationship.

However, when inhibition has become the de facto setting in a person's manner, stiffness and lack of spontaneity produces an unnatural self-repression. Life looks gray, dull, and rigid, without space for relaxation or play to burst forth in natural ways. When children are repeatedly shamed or criticized, they're unable to act freely in daily life. Always watching over their shoulders to see who's judging them, they sink deeper and deeper into self-consciousness, too paralyzed to try the simplest things. Breaking these old restraints is a necessary task for sexual joy and pleasure. Having the courage to stand up against self-censorship by recognizing these inward chains as leftover oppressors from the past calls forth a new strength that invites you to fight for your life. This battle is a lesson awaiting you so that you can sing, dance, and make love in the most uninhibited ways imaginable.

DAILY HEALTHY SEX ACTS

- What chains from the past bind you from expressing your sexual desire? Do you know how they got there? Imagine yourself breaking free from those constraints. What do you look like? Who's there to witness your freeing yourself?

- Make a collage out of magazine photos that illustrates what freedom from inhibition looks like for you. Share it with a fair witness.

> *"Trouble looms when monogamy is no longer a free expression of loyalty but a form of enforced compliance."*
>
> — Esther Perel

Monogamy—the practice of mating with only one person—can create a sanctuary of inner peace, security and well-being for both parties, provided the partners treasure a psychological and emotional commitment in addition to a sexual one. Monogamy may require tremendous tolerance and patience, but practicing these qualities can bring profound growth and personal transformation. However, in our highly repressed, conformist culture, praise of monogamy may be loaded: It is routinely touted by some factions of society as being morally superior to other lifestyles such as polyamory or open relationships. Yet in reality, society consists of many different kinds of people with varying needs and ways of being happy.

AUGUST 14

MONOGAMY

If we look to nature for examples of marital diversity, we discover that while swans, gibbons, wolves and bald eagles all mate for life with one special member of their species, most animals like lions and squirrels prefer a plethora of partners. What causes confusion is when a lion tries to live as a swan or vice versa just to please others.

So-called religious authorities may demonize non-monogamous relationships, but polyamorists are just as likely to live with integrity and compassion as their more traditional counterparts. Another dominant and highly destructive societal myth maintains that men are biologically non-monogamous, while women are interested only in finding a life-long partner. In truth, a person's predilection towards a certain lifestyle has nothing to do with gender, age or ethnicity, and social stereotypes only inhibit us from discovering an authentic expression of our sexuality. The need for open communication, setting healthy boundaries, and treating others with respect remains essential regardless of whom—or how many—we sleep with.

DAILY HEALTHY SEX ACTS

- Write down all the words you associate with monogamy. Now write the words you associate with polyamory or open relationships. Are these words accurate? Do they reflect a certain bias? If so, do you know how you came to hold these views?

- Can you accept that people choose to experience love in different ways? Can you hear that truth from others, from your children, or from your partner?

- If you are in a monogamous relationship and have cheated on your partner, ask yourself how you came to be in this situation. There's no good excuse for deceiving another—especially a lover.

"Love takes off the masks that we fear we cannot live without and know we cannot live within."

— James Baldwin

15 AUGUST

FACADE

Have you ever wanted to tear down someone's facade? Any conflict can trigger old feelings of not being listened to, of being misunderstood. Worse yet, another's deceit and dishonesty can be crazy-making.

At times, we all feel as though there's a vital truth, a living heart, a spiritual wealth that's being denied us. If we could only "break through!"

Yet in reality we all wear masks, to our benefit or harm. The ability to manufacture elaborate, serviceable and invisible psychological constructs is an instinctual coping mechanism that lets the ego function. We can't peek behind all facades, but we can make strides toward a healthy process of confronting our own masks of deception and denial. The personal self mirrors the spiritual self in that both become concealed by falsehood. How often do you cover your personal truth?

What's your neutral state when no one is looking? When we're with people, it can be tough to keep that neutrality. We might feel that we must demonstrate explicitly when we're upset, or not upset. This perceived need may stem from our family of origin, from how we learned to be heard when a simple "no" wasn't enough. We may have learned to mask certain feelings, or portray feelings that weren't ours. But as adults we each need to learn to state our personal truth without having to prove it or shout it. If we don't honor our truth, how can we expect anyone else to do so?

When we can simply express our feelings without false display—especially during sex—we'll be able to experience them. We'll become conduits for our real emotion and deepest pleasure. But if we're wrapping ourselves up to conceal any vulnerability, whatever happens to us has to go through all those extra layers. Sometimes love doesn't even reach where we truly live.

DAILY HEALTHY SEX ACTS

- When do you hide behind a facade? Think of your physical neutrality when alone, and then notice any changes as you interact in the world. Can you reveal your neutral state in public, or do you put on a face?

- The intention to drop all pretenses is a powerful undertaking. Let others know today that you would like to share beyond the facade, to take down your mask. Without any expectations, communicate to one person your willingness to interact on a deeper level.

> *"It looked as if a night of dark intent*
> *Was coming, and not only a night, an age.*
> *Someone had better be prepared for rage."*
>
> — Robert Frost

RAGE

The violent, uncontrollable anger known as rage signals danger. The very word telegraphs an unstoppable superhuman power destroying anything in its path—a "raging" hurricane or epidemic. Like a force of nature, human beings can erupt in rage, sending everyone around them running for safety. The human brain is wired for war and, just as in any other mammal, attacks when enraged. Angered, we "see red" because the primitive part of the brain is so activated that it paralyzes its slower but more accurate operating system. When that thinking part of the brain is "hijacked" or impaired, our lower, more animalistic part takes over and we behave in beastly ways. So chronic rage is a mental dysfunction because one part of the brain cannot be regulated by the other.

Rage stems from a combination of anxiety, pain and shame. But expressing these emotions makes us feel vulnerable and we fear being seen as weak—a terrifying proposition for anyone who grew up with a rageful parent. With years of feeling unsafe, and without any model for trusting others or talking about emotions, many abused children now living in adult bodies armor themselves against the world with a shield of anger. Activated by the smallest incident, their rage is out of control. Trying to console them in that state is hopeless and sometimes hazardous.

But this isn't the case with everyone. In other cases, rage—when used appropriately—can be the force that motivates us to greatness. Rather than "getting even" with destructive energy, a righteous indignation can power noble ambition and generous dreams. Throughout history, wise men like the Dalai Lama have met great injustices, and strong women like Indira Gandhi have moved mountains, when fury fueled right action.

 DAILY HEALTHY SEX ACTS

- If you suffer from explosive bouts of rage that terrify your loved ones, take action today and seek help.

- Notice the impulses that catapult you toward the feeling of rage. What activates you? Can you do something different to calm yourself down or take a time-out?

- If possible, use any rageful impulses today to accomplish something productive.

"Don't you long for something different to happen, something so exciting and new it carries you along with it like a great tide, something that lets your life blaze and burn so the whole world can see it? "

— Juliet Marillier

17 AUGUST

LONGING

Longing is that ache, that unmet echo, those unfulfilled needs. It's such a romantic notion. In poetry, everyone longs for everything else. Sometimes when we want something so bad, the joy of anticipatory longing is even more exciting than actual fulfillment. Certain people seem to be hopped up in this constant state, always with something to long for on the horizon—the next purchase, the next party, the next partner. Life eternally poised in possibility. What a way to feel alive, without actually doing any living.

Longing becomes its own orientation. Just as someone traumatized scans for danger and someone betrayed snoops for proofs of infidelity, so someone who has been deprived forever longs for *something* else. They can land the loving partner, the ideal job, the dream house and still get lost in longing. It's an addictive mind-state. Oftentimes spellbound states of wishing during childhood provided an escape or distraction from harsh reality. Intense longing might be preceded by an inability to handle ambivalence, usually described as life seeming "so blah." Longing is a cover-up for the inability to understand and express authentic needs.

Many times the needs underneath our longing remain unmet because we've never been able to articulate and share them. Early attempts might've been met with shaming, or perhaps we witnessed another's rejection and came to the conclusion that honesty results in pain. To bring the source of longing into the light of awareness rewires the brain pattern that constantly longs for relief without ever taking the obvious actions that would bring relief. Acknowledging our true needs doesn't guarantee they will be fulfilled, but moving beyond the fear that freezes us in a state of unfulfilled longing might elongate our capacity for inner peace.

DAILY HEALTHY SEX ACTS

- Have you ever deeply longed for a person or object? List the first four examples of longing that come to mind.

- Summon the feeling of longing. As your nervous system becomes activated, look for similarities to the state of being triggered by danger, such as witnessing an argument or accident. Today, look for any triggers preceding each moment of longing.

- Longing is not loving, although they may coexist. The next time you feel longing, visualize sending out rays of love to everyone in need. Get yourself out of deprivation and into action.

"Venereal: From Venus, the goddess of love, this word refers to the reality of desire. With the rise of Protestantism and science, the word 'disease' was tacked on in a revealing combination of categorization and moralizing. 'Which disease?' 'The disease of love.'"

— John Ralston Saul

SEXUAL HEALTH

Sexual arousal can come on like a tempest, sweeping us off our feet and washing away all thoughts of precaution or self-care. We want to stay 'in the moment' and not kill our joy with a frank discussion about sexually transmitted disease. What's more, our partner may have no interest in using protection, leaving the burden of safety to fall solely on our shoulders. When we are truly enamored, it can be difficult to speak up. "I'll be more careful next time," we might tell ourselves. Unfortunately, for anyone practicing casual or anonymous sex, STDs are a distinct reality. The willingness to talk about our status, our fears, or our desire for protection is a sign of sexual maturity; it can only lead to greater heights of intimacy and pleasure, pleasure we could never fully enjoy when secretly preoccupied with anxiety over contracting or passing on a disease.

Part of the reason it's so difficult to discuss sexual health is because of the shame and stigma we may attached to STDs—and to sex talk, for that matter. We may have been told that people who have them are unlovable, bad, or sinners. Or we may be racked with guilt or fear about spreading one. Again, as uncomfortable as disclosure to a current or potential partner may be, it can only bring us relief and peace. After all, STDs do not discriminate, and although unwanted, they remain part of human experience. Acknowledging our own humanity and vulnerability is essential to achieving sexual health, both physically and psychologically. When and if symptoms flare up, we can take the opportunity to comfort ourselves and affirm our self-worth. We can also become beacons of information and hope for others, spreading education about sexual health to our communities and using our experience to empower and enlighten others on a similar path.

 DAILY HEALTHY SEX ACTS

- Can you list ten STDs off the top of your head? Do you know the symptoms and treatments for each? What associations do you have with each, and are your perceptions based on personal experience or prejudice?

- How comfortable are you sharing and asking details about sexual health with a partner? The ability to communicate and ask questions is a basic precursor to all forms of intimacy.

- Recurring STDs can be one clear-cut sign of sex addiction. How do your sexual practices contribute to, or compromise, your sexual health?

> *"By engaging in a delusive quest for happiness, we bring only suffering upon ourselves. In our frantic search for something to quench our thirst, we overlook the water all around us and drive ourselves into exile from our own lives."*
>
> — Sharon Salzberg

19 AUGUST

SATISFACTION

There's no feeling like having our wishes fulfilled exactly the way we want. The satisfaction of a great vacation, celebration, or sexual experience rewards all the effort we put in and gives us a sense of completion and wholeness—of a life well lived. But all too often, fulfilling moments seem to arrive at random, emerging by chance and denying us the feeling that we earned them, that we control the outcome of our labors. Yet if we can accept the outcome of our efforts without judging it against our fantasies, "going with the flow" can bring great satisfaction. Seen this way, life has its own perfection, and if we can be pleased with what we have instead of being stuck on what we want, our thirst for gratification is quenched.

Dissatisfaction, then, is discontent with present reality. Look around you and notice what has you dissatisfied. Are you living the life you want, surrounded with people who love and support you? If you are tolerating anything that is less than satisfactory, you have to explore whether you're *settling* or whether you're *belittling* what you have.

To know whether your dissatisfaction with your mate, home, pet, or car is valid or vapid, first decide if you've got a problem of survival or a problem of abundance. The luxury of being able to sit and read these reflections, instead of using every ounce of strength to find food, wouldn't be available without the affluence that lets us live like kings and queens compared to most human beings. Yet we create suffering for ourselves when we ignore the riches we already have. Look around you, and if you don't like what you see, make a change—it's your life. But if you realize it just might be good enough, go to gratitude and see if your satisfaction level rises.

 DAILY HEALTHY SEX ACTS

- How satisfied are you with your sex life? Have you talked to your partner about what you need? Is the problem with you or with your partner?

- What do your living conditions look like? Do you long for something different? If so, what would make you more content? Are you seeking something from without or can you find satisfaction from within?

> *"Too much of a good thing can be wonderful."*
>
> — Mae West

MULTIPLE ORGASMS

Most people think of multiple orgasms as a sexual utopia rather than as a realistic goal that can be achieved by men and women alike. While orgasm need not be the sole aim of sexual activity, it is certainly an intensely satisfying, revitalizing part of it. How you approach orgasm psychologically makes all the difference in bed. If you can activate your mind-body connection and reset your thinking to include an abundance of orgasms, you are one step closer to the experience. But if your thinking tells you it's impossible or undesirable, your body will surely follow.

A healthy curiosity regarding human physiology and a sense of sexual adventure can relieve, and eventually replace, feelings of pressure surrounding performance. Being present to your own arousal and to that of your partner lets you focus on self-renewal in the moment. You can challenge yourself to reboot at will rather than surrender to exhaustion. Like everything worthwhile, it takes time and effort to develop this power, but it is well within your reach.

On the flip side, the practice of *karezza*, or *coitus reservatus*, can be just as mind-blowing as multiple orgasms. Remaining at the plateau phase of intercourse, prolonging sexual ecstasy, and heightening anticipation for as long as possible is a different, equally incredible tantric state that also requires the practice of a true mind-body connection.

DAILY HEALTHY SEX ACTS

- What effect does orgasm have on your body and your mind? Does it signal the end of sexual performance and interest, or do you maintain sexual arousal?

- Observe your mentality as you attempt to reset your mind and body after orgasm. Like a surfer, aim to catch each wave of sexual feeling, and trust the ocean of eroticism to carry you.

- Have you engaged in sex without the goal of orgasm? Next time you make love, practice the art of *karezza* by backing off from achieving orgasm as a means to attain a deeper erotic connection.

"When hungry, eat your rice; when tired, close your eyes. Fools may laugh at me, but wise men will know what I mean."

— Linji Yixuan

21 AUGUST

SELF-CARE

Self-care is like the airplane oxygen mask that in the event of an emergency we first fasten to ourselves before we can take care of another. If we don't take responsibility for our own care, then we're not in a state to take care of anything else. Many times it's in the rush of personal and social interaction when self-care goes by the wayside. One of the key signs of codependency and addiction is self-abandonment. Are we eating right, getting enough sleep, grooming, exercising, cleaning home and car? How about setting appropriate boundaries, and pausing before reacting? We can have so many issues around these acts, especially if they weren't effectively modeled for our unique autonomous development.

Sometimes we abandon our own care to focus on others with the hope we'll be inspired, blessed, or the person we save will return the favor out of gratitude. Cut out the middleman! The best any of us can do for others is to take care of ourselves, physically, mentally, emotionally, and psychologically. When we feel spiritually healthy, chances are we're better apt to define our genuine needs and goals. It can take time to learn to trust and not sabotage true presence of mind.

One of the most important aspects of self-care is communication, knowing that each person you're with is trustworthy. Sexually, self-care involves attending to your own sexual health and pleasure, and knowing when and how to say no even though your body might be saying yes, and vice-versa! If a past history of ignoring self-care has contributed to major problems you've faced, then an inventory of these issues might be in order. Not to punish yourself, which is the antithesis of self-care, but to truly understand your inclination. Why might you have an uncaring attitude toward your own needs? Where does your negligence originate? These are all substantial questions that you can explore, and are themselves a healthy part of self-care.

DAILY HEALTHY SEX ACTS

- List the priorities in your life. Consider how each priority impacts your self-care. Address any discrepancies. See that you're getting enough food, water and sleep each day. Usually if we think we're saving time by ignoring our own needs, our lack of energy will create the opposite effect.

- Do you need to discuss your unmet needs with your partner? If a partnership isn't reciprocal, it's not a partnership. State your needs, and listen to the needs of your partner. See any conflict through the lens of respective self-care.

> *"Love is much more fundamental than any kind of thinking or believing. It is the root and basis of who you are, at the most fundamental level. This means that anything other than love as an expression of your being is artificial and unnatural and is a result of not knowing who you are."*
>
> — Bill Harris

AUTHENTICITY

Living in authenticity is one of the great challenges of being human, and living an authentic life is an aspiration. So prepare to blunder along the path! Risking telling the truth at all times requires both courage and finesse because truth-telling can be hurtful to others, especially those who are fragile. One sure way to measure how fully you're in your truth is to track the sensations in your body. Trust your gut over your thoughts and pay attention to what answers arise for you. Also notice what happens to you when someone asks you a question that puts you on the spot: Do you answer authentically or do you veil your answer to accommodate their feelings? If you choose the latter, what does that do to your feelings about yourself? It's possible to stand in your authenticity by making it a practice to pause to see if there's a more "politic" way to speak your truth without hurting others.

Scores of comedians cite the supposedly typical scenario of a woman putting on a new outfit and asking her husband if it makes her look fat. The gag is that the woman doesn't want to hear the truth, and that the man should know he'd better lie. Such jokes make both men and women look like simpletons whose relationships are founded on manipulation. How would you answer such a question from your partner? Can you handle hearing an authentic answer, and can you give kind, authentic answers?

DAILY HEALTHY SEX ACTS

- In what ways are you inauthentic with yourself? Do you lie to yourself about how much you eat, work, or sleep? If so, ask yourself why, and then take this opportunity to stop lying to yourself.

- Spend a day noticing when you bend your truth in order to accommodate people around you—especially your partner.

- Practice speaking your truth in kind, authentic ways.

"In Tantrism, the first thing is having the experience of touch, of profound contact with things, with the universe, without mental commotion. Everything begins there: touching the universe deeply. When you touch deeply, you no longer need to let go. That occurs naturally."

— Daniel Odier

23 AUGUST

TANTRA

The basis of all Tantrism is the worship of the female and male principles found in all aspects of nature. In East Indian tradition, worship ceremonies can be as simple as thanking the Mother Goddess or as elaborate as gathering in a temple with hundreds to shower the gods with flowers and incense. But in any ritual, the symbols of the male and female—the *lingam* and *yoni*, signifying the penis and the vulva—unite as the creative powers of god and goddess. There is no feminine without the masculine and no masculine without the feminine. The creative principle arises out of the Mother; and when the *lingam* and *yoni* join, the universe is in harmony.

Missionaries misinterpreted the sacred texts of Tantrism as disgusting guides to sexual activity. But Tantric sexual ritual with one's spouse was a sacrament whose purpose was release from the cycle of birth, death, and rebirth. Breathing, meditation and liberation were key ingredients in this Tantric practice—not simply the hedonistic seeking of pleasure through sex. Tantric rites were complex, combining worship, meditation, ritual, wisdom and sexuality; Tantric texts cover topics from cosmology to breath, from charms and purification rites before sex to meditation, poetry, health care, child-rearing, magical spells, and more.

Intentionality in your sexuality is part of *your* sexual practice, too. Gay or straight, when you set intention before you have sex, you commune with your partner and with the masculine and feminine *energies* of the universe. Whether or not you choose to say a prayer, set an intention for healing or for fun. In that way you are choosing to attend to your beloved, your relationship, yourself, and the divine. By being present with the wonder that you are, you give homage to the Mother Goddess and Father God for the miracle of your existence.

DAILY HEALTHY SEX ACTS

- What rituals would you like to include before and after your sexual practices?

- What sexual practices do you hold dear? Have you introduced those to your lover? What practices can you co-create that suit you both?

- Don't hold on to a fixed belief about your sex together. Delve into the unknown and see what emerges between the two of you.

"For flavor, instant sex will never supersede the stuff you have to peel and cook."

— Quentin Crisp

QUICKIES

Quickies often speak to impatience with people and circumstances. Whether we're single or in a committed relationship, a passionate sexual conquest with an equally willing partner represents one area where it seems possible to exert personal control. The allure of wild, hot, spontaneous sex gives the wonderful illusion that life is working out the way we want it, without our having to be present for others who may be confusing or draining, who don't possess the tools to keep boundaries and sustain our arousal, or with whom we get stuck somewhere we don't want to be. Who needs such congested traffic or mind states? We want life to hurry up, we don't have time to wait—let's just get to the good stuff!

Let's face it, we don't always want to go through the rigmarole of relating, connection, intimacy, or even interaction. It's why fast food is so popular—we don't always want to interact with a waiter or shop for groceries and make a meal. We just want to grab it, eat it, and be done. But a lot of times when we think we're saving ourselves time and trouble—often by not practicing care and mindfulness—we're actually wasting more time and creating more trouble in the long run. It's like taking a shortcut that leads in the wrong direction from where we really want to go. We all really want to receive the benefits from acts of intimacy and deep caring, but we often take the shortcut to convenience and momentary relief, and find ourselves even further from our desired destination.

DAILY HEALTHY SEX ACTS

- What are the joy of quickies? There's no one way to have sex, and couples often engage in a variety of sexual styles. Today, discuss your erotic needs with your lover.

- Take a moment to consider where you are taking shortcuts in life, and whether these shortcuts lead you to your goals or away from them. For instance, if you want to save money for a vacation, how do your daily spending habits support your savings goal?

- Do you take shortcuts in relating to others? If you desire healthy relationships, then support this desire by taking the time to connect with the people in your life.

"As long as sex is dealt with in the current confusion of ignorance and sophistication, denial and indulgence, suppression and stimulation, punishment and exploitation, secrecy and display, it will be associated with a duplicity and indecency that lead neither to intellectual honesty nor human dignity."

— Alfred Kinsey

25 AUGUST

SEX EDUCATION

For many children and teenagers, sex education class provides the only place they can hope to receive accurate, non-judgmental information about their bodies, untainted by religion, politics, or the entertainment and advertising industries. Sex is a natural and integral part of life, and young people must have the subject demystified in order to come to their own conclusions about what is and isn't healthy behavior. In an open and safe environment, youths are motivated to continue their sexual education into adulthood, staying informed and conscious at each stage of their journey. Indeed, studies have shown that those who receive "sex ed" actually wait longer to have sex, refuting the feverish notion that information leads to indulgence. Rather, information is empowerment. But if a child has been exposed to shaming, damning or exploitative notions about sex, these wounds may cause pain throughout a lifetime and give rise to compulsions, repression, or both.

If we didn't receive the sex education we needed, it's never too late to learn. Even reading this book, or hopping online, starts the lifelong process of knowing. We can seek out sex-positive role models and mentors who have the ability to heal our ignorance and embarrassment with a gentle, well-timed joke or explanation. Sex education should feel like an exhilarating adventure rather than a boring clinical lecture. After all, every single one of us was born through the miracle of intercourse. We owe our lives to this fascinating process, whether we are gay, trans, bi, straight or other. We may be just beginning our education, or filling in the gaps at a late age, but learning is always best nurtured through encouragement, kindness, support, stability, appreciation and healthy boundaries that engender trust—many of the same qualities that make for healthy sexual relationships.

 DAILY HEALTHY SEX ACTS

- Did you receive formal sexual education? What areas were stressed, and which were ignored?

- How can comprehensive sexual education be taught in schools around the world? Today, write about your own sex ed classes. Did they help or hinder your sexual maturation? If you feel safe, share your story in online discussions or print publications to add your piece to this political puzzle.

- Most sex ed focuses on biology, without exploring the psychological questions about personal sexuality that paralyze so many. What would you still like to learn about sex and, in particular, your own sexuality?

"The secret self knows the anguish of our attachments and assures us that letting go of what we think we must have to be happy is the same as letting go of our unhappiness."

— Guy Finley

EXPECTATIONS

"Let go." This is the call to happiness in most teachings. Expectation can be a way to avoid the present, and anticipation can bring overwhelming nervous excitement. Let go. See what plays out between you and your environment.

We've all planned vacations with high expectations, only to be disappointed that our experience didn't meet them. The let-down was not caused by the place we visited or the experiences we had there. The problem was having held expectations that catapulted us into the future so far we could not stay in the present.

Let go; be here now. Drop your expectations about what "great sex" is and see what happens next time you connect with your beloved. Stop worrying about his or her orgasm or how you think the sexual experience should go. Allow each happening to have its own unique imprint and don't measure it against the last time or how you think it "should have gone." Let go of your unhappiness about your sex life and enjoy!

DAILY HEALTHY SEX ACTS

- Drop your expectations about your next sexual encounter with your partner.

- Show up in the present moment, breathe, and let nature take her course.

- Stay present in your body and with your partner, and be willing to step into the unknown and see what unfolds.

"To love is to know the sacrifices which eternity exacts from life."

— John Oliver Hobbes

27 AUGUST

SACRIFICE

If love were an altar, what parts of yourself would you be willing to sacrifice? It's not hard to see how ancient civilizations, traumatized by the harshness of early human existence, might have assuaged their fears through the ritual of offering treasured possessions to the gods in a symbolic gesture reflecting the surrendered individuality required for their survival. But we also engage in quite healthy and necessary sacrifice by giving up short-lived pleasures for long-term goals. At a basic level, we all surrender childhood innocence and animal instincts in order to grow up, to live successfully in society, and to become our best selves. We also know that joining in romantic relationship with another demands basic sacrifices which can feel difficult: Just for starters, we must forfeit our single-hood and our refusal of accountability, all of which may have served deep psychological purposes. In fact, part of being in relationship with someone, whether romantic or platonic, is sometimes having to forgo personal desire for the greater good.

But when a sacrifice is made not for mutual benefit but to a false god—a delusional mind state—it creates pain and resentment. We all know the martyr who sacrifices personal fulfillment for the sake of enabling others, or the killjoy who abandons pleasure for accomplishment and discovers too late that life has passed. Couples may sacrifice real intimacy for sexual relief, and be surprised to find their emotional connection weakening. Healthy sacrifice requires open discussion and open-handed motives to determine whether our actions in fact serve the greater good—a good which must include our own higher selves.

DAILY HEALTHY SEX ACTS

- List the major sacrifices you've made in relationships. Do you harbor any lingering resentments or regrets? Next to each sacrifice, write what you were hoping to achieve. Own your choices and the inner qualities you were seeking to cultivate.

- History abounds with stories of unthinkable sacrifice for noble causes. Determine which sacrifices you need to make for the noble cause of your best self: Using your time more wisely? Learning to unwind? Eating healthfully? Consciously sacrifice the habits holding you back by surrendering them to a Higher Power. Sometimes we must aim beyond the goal to reach our real mark.

> *"Lots of people want to ride with you in the limo, but what you want is someone who will take the bus with you when the limo breaks down."*
>
> — Oprah Winfrey

DEPENDABILITY

Having people to depend on gives us a metaphorical backbone, a feeling that we're never alone. For some, growing up with unreliable, immature parents created hyper-responsibility because their very lives depended on self-sufficiency. Others became helpless, accepting their deprivation and remaining self-neglectful well into adulthood. Dependability is a basic need for children and not too much to ask for in adulthood. When we ask for our dependency needs to be met, we allow people closest to us to care for us. The knowledge that we can call a trusted other and know that he or she will be there at a moment's notice, no questions asked, telegraphs to us that we have value. And just as dependability signals true friendship, it's one of the primary qualities in a love relationship because it makes us feel safe, loved, and cared for.

It's easy to be dependable when the requests made of us cost little effort or gain us pleasure. Following through on plans to vacation with someone is a form of dependability but has the dual purpose of satisfying our own desire. But the call to be dependable can be inconvenient when it doesn't serve mutually—even little chores like picking up our partner's dry-cleaning or taking her or his pet to the vet. Being of service when our lover is sick or challenged by a death in the family is where the rubber meets the road. Life is unpredictable. When we're called to participate in painful events it can feel scary or burdensome to suspend our lives and go to a loved one's side. Every day we expect dependability from our cars, co-workers, and computers. So we should hold ourselves to the same standard of dependability we expect from associates and machines when beloved hearts are at stake.

DAILY HEALTHY SEX ACTS

- When was the last time you asked someone to do something for you? Did he or she come through? How did that feel?

- Who in your life has been undependable? How did their lack of reliability affect you?

- How dependable are you where your relationships are concerned? Today, practice dependability by offering someone close to you a service that may inconvenience you.

> *"Never apologize for showing feeling. When you do so, you apologize for the Truth."*
> — Benjamin Disraeli

29 AUGUST

EMOTIONAL TRUTH

Being emotionally honest can be tough because, first and foremost, it calls upon us to be true to ourselves and, secondly, it can upset those on the receiving end. Speaking our truth is actually a two-part process that asks us to garner our strength for making an honest statement *and* for tolerating the other's—sometimes unfavorable—response. But being emotionally honest frees us from emotional distress and bodily stress, making it an act of self-care and giving us a sense of liberation and pride. Claiming these feelings is one of the greatest gifts we can give ourselves, yet most of us were programmed to keep our feelings and opinions to ourselves, so doing the opposite feels scary. We've been warned not to "hurt other people's feelings" or were taught to circle around the truth and even to manipulate others to get our needs met.

One of the perils of emotional honesty is the risk that we'll have to soothe *ourselves* if another gets wounded, hurt, angry, or rejecting. Confrontation is understandably anxiety-producing, but its dangers are inherent in human relations, which can be messy. Truth-telling comes with a price that sometimes we, and those around us, don't like. There's no easy street in life, just emotional obstacle courses designed to make us and our principles stronger. Consider that telling people you're angry at them or that you love them are both confrontations requiring you to screw up your courage and brace for their response—understanding, anger, adoration, shame, or a myriad of other emotions that you can't control.

Intentionally taking your own shape, not the shape you shifted in and out of as a child to accommodate adults, is your goal. Not everyone will like that shape, but at least, they'll respect you. More important, you'll respect yourself.

DAILY HEALTHY SEX ACTS

- Think about a situation in the past when you took the easy way out by not speaking your truth. Afterwards, did you feel short-changed or that you had failed yourself?

- Today, look for small opportunities to speak your deeper truth and do so. Notice the reactions from the people around you. How do they tolerate it? How do you tolerate their reactions? Notice how you feel in response to their reactions.

"One's destination is never a place, but a new way of seeing things."

— Henry Miller

It's important to travel, even locally, to new surroundings, otherwise we're just armchair adventurists. We can sit around and wonder about our world's diverse cultures and infinitely varied experiences. But to displace ourselves physically into distant, new worlds has a demonstrable effect on *us*.

Similarly, we can read self-help works and discuss our love lives with friends, therapists, and support groups *ad infinitum*, but if we're not traveling to our personal destination we're just thumbing through guidebooks without leaving the hotel. We need to risk taking that first step away from the comfort of home even to discover, and then fulfill, our true potential.

Relationships also benefit from stepping out of the habitual routine, whether through a dream vacation or a local hotel reservation. Our lives and loves can suffocate from sameness—we wake up in the same bed, walk through the same rooms, live the same lives. Creating new experiences to share injects novelty and new visions into familiarity.

What do we give off when we're traveling that creates such erotic opportunity? Foreignness often rouses the nervous system into overdrive as we scan for danger. In addition, our nervous system sets off a host of neurophysiological processes such as heightened perception, which can make us more visually aware and emotionally more present. For this reason, strangers we see on vacations often look familiar. When we're attentive to a fresh environment, we tend to see more deeply into others, and to make ourselves more known.

DAILY HEALTHY SEX ACTS

- We're all travelers. Today, walk or drive on new streets. If you've always wanted to visit a local site, make time in your schedule to do so, and make it a mini-vacation. Bring your adventure senses and glimpse a new world.

- Relationships can strain under the reality of world travel. How do you navigate bumps along the road? Recall any stresses on the road. What did they reveal about the relationship?

- Every few months, plan an overnight stay at a hotel with your partner, or swap homes with a close friend. Take the pressure off those once-in-a-lifetime trips by starting with small excursions. Oddly, liberating ourselves from familiar routines takes practice!

"Open your heart and take us in,
Love–love and me."

— William Ernest Henley

31 AUGUST

OPEN-
HEARTEDNESS

Every person possesses the potential for open-heartedness—for inclusive understanding and acceptance of another. The real art is to stretch into open-heartedness right when you feel most like isolating and shutting down. It's so easy to close your heart, especially against a partner (and against all humankind, at times). We call withholding love "being cold" while open-heartedness is called "being warm," and it's possible that vital energy is in fact shared when you open your heart to another.

But first, open your heart to yourself. Show yourself love even when—especially when—you fall short, because shame, disappointment, or regret can never open your heart.

There's a saying that indulging anger is like picking up a blazing ember to throw at someone—you get burned in the process. It's the same with close-heartedness. You might want to close your heart to protect yourself from intimidating or hostile forces, and yet closing your heart is one of the most hurtful acts you can do to yourself. *Closing your heart as a form of protection is a contradiction.* Your only true protection in any challenging situation is to open your heart so you can keep the vital energy flowing inside you.

DAILY HEALTHY SEX ACTS

- Share with a partner or friend: What opens your heart? What closes your heart?

- With your hands, feel the vibration of your own opening heart. Imagine that vibration expanding and basking everyone you encounter today in its warmth and energy.

- Practice synchronized heart-opening with your beloved. Explore together what it feels like to close and open the vital energies of loving hearts.

September

"Certainty is knowing that this system works, and because it works, I'm in the right place right now, regardless of how it looks. And since I'm in the right place, at the right time, every time, I need to be good with where I'm at—no matter what."

— Yehuda Berg

1 SEPTEMBER

CERTAINTY

Certainty is faith that an answer to any problem exists. With certainty, we can approach difficulties as challenges. To behold in loved ones the certain attributes of their best selves is an affirmative act. But how frequently does our daily behavior contradict even our surest beliefs? If we believe in the power of unconditional love, we must certainly embody this belief or endure an ambivalence of our own making.

There is much we can't know in this world. There's a tale about a god who greets a man with the promise of riches if the man can keep silent. The god commits escalating acts of mischief, but when he slays a traveler the man angrily renounces the god and the reward. Finally, the god reveals his hidden agenda: slaying the traveler, a villain seeking to destroy the next town. The moral isn't that killing may be justified, but that ethical certainty is subtler than our perceptions, because we are ignorant of so much.

But the imperfection of human knowledge is not a call to chaos. We are most assuredly guided to mindful actions by internal morality, for those thoughts and feelings are knowable. We may not see whether we're making the right decisions or whether a person is right for us, but we can be sure that the questions have entered our awareness. This distinction is both subtle and certain. We spend so much of our lives questioning the meaning of external reality that we often ignore our own inner reality. Follow the flow of your thoughts, and pay particular attention to contrary cognitions. You may be certain that the work of reconciling contradictory inner messages will bring new levels of understanding, self-actualization, and a certain serenity.

DAILY HEALTHY SEX ACTS

- Today, summon certainty for all that you do. Connect with your intentions and trust that by following your instincts with an open heart you are fulfilling your destiny to affirm your inner truth.

- Recall the most recent experience of certainty in your life. How did it feel in your mind and body? Write down similar experiences throughout your life. Although doubts may surface, try to summon this surge of certainty through the expression of treasured values today. For instance, when you smile at your beloved, smile with such certainty.

"For every beauty there is an eye somewhere to see it. For every truth there is an ear somewhere to hear it. For every love there is a heart somewhere to receive it."

— Ivan Panin

RECEPTIVITY

Our capacity to receive—be it love, money, friendship, compliments or presents—stems from our ability to acknowledge our own worth. So often we carry within us a deep sense of being undeserving, and whether that feeling is conscious or unconscious, it makes us repel the very affection and abundance we so desperately seek. The world around us reflects our inner vision; if we have a poor self-image, we'll be blind to gifts from others since we have grown visual receptors only for rejection, mistreatment and unkindness, never seeing the love.

Sometimes a good first step is to begin sharing our gifts and attributes with ourselves through the use of positive affirmations and meditation. We must do this work for ourselves before becoming involved with partners, otherwise they simply become a convoluted means to our same, habitual end of misprizing ourselves: We'd use their constant validation and praise to feel momentarily good about ourselves, but this dynamic would not foster receptivity as much as codependence.

To practice receptivity, we can also practice actively appreciating the good in others, celebrating them and offering support and encouragement. We can make a point of meeting another's gaze and allowing ourselves to receive that connection. We can hear others out, even if we suspect their ideas are off-kilter. In these practices, receptivity brings openness—taking in new points of view, suggestions, strategies and possibilities—and allowing them to alter and affect us deeply. We can become highly receptive to change and growth. We can encounter a mystery and open our hearts to the grand uncertainly of life on this planet. In the end, receptivity is intense aliveness in which we deny no one and nothing, and thus receive everyone and everything.

DAILY HEALTHY SEX ACTS

- If you opened your body/mind/spirit to receiving love and abundance, what would you have to give up? Today, choose to open yourself to all unknown possibilities.

- When we think we know everything about sex, or make assumptions about our partner, we're no longer receptive. Today, how can you give up false omniscience and embrace true openness?

- Ask your partner for one pleasurable act that you ordinarily wouldn't be receptive to. Notice your discomfort with asking. Then notice what you feel when receiving. Give the gift of receiving today.

"This is love: to fly toward a secret sky, to cause a hundred veils to fall each moment. First to let go of life. Finally, to take a step without feet."

— Rumi

3 SEPTEMBER

IMAGINATION

All desire requires imagination, the ability to form mental pictures. Lovers' comfortably inviting each other into the world of their imagination is a wonderful sign of trust and intimacy. Imagination is also indispensable for developing consideration toward others through the ability to imagine the impact our actions may have on someone. So imagination creates consideration, which creates trust, which creates more imagination! One rule of improvisational theater is to answer "yes" to any creative impulse. This permission lets stories deepen and bloom. In relationships, similarly open-minded imagination allows for love to blossom. Rather than, "Yes, *but*—", it's "Yes, and *how about this!*" When we allow room for the imaginative impulses of our beloved, we may glimpse their mind's eye as sacred, just as our own consciousness comes from a higher place. We don't create the treasured and trustworthy people we know, or when and how they enter our lives, so why would we try and control the visions they have to inspire us?

We must learn to accept and cherish our own creative impulses. How often do we reject our nascent inventive offerings out of shame for their primitiveness? All creative impulses are psychological impulses. Imagination lets us receive all that comes to consciousness as raw material, as clay for our life sculpture. Everything has worth for the purpose of revealing and healing self. It takes as much imagination to conjure the fear that represses authentic expression as it does to summon the faith that supports self-acceptance. *Active imagination* is a therapeutic technique that encourages unconscious mental and emotional content to come to the surface in order to discover the true self. Sometimes unleashing imagination may lead us to forge meaningful connections with the world, and sometimes the mere act of validating creative impulses will give birth to hidden material underneath, revealing our true gold.

DAILY HEALTHY SEX ACTS

- Trust your creative impulses.

- How often does what you imagine match up to reality? Today, take note of the imaginative projections you place on the future and whether they hit the mark. Re-imagine yourself.

- Is life a loving or hostile place, do you imagine? Affirm that all's well. Even when life seems bad, imagine the good underneath. Imagine a loving world today.

> *"When we deny the spiritual dimension to our existence, we end up living like animals. And when we deny the physical, sexual dimension to our existence, we end up living like angels. And both ways are destructive, because God made us human."*
>
> — Rob Bell

DENIAL

Denial is an insidious habit that keeps us from learning painful truths. Whatever we can't admit, ironically, engulfs our experience of reality like quicksand. We become the proverbial ostrich with its head buried in the ground, refusing to recognize realities about a situation or person. When we deny any part of our selves—past abuse, current problems, or sexual identity—we split ourselves into shards. And this splitting is the life-force of addiction, essential for it to grow, metastasize, and suffocate us.

Borne out of unbearable pain, denial is constructed of distorted pieces of our psyche convincing us to minimize, justify, and rationalize reality. Together, these workings of denial shield us from horrific memories or unacceptable present circumstances. When life becomes too heavy to bear we may turn to substances or processes to mitigate the misery. What may start out under the guise of youthful experimentation can lead to excess and even addiction, until one day we realize that our ability to choose vanished long ago, and shackles manifest around a wholly unrecognizable self. Empty and adrift, we flounder without direction, grabbing onto grandiose ideas of what we would like to be or who we would like to be with.

Often, the only way we can awaken from the stupor of denial is by "hitting bottom"—experiencing an intolerably humiliating or near-death event. Waking up may mean we see that a toxic relationship we've been hanging onto must end. Facing the ensuing loneliness, along with the other unhappy realities of our life, is imperative for healing to begin. This process, sometimes called "withdrawal," sees the denied pain of the past rise to the surface once the object of desire—person or substance—has gone. Exploring the pain with trusted others is the next difficult task that lets us breathe free.

DAILY HEALTHY SEX ACTS

- Do you find yourself minimizing, justifying, or rationalizing past situations or current people or behaviors in your life? If so, what are the distortions you tell yourself so as not to upset the status quo?

- What one thing do you need to give up in order to step out of denial?

- If you're unsure about a relationship or behavior you're engaging in, ask your closest friends what they think. Put down your defensiveness and listen with an open mind.

"Love leads to present rapture, —then to pain;
But all through Love in time is healed again."
— Charles Godfrey Leland

5 SEPTEMBER

HEALING

Like all organisms, the human organism is encoded to move towards health and healing. But any type of healing takes time, and psychic healing especially requires sustained effort and a lot of deliberate repair work. Love is the remedy that will make your relationship sound or whole again, but you must take great care and have great patience to restore its health, particularly if you or your partner's sexuality was vandalized in childhood or if there's been a betrayal in the relationship.

The road to healing begins with your commitment to stop hurting yourself, to tend to your partner's heart and pain, and to ask to be tended to if you're in distress. Long after you've done the repair work you both may need to do, you must keep a keen eye on the love you and your partner need in order to keep moving forward in the relationship. When this care is done consciously, when you feel you can trust of your partner to be solid for you, and when reactions aren't taken personally, sex can be a powerful arena for healing old wounds.

DAILY HEALTHY SEX ACTS

- Assess where your partner might be hurting. Does s/he need reassurance? If so, how—a kind word, compliment, gesture, or laugh?

- How current are you with where s/he is in the internal healing process? Get curious, ask questions, then follow through with actions that demonstrate your love.

- Be curious about your partner's experience before, during, and after sex. What does s/he need? Be honest about what you can and can't give.

"When we look into our own hearts and begin to discover what is confused and what is brilliant, what is bitter and what is sweet, it isn't just ourselves that we're discovering. We're discovering the universe."

— Pema Chödrön

UNIVERSALITY

If we focus primarily on the world of appearances, it's easy to be overwhelmed by the multiplicity of objects. Everything we see is different and diverse, for all things are unique in time and space. Phenomena appear to our senses through separateness—a process which may confirm any feelings of alienation and disharmony we may carry. Yet when we are filled with inner calm, the whole world seems to unfold toward us with a unified, measured grace. As we process, so we perceive. *Self-consciousness* usually refers to knowing one's little self—a private awareness to which one has sole access. But the more you seek within, the more you find your universality—the synchronicity of your life with the larger picture. Ironically, it's only by looking within that we can connect without.

When troubled, we often turn to the restorative quality of nature to find universal principles of growth, transformation, cyclicity, and other *archetypal* processes characterizing the great patterns of our universe. To conjure the significance of archetypes, imagine you were to ask people from different cultures to describe a tree. You might get one list of attributes specific to each culture, and another list of shared attributes like roots, trunk, bark, and branches. The identical words embody the *archetype* of a tree, because they indicate a universal experience.

How often does a lover's kiss seem to suspend the specificity of the moment to align with all sexual embraces in existence? The ripples made by erotic love extend throughout the circle of life. Our relationship with the whole world is mirrored in love, family and other interdependent systems that are microcosms of universality. "All for one, and one for all!" is the famous phrase that underscores a fundamental psychological need to make overarching, unifying sense of our personal universe.

DAILY HEALTHY SEX ACTS

- Have you ever felt alone in your experience, but later realized it was universal?

- Do you keep anything secret that might prove universal if brought to light? Today, reveal your truth, and find you're in good company.

- What main themes, or archetypes, recur in your life? Does your relationship with a parent or sibling reappear in many forms? Do you encounter the same problem in different situations? Today, seek solutions in others' universal experiences.

> *"You have to accept the fact that part of the sizzle of sex comes from the danger of sex. You can be overpowered."*
>
> — Camille Paglia

7 SEPTEMBER

SEXUAL DANGER

Is there a safe way to invite sexual danger? As long as we remain mindful and present, aware of what we're doing and why, we can find healthy ways to express these needs with a partner. When the pursuit of sexual danger becomes a means of self-sabotage or self-harm rather than a path to reclaiming more authenticity, it ceases to be a viable source of sensual self-expression and loses its positive qualities. Questionable sexual danger includes acting out consensual rape fantasies, having sex in a taboo—sometimes an illegal—location, and extreme paraphilias such as erotic asphyxiation. The consequences of these acts can include retraumatization, arrest, lifetime sex-offender registration, and even death.

A number of studies have shown that our brains have a hard time differentiating between sexual arousal and fear. Danger triggers a release of adrenaline that heightens our senses and renders us hyper-engaged. It even releases neurochemicals that actually make us more receptive to bonding because we're looking for safety.

For some, pushing the limits of danger can be a huge turn-on, while for others it can represent a fleeing from reality and an unhealthy restaging of past traumas. Sometimes society oppresses us with so much shame, prejudice, rules and judgments that the simplest sexual acts take on an aura of danger, even though they are not unnatural. If we removed those external influences, the forbidden activity might even lose its allure. In all these, we may just be seeking a way to defy repression or to reintegrate hidden, compartmentalized aspects of our sexuality. For we desire to express the elements of our selves that we must routinely hide from friends, family and co-workers, and thus to experience a fuller sense of self.

DAILY HEALTHY SEX ACTS

- List everything you find dangerous about sex. Have you ever engaged in consensual sexual danger, such as public sexual activity or role-playing, as a means to experience heightened feelings? What psychological needs could have been driving those actions?

- Consider the relationship between fear and attraction in your love life. Do scary moments—car accidents, horror films, natural disasters—lead to greater closeness? Do you ever seek out or highlight danger to make that happen?

"Tis true, my form is something odd
But blaming me is blaming God.
Could I create myself anew
I would not fail in pleasing you."

— Joseph Merrick

BODY IMAGE

How sad that so many people have crippling body image issues to which their only solution is, "I have got to look better." But we're all built into bodies that have innumerable socially unacceptable realities like susceptibility to illness, elimination, and deterioration, to name only a few. To deny any aspect of your actual body and functions is to cut yourself off from life and reality—not only from your own, but from others' as well.

Bodily ideals, although diverging wildly in different cultures and periods, challenge and judge every individual— even the seemingly "beautiful." While such aesthetic standards can encourage healthy self-improvement, they often impair self-acceptance. We have constant proof of our corporeal failings—and of our inevitably temporary and comparative successes. An exalted, unrealistic sense of one's bodily perfection cannot substitute for a realistic, healthy body image. How can you separate your identity from your body, and show your body as much kindness and compassion as you might show an honored guest? If you aim to grow your psychological capacity for healthy relationships, learning to love your body unconditionally is a good place to start—after all, you're rather attached to it!

DAILY HEALTHY SEX ACTS

- Look in a full-length mirror and note your reaction. Does your body consciousness react like a being that's connected, present and mature, or like an overly disciplined or neglected child?

- Ask your body consciousness how you may forge a meaningful connection to your body over time.

- Send love to your body. Promise to love, esteem and care for your body in any condition, *at least* as much as you love, esteem and care for others in your life. Allow your most loving energy to flow through your body today.

"If you can see your path laid out in front of you step by step, you know it's not your path. Your own path you make with every step you take. That's why it's your path."

— Joseph Campbell

9 SEPTEMBER

SELF-KNOWLEDGE

When we consider the meaning of *intimacy*, it's useful to recall that the ability "to *intimate*," or express, an emotional truth to another necessitates a functional process of self-knowledge. Like so many of our qualities (honesty, health or happiness, for example) self-knowledge is an ongoing practice rather than a destination. We don't expect even smart people to know everything, and similarly the ancient aphorism, "know thyself," doesn't mean there's any cheat sheet or code that can crack open the vault of your own being once and for all. Rather, you embrace the seeking of knowledge as a cherished value, and exercise your intellectual muscles to expand and apply it to real life.

"To know" someone in the biblical sense means to have sexual relations with that person. By extension, one might assume self-knowledge refers to some kind of masturbatory act! But, no. However, there are those who decry any introspection as navel-gazing self-centeredness and, for some, this might be the case. Acquiring self-knowledge without resultant action is like striking a match for heat without lighting a fire—it fails to fulfill its purpose. Self-knowledge requires awareness, development *and* implementation. Any time you find yourself yet again in a familiarly disappointing situation, such as ending up in bed with a partner who doesn't satisfy you sexually or emotionally, ask yourself if this might point to a lack of self-knowledge. Only when we know ourselves may we truly know others. Self-knowledge is not a magic wand, just as knowing you have an illness doesn't always cure it, but it will certainly allow you to make healthier decisions for yourself.

DAILY HEALTHY SEX ACTS

- What do you know about yourself? Jot down a quick list. Now, list what you don't know about yourself. Sometimes knowing what you don't know about yourself can be as important as knowing what you do know.

- The process by which you get to know yourself is key. Write down your own process for knowing, as if you were to impart this wisdom to others.

- What do you know about yourself sexually today? Make a list. Do your actual sexual experiences today mirror your hard-won erotic self-knowledge? Put your ideas into actions, and live what you really know.

> *"The hypothalamus is one of the most important parts of the brain, involved in many kinds of motivation, among other functions. The hypothalamus controls the 'Four F's': fighting, fleeing, feeding, and mating."*
>
> — Marvin Dunnette

BRAIN POWER

We've all heard the phrase, "Use it or lose it," and it couldn't be more accurate regarding both our brains and our genitals. The hypothalamus is one of the major connectors between the brain and the body, motivating us to all kinds of actions, including sex. For this reason we often refer to the brain as the biggest sex organ in the body. When we see an image or person that excites our mental sexual template, signals go through the hypothalamus down to the genitals. Well after we've taken in the data, seconds, even minutes, pass before the genitals are aroused. Exercising discretion about which and how many images we take in and what sexual situations we enter means we're using our "brain power" rather than being run by our genital power. With good brain-power (or impulse control) you can enjoy beauty and sensuality all day long without over-taxing or abusing your brain/body.

While letting endless sexual images of all types run rampant in our mind can create sexual problems, depriving ourselves of sexual energy and attraction can create another kind of sexual problem. If we don't use our genitals, meaning if we don't have healthy, regular sexual contact for the purpose of pleasure and connection with a lover, it can eventually take longer for us to get aroused by sex. Remember, your body is your temple, so don't deny yourself pleasure—use it, or lose it.

DAILY HEALTHY SEX ACTS

- Are you overtaxing your brain/body by looking at too many pornographic images or masturbating compulsively? Are there other ways you let your arousal run you instead of using your brain-power?

- Be honest with yourself by looking at your sexual habits and assess whether you're out of control with sexual behaviors.

- Do you deny yourself sexual pleasure? If so, why? When did that begin? Do you need to share your excuses or fears with someone? Do so today.

"Each one of us needs to discover the proper balance between the masculine and feminine energies, between the active and the receptive."

— Ravi Ravindra

11 SEPTEMBER

EQUILIBRIUM

Equilibrium is the artful balancing of opposites whose end result is mental, emotional and spiritual poise. Such steadiness touches all aspects of our identity, from the expression of our genders to the roles we play in relationships. As youngsters we may have perceived ourselves in stark polarities, led to believe we must choose a narrow interpretation of our self that fits into a single, easily-checked box. Indeed, society often prefers us to be one thing *or* the other. As a result we may have grown comfortable with our femininity, but shrink at the more masculine elements of our personality. Or maybe we've become content to call ourselves athletic while quietly disowning our intellectual abilities. With honest reflection and exploration, however, we can learn to embrace a vast, varied, and evolving palette of traits that paints our self-image expansively and fully.

Like individuals, healthy relationships thrive on balance. Practicing equilibrium with a sexual partner can be a harrowing *and* a wonderful adventure— one in which we risk inhabiting new mindsets, behaviors, and emotions. If we're used to having our partner initiate physical intimacy, what would it feel like to take charge ourselves for a change? Creating balance between leading and following can strengthen and nurture a blossoming bond. If we are more at ease when we are giving pleasure, we can practice opening ourselves up to being the receiving party, and may discover that we don't always have to be the one in control. In the same way that a spinning top effortlessly changes direction without tipping over, equilibrium ensures spontaneity and variation in our sex life. It empowers us to stretch beyond our perceived limits and to own every nuance of our sexual makeup—even those we never admitted before.

DAILY HEALTHY SEX ACTS

- Right now, imagine perfect equilibrium between your inner and outer reality—your left and right brain in sync; your feminine and masculine energies in balance and at peace.

- Visualize the world at peace. Do-gooders and wrong-doers, progressives and conservatives, women and men—all polarities in this world at peace, just for now.

- Seek equilibrium in your love life. If you initiate, follow. If you focus on your own pleasure, focus on your partner's. Switch positions, and energize *the other side of yourself.*

> *"Let me never fall into the vulgar mistake of dreaming that I am persecuted whenever I am contradicted."*
>
> — Ralph Waldo Emerson

VICTIMHOOD

"It's their fault." "No one understands me." "Everyone's against me." Sound familiar? Victim states perpetuate past trauma states, where mental distortions combine with triggered feelings to fabricate a sense of persecution. In such addictive mind-states, we hear censure in every comment. Everyone turns into our distant father or critical mother or abusive ex-lover. Early physical or psychological violence echoes throughout the lives of those who habitually assume the mantle of victimhood even when victimization has ceased. Shell-shocked from past hurt, they exist perpetually hopped up on the chaotic adrenalin that trauma released. Even when pity-seeking seems a conscious choice to elicit special favors—a ploy perfected by con artists and sociopaths—it's never really a free choice. Offered healthy options, who would elect the pain of self-induced oppression?

Knee-jerk victimhood is a coping mechanism common to youngest siblings or abused animals, who automatically whine, cry and mew at the slightest provocation. Their compulsive state of victimized tension may be exacerbated by our unhealthy cultural paradigm of punishing the victim. So how can we each free ourselves from playing the victim in a way that's not shaming? Because the last thing any victim needs is to be shamed. Anyone who's worked with abused animals knows that shaming or scolding won't bring them to health. It takes a lot of patience, love, and reliability to create a sense of safety so they can start to trust again. For human beings as well, we need to see life as a returning from victimhood. Suffering may be part of existence, and surely we are all broken on some level. But love and time and safety helps us heal ourselves and others.

DAILY HEALTHY SEX ACTS

- One way to uncover and address the inner victim is to watch out for verbal extremism in the words you choose. Today notice when and how you use the words *Always* and *Never* in conversation, and try to find more exact, realistic terms to describe what you're experiencing.

- Send healing love to the universe today and everyone who touches your life from the people you see on the street to the unseen artisans who constructed the rooms you inhabit and the vast web of circumstances, good and bad, that have led to each moment.

> "Wanting things to be otherwise is the very essence of suffering. We almost never directly experience what pain is because our reaction to it is so immediate that most of what we call pain is actually our experience of resistance to that phenomenon."
>
> — Stephen Levine

13 SEPTEMBER

PAIN

Pain can be mostly emotional or mostly physical, but always combines some of both. When a love relationship ends, we feel *broken-hearted* because we literally feel pain in our heart. Attachment patterns that are woven when we fall in love and when we love over time are formidable ropes that bind us together, so severing them can feel just like losing a limb because we can't separate brain/mind/body pain.

Sexual pain, whether unconsciously elicited or intentional, differs from other sorts of pain. Pain tolerance is as unique as fingerprints and can be trauma-based or chosen. It's not uncommon for unresolved trauma to manifest itself in the body, creating conditions like painful intercourse for women or performance anxiety for men. How we navigate painful sex can spell the difference between a lifetime of healthy and a lifetime of unhealthy sexual practices. For some, unresolved trauma has become part of a sexual/pain arousal template. When psychological pain follows physical pain during sex, it's a message that the habit of pain is out of alignment with one's real self. Ignoring that pain by continuing those sexual behaviors will lead to exhaustion and despair. But for others, sexual pain during consensual sexual play states that are considered mutually fun shows that a couple has talked about what turns them on sexually. Practice discernment.

When biomechanical problems like back, knee, or post-surgical discomfort get in the way, it's time to learn different sexual positions, incorporate breathing exercises, and slow down. Cultivate mental health through conversations with your partner to create an atmosphere of relaxation, and you will help expand pain-free sex even after injury. In these instances, we have both to grieve the loss of the body's mobility, and avoid the additional pain of comparing our self to how we once were or to other people.

DAILY HEALTHY SEX ACTS

- Are you engaged in psychologically or physically painful sexual practices? If so, when did you start them? Why? Is it time to talk to someone about how you can have a healthier sex life?

- If you have physical ailments, take the time to investigate what positions feel most comfortable and what care you can incorporate (like propping your back up with a pillow) in order to have more enjoyable sex.

"Pity me that the heart is slow to learn
What the swift mind beholds at every turn."

— Edna St. Vincent Millay

Some people reading this reflection are in recovery for sex addiction or love addiction. But one person's recovery is everyone's recovery. We don't have to be addicts ourselves to recover from toxic views, beliefs and messages that do not serve us. All of us are aware of the toxic extremes of sex and love, which can result in sex crimes, stalking, rape, emotional anorexia, heartbreak and suicide. The too-long list of toxic sex and love is ages old and universal. It's the way that humans have always and everywhere related to other humans by objectifying, exploiting, and controlling them. So we all can recover from misinformation and unhealthy ways of feeling and behaving.

Sobriety and *recovery* often seem interchangeable terms, but are in fact very different. Sexual sobriety means ceasing to act out unhealthy sexual behaviors, while recovery means recapturing one's sexual health. This definition of recovery assumes that we're all naturally born with sexual health, however impacted by genetic predispositions or physiological conditions, which psychic trauma has damaged. But we cannot regain sexual health—our sexuality—unless we take steps to create the improved conditions that will imprint our brains with healthy patterns.

DAILY HEALTHY SEX ACTS

- What is your sexual health? Imagine how you might function in your sexual, emotional and relational prime. Write a list of what's stopping you. Do you have blocks, a lack of opportunity or other challenges?

- Research every obstacle to sexual health on your list. How do people recover from similar problems? Order books, schedule consultations, or sign up for workshops. The surest path to the full recovery of your sexual health starts with the first step.

*"The tragedy is when you've got sex in the head
instead of down where it belongs."*

— D. H. Lawrence

15 SEPTEMBER

PREOCCUPATION

Preoccupation is a hallmark of addiction, as it's a great way to distract the mind from painful feelings. It's often remarked that our society is sexually preoccupied, which similarly points to unresolved sexual issues or trauma in our shared history. Of course, mental concentration can be very healthy and effective for uncovering real truths, but the same process can slip into preoccupation or obsession.

While healthy concentration invites in new ideas, preoccupation holds hostages. Healthy concentration focuses awareness on a mental object in order to suspend self-consciousness and integrate content from the subconscious mind. Conversely, preoccupied persons become overpowered by subconscious content. Whatever self-awareness they possess gets projected onto the mental object of their attention, turning it into a "fetish"—an object which contains their own subjective properties. When there's excess pain or trauma and it's no longer safe to be feeling one's subjective feelings, when there are no tools to process and regulate difficult feelings, they have to be objectified, dissociated from, and cast out onto something. This is the root cause of preoccupation.

Preoccupation always seems to promise that good can come of it and that by indulging in it, it will resolve itself. But a preoccupied state in fact perpetuates a negative cycle. The only way to bring healing in such a situation is to leave the preoccupied state, either in the short-term through some kind of disruption, or by developing present awareness over time.

DAILY HEALTHY SEX ACTS

- Observe your thoughts today. What thoughts are productive, and what thoughts are the echoes of stress, anxiety or escapism? What physical sensations accompany such thoughts?

- Breathe into your dissociated thinking. Send oxygen to your brain. Feel your body.

- Choose one or more areas of your life that could benefit from healthy concentration, such as a specific issue in your love life, your sex life, or another area. The next time you find your mind drifting into random sexual, romantic or relational preoccupation, harness this energy to focus on these chosen issues, and to invite greater meaning into your life. Actively engage in brain play!

"Why do you take by force what you could obtain by love?"

— Chief Powhatan

The force of our most sacred feelings expressed through sexual acts leaves us even more empowered, for we have broken psychic barriers to bond with another. But without that other's healthy consent, *force* is just domination over something or someone by manipulation or violence. Using force against the innocent—whether children, vulnerable people, or animals—to engage in sexual acts is one of the vilest forms of control, and we should adopt zero tolerance for such atrocities the world over.

Forcing sex in a relationship—marriage or not—is as violent as any other act of domination and is never okay. We don't own our partner's bodies or sexuality and don't have any rights to them. Passive-aggressive behaviors can also be a form of force—a sneaky way of angling to get what we want. And, just like the blind force of nature, destruction ensues when we exert our sightless might over a situation or person.

For these heinous behaviors mirror humanity's collective anger and self-loathing. Forcing anything in life is a self-centered attempt to manipulate what life has in store for us. Trying to outsmart the universe and the path laid out for our highest good and growth surely pulls us down the road to suffering. When we force anything we're operating out of a belief in our own inadequacy and the fear that we won't get what we want or need. This mentality of scarcity, lack, and limitation makes us rage or cower, as if every opportunity were our last one.

Consider that we live in an abundant universe, one that has an infinite supply of good for us once we open our hearts to it. Surrender to what life has in store for you and step out of trying to force any outcome.

DAILY HEALTHY SEX ACTS

- Describe the different levels of force during love-making that most turn you on, and why. Do you seek to conquer/be conquered and does this affect your capacity for a heartfelt connection?

- Consider the ways you try to control your life. When do you use force to get what you want when you want it?

- Are you domineering or passive-aggressive? What do you need to do in order to lessen these destructive behaviors in your life?

"Love suffers long and is kind; love does not envy; love does not parade itself, is not puffed up; does not behave rudely, does not seek its own, is not provoked, thinks no evil; does not rejoice in iniquity, but rejoices in the truth; bears all things, believes all things, hopes all things, endures all things."

— Paul of Tarsus

17 SEPTEMBER

QUALITY

When we set sail in our youth, we scan for a multitude of adventures, often deliberately sacrificing quality for quantity. What better way to spend our early years than trying on different personas, visiting faraway places, eating exotic foods, and partying until sunrise? When quantity seems more important than quality, we settle for mediocrity in order to sample the full buffet of life.

But something shifts with time and age. Wisdom seeps into our rough edges and brings life into view through a surprisingly different lens. We begin to crave distinct attributes in our experiences, and judge them by higher standards. Intrigued by our own potential, we start to measure our successes by those we admire and hold ourselves to a new criterion of excellence. When we expect such quality from ourselves, we attract people who also demand quality of themselves.

In time, the excellence of our human contacts becomes a rare and valuable jewel. No longer fickle, we transform our lust for raw energy into a desire to deepen connections with chosen ones. We choose differently, too. Rather than seeking multiple sexual encounters with numerous people, we settle ourselves down and look for the quality in another that sparks powerful qualities in ourselves. That certain something can have us falling in love because we are choosing to embark on a wisdom path—one in which we forge ourselves through the experiences we have with our partner. And, there's a paradox in our choice. New love is heady and strong, but ripens only with age. Similarly, sex is like fine wine that becomes deep and bold only over time. The quality of our sexuality changes through our life because the quality of our connection to our partner grows infinitely more interesting than the quantity of sex we have in a week.

DAILY HEALTHY SEX ACTS

- What standards do you hold yourself to in your life? Are you tolerating anything less than the qualities you desire in yourself?

- What qualities do you love and adore in your partner? Think about any qualities you have difficulty with and share them with a trusted friend. When you've found a compassionate way to talk about them, share your thoughts with your partner.

- Are you going for quantity or quality in your sex life? Which do you like better, and why?

"Grow old with me!
The best is yet to be."

— Robert Browning

As time marches on, the accumulation of our experiences etch themselves on our bodies, minds, and souls. The physical body slowly but surely begins to lose its shape and form, while the wisdom of the soul expands and outshines what once was. How many times have you met an elder, perhaps in another culture, whose eyes radiated grandeur, beauty, and a life well lived that rocked you to your core? The weight of responsibility in life can sometimes feel crushing but, to judge from such elders, "What doesn't kill us, makes us stronger." The process of enduring, learning, and growing ultimately leads to a lightness of being. Often those same elders have a mischievous gleam in their eyes, an almost childlike quality that reflects back to us the look of freedom and peace.

But aging with grace and dignity is no easy feat as our consumer culture consistently bombards us with messages glorifying eternal youth. Youth, however, is a state of mind and heart, grounded in happiness and gratitude and born out of a willingness to embrace our age and celebrate the privilege of growing older. Notice how much more experience you have today than yesterday, and how your changing face and body reflect your wisdom. Embrace all of who you are and let the lightness of your being radiate forth to all those you meet. Take a risk during sex and make yourself vulnerable by letting your lover see and feel your inner youth and ancient wisdom, and together you'll open to the ageless, timeless souls that you are.

 DAILY HEALTHY SEX ACTS

- Take an inventory of your entire body starting with your feet and going up to the top of your head. Notice the changes in the shapes, forms, and texture of your skin and hair.

- See the child within when you look into your own eyes. Smile at him or her and know that your essence is timeless.

- Make peace with nature's way, and remind yourself of the wonder and awe of being alive on this day.

"They say it is to know the union with love that the soul takes union with the body."

— Tiruvalluvar

19 SEPTEMBER

SEXUAL UNION

In union is both unity and unanimity—the joining of two separate but equal wholes to create a single experience. We each come into this world alone and leave the same way, but for that one brief hour, whether we have sex or simply lie in our lover's arms, we know oneness with another, a momentary suspension of the awareness of our innate individuality. Our hearts beat as one; we may orgasm at the same moment; our breath may so align that we can no longer distinguish where one of us ends and the other begins. Sometimes the union manifests more emotionally. We share a private joke with a lover that no one else would ever get, and weep over a common misfortune.

The profound process of merging with a second consciousness while melding in physical intimacy can feel like a spiritual event. For that reason it can become a great obsession, addiction, or source of craving, taking us back to the primal vulnerability of infancy. Indeed, the mystical and symbolic act of sexual union may draw its power from a secret longing to return to our earliest experience, for each of us begins our journey in an Edenic state of symbiosis, only to be ejected through the womb and thrust towards independence. We cry our lungs out, for the separation is grievous. As babies, we keep an intense yearning to know the world by placing every thumb, toy or household item into our mouths, merging on a very concrete level with our surroundings. Even in adults, this longing continues. But we can remind ourselves that without a strong sense of self, sexual union is merely a collapse of identity rather than the harmonious celebration of two autonomous beings finding mutual sanctuary together.

DAILY HEALTHY SEX ACTS

- Describe your union with your lover during sex, listing all the adjectives that come to mind. Is the energy between you active or passive? Anxious or relaxed? Considerate or indifferent?

- If you want to change, and charge, the energy between you, focus your erotic intention on your contribution to the sexual vibrations you create *together* rather than on your or your partner's energy. Make love to the energy of your combined love.

- Has your experience of sexual union ever overflowed into a *mystical third*—the intersubjective field of consciousness created by two merging identities?

"Perhaps all the questions we ask of love, to measure, test, probe, and save it, have the additional effect of cutting it short."

— Milan Kundera

TESTING

It seems most of us test our partners almost instinctively. This unconscious testing differs from taking realistic, conscious measures to gauge a partner's trustworthiness, because the very act of secretly testing trustworthiness is a contradiction, and reveals that you don't in fact trust your partner. Whenever you set up obstacles "just to test" a partner, you're really just setting up obstacles. Even if your lover successfully gets past your obstacles to pass the test, all you have really confirmed is that you've trained your partner to expect and permit obstacles in the relationship.

In fact, when you test others you're actually testing yourself: Do you operate from the viewpoint of the greater good, or from a place of ego and preconception? They say you teach what you most have to learn, and it's also possible that you test what you most fear you will fail. Any test we set for others is steeped in our own subjective doubts. In scientific methodology, this is called "confirmation bias:" the human propensity to accept "information" that confirms what we already believe.

Perhaps life delivers so many tests that we don't have to add our own trick questions. A healthy way to evaluate a partner's trustworthiness might be to observe how s/he responds to life's constant challenges. Another unimpeachable test is to meet one's partner in simplicity, to tolerate intimacy, security and safety with that person, and to build trust together.

DAILY HEALTHY SEX ACTS

- Do you put your lover to the test for proof that you are loved? If so, why?

- If your daily life were a test, how would you score? As you behave in trustworthy ways, you will be more inclined to trust the world around you because life tends to mirror personal actions and secret motives back to you.

- You know what you need to do today. Trust yourself to act accordingly.

"Nothing in the world can bother you as much as your own mind, I tell you. In fact, others seem to be bothering you, but it is not others, it is your own mind."

— Sri Sri Ravi Shankar

21 SEPTEMBER

MINDFULNESS

To be mindful is to be dead center in the present. Gurus and teachers from the beginning of time have pointed the way to this single moment where the past and present collide with the future, by reminding us to be *here now*. Infants and children model how to be present in the here and now. You've probably noticed that when a baby is hungry he cries, when her diaper's wet she fusses, and when something catches his eye, he laughs with delight. Their capacity for self-referencing has not developed yet, so they have no choice but to express purely present awareness. To be mindful, then, is to tame the thoughts scampering through our minds every minute by focusing on what's dead center in our immediate experience.

Sight, smell, sound, taste, and touch are all portals to the present. Next time you're watching a sunrise or seeing your lover's face, really *look*. Make contact with the full essence of your being as if you've never seen the sun or those eyes before, and notice what happens in your body. Smell the nape of her neck, his hair and skin, and take in the effect it has on your arousal system. Listen to the sounds of pleasure that arise during your love-making and the feel of your lover's body above and below you. Taste her tongue and let your tongues mingle, focusing only on that sensation. Concentrating on your body is a mindfulness practice designed to give you permission to experience your pleasure. And the key to mindfulness (perhaps ironically) is to get out of your head and to resist the rule of thought. Simple awareness of what's in front of you—what you're seeing, smelling, hearing, tasting or touching—brings you into the eternal now.

DAILY HEALTHY SEX ACTS

- Sit quietly with your eyes open. Really see your surroundings. Now, notice your other senses, and how your noisy thoughts distract you from them. Be interested only in the sensations and senses in your body.

- When you eat your next meal, do so in silence. Make it a practice to taste each morsel of food as you gently chew. Don't chew your thoughts! Savor each swallow before going on to the next.

- Treat your lover the way you treat your meal. Touch him or her carefully and deliberately, take him or her in, and savor every moment.

> *"The omnipresent process of sex, as it is woven into the whole texture of our man's or woman's body, is the pattern of all the process of our life."*
>
> — Havelock Ellis

ANATOMY

Recall your first experience with your own sexual anatomy and how you came to discover your genitalia. How lucky you are if this time of healthy exploration was supported as normal by your parents! For others, messages of shame may have shrouded your natural curiosity and left you confused, humiliated, or disowning your sexuality. Some parents take the middle ground between these two attitudes by anthropomorphizing sexual parts with "cute," inappropriate labels. Some parents talk to their children hurriedly about their regions "down there" due to their own shame.

Whichever scenario you grew up with likely stayed with you into adulthood. If your sexual messages were skewed, you're not alone. These disembodied terms get transmitted from generation to generation. Yet, like your fingers and toes, your genitals are God-given body parts. When we don't learn about them in healthy and accepting ways, genitalia becomes imbued with so much psychic weight that by the time we're adults, just being naked in front of another can be paralyzing.

Undoing early childhood messages about our bodies can be formidable, but appreciating our size, shape, weight, skin and hair texture is a way to honor the temple of our body. It's a fact that no two women have the same clitoral formation or breast nipples, just as no two men have the same shape penis. In general, our sexual anatomy functions the same as others of our gender, but appearances can be markedly different. Oddly, anxiety rises with the simple act of naming sexual body parts, but not when we discuss the anatomy of, say, the leg. The judgmentalism we apply to sex and sexual organs are often the legacy of shame carried over from a parent, our childhood, or the sexual politic of the day. Releasing self-consciousness about our sexual anatomy is essential for an erotic sex life.

DAILY HEALTHY SEX ACTS

- Can you face your sexual body and name each body part from a neutral place just as you would label the various parts of your arms and legs?

- How do you feel about your vagina and breasts, or penis? Do you disown or demean your genitalia? If so, why?

- Make a list of all your body parts and general appearance, such as your height. Start from your head and work down to your feet. Which parts do you like and which do you dislike? Share this list with a trusted other.

"Better keep yourself clean and bright; you are the window through which you must see the world."

— George Bernard Shaw

23 SEPTEMBER

PERCEPTION

Perception, like a camera lens, is a filter that can enlarge, distort or enhance a scene, altering our sense of reality. If we're unable to examine that lens or acknowledge our subjectivity, we become its prisoners, blindly reacting to people and situations. Sometimes we go even further and surround ourselves with people who share our particular warped lens, mistakenly believing their consensus proves our lopsided assumptions correct.

Our perceptions reflect core beliefs because our unique experiences and backgrounds always color them. Yet with an open mind and heart, we can extend our initial impressions to find a more balanced, informed version of the truth. True perception, therefore, is a process rather than a fixed state. Meditation clears the grime from our lens and sets us on the path to enlightenment. Only through the humility of continually asking questions such as, "What if I'm wrong? What am I missing here?" can we begin to have a new experience of living in and interacting with the world.

We've all made relationship choices we thought were right but turned out to be wrong. What we thought was healthy turned out to be emotionally unhealthy. So how do we handle these failures of perception? The first step is another valuable gift of meditation: to learn to observe life and relationships without identifying with the observations. We can have compassion for ourselves and for our failed loves, and admit that being human means sometimes making mistakes. Additionally, we can learn to participate in a shared narrative with others, gaining insights and solutions we were unable to come up with on our own.

DAILY HEALTHY SEX ACTS

- Your perceptions can be the key that unlocks the door to the real world. But it's also possible to become imprisoned by them. Do your habitual perceptions reflect more your treasured goals or your past traumas?

- Today, experiment for five minutes at a time by perceiving the world from opposing vantage points, as if you're wealthy, then impoverished; ostracized, then beloved; and sexually frustrated, then fulfilled. What different perceptions do those different conditions create in you?

- Truly perceive the abundance of your most heartfelt ideals in every person, in each passing moment.

"The poet is in command of his fantasy, while it is exactly the mark of the neurotic that he is possessed by his fantasy."

— Lionel Trilling

FANTASY

Fantasy is a form of dissociation and a way to imagine the impossible or improbable. Lost in a world of unreality, buffered from human connection, fantasy is a solo act that shields us from interpersonal exchanges. Children turn to fantasy when under duress as a way to escape the inescapable. A household fraught with neglect, yelling or violence creates fertile ground for the child to construct unconscious wishes filled with magic, adventure, and hope of a better life. Unfortunately, chronically living in fantasy creates patterns in the brain that may be difficult to break in adulthood, especially where sexual fantasies are concerned.

Being so possessed by sexual fantasies that you avoid your partner and the possibility of connection with him or her will create problems in your relationship over time. Healthy sex requires a solid level of psychic presence, where creativity and imagination can playfully emerge between two people. Being held hostage by habitual sexual fantasies or persistent pornographic images in your head will thwart your being freely present with your partner.

In contrast, when you're present with your partner, you can co-create your fantasies. And when you're in command of your fantasies, you can play them out, talk about them afterwards, and learn from each other what was arousing, what worked, what didn't, or what may have been problematic. Being present lets you use your sex life consciously and as a way to grow, change, and connect.

DAILY HEALTHY SEX ACTS

- Learn about your psyche and inner patterns by challenging your fantasies. Ask yourself, "Are these old patterns or traumas I'm acting out? Or are they arousing and congruent with who I am as an adult person today?"

- Share your insights with your partner to deepen your intimacy with yourself and with one another.

- Take time to talk about what types of fantasy you might like to co-create with your partner. Are they playful, naughty, or exotic? Start with one sentence, then take turns building on that theme and see where it leads you.

"What of people who aren't able to form close and strong relationships? And people who cannot find fulfillment in their lives, or those who have lost hope, who live in disappointment and bitterness and find in life no joy, no love? These, it seems to me, are the real disabilities."

— Fred Rogers

25 SEPTEMBER

DISABILITY

While we've all found ourselves sexually uninterested due to back pain, menstrual cramps, or a depressed mood, we also knew that our desire for sex would return once our body/mind healed. But those of us with disabilities won't experience returning to an abler state. We have to accept impairments we have, and accept our self.

A common error is that physical or mental disability hampers sexuality. Yet everyone, regardless of abilities, is a sexual being, and human sexuality is not one-size-fits-all. In fact, there is no such thing as ideal sexuality. We all have a full capacity for sexual experience and expression, and can define for ourselves what our own personal sensual ideal is. In fact, disabilities can reveal creative ways to be sexual and to experience pleasure and joy.

Sexual limitations may result from physical or mental differences, but our psychological limitations are usually the biggest roadblocks to sexual health. We tend to measure ourselves against the endless images of human perfection we see every day. But when we move into true acceptance of our human foibles and fallibilities, we liberate our self, because we no longer compare our self to anyone else's self. Regardless of whether our body parts match those of most people, whether our mood shifts more than others', or whether our immune system functions optimally we are, on a cosmic level, perfect, whole, and complete—just as we are. Remember, our sexuality is a gift from the divine, so let's not shortchange our self! Finding out what brings us pleasure, learning about our erogenous zones and sharing that with our lover, admitting to our self who we are and what turns us on lets us celebrate our humanity without shame and in gratitude for what we *do* have.

DAILY HEALTHY SEX ACTS

- What are your sexual hang-ups in relation to your physical or emotional body?

- Are you stuck on the idea that you have to have intercourse to be sexual? If so, what do you need to do in order to get into reality about how your body and mind function?

- What holds you back from exploring what's pleasurable for you?

- Admit to yourself what brings you pleasure and share it with a trusted other.

> *"Addiction starts in the most primitive parts of the brain. In our lizard brains, that drink or that drug or that date feels like survival. To the love addict, love really is like oxygen."*
>
> — Ethlie Ann Vare

Love has been called a motivation system rather than a feeling—a cascade of chemicals, especially dopamine, that drives us toward mating. The love addict seeks romantic love, while seeking lust is the domain of the sex addict or love avoidant. Romantic love is what love addicts live and die for. Starved for affection as children or emotionally abandoned, they abdicate all self-care once in the relationship of their fantasy. Many love addicts avoid calm, mundane experiences, preferring to stay liquored up on the dopamine high that makes them feel alive. Obsessive by definition, they will be unable to eat or sleep, will feel love-sick, and may even want to die when they don't get the response they believe they need from the object of their desire.

When they do find a partner (usually as incapable of intimacy as they are), they dedicate themselves irrationally to that person, worshiping him or her even after they are, inevitably, disappointed or abused. The fantasy romance they've constructed lets them lose themselves in dependency and, in return, they expect to be loved unconditionally—the remnant of a childhood need that no partner can meet. Jealousy naturally ensues because love addicts demand an unhealthy total bond and thereby guarantee the rejection that replicates their earliest abandonment.

Ironically and tragically, when love addicts actually attain the intimacy they desperately chase, they become terrified of the feelings accompanying real connection, and they run. Real relationship brings up the twin faces of their terror—abandonment and intimacy—and the jig is up.

Healing from love addiction is formidable work. The love addict can enter recovery only in withdrawal, an agony so great it's described as physical pain. If not in enough pain, love addicts will tough it out, set their hearts on another object, and begin the cycle again.

DAILY HEALTHY SEX ACTS

- Have you hit an emotional bottom in your current relationship? Is it time to get help? Can you commit to acting on your behalf today? If so, whom can you ask to help you?

- Describe the behaviors you want to stop: drinking or smoking pot; chasing after unavailable people; having indiscriminate sex.

- Ask yourself whether you reside in reality or fantasy. Taking action to attend a 12-step meeting or to call a therapist is a declaration of living in reality.

"What I like most about change is that it's a symbol of hope. If you are taking a risk, what you are really saying is 'I believe in tomorrow and I will be part of it.'"

— Linda Ellerbee

27 SEPTEMBER

HOPE

Hope contains within it the powerful notion of potential. Although we cannot yet see the towering majesty of the oak tree, we see in the acorn our hope for it. Just so with relationships: We intuit a connection and begin to imagine the future we've always hoped for. But how can we nurture our hope amid a sea of doubt, cynicism and pessimism?

According to the Ancient Greeks, the gods punished humankind by stowing all evils in a box for curious Pandora to open, as they knew she would, and thereby unleash those miseries upon the world. After the evils took wing, all that remained in the box was *hope*. But how can mere hope defeat everything that boiled over from that unholy box?

One way we counteract the poisonous powers in Pandora's box is by carefully choosing our words to offer the greatest support, affirmation and acceptance of others' hopes. We can employ gentle suggestion rather than coarse declaration to create harmony in our relationships. By reining in our demands and allowing room for another's hopes to exist alongside our own, we ensure a peaceful and fruitful future with that person. We can also develop an independent source of security within ourselves, basing our hopes for intimacy on our own capacities for trust and communication rather than solely on our partner, thus breaking the hopeless shackles of codependence.

For relationships require the tremendous resilience born of hope. When we stay unconditionally willing to remain teachable despite prior trauma, we're using hope as a healthy tool to sow the seeds of happiness. Like a surfboard used to ride the ever-changing waves, hope can be the greatest catalyst for action. When we stop fearing change and instead embrace it, we grow mentally, physically, spiritually and sexually within a partnership, just as we had hoped.

DAILY HEALTHY SEX ACTS

- Dissipate false hope by taking an honest assessment of yourself. List your assets and shortcomings, and let this information bring you a clear understanding of what you expect and desire from others.

- Do you feel safe to share your hopes? Who knows your true heart's desire or your secret dreams? Today, let your hopes shine so they may be seen.

- Imagine each of your loved ones' deepest-held hopes. Is what you imagine truly *their* hopes, or your hopes for them? Make it a relational practice to find out from others, "What's your dearest hope in life?"

> *"I thank God I was raised Catholic, so sex will always be dirty."*
>
> — John Waters

To liberate one's sexual expression from the shackles of social propriety can create an exciting state of arousal. Stretching one's personal boundaries may come from trying novel sex acts or role-play. To do this with a willing partner may be especially gratifying. How can lovers participate in riskier, more outrageous sex play and emerge the healthier for it?

As an example consider talking dirty. Of course, the definition of obscenity fluctuates between and even within cultures: today's commonplaces were taboo in previous generations. But explicit language becomes acceptable through more than general cultural change. When two people are connected, smut can become the language of love, not just a pornographic exercise. If we examine dirty words through the science of neurobiology we find that, while most language functions as a reason-dependent, left-brain activity, curse words are often controlled by the affective right brain, representing spontaneous emotional content struggling for expression. So it's quite natural that swear words and colorful vocabulary should emerge in our most meaningful conversations.

We speak to people to whom we're deeply connected differently than how we speak to someone distant. We *relate our story* the same way we *relate to* the listener. Limiting ourselves to strictly wholesome communication can come across as preachy, staid, or controlling, even if our intention is to use healthy communication skills. How often have we heard teenagers tell well-meaning parents, "Stop speaking 'self-help'!"

To truly connect with others, we must cultivate a shared language that no one party controls and in which all feel engaged and understood. There is nothing inherently wrong with any style of speaking, or acting, provided it's harmless and consensual. And if occasionally acting smutty or talking dirty helps *both* lovers connect in a more arousing and heartfelt way, then, yes, swear with *care*.

DAILY HEALTHY SEX ACTS

- Take one minute alone to unleash an impulsive string of obscenity and kinky thoughts. How does this make you feel? Aroused? Uncomfortable? Concentrate on these feelings. Might they correspond to an emotional event in your past or present? Just for today, mentally release yourself from that baggage.

- Today, notice all your interactions, and rather than getting stuck in one-sided conversation (or sexual contact), seek out ways to relate to your companion uniquely and truly.

"When you make a commitment to a relationship, you invest your attention and energy in it more profoundly because you now experience ownership of that relationship."

— Barbara de Angelis

29 SEPTEMBER

COMMITMENT

When most of us think of making a commitment to someone or some cause, we assume we're limiting our options. But, paradoxically, commitment can open the path to freedom. Consider our daydreams: We can muse forever about what it'd be like running our own business, entering the theater, travelling in foreign lands, or going back to school, but until we make a commitment to any of them and plunge into action, we'll never know. We can be enslaved to fantasy and never freely experience life's bounty.

Life, and logic, requires that we give up one thing for another. You can't simultaneously live a single life and be married, any more than you can live simultaneously in Paris and on a Hawaiian island. Each choice will enrich your life and each choice will demand your sacrifice of another choice; it turns out that we can't have it all. Likewise we can't know what a committed relationship is like until we get into one. We can speculate or avoid it all we want, but until we make a commitment to experience it, we won't know its real pros and cons.

Floundering and procrastinating can create feelings of agitation, of being stuck, of watching life pass us by. Making a commitment moves us into action and, curiously, the more we commit to another person, career, or endeavor, the more we find who *we* are. Commitment can lead to a newfound freedom that inspires creativity and expression, and we learn from this stretching what we're really capable of. In a healthy love relationship we feel safe enough to explore our skills and talents. Commitment, then, gives us a safe container—boundaries strong enough to expand—freeing us to become and discover our true self.

DAILY HEALTHY SEX ACTS

- What one thing do you most want to experience? What one thing do you need to do to turn that desire into action?

- What stands in the way of making a commitment to your dream?

- Talk to a trusted other today and commit to taking one action towards your preferred life.

"Hitherto your eyes have been darkened and you have looked too much, yes, far too much, upon the things of earth. If these so much delight you what shall be your rapture when you lift your gaze to things eternal!"

— Petrarch

SPIRITUALITY

We each have a Higher Power, whether we endow it in people, objects, or abstract spirit. It's our heartfelt, and sometimes unconscious, ideals. It's not the lofty principles we espouse but ignore while engrossed in lowly ones—not our declaration that we're for world peace, while we focus on past slights and operate in the *spirit* of retribution rather than reconciliation. It's been said that our first action and thought when we wake up in the morning is our true Higher Power. If we perceive the world's beauty, we live in a beautiful world.

Most of us strive for such awakenings, but struggle with spirituality morning, noon, and night. So take a moment to affirm the truth that everyone is beautiful yet has room to grow, and you'll create room for yourself to be beautiful and to grow. For spirituality, like life, is a mirror—to believe it, begin to see it. Since our eternally free choice determines our experience, we must learn *to preach what we practice* in order to revere our actual desires as our spiritual beliefs.

But what if our desires are bad? In Jungian theory, God—whether seen as a symbol or reality—governs the structure of one's psyche. Jung also called God our "heaviest wound," who "appears as our sickness from which we must heal ourselves." Twelve-step programs speak of the "God-sized hole" people try to fill with alcohol, drugs, sex and other people rather than *their own spirit*uality. For too often our actual God was edged out earlier in life, and our good desires were dethroned in our heart. Regardless of the innumerable spiritual theories or theologies, the behaviorally modifying practice of seeking daily, conscious contact with our Higher Power disrupts deeply-etched, unhealthy psychological patterns by regularly returning us to our own positive state of pure Spirit.

DAILY HEALTHY SEX ACTS

- What are your spiritual beliefs? Do you believe in a deity, sentient energy, or the lack thereof? How might your belief symbolize your present psychology?

- Describe the spirit of your ideals. An atheist might value freedom. An agnostic might value open inquiry. For each belief, there's a spirit of intention. Today, bask in the true spirit of your professed spirituality.

- Shared practice reaffirms and develops individual spirituality. Even couples with divergent religious ideologies can share spiritual principles to guide their lives—the highest being love. Today, share your spirituality with one you love.

"People ask what they must become to be loving. The answer is 'nothing.' It is a process of letting go of what you thought you had become and allowing your true nature to float to the surface naturally."

— Stephen Levine

October

"I had to give up the fantasy, the enormous life consuming fantasy, that someone or something was going to do this for me—the fantasy that someone was coming to lead my life, to choose direction, to give me orgasms."

— Eve Ensler

1 OCTOBER

SELF-EMPOWERMENT

Life is filled with challenges and strife, which we can use in service of shaping our character, rounding out our rough edges, and forcing us to grow. Taking the "bull by the horns" in life means we set ourselves a course of possibility and vision, and to do so we must step out of our comfort zone. It can also mean that we aren't relying on a lover or partner to make us happy or to bring us sexual blossoming.

Waiting for Prince Charming to swoop in and elevate our dreary lives is a disempowering, grandiose and childish fantasy that only serves to leave us weak and victim-like. Yet many fairy tales conjure images of knights in shining armor and Cinderella-like endings that will rescue us from the hardships of life. Like all fairy tales, these stories are filled with oft-misinterpreted metaphors for life, but bear no factual semblance to adult reality. So they can cripple us in immaturity if we stay attached to them.

Living a life of self-empowerment means that we willingly live in discomfort, anxiety, and sometimes even in fear because we recognize those feelings as a personal crucible for growth. Such growth is essential to realizing—that is, to making real—our own dreams and visions. Independent people know that challenge is a genuine part of reality, and that only by managing it ourselves will we manifest our true selves. Holding the paradox of fear and faith simultaneously is the task of the visionary; create your own fairy tale today and empower yourself to live the life you imagine!

DAILY HEALTHY SEX ACTS

- What fantasies are you harboring—perhaps about being saved from your lot in life—that need to be dashed?

- Are you sexually disempowered? If so, how? What small step can you take today to get into reality and empower yourself? Try talking to a friend, your partner, a health or mental health professional. Take your sexuality into your own hands.

- Do you discount your current relationship and live in fantasy about a perfect one? How might living in fantasy keep you from appreciating the relationship you already have?

"The fact that you are willing to say, 'I do not understand, and it is fine,' is the greatest understanding you could exhibit."

— Wayne Dyer

UNDERSTANDING

Being misunderstood creates the frustration, shame, or anger that we have all felt at one time or another. Communicating our passions, whether intellectual or emotional, feels almost impossible when we're misperceived, especially when the relationship stakes are high. Arguments ensue when others make incorrect inferences about our intended message or operate on assumptions before we've even completed our thought. And as a listener we can perpetrate the same pain by interrupting or by ignoring the other's perspective. Whether we're presenting our view or listening to the position of another, exercising our understanding lets us sympathetically grasp and tolerate other people's feelings.

Misunderstandings can occur in a relationship when we take our partner for granted and don't extend the same graciousness and forgiveness to him or her that we freely give others. We thoughtlessly trample on a partner's opinions when we presume to know what she or he is going to say before it's said. This dismissive attitude diminishes a person's sense of worth, makes him or her lose respect for us and, inevitably, destroys sexual attraction. When we make the effort instead to comprehend our partner's perception, we transmit the clear message that he or she matters deeply to us.

To be really interested in your lover means to pay close attention to what she or he says and does. By staying curious and asking questions about his or her points and positions, you gain a deeper understanding of who your partner is and, therefore, of your relationship. This practice of *understanding*, rather than *reacting*, creates a vital energy between you and kindles an implicit knowing of each other. Soul-to-soul, body-to-body understanding transcends words and may be the stuff that chemistry is made of—and it's the kind of chemical bonding you can practice.

DAILY HEALTHY SEX ACTS

- Pay attention to whether you pay attention to your partner. Are you present, judgmental, interrupting, or understanding?

- What's it like for you when you feel misunderstood? What past wounds does it evoke in you? Do you just react, or have you sorted out the past so as not to bring it into your present relationship?

- Who most needs your understanding today?

"Everything has beauty, but not everyone sees it."

— Confucius

3 OCTOBER

BEAUTY

In ancient civilizations, beauty was conceived as the state of being ruled by gods. When we see inner or potential beauty in ourselves and around us, we invite this godly state of being into our life. This perception plants a seed of beauty that will sprout and grow. You are the beauty that you long to be if you conceive of yourself as beautiful by feeling lightness in your heart and soul.

Ask yourself what qualities you attribute to whatever pleases you and satisfies your aesthetic sense, and consider whether you experience these same qualities internally. To help in this, recall that often our external environment expresses how we feel about ourselves. So take stock of your living environment and consider how you might arrange it to invite more divine beauty into your life. You can also plant seeds of beauty within you by selecting beautiful foods to nourish your body and taking walks in nature to feed your soul.

When you truly feel beautiful, you're no longer dependent on the favor of the gods. Instead, you are putting into practice your desire to have and create beauty all around you. Bring your aesthetic sense to your sex life, and experience yourself as a place of beauty to share and express with another.

DAILY HEALTHY SEX ACTS

- Find a way to radiate your inner beauty today.

- Smile at everyone you meet and recognize your own beauty in the sights you see in nature. When you're in awe of the vast blue sky, recognize your own inner vastness. When you stand in wonder of the blanket of snow on the ground, see that as the wonder of your own self.

- Find your own, unique ways to spread beauty wherever you go.

"The opposite of loneliness, it's not togetherness. It is intimacy."

— Richard Bach

EROTIC INTIMACY

In the spaces between two people who share familiarity and closeness, lives intimacy. A vibrant atmosphere that weaves connection, mutual understanding, and the sense that the other perceives you as nobody else does—these ingredients make the heady cocktail out of which love and eroticism emerge. This most private and personal space can occur with a lover during sex, in a cozy restaurant, or on a walk along a lake. How do you make yourself known?

Intimacy reveals our inmost self—our inner sanctum which we ourselves often discover only in communion with another. How many times have you had a revelation about your sexuality while having sex, or learned about an essential value you hold while in deep conversation with someone you love? Intimacy means to make known, but it teaches about ourselves as well as the other. When we stop hiding from ourselves and begin to tell the truth about who we are, we make ourselves vulnerable to see into the depths of our own soul.

Such openness can be frightening because there's the possibility we'll discover something unsavory, distorted, or out of sync with whom we think we are lurking in the corners of our psyches. Courage is a requisite for this most intimate of all tasks, as are a willingness to venture into the depths of the unknown and the faith that we will emerge changed for the better.

Strip down to your nakedness and bare the raw truth of who you are. Don't be surprised if you find that in this most exposed state you connect to yourself, your lover, and the divine in unimaginable, powerful, and erotic ways.

DAILY HEALTHY SEX ACTS

- Expose your true self to yourself. Think about a part of you that feels stuck or scared. Close your eyes and locate the feeling in your body. Dive deeply into the feeling and see what arises. Write down your experience.

- Share your deepest, darkest secrets with your lover. Strip off your armor and stop worrying about looking good. Dare to expose your truth.

- From this place of vulnerability, open your heart to love and to be loved.

"And think not you can direct the course of love, for love, if it finds you worthy, directs your course."

— Kahlil Gibran

5 OCTOBER

DIRECTION

Either we invest each moment with ego, or we let go. Out of fear, we vainly seek impossible surety in an ever-changing universe; or, out of faith, we respond to our calling, assured of success because we connect to a higher being. When we're full of ego, we hear only what we want to hear, which frustrates everyone in our lives—including ourselves. This self-induced deafness to others blocks our own greater selves. Imagine being stuck at any childhood age and refusing to grow up. Playing make-believe at four is cute; at forty it's a problem. Unfortunately we have to struggle to progress beyond our programming. Like animals instinctually returning to their birthplace, we often instinctually repeat ancestral errors—the family curse passed through generations. Of course, as humans we can reprogram ourselves and fulfill our potential. But early attachment patterns impact how we assimilate new information. It's not enough to seek the teachings of professionals; we have to be able to follow their directions.

How often do we seek advice and then refuse to follow it? Understand: Most of our problems touch our process, not our position. When we become stuck—in consciousness, then life—it's because of an immature or obsolete psychological process. The very act of seeking help outside that system is our first healing step. And when we seek direction, unless it conflicts with our deepest values we must somehow integrate it. Healing comes not from the brilliance of the advice, but from our courageous will to follow where it may lead. Unless we change direction, we end up right where we are, because the thinking that created conflict cannot solve it unaided. We need a Higher Power—in this case, taking direction from someone who has heard, and healed, similar issues.

DAILY HEALTHY SEX ACTS

- Can you follow direction? What feelings does the idea of surrendering to direction from a therapist, sponsor, or trusted friend bring up?

- Are you more directed by egoic concerns setting you apart from others, or a greater good that connects you to community?

- What if the world brought you to each moment to receive instruction? Today, take direction from all that's good and healthy in your immediate environment—before, behind, above, below, and beside you. Tend a garden that needs weeding. Spend time with loved ones. Make an overdue phone call.

> *"Civilization is a process in the service of Eros, whose purpose is to combine single human individuals, and after that families, then races, peoples and nations, into one great unity, the unity of mankind. Why this has to happen, we do not know; the work of Eros is precisely this."*
>
> — Sigmund Freud

EROS

Greek mythology identifies *Eros* as the principal love force uniting the universe. Ἔρως or Eros designates intimate love and is also one of the main Greek gods (known to the Romans as Cupid.) In some myths Eros is the winged son of Aphrodite, the Goddess of Love; in others Eros is a primordial creation god preceding humanity, literally binding the world together through *erotic* love. According to Plato, the principle of Eros is our innate drive for wholeness that ranges from personal to universal levels of experience and expression.

In the classic tale "Eros & Psyche," the god appears as an invisible lover (an emblematic theme throughout literature). Eros would appear only under the cloak of night to make love to his stolen bride, Psyche, on condition that she never lay eyes on him, and would fly away at daybreak. This drama symbolizes most people's tendency to relegate the erotic impulse to dark, isolated encounters that "steal" our entire awareness in the moment, only to dissolve with the return of full alertness. The ultimate union of Eros and Psyche represents one's capacity to integrate such magical loving intimacy with one's "*psych*-ological" waking consciousness. In the story, this union gives birth to a daughter named Pleasure. Remember Eros is a god, while Psyche is a mere mortal destined to become a god. Similarly it is through our deepest desire (Eros) originating from our deepest Self that our consciousness (Psyche) is raised to higher levels, resulting in ongoing pleasure, or enlightenment.

DAILY HEALTHY SEX ACTS

- Anteros is the brother of Eros, born solely to drive Eros onward (through rivalry) from his cherubic childhood to the fulfillment of erotic adulthood. Anteros is sometimes called the god of slighted love, punishing all that is bitter, resentful, fearful and covetous in human relations. Do you tend to let Eros or Anteros rule your love life?

- Imagine your own personal Eros, your god of love. With what qualities do you endow the conscious living energy that rules your love life? Invite the ideals of your healthiest love god to illuminate the world.

- Try to see beyond the veil of superficial appearances to glimpse the invisible, uniting spirit of intimate love within others.

"Can you walk on water? You have done no better than a straw.
Can you fly in the air? You have done no better than a bluebottle.
Conquer your heart; then you may become somebody."

— Khwaja Abdullah Ansari

7 OCTOBER

ACCOMPLISHMENT

Our capacity for accomplishment and intimacy are remarkably intertwined. The passion we have to accomplish great acts sets the bar for our ability to share affection and pleasure with others. Where is the passion you feel for your own life? Know that whenever we complain that a relationship has "lost its spark," it's been preceded by an internal loss of passion for our own life. Even in the face of failure or frustration, we make choices that affirm our independence and ideals— the very stuff of accomplishment. Letting go of "what should have been" to accept "what is" centers us solidly in reality, allows us to learn from our errors, and makes real our potential for impact in the world. And keeping personal autonomy and aspirations alive and strong lets us keep our love that way as well.

Accomplishments generally bring a better life. But worldly attainments themselves don't bring love, intimacy, serenity, or the capacity for relationship. To develop emotional and erotic intelligence we need to practice enlarging our inner passion at every moment. It doesn't matter what's going on in our world, or even how we feel about ourselves in the moment. In fact, the best time to accomplish something may be when we least feel like trying, because the hopeless part of ourselves most needs the light. Through the act of reflection, we open up to our inmost self and our inner passions. When we bring this awareness to our every accomplishment, our outward successes reflect our inner loves. This outside-inside mirroring magnifies the flame in our hearts. And that flame keeps love burning in our most intimate relationship.

DAILY HEALTHY SEX ACTS

- Plan a party with your partner or a friend. Experience working together as a team and see what unfolds. Afterwards, share your pride of accomplishment for a job well done, and celebrate your success together!

- Disconnected sex happens because people are disconnected from their lives, and addictive behaviors always mask the fear of failing to fulfill inner potential. What have you accomplished with your life? How do you measure your accomplishments, and what feelings come up for you when you do?

- Today, set out to accomplish this one task: Talk to one person and, for just one moment, smile deeply from your heart, sharing the uttermost passion you feel for your life.

"Could two live that way? Could two live under the wild rose, and explore by the pond, so that the smooth mind of each is as everywhere present to the other, and as received and as unchallenged, as falling snow?"

— Annie Dillard

CO-REGULATION

We cannot underestimate our life-long need to connect with others. From infancy, we're designed to rely on our primary caregiver, typically our mothers, to regulate our unformed brain, heart rate, and nervous, immune, and every other system with nurturing for our optimal development. And the infant regulates the mother's system so that her brain/body produces hormones letting her, in an elegant loop, give the infant what it needs. That process of co-regulation between mother and infant is a requirement, not an option, for the infant's survival.

As we grow, our systems begin to stabilize according to the regulation we receive from our parents. If we're lucky, we mature into secure, stable beings. If unlucky, we struggle with our own regulatory challenges and may turn to drugs, alcohol, sex, food or other externals to regulate our anxious or depressed systems. If this goes on long enough, we can find ourselves in addiction. Living in isolation or addiction is self-destructive, while turning to responsive people to soothe our pain is constructive.

Even for adults, one of the most important reasons to be in any relationship is for co-regulation. When upset, hurt, or angry we need another person to hug us and assure us that "everything is going to be okay," which helps us settle down. Celebrating milestones or experiencing setbacks are times when we most need friends, trusted family members, or our lover. A healthy, balanced life requires connection and community, as much as self-regulation and autonomy. Seeking soothing in sorrow, or validation in victory, invites those around us to share their wisdom and love. Like the mother/infant loop, we give and receive regulation when we're in caring relationships with others. Co-regulation is what makes love, and the world, truly go around.

DAILY HEALTHY SEX ACTS

- Do you isolate, or use substances or processes to auto-regulate your pain? Or do you ask others to help you get your needs met?

- Is there a part of you that needs to be held so that you can have a good cry? If so, reach out to a trusted other today and let someone regulate your pain.

- Spread some love today by making yourself available to your partner, family members, or friends by lending an ear and opening your heart.

"Slowly, but very deliberately, the brooding edifice of seduction, creaking and incongruous, came into being."

— Anthony Powell

9 OCTOBER

SEDUCTION

Long before flesh touches flesh, the seducer, radiating eroticism and desire, strategically encircles the intended object. Like a spider spinning a web to catch its prey, he or she manipulates an imbalance of power to pursue the vulnerable—dynamics that some find highly arousing. For the seducer is rarely concerned with consent. What matters is the emotional high gained from the chase and conquest. Secret obsessions with power and validation, not the quest for reciprocation, drive seduction, which makes it not just a selfish but also a solitary game. Indeed, regardless of the seducer's success or failure, non-consensual action always reaps a false harvest. Obsessed with the products of love and not the process, seduction yields a lonely caricature of intimacy.

The term springs from the Latin *seducere* meaning *to lead astray* and, after the mid-1500s, referred to the act of convincing a woman to surrender her chastity. The very idea of seduction itself, of seizing or of being seized, can seduce us into a state of anticipatory gratification. In the ideal realm of the silver screen, sensual pursuit provides the perfect playground for our voyeurism and lust for intrigue. But real life is not play-acting. Seduction prizes the thrill of victory rather than the joy of giving and receiving affection. It turns one person into the actor and the other into a prop. In this scenario there's no happy ending and no exchange of energies because seduction is a one-act play and a one-way street.

Seduction will always be a key ingredient in healthy, erotic role-playing, but as a primary means of meeting, knowing, and loving a partner, it falls short. Instead of posturing as the world's most irresistible lover, we can take the greater, but worthier, risk of letting others see our humanity, our fallibility, and our innocence.

DAILY HEALTHY SEX ACTS

- Have you ever been seduced into a course of action by another, perhaps a night of debauchery, an important life decision, or a sudden sexual encounter? Seduction can evoke many responses, from pleasure to horror, that often co-exist.

- Affirm the sanctity of your well-being and integrity, and that of others. Is there a way to integrate the sexy glow of seduction into your erotic play while still respecting the best interests of all involved?

*"The so-called rational animal has a desperate
drive to pair up and moan and writhe."*

— Steven Pinker

SEX DRIVE

There's a familiar witticism that driving and asking for directions—or not—reveals the basic incompatibility in any relationship. Beyond the humor, this joke points to a common underlying issue: a couple's inability to stop and ask for directions about their respective sex drives. We are all propelled to satisfy sexual and emotional desires, along with other deliberate and unconscious goals. But it's a sad truth that some are driven to extremes in the pursuit of satisfaction, while others feel less urgency.

Exhibiting less pressure to pursue sex does not mean a person has less of a sex drive, just as not wanting to be stuck in a conversation you find uninteresting doesn't mean you have a low communication drive. In addition, the sex drive includes both physical and psychological aspects, and there are prescribed ways to assess, heal and satisfy its multiple facets.

Understanding the psychological sex drive involves specific questions: How often do you need to have sex? How do you define sex in plain terms? What does sex mean to you and express to you? Learning about the physical sex drive requires considering other questions: What is the body actually capable of? How does sex affect the body physically, and what are the effects of alcohol or drugs on its health and physiological functioning? Comprehending this dimension of the sex drive requires further inquiry: What level of physical health does the body possess in other activities? How powerful is the natural sex drive without any supplements or medications, and how do such substances affect it? To get the right directions for your sexual experience, take time to recognize these important road signs to your and your partner's drives.

DAILY HEALTHY SEX ACTS

- Take time to review your sex drive. Answer the above questions, and share the responses with your lover.

- How are you driven into action by sexual energy today? Compare this with your sexual energy in the past. How has your sex drive changed over the years?

- If your sex drive seems to take precedence over every other aspect of your life, search for and take an online "sex addiction screening test" today.

"I do think the heart can balance out the mind, if your heart is in a good place it can give you the strength to do the right thing and behave the right way and overcome the mind."

— Alexis Arguello

11 OCTOBER

BALANCE

Bringing life into balance is an ever-changing task because life is ever-changing. It's unlikely that anyone actually lives in perfect balance, but it is possible to seek balance in all areas of our lives. Like a tightrope walker, those who pursue balance must negotiate it step by step, with thoughtfulness and the ability to breathe through stressful moments.

Oftentimes, just when one area of life comes beautifully into balance, another shifts out. Being flexible enough to "roll with the punches" allows for dynamic equilibrium and less rigidity—other qualities essential to tightrope walkers! If one area of your life becomes unmanageable at any time, you're clearly out of balance. It's good practice then to use your heart instead of your head as a way to regain your poise for decision-making and increase your internal flexibility. You might be surprised to find that your personal balance may look and feel differently than you once thought.

DAILY HEALTHY SEX ACTS

- Take stock of the areas of your life that seem out of balance. The areas may include health, exercise, diet, order and cleanliness in your home or office, or problems in your primary relationships. Choose one area to address, then move on to the next.

- Notice whether you can sustain balance in multiple areas over time, or if you have particular difficulty with one area.

- Seek help if you think you have areas that are consistently unmanageable.

"Heaven knows we need never be ashamed of our tears, for they are rain upon the blinding dust of earth, overlying our hard hearts."

— Charles Dickens

SORROW

When we fight the urge to mask our sadness with a happy face, when we can sit with the emotion of sorrow without self-pity or self-abandonment, we fling open the shutters of denial to the whole truth of our experience. Fear of depression, of inviting so-called negative energy, or of falling into an emotional abyss can create shame for even acknowledging sadness. Yet who among us is immune? The invitation to feel real sorrow does not exile us to permanent melancholy or gothic gloom. And the narrow social stance that measures our worth solely by positivity prevents true feeling—the only act that could integrate our sorrows rather than bury us in them. To shine the light of attention and acceptance on our darkest moments brings us closer to wholeness. Sharing emotional truth with trusted others, as we feel it, breaks the chains of isolation.

Personal grief is a microcosmic reflection of world sorrow. Everywhere people suffer for all the reasons under the sun—death, loss, lack, injury and insult—and their suffering is our suffering multiplied. In fact, our potential for identification with others' very real lives is the greatest source of joy and communion, and also of pain and helplessness. To deny the true impact of our own and others' sorrow ultimately leads to destructive avoidant behavior and to a half-life of unreal relationship at best, and sociopathy at worst.

At the same time, we don't need to deprive ourselves of happiness and pleasure in the face of world sorrow. Maturity contains both delight and sadness, and embraces these polar truths as part of livingness. Many of us did not learn self-empathy for our sadness. The more we develop a psychological language for our sorrow, the more depth, meaning and joy we find in life and in relationship.

DAILY HEALTHY SEX ACTS

- How did you cope with sorrow in childhood? Recall times you acknowledged sad feelings and shared them. Now, recall the moments you hid your sorrow in isolation.

- What messages did you learn about sorrow? List all the words you associate with sorrow. Do these beliefs still serve you today? Can you accept your sorrow without shame?

- If you've felt stuck in sorrow, seek out solace. Sometimes sharing the truth about your emotional states throughout the day can regulate difficult feelings, and sometimes it's the first step toward necessary healing.

"Though lovers be lost love shall not."

— Dylan Thomas

13 OCTOBER

DISAPPOINTMENT

Expectation is the springboard for disappointment and displeasure, especially when our desire to control what we aspire to gets wrested out of our sticky fingers by life and frustrates our dreams. A life lived in fantasy or in the throes of love addiction is tragic because it keeps us from ever having our feet on the ground solidly enough to be embodied and present. Constantly pursuing perfection steals the gift of what's in front of us right now on the altar of our life. How often have you fixated on an ideal way you wanted your partner to behave or look, and were so disappointed when they showed up, instead, as themselves? Clinging to your reigning fantasy blinds you to the infinite richness and texture of real human beings, and leaves you an emotional pauper. Standing in reality with a willingness to accept the bounty that comes your way is the only antidote to disappointment.

Yet no matter how hard we try, we're often captivated by that cultural set-up for disappointment, the "Happily Ever After" story. From childhood, we're told that once we find our soul-mates, we'll skip down the aisle of marital bliss onto easy street. We uphold this myth with fervor, even in the face of the failure of half of all marriages. Holding the possibility that love can last forever while recognizing that it, like everything alive, will change over time liberates us from the unrealistic, childish hope that people will be different than they are. When we accept that beautiful and extraordinary moments come when we least expect it, and are most surprised by it, we allow life's true magic to happen. To accept—more, to be glad—that reality rarely mirrors our fantasy or expectations, paradoxically allows great possibility and less disappointment every day.

DAILY HEALTHY SEX ACTS

- Make a list of the last five times you were disappointed. Is there a pattern wherein you set yourself up to have a "bad" experience? What part do you play in your disappointments?

- Being in relationship with other human beings guarantees that we will be regularly disappointed due to human fallibility. Do you allow for human error or do you expect perfection, trying to control others and outcomes?

> *"Most of us don't stop to think about what to look for in the dating process, and yet the choice of who to go out with and continue dating is probably one of the most important decisions we'll ever make in our lives. It is also, all too often, one of the most unconscious choices made."*
>
> — Nina Atwood

DATING

To succeed in dating, it's essential to identify the common denominator in all your relationships. The first thing that comes to your mind may be the traits you seek in all your candi-*dates*. But the real common factor is *you*. All the thrills and stresses of dating reflect our expectations about human connection. From a very young age, we developed specific ideas about relationships. Some of us experienced abandonment; others were smothered. Our experiences shape what we seek, and fear, in a mate. Building a relationship thus requires self-understanding. We must first know ourselves intimately if we hope to connect with another authentically.

Self-understanding also helps us evaluate our dates, letting us process and learn from our feelings when we're together or apart. But when sex is introduced too early, the neurochemical intensity can distort our awareness, making it hard to distinguish between attraction and compatibility. *Attraction* is that immediate but unmistakable warmth drawing us to someone. *Compatibility* is discovered as we relate, day to day, in happy harmony with someone. In the long run, relationships flourish more through companionship, trust and honest communication than anything else.

When sizing up a possible partner, if we think too intellectually about who "would be good" for us, or conversely rely too heavily on the chemistry of what "feels good" to us, our perception becomes unbalanced. It's best to judge slowly, deeply, and in detail. Get to know someone in a leisurely way, as though you were reading a wonderful book for the first time. Savor each turn of phrase and page, and trust that the happy ending will unfold if you have faith in the dating process and stay true to your core goals and values.

DAILY HEALTHY SEX ACTS

- What qualities do you seek in a date? If you're attracted to just one type—by age, race, or creed—question and write about your exclusivity.

- Write two lists: everything you *want* in a partner; and everything you *don't want*. Highlight deal-breakers and deal-makers. Then re-order each list by importance. When dating, ask yourself, "Is this person's trait a deal-breaker? A deal-maker?" Update your lists as you update self-understanding.

- If you regularly bail during the dating period, 12-step slogans "Go until you know" and "Date 'em 'til you hate 'em" remind us to abandon perfectionism and to tolerate the imperfect intimacy of healthy relating.

"Care and responsibility are constituent elements of love, but without respect for and knowledge of the beloved person, love deteriorates into domination and possessiveness."

— Erich Fromm

15 OCTOBER

DOMINATION

Sexual relationships are complex. Sadly, humans often play out patterns and projections in personal relationships. So it might be difficult to glimpse where you and your partner are overly controlling or compliant. Much of your relational style results from your experiences growing up. But the mind on which this programming was imprinted—your mind—will always reveal your own psychological makeup: your innate orientation to certain attributes over their polar counterparts (i.e., thinking vs. feeling). Domination begins within.

Ancient Egyptians believed in the "Weighing of the Heart," where the heart of feeling must be balanced with the feather of intelligence, or the soul is destroyed. Indeed, no one wants to feel dominated by either uncontrolled thoughts or feelings. "Acting out" (whether with food, sex, drugs, or other deflecting behaviors) results compulsively when one's internal equilibrium has been compromised. Health strives for inner balance and outer reciprocity, also known as co-regulation, which is not a frozen stasis of harmonized equality but a constant recalibration towards mutual intimacy.

Some people use domination sex play to explore personal boundaries. Such consensual relationships require a "safe word" for when either the "sub" or "dom" feels triggered, so all domination activity ceases immediately. However, all relationships have aspects of control and compliance, and we all have safe words, but not always the prior agreement to halt when someone's in pain—not just physical pain, but the pain of confusion, abandonment, over-thinking... the pain of honesty and empathy. Together we can all develop conscious safe words for such circumstances ("I need space," "Let's talk") so sexual love may move forward with trust, safety and informed consent.

DAILY HEALTHY SEX ACTS

- Do you dominate others? Do you need to one-up them? Or are you dominated and held hostage? Notice your relational attitude today with others and make adjustments where needed. Does this mean you need to assert your personal truth and set a healthy boundary? Or should you apologize for trying to force your way, and practice attentive listening? Find your balance.

- Make an attempt to liberate your own underdog traits and try to compensate by practicing the opposite quality. If you're more of the thinking type, *feel* your way today, and vice versa.

"It is easier to forgive an enemy than to forgive a friend."

— William Blake

BETRAYAL

Deception, dishonesty, and deceit are painful to experience, whether we're on the receiving or giving end. The more deeply we are in relationship with another, the more we open ourselves up to be hurt. In life, we inevitably hurt and disappoint those we love; this seems to be the nature of human relatedness. Yet when we *deliberately* set out to deceive another, we step out of our integrity, violate the other's trust, and activate shame in ourselves. Betraying another is almost always the result of an earlier experience of betrayal in a cycle of abuse. Being betrayed by a trusted other, especially by a lover, is one of the most painful experiences we can endure.

If you have betrayed another or have been betrayed, take stock of what you did or how you reacted. Then take the necessary time to forgive yourself or another. Whether the two of you stay involved in each other's lives or part ways for self-protection's sake, it can take years to restore trust or to forgive someone who's betrayed you. There's no prescription for how long these processes take, so don't force or rush these complicated matters. Give yourself a break, take the time you need and as nature takes her course, you will naturally heal and become stronger.

DAILY HEALTHY SEX ACTS

- Make a list of persons you have betrayed in your life. Have you made amends? Have you forgiven yourself for your misdeeds? Today, take one step toward repairing your wrongdoing.

- If you've been betrayed, how do you protect your heart today? *Betrayal trauma*, a form of psychological trauma, requires healing—sometimes through professional help. Have you forgiven the betrayer? If not, why? Holding on to resentment, hurt, and anger is a form of drinking your own poison.

- Let go today and let nature take her course.

"To forgive is to set a prisoner free and discover that the prisoner was you."

— Lewis B. Smedes

17 OCTOBER

FORGIVENESS

Like almost everything else, forgiveness begins at home. Self-forgiveness is a form of self-compassion, and without it, we flog ourselves for every little wrongdoing. In addition, we come to treat others the way we treat ourselves. Listen to your judgments of others, and remind yourself that you're actually projecting your judgments of yourself onto them, probably unconsciously operating the way you were programmed in your family of origin. Everyone makes mistakes all day long. Own yours! Apologize when you can, then start over with a greater understanding of what you did wrong. When you begin to forgive yourself for your imperfections, you begin to change positively from the inside out. And when that happens, forgiveness naturally flows outward to others.

But forgiveness for ourselves—or from another—is a natural process. It's not something either "should" do; it happens when we are ready. Like in any dynamic development, glimmers of forgiveness may emerge unexpectedly, then, just as suddenly, recede. Stay open but keep moving forward. If you've hurt another, don't compound it with impatience. Let the other come towards you when she or he is ready. Meanwhile, give yourself permission to forgive your past mistakes. Remember, forgiveness doesn't happen all at once—it comes in stages and may never feel complete.

Forgive only when your heart tells you it's the right time. Forgiving prematurely can hurt you further because forgiving too soon is a lie. You aren't on anyone's timetable but your own. Take your time and stay present. Just remember that waiting too long, holding onto anger, can be toxic to your system and create resentment that keeps you sick and stuck. Suffering doesn't make you a better person, and obsessing over the past won't heal your heartbreak, but forgiveness of yourself and others can do both.

DAILY HEALTHY SEX ACTS

- Make a list today of all the negative things you say to yourself about yourself. How often do you judge yourself for who you are or how you do things? Every time you hear self-criticism, think to yourself, "I forgive myself; I am perfectly imperfect."

- Pay attention to the way you judge others. Is this a reflection of your inner dialogue with yourself?

- Today, forgive someone who has harmed you. Let go, let God!

> *"I would like to no longer dance to anything but the rhythm of my soul."*
>
> — Isadora Duncan

RHYTHM

Every living thing has its rhythm. To find a rhythm, we feel it first and think about it later. Today we feel rhythms from all over the globe, and it's improving more than our dancing. Sure, our unprecedented exposure to other cultures translates somatically into moving our bodies to different beats. But that new bodily learning really grows from greater valuing of others' ways of life. Where there's xenophobia—fear of the stranger—it's impossible to appreciate and incorporate new rhythms, which mark the beat of individual or group patterns. Perhaps worse, some of us remain scared of our *own* rhythm, which may express *rhythmic trauma*—early disruptions of our natural movements that nonverbally communicate our continuously repressed tempo. But coursing through our souls, there is always a deeper rhythm, be it ancestral, astral or astrophysical.

In relationships, we memorize the rhythms of walking together, talking together, and talking as a couple to others. There's the rhythm of intersecting routines and reuniting after a long day. And one of the most profound aspects of sex and love is the erotic reverberation with another's base rhythm—at its core level, the blended heartbeats harmonizing our life forces. Holding one another in our arms and our affections actually brings hearts into attunement, soothing and regulating nerves and emotions. Like yogis, we raise consciousness through our very vibrations.

In contrast, sensing we're "out of sync" with others may frighten us into thinking that we're permanently out of step with humanity. But if we hear all the rhythms that inform our lives, we can realize that life is a series of ups and downs, of upbeats and downbeats. When we affirm all the different drums that friends and strangers march to in our world, we find we're perfectly in time with the deeply fulfilling, divinely orchestrated rhythm of life.

DAILY HEALTHY SEX ACTS

- Today, observe the rhythm of passers-by on the street, at work, everywhere. Summon loving acceptance and let their tempos move you emotionally and corporeally. Try to assimilate new ideas by trying out the rhythms of those you encounter.

- Imagine the rhythm you share with your beloved during sex. What's the internal pace of the love-making you like—is it a symphony, a hymn, or a hard rock ballad? Take responsibility for the rhythm in your sex life by tapping into desired rhythms throughout your day. Know that the rhythms you express make way for the rhythms you receive.

"Love is like a friendship caught on fire: In the beginning a flame, very pretty, often hot and fierce, but still only light and flickering. As love grows older, our hearts mature and our love becomes as coals, deep-burning and unquenchable."

— Bruce Lee

19 OCTOBER

HEAT

Sexual love is a sensual fire that heats or scorches. Just as fireplace flames mesmerize with their graceful, unpredictable dance, the experience of sex and love bewitches. Above all, shared sexuality is *alive*! On Earth, all that's alive has some heat, while the absence of life spells cold death. When sex is good, we say it's *HOT*, while withholding sex is *frigid*. Human thermodynamics involves the actual transfer of energy between lovers as heat is exchanged, absorbed and released. Factors contributing to the temperature of any individual—that person's *temperament*—include personality, background, and culture. We've all met people who radiated such sexual charisma that lava may as well have been flowing from them! You may have been burned by the heat of a lover, and felt left out in the cold when it was over. At what point does someone's sexual heat turn into a tool of manipulation, an amorous arson, preventing cooler heads from prevailing?

The Greek philosopher Aristotle theorized that an animal's "vital heat" determines its reproductive style. Indeed, female animals at their peak of fertility are said to be "in heat." We all have moments in our lives when our capacity for intimacy ignites, as though an engine purrs inside our hearts, melting our defenses and moving us into a deeply connective state with the world. When this happens with our sexuality, all we touch turns to gold. The back arches easily, and we receive and project sexual energy that brings us to a highly eroticized state on the brink of going supernova!

DAILY HEALTHY SEX ACTS

- Heightened sexual heat is almost always the result of an inner breakthrough. What are you doing to create warm feelings in your own life, and how do you bring these feelings to the bedroom?

- Telling the truth can be hot. Exploring fantasies can be hot. Take the temperature of your turn-ons, and ask your partner to share his or hers. See the truths you receive in terms of energy, and let the magnifying glass of your awareness turn up the heat where you may be feeling cold.

> *"Electric flesh-arrows... traversing the body. A rainbow of color strikes the eyelids. A foam of music falls over the ears. It is the gong of the orgasm."*

> — Anaïs Nin

ORGASM

The French call orgasm or, more accurately, its sometimes melancholy aftermath, "la petite mort"— the little death. Orgasm is a muscle spasm setting off a blast of neurochemicals that can leave us ecstatic, seeing stars, or sensing we've merged with the divine. It gets a lot of attention as it's set up as the ticket to "great" sex and even happiness. But there are many different kinds of orgasms, and we experience them according to how our individual bodies are wired. Some report full-body orgasms, simultaneous orgasms, multiple orgasms, genital orgasms, vaginal orgasms, and mental orgasms. Whatever your experience, remember not to compare yourself to others but to build upon the way your own body responds.

Experimenting with masturbation in privacy allows us to discover what brings us to orgasm. Then it's up to us to communicate our preferences to our lover. Some orgasms just happen, while others require concentrating on the body's sensations. But simultaneous orgasms require mutuality between you and your partner. When you're connected to your bodily rhythms and make eye contact, you can sense that both of you are moving toward orgasm. This form of orgasm can't be forced, but requires that both parties are dialed into each other and know what to do to attain orgasm, which might be as simple as pelvic breathing, thrusting faster, or genital stimulation.

Immediate post-orgasm reactions range from laughter to exhaustion to crying. Some pull away, some move close. Orgasm is one of the times in life when we willingly give up control. This can be either scary or exciting depending on our sexual history and on whether we learned to trust or mistrust people with our sexuality. In any case, orgasm reminds us that things in life happen all the time that are, blissfully, beyond our command.

DAILY HEALTHY SEX ACTS

- What type of orgasms have you experienced?

- What type of orgasms would you like to experience?

- How well do you know what brings you to orgasm? Communicate that knowledge to your partner.

"Sexuality is something that we ourselves create. It is our own creation, and much more than the discovery of a secret side of our desire. We have to understand that with our desires go new forms of relationships, new forms of love, new forms of creation."

— Michel Foucault

21 OCTOBER

SEXUAL LIFESTYLE

To affirm one's inner sexuality and identity through a lifestyle choice is one of the healthiest acts of individuality possible. Just as there are many personal styles, there are many sexual lifestyles. Your particular sexuality develops as you define what you like and dislike and discover a safe place to practice what really feels good—what isn't just socially acceptable or convenient on the one hand, or shocking and provocative on the other. But should there be limits to allowing people to practice whatever feels good?

Consider sadomasochism. Physical pain play might be a healthy and indispensable container for certain psychological feelings. But some lifestyle choices are a reactionary response to earlier issues that remain unexamined—retraumatization packaged as sexual extravaganza. Indeed, for some whose arousal template includes sadomasochism, such practices are a replay of childhood trauma. For them, this lifestyle might lose its appeal when the emotions driving it are released through a therapeutic process. Others, though, may work through their trauma and find that this style of sex still works for them.

The key to assessing any problematic sex act—meaning an activity that causes shame or provokes deception—is to unpack it fully to find the life inside. As long as the style of sex is consensual and does no harm to oneself or others, there is no rational reason for anyone else to interfere. Diverse expressions of sexuality might not always be religiously or socially approved, but adherence to a religion or social nicety is equally a matter of choice as is sexual lifestyle.

DAILY HEALTHY SEX ACTS

- Is your current sexual lifestyle a conscious choice? If not, how would you choose to express your sexuality if you had no barriers?

- There are online groups for lifestyle choices of all kinds. Search out trustworthy people who share your interests today to add greater depth, meaning and support for the life you choose to lead.

> *"Our erotic knowledge empowers us, becomes a lens through which we scrutinize all aspects of our existence, forcing us to evaluate those aspects honestly in terms of their relative meaning within our lives."*
>
> — Audre Lorde

EROTIC INTELLIGENCE

It's hard to measure our *erotic intelligence*, in part, because the term itself conjures up different meaning for everyone, depending on her or his sexual history. To clarify, recall that *erotic* means arousing or seeking to arouse sexual love, desire, or pleasure, and that *intelligence* means the skilled use of reason. Deliberately seeking sexual pleasure with the skilled use of reason means we're thinking about what we like or dislike sexually, and why. While eroticism begins with concern for our individual pleasure, arousal translates it into action that we convey to our lover. As we move out of our self in a loving connection with another, we take an ordinary sex act and elevate it to the realm of the erotic.

As we mature, erotic sexuality emerges in a wholly individual manner. Our caregivers may have effectively demonstrated almost every social behavior through modeling, but they couldn't model healthy sexuality directly—it's one of the few areas in life where we are fully on our own. The actions we consider erotic are as unique as our fingerprints, perhaps set from the beginning and waiting to blossom upon exploration and use. Once activated, eroticism is like an exotic shimmy fashioned of pulsing, moving, and flowing personal energies. This dance requires a strong sense of who we are sexually and how honestly we've revealed our sexual self to our partner.

As sexual adults, we unleash our ravenous self while staying connected to our partner. Sharing our deepest, most carnal desires makes us vulnerable and invites deeper intimacy. In so doing we hope our partner will applaud our courage, know us more deeply, and expand our emotional and erotic intelligences so we can transform and self-actualize throughout our sexual lives.

DAILY HEALTHY SEX ACTS

- Share your sexual self with your partner: Connect on a heart level by revealing something you desire but worry your partner may judge you on. It can be as simple as flirting, or planning and engaging in a ritual that you find erotic.

- Notice how well you tolerate the possibility of being rejected or shamed by taking a sexual risk. Is that fear your partner's doing? Your upbringing? Your own self-judgment?

- How has your erotic intelligence developed over the years? Who are you sexually today compared with the past? How would you like to flourish erotically in the future?

"Obsessed by a fairy tale, we spend our lives searching for a magic door and a lost kingdom of peace."

— Eugene O'Neill

23 OCTOBER

FAIRY TALES

In fairy tales, love is an ideal, perfect relationship that was destined to be. It's easy to forget the dark conflicts and dangers that fairy tales also present. If fairy tales really dictated our lives, true love would require early abandonment, voluntary isolation, dubious acquaintances, hazardous tests, fatal mistakes, terrifying evil and horrendous sacrifice. Yet most lovers focus only on the tales' perfect happy endings as a template for achieving their hearts' desire.

How much do fairy tales—in all their fantasy facets—inform our lives? Certainly in a deeply psychological manner, fairy tales express universal inner experiences in symbolic language. One message they share is that, regardless of circumstance and appearances, each of us plays out a profoundly meaningful story whose every moment is vital and whose every act has consequences. But this insight doesn't mean we should run to slay the neighborhood dragon or devote our lives to a lover held hostage by another. One of the most dangerous pitfalls of fairy-tale romance is losing our good sense through the misinterpretation of reality... as fairy tales themselves so often tell us!

DAILY HEALTHY SEX ACTS

- Do you hold your partner to fairy tale standards only to have him or her routinely disappoint you? If so, take time today to get into reality about who s/he really is. Do you like what you see?

- Seek out real, solid information today. Ask follow-up questions to settle any vagueness in all your relationships.

- Find your way out of the maze of misunderstanding to find the amazement in shared values, shared goals, and shared lives.

"A sex symbol becomes a thing. I just hate to be a thing."

— Marilyn Monroe

OBJECTIFICATION

An object is a thing, usually made of material that can be seen and touched. But an object can also be a person we direct feelings towards. Thus, the one we love can be our "love object" in the most literal sense of the word. But when we target a person as an item of our physical desire—a sexual object to be had—we've reduced him or her to a thing to be used for our gain. We all recognize this type of objectification as cold and calculating, serving our carnal needs without any regard for the other. But we often ignore that when we become habituated to this pattern of sexuality we have, ironically, made *ourselves* into objects, and will find ourselves being used sexually or otherwise, and discarded afterward. Over time, such sexual encounters bring despair to both parties.

In contrast, when love and attachment inspire objectification, being the love object can be exciting and fun. All too often people feel offended by being objectified in any way. But when we comfortably embody our sexuality, objectification by our lover feels like a compliment. To achieve that experience, we must leave any shame about our body or sexuality out of the bedroom. Confidence, self-knowledge, and an appreciation of our sexiness and beauty let us view, and give, our self as a love object in a healthy way.

Receiving adoration for our corporeal body requires a high level of self-love. Typically we associate using one's body seductively as a power trip. But when we transform our energy into genuine, relationship-based power we experience our self differently, as an admirer—like our lover—of the body we were given at birth, the body that transports us through life, the body that is the altar of sexual pleasure and delight.

DAILY HEALTHY SEX ACTS

- In what healthy ways do you objectify your lover? When you look at your lover's body, what do you see? What do you tell him or her about the effects his or her body has on you?

- In what healthy ways do you objectify yourself? How do you adorn and prepare yourself for sex? How much effort do you put into cultivating your consciousness and your appearance for yourself, and how much do you do it for your partner?

"Tis well to be merry and wise,
'Tis well to be honest and true;
'Tis well to be off with the old love,
Before you are on with the new."
— Charles Robert Maturin

25 OCTOBER

CLOSURE

Do you grieve your losses at length or do you immediately replace them? We've almost all had the experience of losing a cat or dog that meant the world to us, and before we've had time to grieve, some well-meaning friend suggests that it's time for a new puppy or kitten. If you didn't have time for emotional closure regarding how that animal's companionship enriched your life, then the idea of a new pet can feel wrong, insensitive, and disrespectful to your process. Likewise, without taking time for proper closure to a relationship— whether it lasted three months or thirty years—we're likely ignoring our feelings of grief and loss.

Ending a relationship teaches us many lessons—both good and bad— about how we love. Recognizing the ways we're giving or controlling, when we're driven by fantasy over reality, how we're selfless or selfish, or where we fold or withhold provides us with valuable data on who we are. Don't shorten your learning curve by moving on with someone new before doing a proper emotional autopsy on your last relationship. After all, you were (or thought you were) in love with that person at one time. Once you feel complete with yourself about your prior romance and feel like you've had proper closure with your former partner (meaning you're not holding on to any anger or resentment), then, and only then, is it time to move on with the new.

DAILY HEALTHY SEX ACTS

- If you've recently broken up with someone, allow yourself all the time you need to grieve before you move on. There's no prescribed time for this; you'll know it in your heart.

- If you ended a relationship and immediately jumped into a new one, ask yourself if you're still holding any anger, resentment or contempt about your previous partner. If so, you're likely dragging that energy into your current relationship. Take time to sort out those feelings, and do what you need to do for closure.

> *"For the past twenty years you and I have been fed all day long on good solid lies about sex."*
>
> — C. S. Lewis

SEXUAL MYTHS

Sexual myths are falsehoods about sexuality that are propagated throughout our culture. Many of these sexual distortions carry strong undertones of prejudice—sexism, racism and homophobia—that rob individuals of their individuality. Common stereotypes include "men are all dogs," "women are less interested in sex," "gays are promiscuous," certain races are frigid or hung, and certain sex acts are indulgent, effeminate, or immoral. Other distortions clearly function as tools of organizations or of religious or political figures to shape public opinion through dogma and to control their followers' lives.

Some sexual myths work like a horror film—knowing perfectly well it's fake, we still allow ourselves to get scared. An example is the myth that masturbation will make you go blind. We know it's ridiculous, and yet we might still let ourselves feel a certain apprehension because there's something inherently frightening about sexuality. Especially in adolescence, when we try so hard to conform to programmed norms—familial, social, or institutional—it's scary when puberty hits and we discover how differently we are wired.

Sexual myths—like all myths—are meant to provide a map through chaotic times. But mythical maps reflect the culture creating them more than universal truth. During the Middle Ages, a time when much was unknown and to be feared, sexual myths reinforced fear of the unknown with theories that today seem terrifyingly ignorant. For some people today, porn can be one of the biggest sexual myth machines that exist, providing a formulaic template for sex that many people strive to emulate in real life for lack of a more educated, connective, and multidimensional sexuality.

DAILY HEALTHY SEX ACTS

- What are sexual myths you've encountered, and how do you think *and feel* about them today?

- Examine your mentality for sexual stereotypes. Consider the people that inhabit your world and the roles in which you are casting them. Do these fixed perceptions bring you into greater intimacy or alienation?

- If you were to write your own sexual *narrative*—a true and honest story— what would that look like so far, and what is happening now? What would be a great way to develop this narrative into the next stage of your life?

"Sometimes your joy is the source of your smile, but sometimes your smile can be the source of your joy."

— Thích Nhất Hạnh

27 OCTOBER

JOY

Joy is a vitality state that lifts our spirits, rendering the "incredible lightness of being" a tangible sense in the body. Many experiences and persons can bring joy into our lives, but one of the simplest yet most powerful joy states comes in the presence of a baby. Babies bring joy to the world with their innocence and laughter, recalling in us the lack of inhibition and the play states that make us giggle with glee. Unencumbered by trauma and stories of misery or pain, we bathe in the essence they project—the essence of who we really are.

When was the last time you touched a joy state in yourself or shared that state with your lover? While people and experiences can cheer us up and bring momentary pleasure, the true test of whether or not we will live in happiness is whether we *cultivate joy* in our lives. Our overly stimulating culture can actually steal joy from us, cramming our psyches with endless messages and images that crowd out our soul. The secret to joy is that you must find it within yourself. Hiding in your heart, at the center of your being, this precious, original self-state awaits. But finding your joy can be challenging. Past wounds and hurt sit on top of it and can crush or numb it. Don't despair. In a game of internal hide-and-seek, you can discover your joy by simply and quietly putting your attention on your heart. Don't strain to find it and don't give up on it. In self-love and compassion, sit still and wait for the stirrings of joy to reveal itself to you.

DAILY HEALTHY SEX ACTS

- Take the time today to sit quietly with your eyes closed. Mentally scan your body, and notice where you might be feeling any tension. Breathe into the tension to acknowledge it, then dive further into the feeling below it. Don't chase the feelings; just notice them.

- What do you know about your joy? What has brought you joy in your life? Do one thing today that makes you want to jump for joy!

- How does joy inform your sex life? What pleasure states do you share with your partner that make you both feel vitally alive?

> *"I need sex for a clear complexion, but I'd rather do it for love."*
>
> — Joan Crawford

SECRET MOTIVES

Sex can be used as a secret means to achieve some other ambition and, likewise, certain achievements can actually be a means of getting sex. Spy films are often structured on this pretense, and function as modern-day cautionary tales about interpersonal intrigue run amuck. What common motives secretly underlie sex? Validation, power, security, social climbing, obligation, peer pressure, stress relief, eroticized rage, rebellion—sex can be motivated by a gamut of goals wholly separate from the honest desire to connect with another for mutual care and pleasure.

To engage consciously in sexual subterfuge is to support unhealthy objectification. Such objectification cannot be practiced on others without ultimately objectifying one's inner self. Like the cheater who thinks everyone is cheating on him or her, when we contribute to dishonest behavior we are actually inviting manipulation into our lives. Generally people who feel like they're being played are, in some part of their lives, playing others.

Exploiting any situation or person as merely the means to an end precludes our being in the moment and experiencing life directly. It creates one of the most basic forms of unavailability and dissatisfaction. And even when it's seemingly on purpose and for the doer's benefit, it's always the result of traumatized programming and always backfires. No one would freely choose disconnection as a method to better one's future connectedness, yet disconnection is exactly what happens to practitioners of this kind of opportunism. Cut out the middleman, and let transparency guide you to your true desires.

DAILY HEALTHY SEX ACTS

- Make a list of some of your past ulterior motives for sexual and romantic contact. How have they worked out for you in the past? For instance, did you gain security or power, and at what cost? What might be healthier ways for you to meet your goals?

- Bring awareness to your actions today and consider how often they are the means to a hidden end. It's especially easy to seek intimacy from others through other means. Let yourself be vulnerable today by openly expressing your desire for intimacy to those you trust.

> *"The greatest way to live with honor in this world is to be what we pretend to be."*
>
> — Socrates

29 OCTOBER

HONOR

Honor seems to be a word from a bygone era when men lived by a code of honor and women were granted honor if they honored men's code. But today, to live with honor means to live with a high regard for yourself and for others. Self-respect, or staking your reputation on your word, is a daily test of your honor. Consider how trustworthy you are, and how you measure your own trustworthiness. Socrates' ideal of being what we pretend to be is a provocative one. Most of us don't think we're walking around just pretending to be ourselves, yet to some extent we're all pretenders. So it's a formidable, and honorable, task to attempt to know ourselves deeply—one that requires a commitment to the life-long task of self-inquiry. On top of that, we're in an on-going process of becoming who we are, with no end in sight until that final breath.

To live a life of honor means to live with an undisguised, wholly honest adherence to our principles. This leaves no room for lies or deceit, beginning with ourselves. How many small lies do you tell a day? What are you lying to yourself about, thereby dishonoring yourself? Are you in alignment with who you pretend to be? Set the bar high and aspire to live an honorable life—honor thyself, honor thy neighbor, live on the honor system, and honor the earth.

DAILY HEALTHY SEX ACTS

- Make an honorable gesture toward your lover, neighbor, or the earth today. What does it feel like when you perform acts of honor?

- Find ways to restore your honor and virtue by righting any wrongs to which you've been a party.

- Treat your enemies with respect and don't stoop to tactics that dishonor you—turn the other cheek.

> *"Drink and dance and laugh and lie,*
> *Love, the reeling midnight through,*
> *For tomorrow we shall die!*
> *(But, alas, we never do)."*
>
> — Dorothy Parker

MORTALITY

There's a clichéd fantasy that, if everyone knew the world were about to end imminently, people would throw caution to the wind, kissing strangers and having sex in the streets. How does your apocalyptic scenario play out? Stripped of all pretension, social expectations, and caution, would your usual behavior prove to be just a ruse to ensure your safety and reputation? Consider what would happen if those societal structures no longer mattered. Ideally, we would still seek to behave in a way that reflects our dearest values, even during the darkest of circumstances—*especially* during the darkest of circumstances.

Technically we enter this world alone and we leave this world alone. We also know that death separates, and so may ask, "Why get involved in life if it's all going to end someday?" Yet we want to mark our death and the death of our loved ones. Starting today, we can each secure emotional insurance for that event. Because we do live on. We all live on in the people whose lives we touch, and thus become part of an unbreakable chain. Think of all the mentors and teachers who have impacted your life, and all the people who hold some part of the wisdom you've shared with them. Relationships remain vital in the hearts that experienced them, even after one party has passed on. Every moment we are alive gives us the opportunity to expand our capacity for intimacy and relationship. If this is the truest lesson of a life, we may carry this with us into any kind of death, and through our darkest nights.

DAILY HEALTHY SEX ACTS

- What vital experiences would you want to have if the world were to end, and why? If you are not already experiencing such vital moments today, find a way to be true to your vision while you're still living.

- Reach out to those who have touched your life in a healthy and healing way. Recharge both your batteries, and let them know what they mean to you.

"I lose my respect for the man who can make the mystery of sex the subject of a coarse jest, yet when you speak earnestly and seriously on the subject, is silent."

— Henry David Thoreau

31 OCTOBER

EROTIC MATURITY

Our sexual identity matures over time, as do our political, cultural, and aesthetic selves. In all these areas, maturation demands attention and learning from mistakes. The deep consciousness and refined technique attained in any field can develop tools applicable to sexuality. But unfortunately, the credits don't always transfer. So we see many brilliant artists, athletes and politicians utterly undone by sex and relationships. And many young adults who aspire to sexual maturity before their time dress to impress, assume the postures of popular culture, and mistake the playbook for the event. Further, while age and experience are key elements of maturation, there certainly are oldsters as immature as any teen. So at no social stage can the attainment of erotic intelligence be faked.

Sexual repression or unprocessed trauma keeps many persons paralyzed in an intimacy-impaired juvenile state. Nothing stunts growth like compensating for, rather than confronting, one's sense of sexual or psychological inadequacy. Compensation often goes hand-in-hand with squashing awareness through denial, drama or addictions. Erotic maturity, in contrast, embraces one's vulnerability to shine light on one's sexual self. Having questioned one's sexual inclinations, prejudices, potential and limitations, some sexually mature persons conform with social mores while others may define personal sexuality against the social current. For example, polyamory or open relationships may be a valid lifestyle choice resulting from hard-won self-knowledge. But for those emotionally incapable of tolerating monogamy or intimacy, choosing it may be guided more by stunted sexuality than mature self-awareness.

Erotic maturity arrives through the honest search for intimacy, openness to new ideas, and the integration of individual experience—all marks of being sexual in the world. Every person's journey there is unique and no one needs to be a sex expert. Maturity needs only to create personal comfort and a relational proficiency that imbues all our connections.

DAILY HEALTHY SEX ACTS

- Identify the strengths and weaknesses of your sexuality. Shine the light on any immature attitudes such as bravado, ignorance or inhibition.

- Can you articulate your sexual progress with your partner? Are you aware enough to embrace your partner's erotic path in life? Share your most private sexual truth with someone you love and trust today. Break free of emotional and sexual repression in order to grow up.

November

> *"Having sex is like playing bridge. If you don't have a good partner, you'd better have a good hand."*
>
> — Mae West

1 NOVEMBER

SELF-PLEASURE

Forty-thousand-year-old cave paintings depict prehistoric humans masturbating. Early Egyptians believed the god Apsu created the Milky Way through masturbation. Ancient Greeks taught that Hermes invented masturbation to heal the broken heart of his son, the satyr Pan, after the nymph Echo rejected him. This myth was popularized by the philosopher Diogenes, himself known to masturbate in public to prove that no human activity was so shameful as to require being hidden.

While self-pleasure is well-documented in many cultures, it's also had plenty of detractors cautioning of its medical and moral hazards. These views were firmly rooted in Western civilization until the Kinsey Report and other research helped sway the medical establishment. But as late as 1994, United States Surgeon General Dr. Joyce Elders was fired for commenting that masturbation was a healthy part of human sexuality and might be taught as such in sex education.

The fact is: Masturbation *is* a healthy part of human sexuality, and an inherent gift. The design of the human body gives us free access to our genitals. Whatever your spiritual beliefs, it's clear this function was granted for our enjoyment, whether single or partnered. Masturbation is healthy when we experience joy at delighting ourselves in caring, erotic ways—that is, without shame or self-abuse attached to the act or the accompanying fantasy. For those who have abused masturbation in compulsive ways, it can take time before healthy fantasy can flower and become incorporated into masturbation. Be patient and consult with others who have already walked the path of recovery. If fantasy with masturbation creates problems for you, drop the fantasy and focus on the sensations in your body and your God-given right to pleasure.

DAILY HEALTHY SEX ACTS

- Find a healthy place to masturbate in your home and in your spirit. As you feel self-pleasure, also feel self-love. If shame arrives uninvited, you're in control—just gently ask shame to leave.

- Let your partner watch you masturbate. Notice how you feel being watched as you make eye contact. Experience what it's like to be seen and loved as you express your sexuality.

- If masturbating feels compulsive, ask yourself why. Do minutes turn to hours, interfering with day-to-day functioning? Do you masturbate in public, or while driving? Have you ever broken skin and still been unable to stop? Seek help now to heal sexually addictive behaviors.

> *"The tragedy of sexual intercourse is the perpetual virginity of the soul."*
>
> — William B. Yeats

VIRGINITY

Few interior personal states bear more external social weight than virginity. It's telling that we *lose virginity* rather than *gain sexuality* by our initial sexual experience. For many, leaving their virginal stage can be confusing and anxious. While manuals aplenty detail this much-ballyhooed rite of passage, putting theory into practice involves new skills and processes that need time and effort to blossom. We all know it takes years just to start developing conscious sexuality, but the common social mindset has us becoming sexually experienced with a single sexual act.

The loss of virginity typically refers to penile-vaginal penetration, but this assumption ignores the experience of gays and lesbians, who may define it as the first momentous sexual contact, whether mutual masturbation, oral sex, or anal sex. Indeed, heterosexuals sometimes engage in these same acts and still consider themselves *technical virgins*. In conservative cultures, females who have been sexually active before marriage often resort to hymenoplasty to restore technical virginity and escape sometimes deadly social disgrace. Victims of childhood sexual abuse, incest, or rape might understandably specify consensual sex to characterize *their* first time.

But there are other types of virginity, like that of our ideas. Learning about each sexual act is one part of the process of losing virginity, but so is learning about new feelings. Lovers define and create sexuality together, as it occurs. No matter what happened to us sexually, there are parts of us—physical and psychological—that remain unknown. Many people feel this spiritual concept profoundly—that we can find untouched parts of our being with a partner at any stage. If we have the intent to connect with each other in the deepest parts of ourselves, the ones that have been untouched, we have a reparative way of making ourselves newly sacred, of newly consecrating the sexual act.

DAILY HEALTHY SEX ACTS

- How did you lose your virginity? Was it spontaneous or planned? Did it live up to expectations? Invoke the feelings before, during and after the experience. Where do these feelings show up in your sexuality today?

- Consider whether your initial sexual experiences made you want to gain proficiency or shed innocence. Has this changed over time?

- What part of you goes untouched? Guide your lover there, or simply let in the light of loving awareness now.

"If sex and creativity are often seen by dictators as subversive activities, it's because they lead to the knowledge that you own your own body (and with it your own voice), and that's the most revolutionary insight of all."

— Erica Jong

3 NOVEMBER

CREATIVITY

Through creativity, we fulfill our purpose in life. Through imaginative play as children, we learn our own selfhood and the reality of the world around us. Through original projects as adolescents, we learn our strengths and weaknesses. The act of creation works as a divine mirror, revealing that we receive back what we send out. When we recall the joy and meaning that our most innovative states have brought us, we should conclude that this same creativity belongs in our sex life. But we are our own strictest censors, often repressing creative urges even more than we repress sexual urges.

Creativity is about options. Allowing the free flow of novel ideas gains us a higher perspective, a broader overview than the narrow vantage point of unquestioning assimilation. Rigid adherence to familial, social, or cultural dogma makes it almost impossible to perceive and value personal options. The lack of both healthy sexual education and emotional differentiation imposes paralyzing fears of shame and loss, as well as some of the most black-and-white judgmentalism that ever incarcerated the human mind.

The concept of sexual creativity might intimidate at first, because we fear who-knows-what situations that might arise and what emotional and physical dangers might be spawned. It's particularly intimidating to those who are overly compliant and susceptible to whatever half-baked ideas are suggested. But by strengthening our boundaries, self-trust, and morality, we can safely cultivate a healthy sexual creativity whose acts can bring us deeper connections and greater understanding of others and ourselves.

DAILY HEALTHY SEX ACTS

- Can you recognize the creativity of others? Notice the particular clothes they wear, the interesting food they serve, or the innovative work they do and show your appreciation of these. Let yourself be moved by the unique ideas they are trying to express.

- Can you acknowledge your own creative choices in these areas? Consider what your style and actions express about you.

- Select one cherished trait (e. g. , kindness, honesty, fitness) and let this one trait guide all the choices you make today—your clothes, conversations, entertainments, and meals. Observe the power of your creativity.

"Example is not the main thing in influencing others. It is the only thing."

— Albert Schweitzer

EXAMPLE

People respond to the example we set. However impeccable our words and intentions, people respond to what we actually do. But without a true mirror, we can't see that actual example accurately. When early relationships were marked by codependence, neglect, or abuse, the false mirroring we received warps our perceptions of our self and our actions.

Attachment theory identifies one functional and three dysfunctional basic relational styles: secure, anxious-preoccupied, dismissive-avoidant, and fearful-avoidant. *Anxious-preoccupied attachment* stems from caregivers who were codependent or enmeshed to compensate for their own perceived faults; such lack of differentiation inhibited the child's independent growth and self-knowledge (including ownership of character flaws). Neglectful parenting engenders *dismissive-avoidant attachment*; since the need for closeness was painfully rejected, the child gives up trying to win it by honesty and love. And *fearful-avoidant attachment* results from early conditioning or later trauma by physical, verbal, or psychological abuse; this style greatly distorts our judgment of others', as well as our own, feelings and actions. So the example we grew up with literally becomes our way of navigating the world—it's so deeply rooted, it seems we'd have more luck shedding our skin than setting a new example. Fortunately, the shining examples of many who have transformed their lives to align their words and deeds with their values shows us the beauty, necessity, and possibility of this great work.

What example are you setting each moment? If your actions were to boomerang back on you instantly, would you still act the same? Doing to others an act you'd rather not have done to you reveals a powerful internal conflict you need to address. Only by facing and fixing it can you stop the external conflicts you see as "happening to" you.

DAILY HEALTHY SEX ACTS

- What example do you set when you're alone? Imagine the world watching your behavior at all times—would you want everyone to see you slipping into little comas of rage, panic, lust, or self-loathing? What happens to those secret moments in our lives? Is it as if they don't happen just because we cover them up?

- We can ask for healthy examples when life confounds us. We never have to learn hard lessons on our own. Find a safe space with friends or a supportive community where you can learn to lead *yourself* by example.

"When we honestly ask ourselves which person in our lives means the most to us, we often find that it is those who, instead of giving advice, solutions, or cures, have chosen rather to share our pain and touch our wounds with a warm and tender hand."

— Henri J. M. Nouwen

5 NOVEMBER

EMPATHY

Through empathy we perceive and share the emotional reality of another in that living moment. To bear such witness requires releasing the desire to change another's emotional dynamic, because wanting only to "fix" another's pain may come from our desire to escape feeling it ourselves. Typical defense mechanisms we use to displace empathy include minimizing, maximizing, or distracting.

People who weren't shown empathy in childhood may struggle to practice it as adults. Classic non-responses to childhood distress include, "Stop crying," "Tsk, you're okay," or even, "Here, have a lollipop." Lack of empathy stunts the reparative neurophysiological process that builds secure attachment, and substitutes an endless psychological loop from emotional stasis to disruption to dissociative lapse, over and over again. And it's not just painful feelings that get stuck without the healing connection of empathy. Success may also have rarely received empathy—approval, but not empathy.

It follows that a crucial tool in any relationship is self-empathy, especially as a parent or spouse. If we block self-empathy, especially during our bleakest moments, we're certainly going to be limited in our ability to empathize with others. While empathy lets us see into others, self-empathy keeps us from being invisible. It can be as simple as checking in with yourself during any conversation or situation to voice in your mind, "This is difficult for me right now," or "I am triggered," or even "I feel joyful" in whatever tone speaks to you.

DAILY HEALTHY SEX ACTS

- An elementary step toward empathy is reflecting back what we hear without inserting our own thoughts and feelings. Ask a willing participant to relay an emotional event from the day, and simply try to connect with that experience by repeating key phrases. If the person says, "I felt uncomfortable," then simply repeat, "You felt uncomfortable" in a similar tone. Observe your capacity for bearing witness without trying to fix or distract.

- How do you practice empathy during sexual and romantic times? Truly seeing and being seen by your lover can align bodily pleasure with emotional connection. Sexually experiment by bringing empathy to your bedroom.

"There are politics in sexual relationships because they occur in the context of a society that assigns power based on gender and other systems of inequality and privilege."

— Susan Shaw

SEXUAL POLITICS

People are said to be "playing politics" when they manipulate and use others for their own ends. The politics that seeks power over others for selfish reasons is always based on fear. We all grew up saturated by family politics and learned that certain people address situations through frightening behaviors. To avoid punishment or mistreatment, we found ways to live in progressively complex situations, often by our own maneuvering around obstacles—or manipulating people—to get what we want. The survival instinct demands that we continually re-orient ourselves within group dynamics. But for many of us, this resulted in internalized political drives that inform every other form of politics, including sexual politics with a loved one.

But politics has a nobler meaning as well: the behaviors that make us find healthy values of acceptance and forgiveness within ourselves, and lead us to embody those values in daily thoughts and acts. We may practice loving-kindness, regardless of circumstances, starting with our most beloved. So even our love-making becomes a noble political act that breaks the pattern of manipulation and exploitation. Humility, openness, and goodwill are healthy traits we can cultivate to help us shift from a win-lose paradigm of personal politics to a win-win paradigm of cooperation.

At every moment, a personal politic is happening within you. It can be underhanded and scheming, stereotyping and minimizing; it can seek to divide and conquer. Or we can practice a different politic: one that keeps us present with empathy for all life, and unites ourselves to others through unconditional love.

DAILY HEALTHY SEX ACTS

- We believe everyone has the right to experience healthy sex and love free from trauma, abuse, violence, crime, lies, secrets, judgment, shame, guilt and regrets. This is our shared philosophy and politics. What would you underline, add or subtract from this list, and why?

- How do you define healthy sex and love, and what political statements are you making through your relationships, communications, actions and appearance to practice this philosophy in your life?

"It doesn't matter how long we may have been stuck in a sense of our limitations. If we go into a darkened room and turn on the light, it doesn't matter if the room has been dark for a day, a week, or ten thousand years—we turn on the light and it is illuminated. Once we control our capacity for love and happiness, the light has been turned on."

— Sharon Salzberg

7 NOVEMBER

LIMITATIONS

A limit is a point at which we restrict our actions by our own free choice. We set limits when we tell ourselves, "I'm going to limit myself to one glass of wine with dinner." The related act of setting boundaries—differentiation between ourselves and others—ensures that we can keep setting our own limits freely, so it is crucial for mental health and real relationship. For example, we may say, "My limit is one glass of wine with dinner when I'm out with friends, and my boundary is that if I feel pressured to drink more, I will take care of myself and say 'no,' or leave if I need to." This simple formula will alleviate a lot of problems in relationships when both parties agree that they are entitled to their limits and boundaries.

Limitations, on the other hand, differ. These restrictions on our conscious will are often born out of our fear rather than out of our aspiration to master ourselves. Challenging our limitations is a powerful way to grow and change. When we hear ourselves state, "This is just how I am," or, "I've always been this way," we should recognize that we are giving into our limitations, especially when it comes to sexual experimentation. Blaming or shaming a lover because he or she wants to try something new may indicate that we're hiding behind our limitations. We might then ask ourselves whether we'll really be out of our integrity if we try this new behavior or whether we're taking the easy way out by not confronting our limitations. Demanding that a partner live within our own limitations is a form of emotional hostage-taking. Instead, let's use our awareness of our limitations to further, and freely, develop an ever-evolving adult sexuality limited only by our best selves.

DAILY HEALTHY SEX ACTS

- What are the top three limitation tales you tell yourself? They will typically have a tinge of fear or judgment in them and may sound something like, "I'm too old to..." or, "I think it's weird when..."

- What are your sexual limitations? When did you set those? How did they come to be? Have they helped or hurt your relationships?

- Take on one sexual limitation this week and entrust your partner to help you break through it.

"If love has attachment in it, it is lust. If love has no attachment in it, only then is it not lust. When you are in lust you are not really thinking of the other, thinking of your beloved or lover. You are simply using the other for your own ends."

— Osho

LUST

Certainly most of us have experienced a moment along the path to psychological maturity and self-mastery when lust clouded or coerced our decision-making. We also know that in many religions, lust is a great sin. We have experienced preaching of the perils of lust—mostly fear-mongering threats that can repress true spiritual recovery. There's so much that's unfair about lust, right? Why does one even get tempted? It's like the whole Icarus myth, where a child who has yet to master self-control is given waxen wings and admonished not to fly too close to the sun. Why put people in a situation they can't handle, and then condemn them to fatal suffering when they fail?

Lust inflames a part of the body that feels like a refuge sometimes. It's one place where we are totally alone, where no one can get at us. So it's a place where it feels like we have personal power. Surrendering to lust is unconsciously based on the desire to reclaim a sense of personal power. But, sadly, it's a desire which rarely matches up with our own values. The profound privacy of this conflict is one of the reasons we experience the split between our desire and our values as externally imposed, as a feeling of being unfairly judged by foreign morals. In truth, when you peel away the layers, the clash between our own lustful choices and our own ideals is deeply internal to us.

DAILY HEALTHY SEX ACTS

- Take an inventory of lust in your life. What specific images or events provoke your lust? Write about the feelings that happen in your body and being. Trace back to the earliest times that you felt these feelings. What other feelings can you remember at that time, and how was your lust resolved?

- Recall one past situation that stirred your lust. Imagine a way for the situation to be fully resolved, but that *doesnt't* result in sex or romance. For instance, the high school crush lets you know how wonderful you are, or the models in the underwear ads are fascinated by *your* beauty. What really drives your lust?

*"Sexuality poorly repressed unsettles some families;
well repressed, it unsettles the whole world."*

— Karl Kraus

9 NOVEMBER

REPRESSION

Despite the constant barrage of sexualization, objectification, and exploitation in any given society, its populace is very likely sexually repressed. As most human beings have grown up in a sexually repressive environment, sexual healing won't be achieved by taking one's top off and dancing on tabletops. Were sexuality merely a body part or consensual transaction, perhaps exposing the body part or engaging in the sex act would release inhibitions. But sex is more than a thing to be had! Many of the actions that people try in hopes of escaping the grips of repression—of becoming sexually liberated—actually serve to bury and thus reinforce the original repression, without shedding the light needed for healing to occur. And all sexual repression results in *repression of the capacity for intimacy*.

People commonly complain that their partner is "repressed" and needs to be more sexually open. This comment always raises a red flag: Is there coercion or unhealthy boundaries, or is the partner in fact unusually repressed? Why is this couple not in an intimate enough state to find understanding? The process of identifying mutual sexual needs is where repression really shows itself. For repression is not so much about which sex acts one finds acceptable as it is about the ability to share one's emotional, relational and sexual truth, and to receive another's truth without judgment. If doing so seems daunting to you, that's the degree of repression that still informs your actions.

DAILY HEALTHY SEX ACTS

- Choose to liberate yourself from the shackles of repression. The process, as always, begins within. How do you honestly feel about your capacity for sex and intimacy?

- How has repression shown up in your life? In the lives of your parents? What is one action you can take towards healthy expression that will shed light on a repressed area? You do not need to know how to heal. Just trust the light that you bring to this area of your life to also reveal your next step.

"She knew she was by him beloved,—she knew,
For quickly comes such knowledge, that his heart
Was darken'd with her shadow."

— Lord Byron

INTRIGUE

The word *intrigue* carries a dark, mysterious, even foreboding connotation. It's used to describe the crafty, underhanded plotting of villains in a play. But it also refers to the intricate machinations of a lover seeking to draw another into a passionate affair. Intrigue differs from simpler flirtation in that the object of desire is usually unavailable or perhaps taboo, such as a married boss, a delinquent teen, or a complete stranger. Flirtation may also be "innocent" attention without intention. But intrigue involves sending the unmistakable "signal"—that intangible vibe we all know so well yet struggle to define. It's a certain way we silently undress someone in our mind while carrying on a mundane conversation. Or small clues we leave behind to trigger someone's curiosity or stoke the flames of jealousy. However we do it, our aim is an erotic "high," a hit of validation and recognition, and the unspoken promise that someday we will in fact consummate our desire.

Intrigue may have its roots in childhood trauma and family-of-origin issues. We may have learned early that secretive, duplicitous action rather than direct, honest communication was the best strategy for getting our needs met. Indeed, intrigue always secretes and compartmentalizes our connection with someone rather than publicizing and expanding it.

Despite its shady characteristics, though, we can use this covert and steamy energy to enliven a consensual relationship with a partner. Role-playing is one of the greatest methods for introducing excitement into the bedroom and beyond, freeing us from the ordinary and engaging our imaginations to good avail. In fact, without a healthy outlet for the expression of intrigue, this enticing, illicit passion play may harm us, just as it has harmed so many great—or despicable—characters of stage and screen.

DAILY HEALTHY SEX ACTS

- How has sexual, romantic or emotional intrigue touched you? Do you send out sexual vibes, hoping others will respond? Are your conversations with strangers sparked by the need for romantic validation? Have you ever grilled friends about an ex-lover to keep passion alive with *triangulation*—the indirect communication toward one person through engaging third parties?

- Do any of your acquaintances engage in intrigue? How does it feel to be left out while someone you care about creates intrigue with another? How do you respond? Sometimes the best first step is simply identifying what's happening. Does it make it any less personal to recognize their intriguing as a learned, perhaps even addictive, behavior?

> *"Love is hurt with jar and fret;*
> *Love is made a vague regret."*
> — Alfred Tennyson

11 NOVEMBER

REGRET

Healthy regret inspires us to change our behaviors and, sometimes, our environs. But the regret we just can't shake reveals larger unresolved issues. Ironically, that gnawing regret stems from *euphoric recall* of emotionally gratifying memories. Our nervous system finds arousal through shame as well as delight and, when triggered, we often self-soothe by recalling moments which aren't purely positive. In fact, such memories often possess a retraumatizing element. Thus unconquerable penitence is a by-product of trying to disengage from overwhelming current feelings through familiar fantasies. Recurring lapses into remorse signal that we're ignoring something painful.

Regrets usually center around key people in our lives, especially ex-lovers and family members. As we mull over conflicts with them, reactivity often engulfs our autonomy and integrity. We dismiss any personal shortcomings and construct elaborate defenses in mere seconds, blinding ourselves to our own culpable behavior. In 12-step programs, the amends process requires vigilant self-examination to find our part in every regrettable situation, and an appropriate revisiting through active imagining or direct interaction with the persons involved. This process of finally acknowledging our impact on another's reality additionally teaches us that, first, we don't have all the information and, second, much of reality is not of our making.

Reactive regret blocks the truth that we're exactly where we're supposed to be right now *and* that we can progress. We rail against ourselves for our imperfections, which only isolates us from others and the flow of life. But healthy regret brings the humility to recognize where we've erred and to admit powerlessness over our past mistakes. And with that humility comes the ability to let go of control, to make proper amends, and to move on to doing better.

DAILY HEALTHY SEX ACTS

- Do you regret anything in the past? Do you regret not making more of your present? Tap into the feeling of regret and where it lives in your body. Breathe into that space with the confidence that everything is working out exactly as it should.

- Do your mistakes teach you, or do they only punish you? List past misdeeds and whether they still gnaw at you. You deserve peace of mind. Write a brief letter of acknowledgment or apology, place it in a safe spot, and let it inspire you to greater action, such as confession, restitution, charity work, and self-help.

"But love is never retained by force, nor by complaining, nor by finding fault, nor by any other disagreeable activity. It is either held through the exercise of lovable qualities, or it is lost. Anxiety, and fear of the loss, but make the loss more certain. And in spite of all effort the loss may come."

— C. C. Zain

CONTROL

Whenever we hit on the great idea of influencing our partner's behavior or shaping how our relationship "should" go, we may want to pause and explore whether such thoughts are a sign of trouble. Trying to restrain another's actions and emotions is a recipe for disaster, born from a need to orchestrate outcomes that's itself born of insecurity. We've all heard and used the term "control freak" to describe persons obsessed with controlling themselves and others in order to command every situation. No one likes being around such a person, yet we demonstrate our own controlling traits when we react out of fear that we're not going to get what we want.

The opposite of control is surrender and sexual pleasure is, in large part, all about surrender. Women who can't orgasm and men who have performance problems are usually unable to give up control and to surrender. If at any time during the sexual act you're in your head agonizing about how your thighs look, your penis size, or whether you're "good enough," you're struggling with control issues. Dropping your internal story about not being good enough and instead surrendering to pleasure is the greatest gift you can give yourself and your partner. Get out of self-consciousness and open your heart. Then you can dispense with your ideas about the outcome of your sexual experience and yield to the undreamt-of possibilities of its happenings that are beyond your control. Stay open and give way to the chance that something amazing, healing, and beautiful can occur without your having to direct or control the result.

DAILY HEALTHY SEX ACTS

- Do you try to control the outcomes or circumstances in your relationships or professional life? If so, why?

- When was the last time you tried to control your partner? How did it go? Do you need to make amends?

- Next time you make love, try surrendering fully to the experience by silencing the negative voices in your head and focusing on the sensations in your body.

"Often affairs are like viruses, in that they are opportunistic and they feed on a part of oneself that is kept underground, unknown even to oneself."

— Tammy Nelson

13 NOVEMBER

INFIDELITY

We've almost all heard the insult "Infidel!" shouted on a 15th-century movie set as throngs gather to stone the guilty party. Historically, the word *infidel* has denoted a person not of one's own religion. In the true sense of the word, however, being an infidel signifies lacking faithfulness. While *infidelity* can still indicate disloyalty to a religion, today it usually means cheating while in a monogamous, committed relationship. Despite its being pervasive, most of us abhor falseness in marriage. We cling to the idea, "once married, always married," and see breaking our marriage vows as the ultimate betrayal.

Interestingly, however, only about 3 percent of mammal species are monogamous and form families as humans do. Perhaps that's because different species have more or fewer neurological receptors for attachment than do others; similar variance among human individuals may also explain why some of us appear less suited for monogamy than others. Other fuel for infidelity includes changing societal mores, our endlessly available choices, and expanding life spans which let a relationship last for much longer than may serve some of us.

In fact, human beings are designed to mate and stay attached for a relatively brief period of time—long enough to raise children in a stable environment. Some find the permanence of family life gratifying while others continue to feel wanderlust: Enter the proverbial mid-life crisis! But being unfaithful does not solve our woes, because the pain that invades the attachment system of the betrayed is oftentimes unforgivable. Rather than cheat, consider whether it's time to reinvigorate your relationship or to move on. While either of those propositions will hurt, nothing compares to the ache of infidelity.

DAILY HEALTHY SEX ACTS

- To whom have you been unfaithful? Do they know? What would it require to tell them—courage, strength? What benefit would honesty bring you or them?

- If you've been unfaithful in the past, what was the outcome?

- Are you still getting your needs met in your current relationship or are you comparing your partner to others? If you're in comparison mode, it's time to talk to your partner before you cheat.

> *"We cannot outperform our level of self-esteem. We cannot draw to ourselves more than we think we are worth."*
>
> — Iyanla Vanzant

Our culture is so oriented to transactions that even the idea of esteem—value beyond the material—sometimes seems to be a means to an end. As a result, our respectability may rest on whether or not we are viewed by others as "worth" something, as making it financially, as deserving of approval, as able to amass wealth or fame. This understanding of esteem is in keeping with the dominant paradigm of our capitalist society.

But genuine esteem is not a means to the end of social acceptance. It's a process in itself. Esteem is that little voice in our head that rates, values and judges everything we say, think, and do. It's our narrator and our witness. Because this voice is so private, it seems like it's just us, like it's on our side, like it's all ours. But our natural esteem can become overwhelmed by the power of external society—the voice not of our selves, but of social status and judgment. It can become a faulty filter that informs our reality and the actions we take. It's such an intrinsic filter, it appears to be reality itself—that's how powerful it is.

Endow yourself with healthy self-esteem. What is the feeling tone in your life that radiates in you and makes you shine, that makes you feel whole, that makes you feel your heart? That feeling tone, which we long to hear from others, is *the tone we want to practice with ourselves.* That's where we want to live with ourselves. It doesn't happen from the outside in. That's why it's called *self*-esteem.

DAILY HEALTHY SEX ACTS

- Write yourself a loving letter. Let yourself know all those traits you appreciate. Anything that hasn't been said about how great you are—let it be said now. Mail yourself the letter and imagine your surprise and joy reading it!

- Do a positive play-by-play of your successful actions today whenever you have the opportunity. Tell yourself, "You are a vision of health brushing your teeth!" "You brew tasty coffee, and I love the way you savor every drop." "You are a *dynamo!*"

"We don't love qualities, we love persons; sometimes by reason of their defects as well as of their qualities."

— Jacques Maritain

15 NOVEMBER

DEFECTS

We've got every character defect under the sun, just as we possess every positive trait as well. This rich variety of our qualities creates a stumbling block for many who so fear judgmental "type-casting" that they are loathe to admit key characteristics, whether negative or positive. However, whatever enters our field of awareness is part of us, though we often perceive our own reality only when projected onto others. Early psychological differentiation involves defining ourselves in comparison with others. How many messages about unacceptable behaviors do we inherit along this journey! The ego emerges from adolescence with a definite set of attributes with which we identify, but this list is deceptive. If we were to catalogue all human character defects, we would each be able to recall at least one time at which we exhibited each attribute. And often, we are attracted to individuals whose over-expression of defects that challenge us allows us to hide our own manifestation of the selfsame traits.

Recognizing the universality of every negative characteristic allows empathy and acceptance. The tricky part is to improve our character while accepting our faults. Denying imperfections to save face is counter-productive, for if we hide our real impulses to present an idealized version of ourselves, we're not presenting our real issues and we're avoiding emotional connection with others and our world. The reality of our inner thoughts and instincts can feel naked, shameful, raw, or unwieldy. But exposed to the light with trusted others, these forbidden impulses underneath our defects become transformed. Then we can become integrated into a psychological wholeness. That great work is possible—to contain and reconcile dissimilar extremes, orientations, and aspects without losing our essential, potential unity.

DAILY HEALTHY SEX ACTS

- Reckless. Insatiable. Deceptive. Clingy. Vain. Dismissive. Trivial. Violent. Tactless. Controlling. Impractical. Fearful. Think of one example in your past where you exhibited each of these traits. Whatever memory comes to your mind first will usually provide you with a clear illustration. Know that you have the capacity to exhibit all defects, some more easily than others.

- Share yourself with your partner, who is probably more aware of your defects than you can imagine. Invite your partner to support your mindfulness of how and when your defects manifest, and allow all information received to bring your most hidden defects to light. Step into the light.

> *"To judge you by your failures is to cast blame upon the seasons for their inconsistencies."*
>
> — Kahlil Gibran

FAILURE

When a relationship lasts, we hail it as a success, but if it ends we frame it as "failed." The same goes with failed business ventures, failed careers, failed aspirations. And after too many repeated misfortunes, or because of poor self-esteem, we don't just see what's failed, we think of *ourselves* as failures. Of course, this utterly demeans and denies the true nature of the entire experience, including accomplishments along the way and the constant forging of inner character.

We point this disparaging tendency outward, too. When people let us down, falling short of our expectations or moral standards, we can so easily see them as "complete and utter failures." Think of the lawbreakers who fill our jails or the lawmakers who abandon them there. When people do bad things, we confuse the wrong actions they committed with the persons they are. We mistake doing with being. We're usually more forgiving of our own mistakes as we can see the chain of circumstances leading up to them. But how sad that we ever see ourselves, or anyone, as "failures" simply for not reaching our potential.

It's said that sometimes when things are falling apart, they are actually falling into place. The traumas of our so-called failures allow greater emotional connection by knocking down the false crown of ego and teaching us empathy for others who miss their marks. Often we don't even realize how disconnected we are from other people's pain until we feel some of it ourselves. The truth is that, without connection and empathy, success is hollow and lonely. To attempt any goal, to dare to fail, to grieve the loss of our erroneous self-image, and to understand every other person who's done the same can only be seen as a success in the fail-proof development of our soul.

DAILY HEALTHY SEX ACTS

- Reflect on your failures—relationships, career choices, social events, or fashion faux pas. Then, focus on your proven ability to step out of your comfort zone and take risks. Today, share with someone part of your shameful past from a place of loving self-recognition and appreciation.

- We've all experienced rude awakenings. Do you empathize with others when they're down, or does the smell of shame compel you to join the attack?

- Starting today, stand up for the underdog, the "loser." Sometimes having the strength to show loving support for unacknowledged others turns the tides of our own lives.

"This is what rituals are for. We do spiritual ceremonies as human beings in order to create a safe resting place for our most complicated feelings of joy or trauma, so that we don't have to haul those feelings around with us forever, weighing us down. We all need such places of ritual safekeeping."

— Elizabeth Gilbert

17 NOVEMBER

RITUAL

Rituals contain our deepest feelings and thoughts in the most literal sense. A good ritual is like the bag of endless treasure—it holds all your psychic burdens and provides all your spiritual sustenance. But when a ritual becomes emptied of feeling, either you are no longer paying attention to it or the ritual no longer serves its function for you. Platonic and romantic relationships are often littered with ineffective rituals, as people try to dump daily or lifelong stress into, or draw meaningful support from, relationships which simply cannot contain such intensity.

Modern life brings greater stimulation than ever and so demands greater ritual than ever. We might not be cognizant of this constant inundation but at a cellular level, we are shaken. We already use little habitual rituals we barely notice to help us feel safe: meals, exercise, grooming, or social media. These may contain ambient anxiety for a while—as much as treading water may delay drowning in the ocean.

We might find healthier daily rituals than, say, walking to the corner store for a donut or watching soothing blabber on the Internet. Our rituals might be conscious, purposeful, and bigger than us, such as spiritual or philanthropic practices or 12-step recovery. We might also create a unique life ritual that reflects our dearest search for meaning, and follow it rather than all the daily distractions that rob our focus without replenishing our spirits.

DAILY HEALTHY SEX ACTS

- Like two martial artists bowing to each other in greeting, you and your lover can enhance your sex life with rituals. Do you invite your partner to sexual contact with candles and sensual clothing? Next time you make love, try taking a moment to share from the heart your intentions for the sexual experience and ask your partner to do the same. Let love become a ritual.

- Create little rituals throughout your day. Would this mean eating lunch in a park, closing your eyes and breathing for a mini-meditation, or stopping to smell the roses? Invite the value of sensual experience to change routine into ritual.

"Oh the comfort, the inexpressible comfort of feeling safe with a person, having neither to weigh thoughts nor measure words, but pouring them all right out, just as they are."

— Dinah Maria Mulock

COMFORT

Physical comfort is a state of ease and freedom from pain that registers in the body as relaxation and safety. All infants and children require and deserve comfort in order to develop properly. Soft cooing voices, gentle touch, smiles, cleanliness, and wholesome food all contribute to the growing body/mind. And when these basic conditions are absent in childhood, our need for comfort in adulthood can be so profound that it becomes pathological, driving us to seek mothering from anyone who will have us, to use others to fill our emptiness with sex or love, and to risk becoming addicted to a perceived source of comfort.

Most of us create relationships that provide comfort. A healthy relationship should soothe and reassure in times of struggle. But if we came from difficult families, we find that setting up a supportive relationship is easier than maintaining one, since nurturing it requires diligence and the capacity—which we never learned—to reciprocate comfort. Over time, though, we can build connections to our self and others, and enhance our ability to console ourselves and our partner, or friends and family members, without expecting them to fix us. If we can come to know the people closest to us, we learn exactly what they need in times of distress: a simple smile, a listening ear, an invitation to go for a walk.

Our surroundings reflect our power to self-comfort, our sense of healthy entitlement, and our capacity to comfort others. The smallest effort we put toward making a clean, restful space rewards us richly with physical comfort and peace of mind. Simple favorite possessions breathe life into a home while healthful foods nourish and replenish the body/mind of everyone living there. When we are comforted and give comfort, we create a foundation of strength for living.

DAILY HEALTHY SEX ACTS

- Are you capable of self-comforting in healthy ways? If so, list the ways you comfort yourself.

- How readily available are you to comfort your lover, child, friend, or family member? What do you do that's particularly calming to each one of them?

- How comfortable is the environment you live and work in? What do you need to do to make it more so?

"The greatest pleasure isn't sex, but the passion with which it is practiced. When the passion is intense, then sex joins in to complete the dance, but it is never the principal aim."

— Paulo Coelho

19 NOVEMBER

PASSION

Passion provokes our physiology: Our hearts feel like opening and inner and outer realities converge and align. Passion invokes that state of grace where everyone smiles at us and we tap into a celestial audience. Our true purpose—to fulfill our potential—is evidenced by our passion. How we measure difficulties reveals our passion as well; when a project seems beset by insurmountable obstacles, it's probably not our passion, but hurdles met in accomplishing what we love seem to melt away as we progress. Guided by visions of a greater good, passion energizes us beyond expected limitations.

So it's important that passion be grounded in reality, since many passionate causes are also irrational and misguided, especially in romantic pursuit. Sex is the playground of passion. To transcend personal boundaries and unite in shared ardor is one of the greatest experiences and symbols of living. However, sex is too often a solitary fervor of parties overcome by private sensations who happen to rub up against the other. We hear of lovers who can no longer receive excitement without counterfeiting it through drama, such as make-up sex or the myriad unconscious tricks people use to get high off their own brain chemicals. But intoxication isn't passion.

In fact, even in the most everyday moment we can cultivate and unleash our true passion to create intimacy with our partner. Since we all have embraced at least one passion inspired by another enthusiast, we know the vital importance of personal connection in sparking such fire. To stir another—especially during sex—can be a mindfulness practice. Through it, we affirm such faith in our passion that, even when it seems to be waning, we know it's still there, like the new moon in the night sky.

DAILY HEALTHY SEX ACTS

- Recall those who have inspired each passion of yours, imparting their own exhilaration through sharing. What passions can you share with the world? Today, share the foremost passion of your life with another.

- Imagine what it would be like to have been born and raised as your beloved. How might you feel his or her passions and interests? Anytime you feel apathy for others' interests, trace their experience to embrace their passion.

- Let passion awaken in your heart; allow it to build in your body. Make this a mindful practice, and affirm the spark of love wherever you are.

"Gratitude unlocks the fullness of life. It turns what we have into enough, and more. It turns denial into acceptance, chaos to order, confusion to clarity. It can turn a meal into a feast, a house into a home, a stranger into a friend."

— Melody Beattie

Real gratitude is marked by more than a thank-you card or birthday gift. We're almost all instructed as toddlers to parrot the words "thank you" in response to a gift or favor, no matter how we really feel. But superficial social niceties are far different from the deep emotion of thanksgiving. Only by honestly affirming the light can we act like the light and shine. We feel blessed for our lives and, in that moment, we bless our lives. Truly grateful feelings surge from our core whenever we fulfill our potential in small ways or in grand. To be away from gratitude is to be out of touch with our true purpose. Gratitude is an essential indication that our current actions reflect our real values.

Gratitude is a sign *and* a remedy. In the worst of times, during a material, relational, emotional or spiritual depression, summoning gratitude is a sure way to get our life back on track. Opening our eyes to affirm gratitude grows the garden of our inner abundance, just as standing close to a fire eventually warms our heart. When life demands more and still more of us, gratitude lets us know that we have, and are, enough. The physiology of gratitude induces a regulated state similar to meditation or prayer: slow and steady breathing, blood flowing to the brain, neural pathways rewired. Gratitude as a physical act actually builds a healthier brain.

DAILY HEALTHY SEX ACTS

- Each morning and night for the next two weeks, quickly jot down five things that come to mind for which you're grateful.

- Sit face-to-face with your loved one and share these simple gratitude lists, and ask that person to reciprocate if possible.

- Today, practice an *attitude of gratitude* as you move through the world. Mentally note what you love about each moment. How long can you stay in gratitude before your mind wanders? The second you become distracted, try to notice the situation that broke your focus. Were you in fantasy or anxiety? Try to get back into life, and move toward life with gratitude.

"It is not sex that gives the pleasure, but the lover."

— Marge Piercy

21 NOVEMBER

SEXUAL
TECHNIQUE

What's technique but the ability and desire to refine one's skills? Or, as we say, it takes practice, practice, practice. We think nothing of musicians, chefs, surgeons, and dancers devoting time and study to perfect their craft. Why should it be any different when it comes to sexual experience? All too often, lovers find what they like and repeat. Further exploration can be embarrassing. It might give the wrong idea that we are dissatisfied rather than curious or ambitious. Open and honest sexual discussion might open us to critique and feelings of inadequacy.

Yet we are each responsible for our individual well-being, comfort, and boundaries. Self-care is a prerequisite to any sexual technique, because being paralyzed by insecurity inhibits the maturation of eroticism. With a little consideration and basic research, we all may develop sufficient sexual expertise to give and receive pleasure reliably when with our chosen partner.

Technique is never about what happens, technique is about how it happens. For starters, you might focus on time: What is it like to move fast or slow? Then, consider force: strong or soft? Also, what about attention: focused or diffused? What other key elements of technique in any field might apply to sex? This is one unchartered realm where it's still possible to discover your own expertise of expression.

DAILY HEALTHY SEX ACTS

- Notice the techniques you've developed to feed yourself, bathe yourself, and function throughout your day. Where do you find pleasure and mastery in your routines? Is it the patient way you prepare food, or the smooth manner you turn the wheel of your car? Do you bring these moves to the bedroom?

- How does your body move? Feel the touch of your own fingers, the feel of your tongue against your lips. Move beyond your favorite sensory feelings—even Picasso experimented with different materials and styles. Expand your tolerance for qualitative differences such as pressure, texture, and vibration.

- Now, notice how your lover's body moves.

"Perhaps the great renewal of the world will consist of this, that man and woman, freed of all confused feelings and desires, shall no longer seek each other as opposites, but simply as members of a family and neighbors, and will unite as human beings, in order to simply, earnestly, patiently, and jointly bear the heavy responsibility of sexuality that has been entrusted to them."

— Rainer Maria Rilke

COUPLESHIP

The state of being romantically and sexually connected to another is a sacred calling and one that should not be taken lightly. To love another is a great responsibility, and one that we can easily forget when the thrill of new love has morphed into quieter comfort and connection. All too often, we take our mates for granted and even begin to resent them. By doing so we trample on their hearts in self-serving ways. We may become habituated to bickering and arguing, projecting our hurts onto the person in front of us who has entrusted her or his most tender, vulnerable self to our care.

A key charge when in coupleship is the commitment to understand the depths of who the other was, is, and is becoming, and to tend to him or her accordingly. At the same time, we must commit to delve more deeply into our own dynamic issues, and aim to be transparent about our own evolution. All mammals need initial relationship to survive; human beings need relationship throughout life in order to grow, develop, and flourish.

But romantic passion recedes over time, so creativity becomes another crucial obligation. Conjuring novel experiences to share, keeping our self interesting through unique pursuits, and giving each other enough space to explore the world independently keep coupleships vital. Both planned date nights and spontaneous activities can bring shared laughter and happiness—a sure way to release dopamine in the brain. Sexual novelty will spice things up, further raising dopamine levels and enjoyment of our time together. At our core, we are all tender, feeling beings who need one another to support our emotional, sexual and physical thriving over a lifetime. Tread lightly on your partner's heart. It was given to you for safekeeping.

DAILY HEALTHY SEX ACTS

- When the going gets rough in your relationship, what do you do? Do you examine your own issues, attempt to understand your partner more deeply, or start packing?

- Write your definition of what it means to be in coupleship and ask your partner to do the same. Share your musings with each other.

> *"Too often we underestimate the power of a touch, a smile, a kind word, a listening ear, an honest compliment, or the smallest act of caring, all of which have the potential to turn a life around."*
>
> — Leo F. Buscaglia

23 NOVEMBER

CARING

Caring can feel joyous, a form of poetry in action as we surrender to the purest giving and the delightful receiving that naturally ensues. This poetic action is evident in a mother's eyes as she cares for her child. In that moment, we see a myriad of processes taking place within the dyad which we attribute to caring. Out of that caring emerges love, joy, and fulfillment for both parties. When we are actively working to tend to another with kindness and concern, our labor can melt into divine service, especially when we adopt an attitude of gratitude for being able-bodied enough to help.

Caring comes in the simplest of gestures, like a knowing smile or a brief acknowledgment. Caring is open-hearted, keeping us available to transmit love to a stranger through simple eye contact and without condition. This is not the opportunistic sizing-up of sexual cruising; instead, it's the felt recognition of the divinity and humanity in another individual. This type of connection is greater than the personal; it's a moment of consciousness meeting consciousness.

Caring for a loved one may actually be harder than helping a stranger because it requires a deeper level of mindfulness. When our loved ones cannot look after themselves, their vulnerability can activate difficult, even aggravating dynamics between them and us. But challenging ourselves to be mindful of those triggers while undertaking acts of kindness calls forth the part of us that longs to be needed. Rather than resenting the demands of a sick partner or elderly family member, we can see their distress as a chance to put our capacities for loving and for supporting to good use through our caring service.

DAILY HEALTHY SEX ACTS

- Consider the vulnerable in your life. Who or what could use your caring—a neighbor in need of a meal? A family member shut inside? A yard that's gone to seed? Let their distress bring forward the best in you.

- Who cares for you? Do you ask for help when you need it or do you force yourself to do everything on your own?

- Today, make eye contact with everyone you see and think to yourself, "I love who you are." Notice how this caring thought makes you feel by nightfall.

"Fashion is as profound and critical a part of the social life of man as sex, and is made up of the same ambivalent mixture of irresistible urges and inevitable taboos."

— Rene Konig

CLOTHING

People have been adorning themselves with clothing from the beginning of time, and time and fashion have changed the purpose of clothing. Do you think about your choice of clothing? Do you dress for yourself or for others? If you dress for yourself, take time to look at the choices you're making today. Dressing in the same way you did ten years ago may no longer capture who you are today. Dressing simply to attract someone sexually may be a way that you objectify yourself. Dressing because you love the feeling of the fabric, styles, or colors you choose can be a healthy, creative expression of who you are.

Like colors in the rainbow, there are many reasons why people choose what to wear and when to wear it. What you wear conveys directly how you feel about yourself. Are you tidy, neat and clean in your appearance, or does your worn-out garb suggest some problems with deprivation? Do you rely on the latest fashions excessively, dressing to impress while living beyond your means? Do you wear clothes that are too tight, too youthful, or inappropriate? Do you disown your masculinity or femininity by your choice of clothing? Clothing is tied to sexuality and to money as well as to the acceptance, and celebration, of who you are.

DAILY HEALTHY SEX ACTS

- Take some time going through your wardrobe today. Throw away tattered clothes and donate ill-fitting or inappropriate garments to your favorite charity. If you over-shop, take the clothes you don't wear or those with tags still on them to a resale shop.

- If you haven't bought new clothes in a long time, take this opportunity to look at any deprivation issues you may have about your appearance and body.

- If necessary, ask a friend to help you clean out your closet or visit a department store that offers a complimentary personal shopper.

"In dwelling, live close to the ground. In thinking, keep to the simple. In conflict, be fair and generous. In governing, don't try to control. In work, do what you enjoy. In family life, be completely present."

— Lao-Tzu

25 NOVEMBER

FAMILY

Our ideas of family vary depending on our personal history, and evolve throughout our life. Some of us are born into a family while others are adopted or fostered. But either way, without proper attunement, consistency, and love, children feel empty and scared, wondering if they're wanted. In the best of circumstances, family provides children security, warmth, and a place to flourish with attentive elders who steward them into adulthood. In less favorable circumstances, family can be a place of uncertainty and even danger.

Your family forged you into the person you are today. Patterns of feeling, thought and behavior were set and activated based on a multitude of factors: the region of the country you lived in, the culture or religion you grew up with, the intergenerational abuse you may have suffered. The complexities of who you've become are a tapestry of people, places and events, all of which form a "self." Even the best-meaning parents can create insecure children by simply being insensitive. The process of growing into adulthood requires that we examine these early, set patterns that still hamstring us and keep us acting out immaturely. One of the quickest routes to self-knowledge and, thereby, eventual self-liberation is to get into a committed relationship. In relationship, all of our family-of-origin issues emerge, play out, and can then be healed.

In adulthood we often create our own families by having or adopting children. However, family can also be a group of people you gather together over time, who know and love you, who support you in your endeavors, sexual orientation, spiritual exploration, and other personal choices without judgment. By healing your shame and other problematic patterns from childhood, you will attract like-minded people who will comprise your "family of choice."

DAILY HEALTHY SEX ACTS

- Give thanks for the family you were born into or the family you were raised in whether it was good, bad or otherwise. Recognize that this family is, in part, responsible for your strengths and gifts, not just your shortcomings.

- Take time to be in gratitude for the family of choice you've created and let those people know what they mean to you.

- Tell your partner how grateful you are to have him or her in your life.

"We can only be who we are, and at some point that has to be good enough."

— Panache Desai

ADEQUACY

We exalt the exemplary, but the rare thrill of perfection pales next to the dependable pleasure of adequacy. To feel loved and accepted for ourselves, regardless of what we achieve, creates a sense of warmth and safety that no honor or title can bestow. In youth and beyond, we sometimes despair of anyone's ever staying with us, given all our faults. Yet we stay with ourselves and face our flaws day and night, and most of the time we reconcile ourselves to our shortcomings. We're all adequate for this world, or we wouldn't have existed. Even if we permit certain thoughts of inadequacy to define us, they're just thoughts, a tiny percentage of our reality.

But the loop of psychological inflation and deflation can seduce us into the superlative world of compare-and-despair where, as it's said, we're each the worst piece of shit that the world revolves around. Of all the infinite words and ideas to which we've been exposed, why do we cling to the ones that tell us we're not good enough? For, make no mistake, no one has the power or vantage point to define us by our true worth, not even ourselves—and we're the witnesses of our whole lives.

Adequacy derives from the Latin *adaequatus*—to *make equal*. Adequacy balances the polar extremes of grandeur and depravity, and lives in the interstice of reality and fantasy. We need our heroes and superstars to inspire us to exceed what's accepted as possible. But this ambition makes a poor base for our central identity. Any attempt to express the *best* emotions or the *most* successful thoughts is as quixotic as trying to locate the strongest wave in the ocean. Go with your natural flow as a human in the act of being, by honoring your sacred adequacy.

DAILY HEALTHY SEX ACTS

- Notice today the language of superlatives around you, constantly rating objects and events as *best* or *worst*, and any feelings that accompany such judgments.

- Affirm the adequacy of each moment in your life. Your experience may have been less than ideal, but something carried you to this moment— whether good-enough caregivers, passable life instruction, or sufficient opportunity.

- In your heart, extend the appreciation of personal adequacy beyond your own experience to hold everyone you know. Leave off value judgments that isolate you from loving others and bask in the beauty of shared humility, of shared humanity.

"Whate'er of us lives in the hearts of others is our truest and profoundest self."

— Johann Gottfried Herder

27 NOVEMBER

SUPPORT

Raising children on a strong foundation of ethics is one of the greatest gifts adults can give their offspring. Preparing children for a life of ups and downs gives them a sense of security even in a world of uncertainty. To feel thus supported means children have an internalized trusted adult figure residing in their hearts and souls. Whether a parent, grandparent, or teacher, one such person makes all the difference in a child's life. For without an effective scaffolding to make it from one phase of childhood to another, human beings wobble and hobble along, unsure of who they are and where they should be going. Thus support is a basic human need, one the organism requires in order to mature properly.

Moving from adolescence to young adulthood, we may pick supportive or problematic people, depending on what was modeled to us as youngsters. If we had strong adults to rely on, we learned to stand on our own two feet by heeding our feelings, needs, wants. This facility let us choose a mate wisely and communicate appropriately with our relational partner. But without support from others we don't flourish in relationships; in fact, many support-deprived people tend towards isolation, one of the cornerstones of addiction. If children learn that the adults around them are unreliable, they quickly look elsewhere for help, often choosing peers who, like them, use forms of self-soothing such as drugs, food, alcohol or sex. Isolation and addiction are dead-end streets that leave the wanderer longing for connection and love. The way out of addiction is inevitably through the support of a community of concern which models and teaches—finally—how to trust others. We can never escape our fundamental need for support. This need connects humanity, the truss of recovery, and the road that leads to intimacy.

DAILY HEALTHY SEX ACTS

- Do you have a support system of reliable others or are you isolated? Make a list of those you believe are available to support you.

- Did you choose your mate from a place of strength or weakness? Do you feel supported by that person? Talk to your partner about what you need in order to feel supported.

- What kind of support is lacking in your life—emotional, physical, financial? Whom can you ask to support you today?

> *"When another person makes you suffer, it is because he suffers deeply within himself and that suffering is spilling over. He does not need punishment; he needs help."*
>
> — Thích Nhất Hạnh

People can suffer physically from aches and pains, emotionally from hurt feelings, and mentally from toxic thoughts that distort their self-concept and experience of the world. People even suffer spiritually, regardless of their beliefs: Censored questions and abuses in the name of so-called spiritual principles harm believers and nonbelievers alike, all over the world. So we know there's universal suffering, and we also know that only individuals who acknowledge their own and others' common pain can lessen it. For there's no greater suffering than the unaided, lonely suffering that comes when we deny our connection to others.

NOVEMBER 28

SUFFERING

Yet, while suffering forms part of the human condition, self-induced suffering does no one any good. The "long-suffering" spouse who codependently bears the burden of an imbalanced relationship, or the tortured soul who declares, "I can handle it myself," exemplify self-abandonment. One way to end such pointless suffering is to reconsider our much-vaunted "strength." Maybe we're not meant to *handle* suffering on our own. Perhaps the gift of suffering is to break down the walls that isolate us from one another, so that our own healing through others can guide us to help others in turn. Thus the *wounded healer* passes through a trial of suffering and, with the resulting understanding, learns to lead people from their pain.

And suffering can teach us to heal ourselves. For example, many persons in a therapeutic recovery process have been dealt hard blows in life, but suddenly find immense personal relief when they recognize they now respond differently to adversity. They've substituted new patterns of behavior for their previous, painfully destructive reactivity. Thus, even in the midst of difficulty they feel deeply joyous since they see that, through dedicated self-improvement, they've at last learned how to respond to suffering in a good way both for themselves and others.

DAILY HEALTHY SEX ACTS

- People often ask: If there's a God, how can He allow so much suffering in the world? Realize all world suffering you perceive is a mirror to your own psychological self-abuse, gender imbalance, prejudice, poverty, and hunger. *You couldn't even perceive each suffering aspect of external reality if it didn't already exist within you.* Touch and transmute your psychological suffering, and perceive the world in kind.

- Today, share your secret suffering with others—in writing, art or speech—as a courageous attempt toward healing our collective pain.

"Ideals are like stars; you will not succeed in touching them with your hands. But like the seafaring man on the desert of waters, you choose them as your guides, and following them you will reach your destiny."

— Carl Schurz

29 NOVEMBER

IDEALS

Nature encourages us to find an appropriate mate, but our culture goads us to seek the "ideal" one. So we prowl for an archetypal male or female and swoon over each new possibility during the dating process. In this seemingly endless search to find "the one" we sometimes get caught up in the maze of our imagination, fantasizing about what we deem perfect—or have been taught to deem perfect—and ignoring the person in front of us who may, in fact, be "perfect" for us. For while ideals should guide our aspirations, we shouldn't let them trick us into thinking that we'll meet a truly flawless being who will never disappoint us.

In fact, fixating on what we think we want or need can become the easy way out of staying in reality. Clinging to impossible standards can seem to justify the desire to flee from the present moment, from the "now" that is here, by romanticizing another time, place, or person. This exercise in futility serves only to create suffering because there's no avoiding the reality of what *is*. Don't use your ideals as a way to hide from life, for there is no escape other than to dive into what's in front of you. Ideals can act as guiding principles and have us shooting for our personal best, or they can be clinged to out of fear or grandiose expectations of what we think we should have. Set your sights on the stars, but then "let go and let God" and wait for the simple perfection of the moment.

Treasuring an ideal while simultaneously staying open to all other possibilities creates a space for you to arrive at your unique destiny, whether in seeking a lover, a new job, or a vacation spot.

DAILY HEALTHY SEX ACTS

- Have your ideals kept you sitting on the sidelines of your life, or have they helped you get what you want?

- Do you confuse idealism with grandiosity, feeling like you "deserve" something "better" than what you have? How do you distinguish between being in gratitude for what you have versus settling for that which is less than ideal for you?

- Take a leap and hold a vision for what you ideally would like to have in your life, then surrender your ideas to a Higher Power and see what you receive.

> *"We need to allow ourselves the freedom to figure out what we internally want from sex instead of mimicking whatever popular culture holds up to us as sexy. That would be sexual liberation."*
>
> — Ariel Levy

SEXUAL LIBERATION

There have been many sexual revolutions in history, but the phrase *sexual liberation* conjures images of the 1960s and 1970s. Then, young men and women rebelled against the conformism and repression of the 1950s, casting off its narrow morals and openly experimenting with non-monogamy, group sex, bisexuality, and the "free love" that made traditionalists so nervous. Through their collective, public commitment to smashing the shackles of inhibition, these erotic reformists paved the way for today's greater tolerance, acceptance and freedom of nonconforming sexualities.

That sexual liberation movement centered on human rights that were being crushed by the social-political system. But over time, corporate powers seized the notion of free love and found a way to use it against us. Our culture became saturated with sexual objectification and exploitation, leaving us more confused and lonelier than ever. We could now have as much sex as we wanted, whenever we wanted, but that didn't solve our deeper internal struggles. Worse, such supposed openness didn't protect many of us from sexual trauma experienced at home, in the military, in school, in church, or at work.

True sexual liberation, then, must include the healing work we do to recover an authentic, holistic sexual expression that is not dictated by external powers. Sexual liberation must now come to signify an inner peace that lets us make conscious sexual choices without shame, guilt or fear. After all, we can have orgies until the end of time, but underlying negative emotions we may carry about our sexuality can only be cured through careful examination of our wounds, both personal and cultural. Completing a sexual inventory and sharing it with a trusted individual can remove decades of sexual baggage in mere hours, leaving us free to enjoy a "lightness of being" we never believed was possible.

DAILY HEALTHY SEX ACTS

- Do you consider yourself sexually liberated? Why or why not?

- Consider *from what* you want to be liberated. People often seek sexual liberation to compensate for the trauma of repression or abuse, but no amount of liberation can *heal* trauma. The only thing any of us can do to heal past sexual trauma... is to heal the trauma.

- Today, take one healthy step toward liberating yourself unto your true sexual ideals.

"Like water which can clearly mirror the sky and the trees only so long as its surface is undisturbed, the mind can only reflect the true image of the Self when it is tranquil and wholly relaxed."

— Indra Devi

December

> *"The moment one gives close attention to anything, even a blade of grass, it becomes a mysterious, awesome, indescribably magnificent world in itself."*
>
> — Henry Miller

1 DECEMBER

ATTENTION

It's a commonplace saying that "the eyes are the windows to the soul." It turns out that the eyes are also the windows to our nervous system. The center of the nervous system, the brain, loves novelty, so it's no surprise that when we make close eye contact with a lover, we "see" them as if we're seeing them for the first time. Equally interesting, twelve inches is the optimum attachment distance between a mother and the infant she's cradling. Their eye contact at this precise distance creates a novel experience in the brain, stimulating all manners of function and structure through their shared gaze. It is thought that mothers "fall in love" with their babies and, like lovers, the mother and infant dyad basks in the glory of their felt love for one another, cooing, smiling, and touching. So both the attachment and sexual pathways are the same in the brain, but nature saves the activation of the sexual pathway for the adolescent period.

If you recall your first love, you probably gazed into each other's eyes as you giggled and swooned. Adult relationships require that you risk moving *emotionally*—not just visually—closer in order to create the novelty the brain needs for sexual stimulation. Your close attention on your partner's eyes is a way to re-stimulate mutual attraction. Your challenge is to be willing to "see" him or her, and be "seen" by him or her, in new and different ways.

DAILY HEALTHY SEX ACTS

- In a comfortable setting, like on your bed or sofa, sit face-to-face with your partner so that you have approximately twelve inches between you. Begin by softly gazing into one another's eyes. Notice your attention. Do you drift away? Is it easy or difficult to hold the gaze? Does it come and go? What do you "see" when you're looking?

- Spend some time talking to each other after you've done this exercise.

"The reality is that most of us communicate the same way that we grew up. That communication style becomes our normal way of dealing with issues, our blueprint for communication. It's what we know and pass on to our own children. We either become our childhood or we make a conscious choice to change it."

— Kristen Crockett

DECEMBER 2

CHILDHOOD

An infant is the living manifestation of all things good and perfectly imperfect! When adults see their own beauty and virtues in these soft, curious, and loving creatures, they become filled with joy interacting with them. This mirroring is important because childhood bonds with primary caregivers form early attachment patterns which last into adulthood and shape all our relationships. Therapy and recovery work almost always explore significant or traumatic experiences from that stage, so rich with growth, and examine early conditioning to see if its messages still serve us.

One of the most important aspects of childhood development is the emergence of sexuality. How were the topics of love and sex addressed in your household? Some families are emotionally absent on the subject, with parents who tried to shut out sexuality; other families are enmeshed, with parents who let sexual issues all hang out. These early messages—verbal and nonverbal—affect a child's sexuality at a cellular level. They are the fertile soil from which sexual identity will emerge, whether through imitation, avoidance or defiance.

We all know from our own lives that the actions, emotions, and conversations of adults greatly impact children. Since it takes a village to raise a child, how can we now develop healthy sexuality to set a positive example for the children in our lives? While there is no one definition of appropriate behavior and speech, and we may know better than to repeat our own childhood experiences, resources abound to help us identify healthy messages about sex based on what works best for the psychology of the child in his or her community. We may fine-tune our behaviors through reaching out to caregivers we admire. By consciously practicing our truest principles, we'll develop healthier ways to relate to children responsibly and, with time, to heal our own inner child.

DAILY HEALTHY SEX ACTS

- If you have or were to have children, what message would they receive from your sexual and romantic lifestyle? Are you embodying values you'd want to pass on to the next generation?

- What patterns are you replaying from your childhood? Do they serve you? If not, what will it take to break the cycle?

- Today, let your presence be a healthy model for others. Enjoy the connection this brings with everyone, especially all caregivers and children—who deserve our best selves.

"Love grants in a moment what toil can hardly achieve in an age."

— Johann Wolfgang von Goethe

3 DECEMBER

ABUNDANCE

Measuring abundance only by acquisitions in the world outside our hearts is a tempting trap. But if you cultivate an attitude of inner abundance, it invites opportunities, connection, and sizzling sex. When we feel starved for affection, the slightest gesture from another seems to endow us with fortunate (but fleeting) wealth. Ironically, when we're too well satiated, the human need for validation escalates so that we fail even to remember our past abundance. Both types of deprivation thinking tell us we're not good enough, everything's terrible, and every other pessimistic, victimized message. These deficiency distortions make it seem that other people have all the good sex, the perfect lovers, the better lives. Feeling deprived deprives us of perspective.

Life is truly abundant. The task of loving intimacy requires that we learn to open up honestly about our inner lives and bring content to the surface, so that by clearing away the debris from the windshield we can see clearly. Then we're no longer stuck in our heads but become present for reality. And our very presence is the secret to abundance. That you can even show up and experience this moment indicates your abundance. To accept and honor the abundance of the life-giving property of your own personal reality—which includes even your present problems—is to stretch your mind and thus get room for growth. For your mind is where the real stretching takes place. So many people think about stretching sexually: stretching the technique, the positions, the emotional connection, even the actual body parts. But the real stretch is to nurture an enduring realization of your abundance. What you have to offer the world is enough. Your sexual potential and expression on this day is exactly what it needs to be. Your innermost true nature abounds with love and life.

DAILY HEALTHY SEX ACTS

- Learning to transmute what displeases you into the gold of pleasure is necessary for abundance. Look at your surroundings now. What do you love? What beauty do you see? When you can love and see beauty wherever you are, you connect to abundance, which attracts abundance.

- Acts of loving and being loved—the warm embrace of a lover, friend, parent, or pet—enriches us. Let love show you your abundance. Summon your most secure feelings of past lovingness, and share that emotion with all you encounter today through open smiles, accessible eyes, and abundantly loving vibes.

> *"What is home? My favorite definition is 'a safe place,' a place where one is free from attack, a place where one experiences secure relationships and affirmation. It's a place where people share and understand each other. Its relationships are nurturing. The people in it do not need to be perfect; instead, they need to be honest, loving, supportive, recognizing a common humanity that makes all of us vulnerable."*
>
> — Gladys Hunt

VULNERABILITY

It's only recently that *vulnerability* has come to signify a positive attribute in intimate relationships. The word stems from *vulnus*, Latin for wound, and meant to be open to attack or damage. Most superheroes and gods are invulnerable—that's what makes them superheroes and gods. But each of them has a secret weakness, or there would be no stories. Achilles' mother dipped him in the river of invulnerability as a baby—his entire body but the heel where she held him—thus his one susceptibility gave death a portal. And most of us have many more vulnerabilities than Achilles.

So the fact that a term denoting the weakest link has come to be associated with emotional intimacy is a sign of advancing civilization. There's little need for the physical self-reliance of our pioneer ancestors; the world's threats have become so subtle and pervasive that most historical defense strategies are futile in modern times. As a result, we find that only through identifying, accepting, and processing our fragility with trusted others can we transform weakness into strength.

To embrace vulnerability implies trust. We bravely trust those around us not to hurt us; we must trust loved ones with our well-being, our emotional states, in some cases with our lives. To be hurt by friends and family can be painful, but to be wounded where we make love can leave us withdrawing forever because we're at our most vulnerable when we're both physically and emotionally naked. So in a way, anyone who has sex is vulnerable. Honoring this fact can create a sacred space that further engenders connection, identification, and caring.

DAILY HEALTHY SEX ACTS

- When have you been wounded in sex or love? For every painful memory, recall a moment where you safely received and shared openly with a lover. Affirm the values of safety and trust in your intimate relationships. *Trust those who are trustworthy.*

- Are you vulnerable to flattery, seduction, or back-rubs? List your weak spots—your Achilles' heel— and share with a trusted other. Ask him or her to reciprocate. Be vulnerable enough to express vulnerabilities.

- Think of the most vulnerable people in your life and the larger world. Today, bear witness to their vulnerability. Acknowledge each demonstration of the human condition, lending your empathic awareness to strengthen all.

> *"A holy person is someone who is whole; who has, as it were, reconciled his opposites."*
>
> — Alan Watts

5 DECEMBER

HOLINESS

Holiness is usually thought of as worship in service of the gods. To be holy is to be devout or to hold that which is divine in reverence, in a way that's pure and meaningful to the devotee. It's been said that the surrendering mind creates divinity and that anything you surrender to becomes a god or a place of holiness. How many times have you seen someone surrender to the beauty of nature, paying homage to a sunset or standing in awe before the ocean? If you mocked that person thinking s/he were personifying nature in a way that was silly or weird, you may want to consider whether that person's connection to something seen as holy made you feel uncomfortable.

The Old English word *halig* dates back to the 11th century and is derived from *hal*, meaning whole. Thus, holiness can be thought of as a form of perfection. When you choose to see all of life as perfect, whole and complete, suffering ends. Nature's way—understood holistically—is the way of perfection, comprehending even destruction within it. While in the dark storm of devastation and pain, it's almost impossible even to imagine "perfection," or even that anything good will ever shine again. The ability to reconcile those opposites gives you the power of simultaneously holding the polarities of good and bad, right and wrong, and of acknowledging that one cannot exist without the other. When duality ceases, all is well. Self-centeredness drops away and then you, too, are part of the divine matrix and therefore, holy. Moreover, when you surrender to your lover, s/he becomes a holy place for the divine to twinkle. In the heat of passion, look into your lover's eyes and in them, see your lover's holiness, and the reflection of your own.

DAILY HEALTHY SEX ACTS

- The next time you plan to have sex, create a sacred space together with your partner. Pick and choose the mood, lighting, colors, and scents you want to incorporate into your experience.

- Agree to call forth the divine by surrendering to the god and goddess within each other: "I surrender to the god in you;" "I surrender to the goddess in you."

- Be open and willing to experience a mystical third that emerges as a result of your union. Surrender to your partner—let yourself be surprised.

"We don't see things as they are. We see things as we are."

— Anaïs Nin

DISCERNMENT

To distinguish subtleties is to perceive nuance and detail. Connoisseurs of gastronomy and fine wine aim to discern the most elegant, finest samplings the artisanal world of food and drink have to offer. With years of education and highly tuned palates, they distinguish the best among masses of products.

But unlike the connoisseur, we tend to seek mates based not on education but on past mistakes and youthful follies. Rarely do we school ourselves in human nature or in our behavior. Rather, we dismiss our peccadilloes and their cost to others as we run blindly toward the next attractive person on our radar. Discernment is nowhere to be found in our process. Instead, we grab like gluttons at any piece of flesh that appeals. No wonder we get emotional indigestion when, months later, we wake up next to someone who couldn't be less right for what we want and need!

When you regard a potential mate or your current partner, use discrimination in your attention. If you focus on your lover's strengths and attractive qualities, your recognition of these will bring out the best in him or her. Equally important, you will bring out the best in you, as you apply your most discerning awareness to acknowledge what you genuinely value. Such refined alertness will assist you to evaluate wisely and honestly, and will have you seeing differently once you have chosen.

DAILY HEALTHY SEX ACTS

- When you next walk through a farmers market or the produce section of your local grocer, take time to differentiate *good* fruits and vegetables from *the best*. This is an act of discernment and sensuality. Touch, smell, and taste them (when allowed) before you choose.

- How discerning were you when you chose your current partner? Do you feel resentful because you mistook him or her for being different than he or she is? If so, talk to your partner about that today. Just remember—this is your issue.

- Pay attention to your judgment in all situations you find yourself in today. How might you be more discerning about your choices and decisions?

"Do you want me to tell you something really subversive? Love is everything it's cracked up to be. That's why people are so cynical about it. It really is worth fighting for, being brave for, risking everything for. And the trouble is, if you don't risk everything, you risk even more."

— Erica Jong

7 DECEMBER

RISK

When we attain a peak experience—falling in love, having sex with a stranger, climbing a formidable mountain, skydiving—we stretch our capacity to tolerate risk. This plasticity is life-affirming when it's creative, but destructive when we mistake recklessness for courage. Certainly, intensity is intoxicating and thrilling activities require "guts" and a suspension of good sense—you only live once, right? Right! But constantly taking ourselves to the extreme exhausts our system and, like an addiction, goads us to seek higher "highs" just to feel alive.

For sex to intensify in a long-term committed relationship, you can also seek experiential risk, but as an inward path. Having athletic sex with your eyes closed the entire time is a solo performance and a physical workout, which is fine if that's all you want. But try risking your heart and soul to the extreme by looking deeply into your lover's eyes during love-making, and feel and see who's looking back. Many roll their eyes at the idea of making eye contact during sex: "Do we have to stare into each others' eyes? I want spontaneity!" Yet spontaneity doesn't come without risk. Showing who you really are sexually to your partner, and to yourself, can feel like jumping out of a plane because you risk looking like you don't have it all together. There is nothing suave about revealing the depths of who you are to yourself and to your lover. It can feel scary and it can activate self-judgment or criticism of the other, especially if you harbor restrictive beliefs or memories of past hurts surrounding sex. But if you want the real thrill of extreme risk, challenge yourself to find your sexual pinnacles and perigees with someone you love and who knows you well.

DAILY HEALTHY SEX ACTS

- Are you living at risky extremes in your life? Do those extremes deprive you of other experiences, exhaust you, or keep you from having what you want?

- If you're afraid of risk and tend to deprive yourself of intense pleasure, challenge yourself today to do something extravagant that you've always wanted to do but have withheld from yourself.

- Look into your partner's eyes at the moment of orgasm and see what happens.

"For fast-acting relief, try slowing down."

— Lily Tomlin

The culture at large seems to pressure us at every turn, telling us to look better, drive cooler, make more money, and smell sweeter. We're constantly bombarded with images and messages urging all manner of self-improvement. So it's natural that people point to all the stress "out there." But these external pressures that derail so many of our days really get their foothold in internal pressure. If it weren't for our own expectations, comparisons to others, and fear, we would remain serene in any storm. Serenity sometimes derives from knowing there's nothing more we can do—that we really have done our best. How do you accept imperfection as a natural part of life?

To get relief from such daily—or lifetime—pressure, many people sexualize their stress. Not a bad idea, right? You see an attractive person and feel turned on romantically or sexually. Seems simple enough, but unpacking these moments often reveals anxiety, not attraction, fueling those feelings. For example, let's say you don't like a certain part of your body. Suddenly encountering a person with your ideal body might trigger stress, and you may soon find yourself sexualizing a neutral social situation. We all have distinctive relational deficiencies, which when triggered can become sexualized, releasing dopamine in the brain and inducing a feel-good state that covers up the stress.

Sex itself—the entire concept of sex—can bring stress. Sexuality usually grows in a haphazard way, more like a beguiling patch of weeds than a cultivated garden. We spring from seeds of older plants (our parents) and our many budding relationships sprout up, sometimes without our even knowing with whom we're relating. But a cultivated garden gives a noble setting to the peaceful beauty of flora. Cultivate your sexuality consciously, don't let it become a junkyard for you to dispose of stress.

DAILY HEALTHY SEX ACTS

- Watch when sexual or romantic feelings occur in your day, and try to trace whether they might stem from stress.

- Take an inventory of your recent sexual experiences to find out if relief from stress is a motivating factor. Does stress-relief sex measure up to mindful and mutually present sex?

- Let go. Let go of the notion of "letting it all go." The next time you feel stress or pressure, let go. Let go of letting go. No situation has ever been solved through submitting to stress and pressure.

"The door you open to give love is the very one through which love arrives."

— Alan Cohen

9 DECEMBER

GIVING

We've all known someone who is always giving gifts, doing favors, and desperately anticipating everyone's needs. The reward people get from over-giving is that they look loving and caring. But in reality, they are trying to control everyone around them. Compulsive giving, done out of fear of abandonment, aims to keep people obligated to us and gives us a false sense of power. Such conditional giving feeds the ego with distorted messages that we're special, important, and loved by all. In fact, this kind of giving can be an exhausting defense against having to look at ourselves, and a blockade to real intimacy, which is always based on mutuality.

For giving and receiving in a healthy relationship is a two-way street. To receive gracefully—gratefully—requires that anxiety about abandonment be vanquished by confidence in the other. Accepting gifts or kindness means we can care for our needs and allow another's help, instead of draining all of our energy into caregiving for others. Sexy people privilege their self-care—not in self-centeredness but in a way that shows they take responsibility for themselves. When we take care of ourselves first, we take ownership of what we need. And only once we're balanced can we appropriately give to those around us.

Giving to our beloved during sex means that we surrender to the shared energies emerging between us. We don't control the sexual experience through domination or insisting on our partner's pleasure. Requiring our partner's orgasm is a form of force and control. Instead we give freely from a place of fluidity, and experience freely without setting a program. Generosity without an agenda allows the precious polarities of giving and receiving to ebb and flow mutually.

DAILY HEALTHY SEX ACTS

- What does "giving" mean to you?

- Ask your partner how sexually generous she or he finds you, and listen from a place of vulnerability and openness.

- If you are invested in giving during sex, try receiving. Take turns giving and receiving with your lover and talk about what happens to you afterward.

"The idea of waiting for something makes it more exciting."

— Andy Warhol

Remember waiting for something grand as a child? Whether it was your birthday or the arrival of a special relative, anticipation filled your little being with tremulous excitement, blocking out all other reality. Looking forward to plans you've made to restore your mental health, such as taking a vacation, is a wonderful way to create novelty and to rest from day-to-day responsibilities. Setting goals and at last achieving them supports your hope of realizing your potential and having a richer life. The capacity to hold and wait for good things to come is an internal strength that can bring great fun and joy to life.

But anticipation can become problematic when it runs our lives. The mind seems always to tumble into the future, always to expect the next, new, more exciting experience or possession. Impulses compel us to consume yet another unnecessary thing or get into a relationship or agreement we haven't had time to mull over. Conversely, waiting for something better in the future can overtake the present as an obsession, and leave us discontent with what we already have.

At its best, anticipation emerges deliciously from hope, awareness, or intuition about something yet to come that's even more wonderful than the present. Take heed and let yourself relax into the present moment. See what new excitement emerges freely without your effort, when you don't give over to impulses that say, "I want it now."

DAILY HEALTHY SEX ACTS

- Luxuriate in the present, and notice the moment-to-moment changes around you.

- Set a date with your beloved and notice the anticipatory feelings that arise as you get closer to your date.

- Go shopping and don't buy anything. Stop, look, think about the item and whether you need it, want it, or are lunging at it for a momentary "high." If you decide you need or want the item, wait at least a day before you return to the store and purchase it.

"If you notice an unconscious fantasy coming up within you, you would be wise not to interpret it at once. Do not say that you know what it is and force it into consciousness. Just let it live with you, leaving it in the half-dark, carry it with you and watch where it is going or what it is driving at."

— Marie-Louise von Franz

11 DECEMBER

AMBIGUITY

When we allow healthy ambiguity in relationships, we invite intimacy, which thrives in the open hand. Romantic enmeshment assumes an unqualified accord, and to align with a partner on important issues feels gratifying. But gratification is not relationship. The ability to navigate the unchartered territory of loving requires definite ambiguity. *Definite ambiguity* sounds like an oxymoron, but secure openness is exactly the grasp-free touch that feeds love. To live in shades of gray means to save ourselves from fluctuating extremes. We all tend to self-declarations that may be contradictory: *We're this way. No, we're that way.* Stating our case so rigidly seems to summon its opposite. But since external reality is not black and white, we try to embrace an inner ambiguity that mirrors the real world.

The diversity of individual experience validates ambiguity. Unfortunately, formal education tends to reward only the "right" answers that are not always evident or meaningful in the real world. Exploring the process of our thoughts can be even more enlightening than memorizing and parroting another's script. Dictated paradigms of right versus wrong, good versus bad block the realization of our personal truth. Only through the lens of ambiguity may we each uncover inner certainty.

Whenever we hear the urgency of absolutism, we're reminded how often single-mindedness signals anxiety and lack of serenity. That doesn't mean we should weaken every statement by injecting *maybe, sorta, kinda* and never take a stand. Pick your battles, but don't sweat the small inconsistencies. We never have to defend our principles against the charge of uncertainty, because if they're *really* our principles we embody them in an open, ambiguous generosity that lets us live them in the richly ambiguous real world and with richly ambiguous others.

DAILY HEALTHY SEX ACTS

- Do you rush to know and fix everything? When does solving every problem that comes your way suck the life out of the room? Consider how it feels *not* to know. Can you share when you haven't the answers, or does pride or fear prevent you from acknowledging your ambiguity?

- Recall times you were forced to eat your words, to retract a stated "fact" or opinion. Practice a light touch and let ambiguity guide your expressions.

- It's difficult to accept that people—especially parents—aren't all good or all bad. Today, see the ambiguous human truth beyond absolutes.

> *"You say to me-wards your affection's strong;*
> *Pray love me little, so you love me long."*
>
> — Robert Herrick

DELAYED GRATIFICATION

Like so many powerful acts, delaying gratification holds a paradox. Anticipation can have the delicious energy of tension-building, fueling us with the virility of passion and excitement. At the same time, especially if we're used to dictating outcomes, it can create discomfort and agitation. But if we can tolerate the tension that occurs when slowing things down or deferring an event, we give ourselves time to think about what we really want and we give life time to present it to us.

If you've ever jumped into a relationship and regretted it later, you may consider the power of slowing down the action to gain time. Like the spider that weaves and waits in its web—an intricate structure that captures whatever comes—the Zen master lets life come towards him/her. Patience and delaying gratification are useful actions that buy us time to think about decisions and to savor them. Yet such time-garnering actions that postpone and sharpen pleasure are anathema in a world of fast food and instantaneous experiences. We are pressured daily to grab immediate gratification or be left behind and miss the supposed event of a lifetime.

When it comes to sex and orgasm, the highest level of pleasure is often the anticipation won by delay. The lingering look, long embrace, and deliberate kiss create innumerable possibilities when you slow your rhythms and connect through deep sensuality. Immediate gratification in sex is the mantra of the neophyte. The masterful lover slows to the pace of the unknown and trusts the magic of eroticism to unfold.

DAILY HEALTHY SEX ACTS

- Do you accept every invitation you receive or do you take a beat and think about what you really want?

- The next time you have an impulse to eat something or buy something you probably shouldn't—just stop. Walk away from the food or the purchase and let yourself think about what you really want or need.

- When you make love, notice any anxiety you may have about racing to the finish. Slow your pace to your breath and make contact with you lover. Alter your rhythm to an exploratory one instead of a result-oriented one.

"We are not the same persons this year as last; nor are those we love. It is a happy chance if we, changing, continue to love a changed person."

— William Somerset Maugham

13 DECEMBER

CHANGE

Transformation may be the essential quality of life both in nature and in our self. So we need to keep a fluid sense of our self over our whole lifetime. But change—flexibility—takes all the strength of true courage. A structure that's frigidly rigid will break, but one strong enough to be malleable can bend. In the same way, having a supple vision for your relationship is key to keeping it alive, rich and fulfilling over time, while hanging onto a preconceived plan that doesn't permit changes is a recipe for relational deadness.

For nothing is more dynamic than a living, breathing relationship. The myth of marrying young and living "happily ever after, 'til death do us part" doesn't allow for the rapid changes of modern life or for our increasing life spans. Our jobs and careers alter with our interests; fashion shifts with the decades; children grow; and so do we. Our ever-changing world, and self, requires we stay current with our partner to ensure the vivacity of our relationship. Without diligent tending, it can become stagnant and brittle, leaving us wondering what happened to our love.

Before we know it, years have passed. We've manifested, as best we could, whatever vision we had as a couple—raising a family or building a business. These achievements can give us a sense of accomplishment, but may leave us wondering what to do next. Luckily, newness is always on the horizon, but in order to end up on the same shore together instead of drifting apart, we must be conscious about the decisions we make as a couple. If we pick ones that inspire and invigorate both members of the coupleship, we will breathe new life into it.

DAILY HEALTHY SEX ACTS

- What changes are before you personally and professionally? Do these changes affect your relationship or your sex life? If so, how?

- Create a vision board for your life and ask your partner to do the same. How do your visions and desires line up? What are the non-negotiable items on your lists and how can you deal with conflicts between them?

- Make a commitment to talk about your vision for your life together at least once a year, no matter what stage of the relationship you're in.

"The artist's experience lies so unbelievably close to the sexual, to its pain and its pleasure, that the two phenomena are really just different forms of one and the same longing and bliss."

— Rainer Maria Rilke

Themes of sex and love rule the realm of art. Mirrors of human consciousness, works of art reveal our species' unresolved preoccupation with human relatedness. Characters falling in love and managing, or mismanaging, relationships engage us in our most heartfelt questions. Great art instructs us, subtly and experientially, especially when an artist taps into his or her own existential questions about love and life. Is it any wonder that, while confronting cultural distortions about sex and love, so many famous artists show signs of sex- and love-addicted thinking?

Certainly, the creative mind often wrestles with painful personal issues, whether by choice or design. But it's time to dispel the myth that the artist must suffer to create. How many times have you followed an ill-considered or potentially destructive course of action thinking it will enhance your creativity or give you a story to tell? Instead, look closer at artists like Jean Cocteau, Eugene O'Neill and Stephen King, who integrated their individual problems into their art, sometimes after addressing undiagnosed mental illness or untreated addictions, and thereby produced even deeper pieces. These recovered artists teach us that a creative spirit makes compelling works *in spite of—not because of*—internal drama. The eyes that see to the depths of the human spirit perceive most clearly when waters are calm.

Nevertheless, art can contain our private struggles. Channeling our pain into constructive endeavors is healing, whether we engage in classic arts such as a painting or performance, or in crafts such as bread-baking or gardening. People try to dump unprocessed thoughts and feelings into relationships or work situations, which simply cannot contain them. Art is an infinite container for all personal issues and, for many, a way to stay sane, and to see and show truth.

DAILY HEALTHY SEX ACTS

- What are your favorite works of art? Why do you think they affect you?

- Visit a museum, theater, dance or music recital. Consider any personal issues around sex and love expressed by an artist. Is the work intimate, creating a connection between artist and audience?

- Today, engage in art therapy. Take several meditative minutes to draw, design or doodle while channeling feelings and thoughts you're having about current personal struggles.

*"Kissing Agathon, I held my life on my lips.
It wanted to pass over, poor thing, into him."*

— Plato

15 DECEMBER

TRANSFERENCE

Transference prevents us from engaging authentically with others because we're actually in relationship with our own psychological make-up. For example, we might unconsciously transfer our love, or hatred, of a parent onto our partner, teacher, or child. In the sexual arena, we might unknowingly project negative feelings or irrational hopes surrounding a figure from our past onto our current lover. A common version of such transference is the expectation of "great sex," which sets our partner up to disappoint us because no one can fulfill our implicit fantasies.

Whenever we perceive a situation solely though the lens of our own psychology, we are likely transferring our limited, programmed view onto life and others rather than living in reality and real relationship. It's damaging and costly to transfer some past other's vices or virtues onto our present partner because it keeps us from knowing his or her unique self, and from renewing our own self.

In the early stages of love, we tend to transfer positive attributes onto our lover, obscuring his or her imperfections so the relationship can progress. But eventually we must throw off the veil of transference in order to perceive our partner in the light of objective reality. To see others this clearly, though, means we have found the self-knowledge to recognize our transferred issues as well as the compassion to accept others with their gloriously individual flaws and merits. When you can appreciate the unique qualities of all who exist, and perceive yourself and your partner from the viewpoint of that inclusive totality, your partner *and you* become unheralded, new, creative beings. Dropping your transference sharpens and expands your perception during sex, allowing two independent individuals to become one and to create a cosmic third—to create conversation, rather than maintaining a wholly internal monologue.

DAILY HEALTHY SEX ACTS

- Do you transfer your idealized version of love onto your partner? How does this set him or her up for failure in your eyes?

- Make a simple list today of all of your partner's attributes and why you love being in relationship with him or her.

- What past person's behaviors do you tend to see in others? Today, practice recognizing novel and unique qualities in your lover, friend, boss, co-worker, or neighbor.

"Excitement is not enjoyment: in calmness lies true pleasure. The most precious wines are sipped, not bolted at a swallow."

— Victor Hugo

EXCITEMENT

Life can seem to lose its luster as we age, leaving us thinking that excitement lives only in the domain of youth. We may wax nostalgic for the lightning-bolt arousal of our feelings, ranging from exuberance to agitation. But taking it slow and becoming present with what and who's in front of us can create a different, more mature kind of excitement. Eroticism can build to the frenzied excitement we associate with our younger days, but slow, languorous love-making can, paradoxically, take us to unexplored sexual heights.

Many lovers are always "off to the races:" Hurtling towards orgasm, they miss the excitement of sensual meanderings along the way. Arouse a strong response from your lover and see what shifts and changes might take place in the spaces between you. Allow a sense of play and leisure in these new-found spaces, and be on the lookout for surprises which manifest as spontaneous bursts of joy and love. These safe surprises create excitement because they invite novelty and unscheduled freedom into your rushed lives where you mostly co-exist as companions. When excitement makes an appearance, energies shift from the day-to-day grind to something magical, intriguing, and free from time constraints. Get excited by the unhurried building of passion, and watch the ordinary become extra-ordinary.

DAILY HEALTHY SEX ACTS

- Identify an activity that you usually rush through: Showering? Eating breakfast? Answering emails? Now try it at a slower pace and notice what happens.

- Invite your lover to try something new and exciting, based on what you know they would like, and pay attention to the energy shifts from slow arousal to high excitement.

*"Another world is not only possible, she is on her way.
On a quiet day, I can hear her breathing."*

— Arundhati Roy

17 DECEMBER

POSSIBILITY

We often hear that life is like a river, and as we drift downstream we experience only those possibilities we can perceive and reach. So how can we actually realize whatever potentialities exist but lie dormant? This riddle is key to the very notion of possibility: We never know what may happen! But we can invite wider possibility into our lives by recognizing the proven transformative effects of keeping our eyes and minds open. For when we review our own lives, it's amazing how scantily possible—how miraculous—all the breakthroughs that occurred seemed beforehand.

Many people complain that they feel trapped by circumstance. Yes, some may suffer obvious material or physical impediments, but most ignore a whole panoply of psychological, emotional, and mental possibilities. When it comes to sex, the possibility of pleasure can feel like an elusive quest that's wholly dependent on external factors like the availability of responsive sexual partners. But what is it that actually causes pleasure, and where is it caused? All of us can feel a pleasing touch at one time, but in a different context or mood find the same touch not pleasurable at all. Sexual pleasure, then, may be more psychological than physiological, and so may rely more on our inner harmony and receptivity than on the accidental luck of finding a partner, quite *possibly....*

DAILY HEALTHY SEX ACTS

- When faced with a new possibility, sleep on it to let your unconscious truth emerge. Pay attention to any dreams—specifically the way they make you feel, whether or not you remember them. Allow yourself to know on a hunch. If hunches have led you astray, weigh the decision with at least three trusted acquaintances to get back on track.

- One of the greatest possibilities is the present moment and where that can lead you. Let your integrity and intuition guide you today. Step by step, bear witness to your unprecedented path.

"Speak low, if you speak love."

— William Shakespeare

What are whispers? Even before we learn language, we catch the sensuous, soothing quality of gentle speech. A parent's murmur is one of the earliest expressions of love. Earlier still, in the womb, we sensed the soothing, whispery swoosh of blood flowing through our mother's body. Whispers focus our energy and attention, whether for sharing a secret or honoring the sacredness of a house of worship, hospital, or library. Yet in Western society, most effort is focused on expansion, which is reflected in the voice—delivering endless streams of news, talking over others, getting in the last word. Listen carefully. The sound of most voices is like a grabbing hand. But a whisper seems to release that needy grip, letting go of the drive to be heard by chattering consciousness. A whisper is willing to proceed another way, as its subject often imparts. Just as reversing our physical posture by standing on our head lets blood flow to the brain, whispering reverses vocal force: Instead of pushing words out, it stimulates the listener's auditory muscles to take sound in.

Life is magnified in whispered moments. There are marvelous sea creatures whose existences can be viewed only within the deep blue sea, and similarly we all have dear secrets that can be spoken only in the habitat of the heart. But *what* and *why* we whisper is crucial. A sudden brush, or one covetous thought, and a whisper becomes a sensual invitation or a conspiratorial hiss. The sacred becomes the seductive, ensnaring another through the control of breath. As romantic love and tainted love define themselves through contrast, so a whisper can be a hollow strain drawing us to lust, theft, or murder, or a glorious melody of love, giving, and life.

DAILY HEALTHY SEX ACTS

- Listen. Hearken to the quality of sounds today. Just for this moment, walk toward the whispers. What message does the world have for you hidden underneath the clamor of daily distractions?

- What secrets would you share in a whisper? Even if our life is an open book, we rarely share as we feel. In your truest, most vulnerable voice, reveal to someone you trust and adore your most secret wish in the way it whispers its presence to you.

"The loss of a cherished pleasure is not necessarily the loss of true happiness and well-being."

— Jean-Yves Leloup

19 DECEMBER

FULFILLMENT

The fulfillment we expect from intimacy and sexual communion is really like the harvest we expect when we plant a seed in soil: they both take time to grow. Even a healthy intention cannot sprout suddenly into a fully formed reality. We must nurture the seed of our intention through good times and challenging times. If we want to be present for ultimate fulfillment, we need to be present for disappointments along the way. We cannot constantly uproot the seed to see if it has sprouted. Instead, we must practice faith, which requires care and patience.

When we look around, the only readily visible constancy in life is change and impermanence. If we hinge our inner fulfillment to any external circumstance, we enslave ourselves to fluctuating states: Childhood toys break. Homes and possessions deteriorate. People and pets die. The human condition bears witness that bad things happen to good people. So lasting fulfillment might well seem impossible. But understand that we perceive reality only through the lens of our limited perspective. The suffering we see is what *we see*—yet it is a mirror to an invisible, inner reality.

We're often advised to "be in the now," to live the present moment without expectations or projections. Simply to be. Still, we always bring our self—even in the now—which isn't some dissociated state separate from our experience and hopes. If fulfillment is truly possible, it involves a mode of grasp-less being that contains our future and past. There is nothing more fulfilling than the gift of personal consciousness, that kiss of life. This is our ever-replenishing wealth. May we share our ever-enlightening selves in each precious moment, and may the harvest of this loving act ripple throughout the world of our being.

DAILY HEALTHY SEX ACTS

- What do you hope to receive from these reflections? What are you looking to fulfill? True fulfillment requires open heart, eyes, and mind. If you're looking for a specific material result, what would *that* fulfill? Continue asking this question until you uncover the inherent potential within you that seeks permission to live. Now—live for today!

- What do you find fulfilling? Let yourself immortalize the good times. To combat chronic discontent, write down all your fulfilling moments, past and present, on index cards, and store them like favorite recipes in a special box. These are your *recipes for fulfillment*. Add more as experienced.

"In this very breath that we take now lies the secret that all great teachers try to tell us."

— Peter Matthiessen

BREATH

Breath is our life force, the source of energy that fills our bloodstream with oxygen and our organs with vitality. Most people hold their breath during orgasm and tense up from that poor breathing habit. In fact, many women who struggle with orgasm are often simply not breathing during sex, while lack of oxygen in the pelvic area can induce male erectile difficulties. To control your breath consciously is to control your responses, and it's key to focusing sexual energy. During sex it's important for lovers to stop, relax and notice the sexual excitement in their bodies, to breathe together and feel the radiating warmth. Notice what you feel in this engagement—if time stops and your thoughts quiet down, if the pressures of the day and all of your expectations have, momentarily, vanished. This practice can be considered an ecstatic meditation with your lover, ergo sex may be your opening to a shared spiritual path.

Most mindfulness meditations ask us to focus on our breath. Similarly, your breathing patterns during love-making can be a focus to increase relaxation, vitality, and orgasm. Pay attention to your breath and allow its flow to be easy, natural and fluid. Breathing with each other brings alignment and openness as a couple. Your expanded breathing can carry you to heights of sensation and depths of loving feelings as it modulates your hearts' rhythms and synchronizes your energies. When you breathe to connect and attune, you expand your repertoire for spiritualizing sex. From this vantage point, prepare to meet the sacred in each other. Breathing, prayer or meditation sets the stage for inviting your highest selves to a sexual feast. Let your feminine energy worship the masculine energy and your masculine energy serve the feminine energy. Breathe and release into the erotic unknown.

 DAILY HEALTHY SEX ACTS

- Practice inhaling and exhaling, which will seem like separate activities at first. The more you relax and focus on breathing, the more it will flow in and out. Notice when your sensations heighten and where your tensions release.

- Focus your energy on relaxing and opening your body. Breathe into your abdomen, relaxing the lower half of your core.

- With each in-breath through your mouth, direct energy into your pelvic region or vaginal canal, then exhale through your nose. Continue this breathing during intercourse and stay with the sensations in your body.

> *"What we must work on, it seems to me, is not so much to liberate our desires but to make ourselves infinitely more susceptible to pleasure."*
>
> — Michel Foucault

21 DECEMBER

PLEASURE

In the classical myth told by Ovid, Pleasure is the daughter of Eros, the god of love, and Psyche, his earthly bride made immortal. The name *Psyche* shares the same root as the word *psychology:* spirit or mind. In one interpretation this ancient tale illustrates that pleasure is born from mindfulness (Psyche) and a uniting intention (Eros). Indeed, this sounds like the erotic formula for every coupling from Internet dating and tearoom cruising to sex surrogacy and marriage. It can be counterintuitive, but pleasure requires planning and self-knowledge in the same way vacationing can take as much effort and thought as working.

Sexual feelings set off nerve-bundles and neurochemicals within the body that are more intense and immediate than those which other enjoyable activities activate. Sex creates pleasurable sensations that are distinctly personal. Maybe this is one reason our sex organs are called private parts—not because they must be kept private, but because intense pleasurable sensations are experienced individually. It requires effort to share our sexual pleasure with a partner. But to show pleasure is to grow pleasure, for ourselves as well. Unfortunately our society often disdains any open display of unpretentious sexuality, regardless of whether it's healthy or destructive.

When people compulsively pursue pleasure, especially in sex and love addiction, they're not aware how much of the hunt is actually *un-pleasurable*. Whenever preceding or resulting pain is greater than the fleeting payoff, we should question the effectiveness of the enterprise. We can ask ourselves whether the enjoyment creates valued memories and anecdotes for years to come, or must be crushed and hidden upon consummation. Pleasure of which we are aware, and which we can share, has life and will continue to exist—much like the immortal progeny of Eros and Psyche.

DAILY HEALTHY SEX ACTS

- Consider what brings you pleasure, and how you share your pleasure with others. Do you narrate the enjoyable sensations you receive like making a report? Do you convey your feelings wordlessly, with sounds or facial expressions? Or do you count on their being communicated by themselves, as through osmosis?

- Experience pleasure today, and let yourself show it. First, practice alone and relay your feelings out loud. When you feel comfortable, practice sharing your experience of simple pleasures with other people.

"The chemist of love
Will this perishing mould,
Were it made out of mire,
Transmute into gold."

— Hāfez

SEXUAL ALCHEMY

The ancient art of alchemy strives to elevate the basest metals into noblest gold. Medieval and renaissance alchemists believed in the magical properties of a healing solvent—the elixir of life—that would purify and cure all. Both practical scientists and spiritual seekers, they desired to unite the mundane with the holy. Modern scholars like Jung and von Franz interpreted their work psychologically as a symbol of the individuation process: Transmuting the dross of personality defects and distorted thoughts manifests the true, highest Self.

When we think about sexual alchemy, we conjure up the idea of transforming base lust into golden union. In the black/Nigredo phase of alchemy, we witness the human condition of mutual nakedness: Holding our love in our arms, we touch that soul's pain and sadness, and gently cradle the memories stored in every cell of that body. We behold the eternal youth and beauty of our partner while simultaneously savoring our lover's ancient wisdom. In fact, we revel in all aspects of our partner's being, which leads to the purifying white/Albedo stage where the illusion of separateness dissolves through the power of loving touch. As we make love, affirming the core of sexuality inside every soul, the red/Rubedo phase of healing energy creates a melding fire of eroticism. Of its own accord, the final golden/Citrinitas phase materializes and our two identities merge in a mystical third. That is the alchemy of sex.

At the precious moment of orgasm, we glimpse life without preconceptions, through our god eyes. In fact, some sex magic uses the momentary uncontrollable upheaval of orgasm to cast intentions. Of course, since domination motivates such sex magic and love spells, those efforts rebound to confound the caster. For the true gold of intimacy manifests only through open-handed trustworthiness. In this way, we are all diviners using the magic of sexual expression to craft our own ennobling, enlightening realities.

DAILY HEALTHY SEX ACTS

- What alchemical stages have you experienced on the path to sexual enlightenment? Elevate sex as an art. Let your body be your tools and explore your sensations as precious metals to be combined, purified and exalted.

- Today, transmute the dullest of routines into the most sacred, restorative act through the power of healthy, altruistic intention.

"Perhaps the most important thing we bring to another person is the silence in us, not the sort of silence that is filled with unspoken criticism or hard withdrawal. The sort of silence that is a place of refuge, of rest, of acceptance of someone as they are."

— Rachel Naomi Remen

23 DECEMBER

SILENCE

Sometimes during sex, there's a heightened silence that's sacred. It's a shared silence. An erotic freedom where lovers are almost of one brain, giving and receiving pleasure, connected to a collective power. These deeply sensual states transcend the limitations of sound to draw powerful healing and healthy love as if from the source of life. Artists and athletes know about being "in the zone" during peak performances as they become utterly immersed in what they're doing, capable of incredible feats of focus and mastery. Sexual partners may also enter into the zone, a place of ecstatic silence. There may be noise, but this kind of absorption taps into a sacred silence beyond all sound. We move beyond what we are doing. This state requires practice, attunement, and mutual trust.

There are also times when sex is uncomfortably quiet, a still and frozen silence dissociated from the deed at hand, paralyzed by unwanted thoughts. This truly dead silence is attended by painfully awkward physicality and emotions. It seems the slightest word could crack ice, although the mind is chattering a mile a minute with a million questions. We all know what it's like to become locked out of another's experience in bed.

How do we attain the pinnacle of sacred silence, or break the cycle of repressive silence? The phrase, "What are you thinking?" can invite open-hearted communion, but for less solid bonds this question can toll the death knell—a desperate signal that energies are out of alignment. Intimacy is the act of openly sharing one's experience and receiving the experience of another, and sometimes there are truly no words for what we've experienced together. It takes special care to recognize when we reveal more of who we are only in the silence.

DAILY HEALTHY SEX ACTS

- Find your sacred silence. Are there certain moments throughout the day when you become immersed in what you're doing? Can you share this sacred silence with others?

- To know silence, you must know sound. Listen today for the sounds you make. What kind of sound do your words create? Your movements and breathing? What are the sounds of your thoughts?

- There are ways to invite communication before, during, and after sex that flow like sex itself. Break through the ice of any repressive silence by caressing your partner with loving and erotic thoughts, sounds, words, and silence—in that order!

"When someone loves you, the way they say your name is different. You know that your name is safe in their mouth."

— Jess C. Scott

ADORATION

Adoration comes from the Latin *adoratio*, meaning "to give homage or worship." In our culture, the idea of worshiping one's partner is fraught with fears that worship means subjugating ourselves. But if worship means to adore, to take in, to treat with the utmost respect or to hold in the highest esteem, we should all regard the person we love most in that consciousness. When someone is adored, we cherish and handle that person with great care. We see electrifying adoration when a parent looks at his or her infant, drinking in the child's essence, beauty, mystery, and fragility all at once. Similarly, star-crossed lovers gaze into each other's eyes as if the entire cosmos rested there. The power of this depth of attraction touches us at the core of our being; our very humanity comes alive as if we're seeing our own selves anew. Such an intense human connection seems to telegraph our profound need to see and love another, and in so doing to be truly seen and loved ourselves.

When shame inhabits our sense of self, it makes it very difficult, and sometimes impossible, to take in the adoring gaze of another. And, truthfully, when we don't adore ourselves or treat ourselves with maximum respect, we attract others who don't treat us well.

Dare to adore your lover. Find a way to define adoration for yourself and see if worship flows as an expression of your adoration. Take a leap and let yourself feel what it's like to adore another. Who knows? You may find that what goes around comes around.

DAILY HEALTHY SEX ACTS

- Commit to one adoring act today, whether stroking your partner's face while telling of your love, looking into her or his eyes and telling of your adoration, or making an adoring gesture towards your partner like giving a foot massage or drawing a hot bath.

- Is a family member annoying you today? Put aside your judgments for a moment, imagine that person as an infant or small child, and see her or his inherent value. Tell that person something you adore about him or her, then show it through a tangible gesture: something you do or give to express your adoration.

"The door to the human heart can be opened only from the inside."

— Spanish proverb

25 DECEMBER

CENTER

Personal recovery is an inside job, whether it's the recovery of sobriety, values, relationships, or sexual health. No one can do it for us. But the message that we're dependent on external circumstances for our well-being and sense of self is all-pervasive. In fact, through much of history children were regarded as mere property subject to the dictates of family or state. The idea that newborns enter this world with unique destinies rather than as blank slates for caregivers to script represents a radical, and ongoing, paradigm shift. This novel idea means that the sacred center of our being requires and deserves dedication and attention—to be recognized and free. Unfortunately, living in our true nature often seems not in our nature.

Nothing can throw us off-center more than balancing romantic, familial, social, financial, and personal obligations. When we can't express ourselves through all these activities, we may take obsessive refuge in one of them or transform into another personality to cope. Too often, we change our voice in an attempt to be heard, which muffles its true melody. Similarly when we attract a lover by presenting a made-up version of ourselves, we hide our true center. And, like a top, when we're not centered, our wobbly actions have uncentered—*eccentric*—and unintended consequences.

Each of us has at least one area of our life where we feel mastery—an athletic skill, an art, a talent, a body of knowledge. In our area of expertise, we know to come from our center. In contrast, many of us have never felt centered in relationships and sexual activity. But we can start right now to apply what we do understand of centeredness to cultivate a sense of self that's centered within all the lives and loves we touch.

DAILY HEALTHY SEX ACTS

- What is the central focus of your life? Calculate how you spend your time. Are there addictive or habitual lapses in your day? Unwinding for self-care is fine. But watch for actions that become distractions from your true center.

- Do you lose yourself in orbit around certain people? Conversely, do you have to be the center of attention? Today, make room for all persons to come from their center.

- How do you center yourself? When have you felt most centered—in touch with your true self? Can your lover share in this process, or must you be alone to find your center?

"Every gesture, every caress, every touch, every glance, every last bit of the body has its secret, which brings happiness to the person who knows how to wake it."

— Hermann Hesse

HEALTHY SEX

There are many debates about what constitutes healthy sex and no one person has the final definition—except you. You have to decide what is and isn't healthy for you depending on your past, what you know about yourself today, and what safely brings you pleasure. A general guideline of aspects for you to check is S. A. F. E. : Is it Secretive or Shaming? Is it Abusive to you or your partner, whether verbally, emotionally, physically, or sexually? Is it used to escape Feelings? Does it require an Emotional connection with another?

As you continue to define healthy sex and to develop your own safe scripts, consider that deepening your sense of self and embracing your own erotic, animal nature is a benefit of the sexual freedom you seek. Create a climate with your partner of mutual respect and honor, and notice how you feel after a sexual encounter. An embodied sense of self that feels congruent, whole, and good likely means you're on the right track. As you hone your erotic lovemap, you may dare to demand the experience of staying in the present moment and staying relational with your partner. Seek surrender and vulnerability, and take risks you may have avoided in the past. Challenge yourself to feel deeply and to love with your entire body, mind, and soul.

DAILY HEALTHY SEX ACTS

- Take time to envision your most erotic self. What's missing from your experience today, and what do you need to do to take a step toward your vision? Share this with your partner.

- Talk to your partner about trying something new the next time you have sex. Will this be making eye contact during the moment of orgasm, sharing a sexual fantasy that includes the two of you, or using massage oils? Bring to life one aspect of your vision of your most erotic self.

"Know that although in the eternal scheme of things you are small, you are also unique and irreplaceable, as are all your fellow humans everywhere in the world."

— Margaret Laurence

27 DECEMBER

APPRECIATION

When we come to the knowing that we actually want what we already have, we arrive at a new vista of appreciation. We're bombarded daily by media messages that something better awaits us "out there," usually through purchasing something new or through the fantasy that we'd be better off with a new partner. Breeding chronic dissatisfaction with what we have and chronic lust for what we don't is one of the engines that drive addiction, because more of anything—even something great— is just never enough. This permanent feeling of lack wears down our healthy recognition that we're perfectly imperfect, good enough as we are, and that our partners are unique and loveable as they are.

Appreciation is the antidote to the false feelings of chronic deprivation. If you treat yourself poorly because you think you aren't good enough, pretty enough, physically fit enough, then you're out of appreciation for yourself and your own unique beauty. If you judge your partner as not "enough" in one way or another, then you're out of appreciation for how irreplaceable s/he is.

DAILY HEALTHY SEX ACTS

- Each day, tell your partner one thing you appreciate about him or her.

- If you're not in a relationship, make a list of all the things you appreciate about yourself, and share those attributes with others by putting them into action. For example, if you appreciate your sense of humor, make someone laugh today.

- Take time to appreciate your family members, the life you have, and the world around you. Don't waste time waiting for some future jackpot. Appreciate the bounty you already have.

> *"Every action of our lives touches on some chord that will vibrate in eternity."*
>
> — Edwin Hubbel Chapin

SEXUAL FOOTPRINT

What is the impact of sexuality and sexual activity on ourselves and on our lives? We hear about carbon footprints—the impact of our consumption on the earth. So to trace our sexual footprint, we might examine the consequences of our sexual choices, whether seemingly casual or conscious.

Initial sexual encounters may set a pattern. Understanding and healing damaging formative experiences that were stepping stones in our sexual development is imperative, because sometimes those stepping stones petrify into the expected path, the known and travelled terrain. Every sexual experience builds certain muscles and creates a filter, and excludes other muscles and filters. Over time, experiences create neural pathways while pruning unused ones. Such cultivation affects our entire sexual politic, but is difficult to perceive since we are so immersed in our own experience that it appears as simple reality. Often, sexual experiences before puberty lead to inappropriate sexualization. Adult survivors of incest or childhood sexual abuse can feel guilt or complicity for premature sexual activity. But of course, children do not have the comprehension, capacity, or power to make decisions for their own sexual health. So it's crucial that adult survivors take charge in the present by working through unprocessed trauma.

Mature sex involves an intensely intimate audience with a partner. Yet it often seems there's a conspired agreement afterward to ignore the depth of sensations, to deny the myriad of thoughts as they occur. We align our love-making with an actual person who will go out into the world, our vibrations affecting each other like tuning forks. If we're engaging in dishonest, shameful or anorectic sexuality, then how could we not manifest such a sexual footprint on our destined path? To seek sexual health, we engage in healthy intimacy and bring this capacity to our larger relationship with life.

 DAILY HEALTHY SEX ACTS

- Trace your sexual footprint: List your earliest, and then your most significant, sexual experiences and what you learned from them.

- Achieving sexual health might necessitate healing damage from past relationships. In 12-step, this is the inventory and amends process, which is complex and requires sponsor supervision. For now, simply try to have compassion and patience for others, as you would to heal yourself. Let love mend.

"You may be deceived if you trust too much, but you will live in torment unless you trust enough."

— Frank Crane

29 DECEMBER

TRUST

In the Buddhist tradition of Tantra, *anāhata* is the Sanskrit name for the heart *chakra*, or energy, and means "unhurt." Anāhata is the origin of trust. It evokes an image of our holiest, innermost place that believes in life and in others' goodness. Although we may have experienced trauma, betrayal and abandonment, we can still trust nature to support our every breath and step. As we breathe in and out, we feel the miracle of the human body. The ground holds our feet, the sun warms us, and water refreshes us. Even if we cannot believe in others' love for us, we can trust in the love we ourselves feel and allow it to give our lives meaning. Trust becomes a form of meditation as we consciously focus on what is positive and hopeful. Trust asks that we give others the benefit of the doubt, that we suspend judgment and paranoia, and that we muster the willingness to let go of the past.

To build trust with a partner, we can proceed gently and purposefully, taking care to practice the elegant, silent arts of looking and listening. People show us who they are in myriad ways, from their subtlest body language to their most raucous humor. Learning to witness others from a place of wonder teaches us that we can trust our own instincts and safely navigate all types of relationships. We learn to heed red flags, warning signs and intuition. How often have we sensed that another person is not good for us, but due to lust, laziness or fantasy, we just completely ignored our gut feelings? Trust must be earned and learned. We must build it daily, both with ourselves and the people with whom we choose to be intimate.

DAILY HEALTHY SEX ACTS

- Trust is broken not by our inability to trust, but by our inability to discriminate between trustworthy and untrustworthy. Can you free your potential for unlimited and unbreakable trust, or are you still reeling from betrayal trauma? What do you need to do in order to rebuild trust in humanity, or in one human being?

- In a world of mirror projections, we perceive only what we ourselves are. So we must wield our muscle of trust to explore reality outside our ego. Today, trust entirely in life. See beneath the surface to affirm in each situation the vital heart of unconditional love.

> *"'Last forever!' Who hasn't prayed that prayer? You were lucky to get it in the first place. The present is a freely given canvas. That it is constantly being ripped apart and washed downstream goes without saying."*
>
> — Annie Dillard

IMPERMANENCE

Your time on Earth is limited, so the common advice to make the best of it means there's wisdom and serenity in learning to love and let go. If you cling to the external cultural assumptions of what you need to be okay, it might seem you have a lot to lose, or that what you've got is not enough. Of course, what you have changes constantly. Where you're at can be a dream or a nightmare, a safe, familiar home or a cold, discordant place. Even if you live in the most expensive, secluded home, you might watch the news and be transported to scenes of utter poverty, and that's where you're at. You might be living in your head, in some traumatic memory you've been playing out for most of your life. So your quality of life is a *perceptual* reality.

Nothing lasts forever. Our pain often feels like it will last forever, but thank the stars for impermanence. There's another common saying: This, too, shall pass. What a blessing, because what would we do if negative feelings never left us? Whenever we grieve the sad truth that all we touch will be taken away from us someday, we can also be grateful that suffering is not permanent either. Perhaps the greatest achievement and reward in life is being able to maintain an inner state of peace and acceptance in the face of change, to grow our hearts big enough to handle loss, to love and let go, to feel gratitude for what we have now. The law of impermanence might signify that even our knowledge, beliefs, and inner states must also change, and perhaps this is how to discover who we really are.

DAILY HEALTHY SEX ACTS

- Touch hope. Let your problems go. Are you solving them now? In school, you wouldn't bring homework to a talent show or football game, so why bring your problems to the daily events of your life? Realize the next right action you need to take is on a need-to-know basis. Be present with your present.

- Touch ground today. See what's around. Feel your heart and the flow of life. Look. Listen. Love. What makes a moment, and how long does it last?

- Touch your lover. Feel life for today. Give blessings, and express your deep gratitude for all you have. Trust, it's there.

"Life is nothing but an opportunity for love to blossom. If you are alive, the opportunity is there—even to the last breath. You may have missed your whole life: just the last breath, the last moment on the earth, if you can be love, you have not missed anything—because a single moment of love is equal to the whole eternity of love."

— Osho

31 DECEMBER

ETERNITY

How did the concept of eternity emerge? Perhaps ancients thought the stars or oceans were infinite in time and space. We know better now. Rocks, mountains, suns, sky... all have beginning and end. But perhaps our ancestors were onto something when they came up with the ideas of forever. There's no absolute disproof of eternity, either. What might exist in that repository, where we consign profound emotions and treasured moments? "I will love you forever."

Eternity belongs to poetry. Every moment you experience is part of eternity—the sum total of manifestation. Even if what's perceived is later revealed to be not as it seemed, both momentary realities exist like radio signals echoing into space. That's a gorgeous truth, because it means we all have the right to exist just as we are. Often we hold onto the message that we don't have the right to claim our space. But the eternal actuality of each moment confers a spiritual right to cherish our bodies, to live and love one another, to enjoy fulfilling sex.

For many, eternity is a sacred concept that evokes unseen eyes. Love and sex touch eternity. Emotions of intimacy are experienced as timeless, compared to habitual feeling states, and time spent in love-making expands, compared to regular time. Eroticism touches a deep place within us, distinctive from any other. It tells us there's more to us than meets the eye. The idea of eternity tells us there's more to life than meets the eye. Eternity grants us unknown affinities, for ever-greater intimacy, for seeing into others. When a lover knows your soul at length—for all time—the intimacy might feel earth-shattering, like someone has joined you at the depths of your being, where you never thought it possible.

DAILY HEALTHY SEX ACTS

- What happens to forever? Think of the last time you affirmed eternal love. Where does that moment exist in you today?

- Close one eye. Picture this as the only perspective you've ever known. When you've forgotten your previous view, *slowly* open your closed eye and feel the moment your vision expands. Now... imagine you could open still more eyes to see in every direction, like the all-seeing eye of God. Can you catch a glimpse of eternity?

- If every moment echoes throughout time, if each act is writ in the everlasting script, if all you think and touch and hope and hold becomes your life, then live, live in your eternal soul-light, which is love.

*"Everything must
have an ending except
my love for you."*

— Samuel M. Johnson

INDEX

Alexandra Katehakis, Ph.D. MFT, is Founder of Center for Healthy Sex in Los Angeles, California. A Certified Sex Therapist/Supervisor and Certified Sex Addiction Therapist/Supervisor, she specializes in the field of human sexuality. Dr. Katehakis has incorporated interpersonal neurobiology into her Katehakis Integrative Sex Therapy Model. She is the recipient of the International Institute of Trauma and Addiction Therapists 2018 Leadership Award and the 2012 Carnes Award for significant contributions to the field of sex addiction by the Society for the Advancement of Sexual Health. In addition to co-authoring the 2015 AASECT award- winning *Mirror of Intimacy: Daily Reflections on Emotional and Erotic Intelligence* (2014), Dr. Katehakis has published *Sexual Reflections: A Workbook for Designing and Celebrating Your Sexual Health Plan* (2018) and *Sex Addiction as Affect Dysregulation: A Holistic Healing Model* (2016 published by W.W. Norton & Company). She is a contributing author to the *Routledge International Handbook of Sexual Addiction* (2017) and the Clark Vincent award-winning *Making Advances: A Comprehensive Guide for Treating Female Sex and Love Addicts* (2012). She is author of *Erotic Intelligence: Igniting Hot, Healthy Sex After Recovery From Sex Addiction* (2010). Dr. Katehakis is a national speaker, contributes regularly to online magazines, blog sites and podcasts, and has served as a clinical educator at numerous mental health and addiction treatment centers in the US and Europe.

Tom Bliss grew up in the Pacific Northwest and now lives in Los Angeles, California. He graduated from Pitzer College with a self-designed major in "Multimedia Performance: Life as an Art Form." While penning his senior project—a symbolic play about a playwright being forced to show up in his own symbolic play—he was privileged to experience *Samadhi*, the supreme state of enlightenment through meditation. Upon graduating, he joined the San Francisco-based Chero Company founded by Frank Moore, the wheelchair-bound performance artist/ shaman, whose marathon all-nude "Eroplay" happenings encouraged people to connect freed of social and cultural programming. During the next 15 years Mr. Bliss worked on both coasts as a multimedia performance artist and writer. In 2007, he entered a sex and love addiction recovery program at the Los Angeles Gay and Lesbian Center, and attends weekly support groups through various organizations. In 2009 he completed the Parent Educator Certification Program in Non-Violent Communication (NVC) at Echo Parenting & Education. He has appeared as guest educator on the PBS series, "A Place of our Own," discussing topics ranging from emotional literacy to self-care for caregivers.

CHS

Desiring to create a place where people could heal damaged sexuality and support loving connection, Alexandra Katehakis and Douglas Evans conceived **Center for Healthy Sex** in 2005. CHS began with the belief that all individuals have the right to experience themselves as healthy sexual beings. The organization aspires to move people from shame and pain towards gratitude and joy, recognizing that the process of healing sexuality is a profoundly spiritual path that awakens every aspect of our humanity. The sensitivity and commitment of its staff have made CHS a nationally recognized treatment center.

CHS works to realize a world in which self-aware adults consciously choose healthy, psychologically and spiritually integrated sexual behaviors. All CHS staff—administrators, intake counselors, and therapists—hold a vision for repairing the underlying trauma that has led clients to dissatisfying or destructive sexual activities, so they may at last own their sexual desire instead of having it own them. A caring, non-judgmental, and safe space, CHS allows men and women to heal the past, embrace relationships respectful of themselves and others, and walk courageously into a future that reflects and celebrates their genuine being.

Center for Healthy Sex
10700 Santa Monica Boulevard
Suite 311
Los Angeles, CA 90025
(310) 843-9902
www.CenterforHealthySex.com

Printed in Great Britain
by Amazon

71427490R00239